W9-CIQ-379

Third Edition

Hospitality Marketing Management

Robert D. Reid
James Madison University

David C. Bojanic
University of
Massachusetts—Amherst

 JOHN WILEY & SONS, INC.

New York / Chichester / Weinheim / Brisbane / Singapore / Toronto

To my wife Susan, who brings laughter and love to each new day
 Robert D. Reid

To my son Matthew, my inspiration; my mother and sister for your love
and support; and the memory of my father and brother
 David C. Bojanic

Library of Congress Cataloging-in-Publication Data:
Reid, Robert D.
    Hospitality marketing management.—3rd ed./Robert D. Reid, David Bojanic.
        p.   cm.
        Includes index.
        ISBN 0-471-35462-7 (cloth : alk. paper)
        1.   Hospitality industry—Marketing.   2. Food service—Marketing.   3.
    Restaurants—Marketing.   I. Bojanic, David.   II. Title.

TX911.3.M3 R443 2001
674.95′068′8—dc21
                                                                                    00-027364

Printed in the United States of America.
10 9 8 7 6 5 4 3 2 1

Contents

Preface

Developing the third edition of *Hospitality Marketing Management* has been a rewarding experience. Since the first edition was published in 1983, followed by the second edition in 1989, there have been many dramatic changes in the hospitality and tourism industry. The industry continues to mature and offers today's students many opportunities for successful careers in many sectors of this dynamic industry.

Since the second edition was published, we have witnessed the collapse of the Soviet Union, the fall of the Berlin wall, and many other world-altering events. The changes within the hospitality and tourism industry also have been substantial. We have seen consolidation of brand names with the acquisition of such firms as Hospitality Franchise Systems, which today is the largest lodging provider in the world. Hospitality Franchise Systems did not exist when the first edition was published. In the early 1990s, after more then ten years of patient effort, a Canadian franchise of McDonald's opened its first restaurant on Pushkin Square in Moscow. With more than 25 cash registers, this restaurant soon became the busiest in the McDonald system.

The world of hospitality and tourism continues to change and evolve. In several countries, hospitality and tourism has become the number one industry. Hospitality and tourism is poised to become a dominant industry, both nationally and internationally, in this next century.

It is our hope that this edition will help you to acquire some skills that will help you become more successful in your career.

WHAT'S NEW IN THE THIRD EDITION

There are several changes that have been made in this third edition. Each was made with the goal of improving the text and of making it more useful for managers, students and instructors. Among the most significant changes are enhanced pedagogical tools, additional topical coverage, and a reorganization of material.

Enhanced Pedagogical Tools

- *Marketing Action Now!* Each chapter features one or more situations in which an immediate decision must be made and the reader is asked to take *Marketing Action Now!* In some cases, the action called for is a response to a crisis. In other situations, the *Marketing Action Now* calls for the material presented in the chapter to be applied to a real-world situation. In all instances, the *Marketing Action Now* section asks the reader to review the material in the chapter and take action—now! This presents an excellent opportunity for students to learn by doing.

- *Reorganization of chapters.* Chapter 2 and Chapter 3 in the second edition have been combined into Chapter 2 in the current edition. Material in this chapter is more streamlined and provides a better linkage between the uniqueness of services marketing and hospitality and tourism marketing. A new component has been added to this chapter: the evaluation of service quality. Also, the chapters on marketing research and management information systems in the second edition have been combined to form Chapter 6 in the third edition. This will help the reader to better understand the relationship between these two functions.

- *Focus on applications and step-by-step guides.* Rather than getting bogged down in theory and definitions of marketing terms, this edition focuses on applications. Each chapter is written in such a way that readers learn by doing to the greatest extent possible. Many chapters feature step-by-step models and processes that show the reader how to develop marketing plans, evaluate marketing research, develop sales forecasts, plan sales presentations, and perform other important marketing activities.

- *Key terms and glossary.* Within each chapter, key terms are highlighted within the text and then are listed at the end of the chapter. Further, a glossary of marketing terms is provided in the margins of each chapter for quick reference.

- *More clearly developed chapter objectives.* The previous edition featured a brief outline at the beginning of each chapter. This has been improved upon, with more detailed outlines and specific learning objectives provided at the beginning of each chapter. This provides a better focal point for both students and instructors.

- *Chapter opening profiles.* Each chapter begins with a profile of an individual who has become successful in the hospitality and tourism industry. These individuals are from all segments of the industry and have a wide variety of educational and background experience. The profiles of these individuals are also linked to the objectives of each particular chapter.

Additional Topical Coverage

- *Addition of new chapters.* An entire section, consisting of three chapters (Part 4, Chapters 7–9), has been added. This section provides a strong orientation regarding the management of the product-service mix. Chapter 7 focuses exclusively on the development of new products and services. This chapter deals with such issues as managing product lines, planning for new products and services, and identifying new products and services. Chapter 8 focuses on product-service mix positioning, product life cycle orientation and management, and the adoption patterns of consumers. Finally, Chapter 9 examines service delivery and distribution strategies, and the important area of electronic commerce.

- *New sections added.* Several new sections have been added to the text to make it more current with contemporary marketing practices. Some of the new sections include text on service quality and satisfaction (Chapter 2), organizational buying (Chapter 3), sales forecasting (Chapter 5), ethical issues (Chapters 6, 10, 13, and 14), and consumer price sensitivity and yield management (Chapter 14).

- *Addition of new and timely material.* The entire text has been updated with current material and examples. Facts and figures have been updated to provide the most up-to-date coverage possible, and more illustrations have been added to enhance the presentation of the text.

- *More balanced focus on promotional mix.* There is a more balanced focus on the broader promotional mix in this edition. The second edition devoted more attention to advertising. With the shift away from advertising toward more focused marketing promotions and direct mail, this edition offers a more balanced presentation overall. In addition, a new section has been added in the important area of direct marketing.

- *Increased emphasis on the strategic and tactical pricing strategies.* The pricing chapter has been refocused to provide a stronger orientation toward the strategic and tactical issues related to pricing. The goal is to provide a more practical approach to the pricing decision.

Organization

This edition of *Hospitality Marketing Management* is divided into six parts. Each part is described in the following paragraphs. We hope that you will find this overview of the book useful as you plan your reading and study agenda.

Part One—Introduction to Hospitality Marketing. This part provides a solid foundation in marketing principles, encompassing the first two chapters. The first chapter, "The Functions of Marketing," introduces the marketing environment in which all businesses operate. The marketing environment includes the economic, political and legal, social and technological environments. Important terms related to marketing are introduced so that the reader will be able to understand material presented in later chapters. The role of management in marketing, including planning, execution, and evaluation is presented. Finally, the vital marketing mix is introduced, both from a traditional and a hospitality services perspective.

Chapter 2, "Introduction to Hospitality Services Marketing," defines and explores the unique nature of services. While very different from product marketers, services marketers have to be concerned with intangibility, inseparability, perishability, lack of service consistency, and buyer involvement all of which are unique to services marketing. The important quality element of services is introduced and readers are provided with suggestions for successfully managing in a service environment. Methods to improve guest satisfaction are provided. Finally, the chapter concludes with an examination of the key components of the management of hospitality or tourism firms—operations, finance, administration, human resources, research and development, and marketing.

Part Two—Understanding and Targeting Hospitality Consumers. Chapters 3 and 4 focus on consumer behavior and market segmentation. Chapter 3, "Understanding the Behavior of Hospitality Consumers," examines those variables that influence consumer behavior, namely—culture, society, family, individual roles, needs and motives, individual perceptions, attitudes, learning, and self-concept. The chapter also introduces a consumer decision-making model that marketers can use to understand and influence how purchase decisions are made. The remaining sections of this chapter are new to this edition and focus on the consumer problem-solving processes and techniques, and organizational buyer behavior.

Chapter 4, "Market Segmentation and Positioning," provides the reader with the criteria for segmentation and a discussion of the variables than can be used to segment markets effectively. Segmentation and target market strategies are presented, with numerous examples. Finally, the concept of positioning is addressed, including a four-stage process that can be followed in a practical setting.

Part Three—Marketing Planning and Information. This part consists of two chapters and examines planning, marketing information and research. Chapter 5, "Developing a Marketing Plan," distinguishes between strategic and tactical planning, and helps the reader to see clearly the advantages and disadvantages of a developing marketing plan. The most important section of this chapter introduces a marketing planning process that shows the reader how marketing plans are developed in a step-by-step fashion. Finally, the chapter provides an overview of the qualitative and quantitative forecasting techniques used by marketing managers today.

Chapter 6, "Information for Marketing Decisions," provides the justification for the critical need for information, and shows how successful firms have developed marketing information systems to provide timely and useful information. Internal and external sources of information are explored and the benefits and drawbacks of primary and secondary data sources are discussed. In addition, the chapter discusses the marketing research process and the relationship between marketing research and information systems. Three research methodologies—observation, survey, and experiments—are introduced and the benefits and drawbacks of each are discussed. The fundamentals of sampling and survey instrument design are presented. Finally, the chapter discusses the ethical issues surrounding the marketing research process.

Part Four—Product-Service Mix and Distribution Strategies. This part is entirely new. It is designed to provide a more comprehensive view of marketing-decision making and the development of marketing programs by hospitality and tourism organizations. Chapter 7, "Developing New Products and Services," introduces the reader to methods of developing new and innovative products and services. The importance of product lines and strategies for product development are discussed. Then, a new product development process is introduced, providing a step-by-step approach for developing a new product. Finally, the importance and characteristics of effective branding are presented.

Chapter 8, "Product-Service Mix Strategy," will help the reader to understand the stages of the product life cycle and the adoption stages of consumers. In addition, some other product concepts such as the wheel of retailing and resource allocation models are discussed. Finally, some of the particular elements associated with managing service firms are presented.

Chapter 9, "Distribution, Intermediaries, and Electronic Commerce," is another new chapter dealing with the organization of channels and the systems used to deliver hospitality and tourism services to consumers. In particular, students are exposed to the concepts related to channel management, including a thorough discussion of franchising. Next, a list of common intermediaries is presented and their respective roles are explained. Finally, electronic commerce strategies are provided for service marketing in the new century via the Internet.

Part Five—Promotion Mix. The material in this part has been refocused to provide a more balanced coverage of all aspects of the promotional mix. There is less emphasis on the advertising media and more emphasis on focused or direct marketing. Chapter 10, "Promotion and Advertising," introduces the promotional mix (advertising, sales promotion, public relations, and personal selling) and covers the functions of promotion and advertising. Strategies are provided for promoting over the product life cycle and techniques for establishing promotional budgets are discussed. Next, the fundamentals of planning, evaluating, and managing advertising campaigns are presented. Finally, the societal effects of advertising are discussed, including social and ethical criticisms and economic effects.

Chapter 11, "Advertising and Media Planning," examines the development of media plans. This is followed by detailed discussions of the use, advantages, and disadvantages of the various print media (e.g., newspapers and magazines) and broadcast media (e.g., radio and television). Techniques for success are provided for each of the media alternatives, including direct mail and support media, such as outdoor advertising and brochures.

Chapter 12, "Sales Promotions, Merchandising, and Public Relations," covers two of the less understood elements of the promotion mix: sales promotions and public relations. First, there is a discussion of the role of sales promotion and the types of common sales promotions used by hospitality and travel firms. This includes a list of steps that can be taken to ensure successful sales promotions and a technique for assessing the impact of these promotions. Then, merchandising is presented, including techniques for training and suggestive selling. Finally, public relations is defined and presented, along with guidelines for opening a new hotel.

Chapter 13, "Personal Selling," provides a clear picture of the various sales roles and a profile of successful sales personnel. The reader is exposed to the use of features, advantages, and benefits in selling hospitality and travel services and the markets for group sales. Next, the personal selling process is covered in detail, including methods for handling objections and for closing the sale. Finally, some personal selling tools are provided, and ethical issues surrounding the personal selling process are examined.

Part Six—Pricing Strategy and Menu Design. The final part, consisting of two chapters, explores the vital area of pricing and using menu design as a marketing tool. Chapter 14, "Pricing Strategy," explores the importance surrounding the choice of pricing objectives and pricing strategies, and the relationships between price and demand. The beginning of the chapter focuses on the factors that affect pricing decisions, followed by a discussion of broad pricing strategies and specific pricing techniques. Finally, specific applications of price segmentation are provided, and legal and ethical issues are examined.

Chapter 15, "Using Menu Design as a Marketing Tool," explores the role of menus in marketing, menu-planning considerations, methods for producing a printed menu, and particular issues surrounding menu planning. Some of these issues include accuracy in menus, cycle menus, and methods of evaluating menu effectiveness.

An *Instructor's Manual* (ISBN 0-471-40597-3) with test questions accompanies the text. In addition, qualified adopters can download PowerPoint slides to accompany the book from Wiley's web site, http://jws-edcv. wiley.com/college.

We hope that you will find these improvements and changes to the third edition of *Hospitality Marketing Management* useful in your quest to learn more about the exciting world of marketing in the hospitality and tourism industry.

Robert D. Reid
Harrisonburg, Virginia

David C. Bojanic
Amherst, Massachusetts

ACKNOWLEDGMENTS

We are grateful for the help of all the educators who have contributed to this edition through their constructive comments. They include:

Professor Seyhmus Baloglu
University of Nevada, Las Vegas

Professor John Brady
University of Southern Mississippi

Ms. Lisa Gates
Educational Foundation of the
    National Restaurant Association

Professor Lyle Hildahl
Skagit Valley College

Professor J. Norman Howard
State University of New York,
    Plattsburgh

Professor Tal Moore
Central Missouri State University

Professor Bruce Neil
Luzerne County Community
    College

Professor Howard Reichbart
Northern Virginia Community
    College

Professor Judy Siguaw
Cornell University

Professor Camille Stallings
Pima Community College

Professor Ralph Tellone
Middlesex County College

Professor James Turley
New York Institute of Technology

Professor Elizabeth Vargo
Pennsylvania State University, New
    Kensington Campus

Professor David Whitney
Central Michigan University

Introduction to Hospitality Marketing

Chapter

1

The Functions
of Marketing

❖ Chapter Objectives

By the end of this chapter, you should understand:

1. The various elements of the marketing environment
2. The concept of marketing and the marketing process
3. The marketing mix and the development of marketing programs
4. The external environment and its impact on the firm's operations
5. The difference between the terms *marketing* and *selling*
6. The role that marketing plays in the management of a hospitality or travel firm

❖ Chapter Outline

❖ Chapter Opening Profile

ONE OF THE MAJOR ISSUES FACING the hospitality and travel industry in the near future is the shortage of workers due to low unemployment and a healthy economy. Based on a 1998 study by the American Hotel Foundation's (AHF), national turnover in 1997 for line-level employees was 91.7 percent, 13.5 percent for property managers, and 11.9 percent for supervisors.[1] As a result, experts predict that by the year 2000, the industry will need another 800,000 workers to fill current jobs. The figures for the food service industry are similar, where the average waiter lasts between three and six months.

The majority of respondents to *Hotel & Motel Management's* 1999 Independent Management Company Survey listed labor and human resources as the biggest challenge facing management companies. In fact, respondents indicated that attracting, retaining, and training employees was their primary objective for 1999 and beyond. When unemployment levels are low, it is normally difficult to find good workers. These high rates of turnover and the shortage of workers affect a hospitality firm's ability to provide consistent, high-quality service. Unfortunately, this trend is beyond the control of hospitality firms.

According to a 1998 National Restaurant Association (NRA) study, turnover costs for restaurants average about $5,000 per employee, which is similar to findings in the AHF lodging study. The AHF report cited wages as the major cause of turnover, followed by causes like the lack of advancement, lack of recognition, conflict with management, and better opportunities in other hotels and other industries. Apparently, the higher the wage, the longer the employee is likely to stay with the company.

The bottom line is that employees must be treated well, and firms need to make the jobs more attractive. At the 1998 Hotel Show in New York City, a panel of marketing professionals commented on the fact that hotels were losing good salespeople to other industries with more attractive jobs. It is difficult to maintain a high level of quality and a consistent image with consumers if you can't attract enough good employees. Firms will need to adapt to these changes in the environment and find way to be competitive. The firms that succeed in hiring and retaining the best employees will be in the best position to market products that are valued by consumers.

▲ INTRODUCTION TO MARKETING

In recent years, most of the growth in the hospitality industry has occurred in chain operations or in the industry's corporate segment. The hospitality industry leaders, such as McDonald's, Burger King, Choice International, Starwood Lodging, and Marriott International, continue to increase their share of the market, at the expense of smaller chains and independent operators. While independent operators have continued to prosper, especially in the food service sector, the marketplace is much more competitive. An increased level of competition has meant greater emphasis on marketing. No longer is it possible for an individual to open and operate a foodservice facility successfully on good food alone. To assure a steady flow of clientele, a hospitality manager must possess a thorough understanding of marketing. Without the marketing management skills the hospitality industry demands, a hospitality manager is less likely today to achieve success. With this continual change and increased competition, what are the marketing functions that a successful hospitality manager must fulfill? This chapter introduces basic marketing concepts, and those that will explore specific areas of professional hospitality marketing management.

Marketing Defined

marketing merging, integrating, and controlled supervision of all company's or organization's efforts that have a bearing on sales

The term **marketing** encompasses many different activities and it is necessary to discuss some of the terms used in the definition of marketing, and throughout the text. First, the term **product** refers to all of the goods and services that are bundled together and offered to consumers. For example, computers and automobiles are sold as tangible goods, but they include warranties and service contracts as part of the overall product. Therefore, the term *product* does refer to both goods and services, but it is often thought of as a good or commodity. Another term that is used to refer to the product as a bundle of goods and services, and eliminate the confusion is the **product–service mix**.

product all the goods and services that are bundled together and offered to consumers

A **service** is defined as an intangible product that is sold or purchased in the marketplace. A meal purchased at a fast-food restaurant or an occupied room in a hotel is considered a part of the service segment. Why? Simply stated, after the meal is consumed and paid for or after the individual checks out of the hotel, the individual leaves the facility and does not have a tangible product in exchange for the money spent. This individual has consumed a service that is a part of the hospitality and travel industry, one of the largest service industries.

product–service mix bundle of goods and services offered by a hospitality organization

Each year, millions of individuals spend billions of dollars vacationing and traveling for business and pleasure; when the trip is over, nothing tangible remains. To reflect the role of service industries, such as the hospitality and travel industry, more clearly, the definition of marketing can be expanded to include references to services. This will eliminate the confusion caused by the semantic differences between products, goods, and services that were discussed earlier. According to the American Marketing Association, *marketing is the process of planning and executing the conception, pricing, promotion, and distribution of ideas, goods, and services to create exchanges that satisfy individual and organizational goals.*[2]

service an intangible product that is sold or purhcased in the marketplace

The vast majority of hospitality establishments, however, are being operated to generate a satisfactory return on investment in the form of profits or excess revenue. These profits are used to pay dividends to stockholders and are reinvested by the organization to promote expansion and further development. Even nonprofit hospitality operations, such as selected hospitals, nursing homes, college or university hospitality operations, and government-run hospitality operations, must be concerned with marketing. Managers of nonprofit operations must still understand the wants and needs of their consumers and provide goods and services at a satisfactory level to as many individuals as possible. A universal concern of all hospitality managers is the financial condition of the organization. Whether a manager is trying to achieve a 20 percent annual return on an investment or is instead aiming to break even on a very limited budget, the overriding concern is still financial.

Another factor that any definition of marketing must include is a focus on the *exchange* that takes place between a producer and a consumer. In order for an exchange to take place, both parties must receive something of mutual satisfaction. In most cases, consumers give producers money in exchange for products and services that meet the consumers' wants and needs. However, the exchange can include anything of value to the parties. Before there was a monetary system, people would **barter**, or exchange goods and services rather than money. There are still companies that engage in bartering today. For example, PepsiCo chose to exchange its soft drink product with a company in Mexico for wine and other products to avoid incurring the foreign exchange risk associated with the peso, which was devalued at the time.

barter exchange of goods and services rather than money

The Marketing Process

The process of *marketing* can be best understood by examining the diagram presented in Figure 1.1. As you can see, the target market, or those groups of consumers that the firm chooses to target with its marketing efforts, is at the center of the process. The **marketing concept** is based on the premise that firms determine customer wants and needs, and then design products and services that meet those wants and needs, while at the same time meeting the goals of the firm. This concept is an extension of earlier concepts that focused on the production process as a means to design products and services, or the selling of already-produced products and services. Today, most firms realize the value of customer input in the new product design process. Chapter 2 looks at the issues unique to mar-

marketing concept firms determine customer wants and needs and then design products and services that meet those needs while meeting the goals of the firm

Figure 1.1   The Marketing Process

keting services, Chapter 3 focuses on the behavior of hospitality consumers, and Chapter 4 discusses the process of choosing target markets and positioning products in the market.

marketing mix price, product, place, and promotion

In Figure 1.1 the first layer around the target market, or consumers, is referred to as the **marketing mix**. The marketing mix has four components: price, product, place, and promotion. These four components are often referred to as the 4Ps of marketing, and they are the variables that managers can control. Firms will use the marketing mix variables to formulate strategies for a product or service that are used to form a **marketing program**. This program is the basis on which the firm competes with other products and services. The marketing mix will be discussed in more detail later in this chapter. The product component is covered in Chapters 7 and 8, the place (distribution) component is covered in Chapter 9, the promotion component is covered in Chapters 10–13, and the price component is covered in Chapter 14.

marketing program basis on which the firm competes with other products and services

external environments the economy, trends in society, competitive pressures, political and legal developments, and advances in technology that affect the performance of a product or service

The outside layer of the diagram represents the **external environments** that influence the marketing process. The state of the economy, trends in society, competitive pressures, political and legal developments, and advances in technology all affect the performance of a product or service. Firms cannot control these environments, but they must monitor the changes and trends in the respective environments and look for opportunities and threats. Later in this chapter the different environments and some of the current trends that affect hospitality and travel firms will be examined in more detail.

marketing management cycle involves marketing planning, marketing execution, and marketing evaluation

Firms must continually monitor environments and make changes in their marketing programs. The **marketing management cycle** involves marketing planning, marketing execution, and marketing evaluation. This cycle is discussed briefly in this chapter, and Chapter 5 covers the marketing planning process in depth. To be successful in marketing planning, firms need to conduct research and collect information that can be used to evaluate their programs. Chapter 6 discusses the **marketing research process** used to gather information to be stored in **marketing information systems** and used to make marketing decisions.

marketing information systems computer systems used to store and organize data for use in decision making

marketing research process used to collect information about consumers and markets

Marketing versus Selling

Many hospitality managers engage in activities that they incorrectly refer to as marketing. Many people confuse advertising or personal selling with marketing. Although such activities are without question a part of the marketing function, alone and unsupported they cannot be referred to as marketing. Marketing refers to the entire process that is illustrated in Figure 1.1. Advertising and personal selling are merely forms of promotion, and promotion is just one component of the marketing mix. Managers engaged in activities of this type are merely attempting to sell their products and services.

The product–service mix is composed of all the tangible and intangible products and services that make up a hospitality operation. The product–service mix includes the food, beverages, guestrooms, meeting facilities, table appointments, and personal attention by service personnel, as well as a host of other tangibles and intangibles. This type of activity performed alone is very self-centered, or product–service mix oriented. The focus is only on the hospitality operation's product–service mix, and the goal is to convince the consuming public to purchase and consume a portion of the product–service mix. Little consideration is given to the needs and wants of the consuming public; instead, the hospitality manager is hoping that a sufficient number of consumers will patronize the operation to allow the operation to achieve its financial objectives.

The hospitality and travel industry, especially the food service segment, is filled with examples of operations that have failed because the owners created operations they liked or "always wanted to operate," yet the owners and managers failed to consider fully the needs and wants of potential consumers. The results are predictable: low volume, poor sales revenue, and frequent bankruptcy. Because this mistake is so prevalent in the food service segment, restaurants have one of the highest failure rates of any type of business in the United States.

The difference between selling and marketing is very simple. **Selling** focuses mainly on the firm's desire to sell products for revenue. Salespeople and other forms of promotion are used to create demand for a firm's current product(s). Clearly, the needs of the seller are very strong. Marketing, however, focuses on the needs of the consumer that ultimately benefits the seller as well. When a product or service is truly marketed, the needs of the consumer are considered from the very beginning of the new product development process, and the product–service mix is designed to meet the unsatisfied needs of the consuming public. When a product or service is marketed in the proper manner, very little selling is necessary because the consumer need already exists and the product or service is merely being produced to satisfy the need.

selling firm's focus on generating revenue

Another brief example will illustrate the critical difference between selling and marketing. During the 1970s and 1980s, many chain food service operations became very successful by targeting the under-30 singles market segment. The pattern for success was to develop a "high-energy" lounge style of operation that sold a high proportion of liquor to food. These operations were often called "fern bars" due mainly to the woodwork and plants that typically dominated the decor. For many years, these operations were very successful, generating very substantial sales and profits.

However, by the late 1980s, several factors combined to cause a problem for these restaurants. First, the market segment to which this type of facility was appealing was declining as a percentage of the total market. Those who had previously patronized the fern bars were now seeking a more relaxed atmosphere. Often, the single people who had patronized the facilities were now married, and many had small children. They either did not patronize food service facilities of this type, or they wanted a very different type of dining experience. Second, the *societal* attitudes toward alcohol consumption, especially as it related to drinking and driving, had undergone significant change. Annual per capita consumption of alcohol was declining. Third, consumers' nutrition needs were changing as they started opting for healthier choices. The relationship between diet and overall health and well-being was becoming more pronounced.

With these three factors in mind, the fern bar concept began to change, with less emphasis on alcohol consumption and more emphasis on food sales. Menus were researched and rewritten. Music selections were changed, and the volume levels were reduced. Also, more emphasis was placed on service. In the end, the fern bar evolved to meet the needs of ever-changing consumer tastes. Even the most successful concept will not be successful indefinitely. If the operators of these restaurants had continued to *sell* their product–service mix, they would not have been successful. Instead, they were sensitive to the changes occurring in the marketplace, especially within their target market segment, and were able to adapt their product–service mix to meet the needs of consumers. They found the key to successful marketing: recognizing trends and being ready and willing to make necessary changes to assure continued success.

The Emergence of the Marketing Concept

If a hospitality and travel organization is to market its product–service mix successfully, it is essential that the marketing concept be thoroughly understood and fully implemented. Understanding the marketing concept is not difficult, but implementing it may prove to be very challenging for management. Simply stated, the marketing concept is a consumer-oriented philosophy that focuses all available resources on satisfying the needs and wants of the consumer, thereby resulting in profits. As an old rhyme states,

> *To sell Jane Smith*
> *What Jane Smith buys,*
> *You've got to see things*
> *Through Jane Smith's eyes.*

Clearly, it is difficult to sell something to someone who has no need for it. If the firm adopts a consumer-oriented marketing philosophy, however, the product–service mix will be designed in direct response to unsatisfied consumer needs; as a result, very little actual selling will be necessary. In such instances, supply and demand are in balance, and both the consumer and hospitality providers are satisfied.

Table 1.1 illustrates the two different philosophies of the marketing concept that are often practiced in the hospitality and travel industry. One

| Table 1.1 | **How the Marketing Concept Is Used and Abused** | |

Decisions	*When the Marketing Concept Is Applied*	*When the Marketing Concept Is Not Applied*
Menu Design	"Let's conduct focus group interviews using our current and target market customers to determine which potential new menu items we should add to our menu."	"Let's add two steaks to the menu, that's what I like to eat."
Pricing	"How do you think our guests will perceive the price-value of our new weekend package if we increase the price by 5 percent?"	"Let's increase the price by 5 percent; that's what we did last year."
Guest Service	"I'm very sorry that you had to wait 20 minutes for your breakfast this morning. May I offer you a complimentary breakfast today, or would you like the credit applied toward your breakfast tomorrow?"	"I'm sorry you had to wait, but we were short-handed today. One of the servers called in sick."
Guest Requests	"We don't have any rooms with a king bed available at this time, but I can have one ready for you in 30 minutes. Can I have the bell staff check your bag until then?"	"We don't have any rooms with a king bed left. You'll have to take a room with two double beds."
Reactions to negative guest comments	"That is a very good idea. I'll talk about it at our staff meeting tomorrow and see if we can use your suggestion to improve our service. Thanks for suggesting that."	"Your idea isn't feasible, and besides, it's against our policy."

demonstrates the actions of a manager who applies the marketing concept, the other demonstrates actions that are not consistent with the marketing concept. The key question to ask when trying to distinguish between the two approaches is "Are consumers given priority, or is the operation run to suit the needs of the employees, management, or owners?"

A manager of a hospitality operation has a difficult series of daily challenges. First, a manager is expected to successfully satisfy the needs of the hospitality consumers. Second, the owners expect a manager to maintain the level of expenses within certain predetermined limits that are usually defined in actual dollars or as a percentage of sales. Third, a manager is expected to generate a satisfactory return on investment for the owners.

This return might be the break-even point in a nonprofit operation or a 12 percent rate of return in a commercial operation. Whatever the return, a manager is faced with a series of difficult objectives to achieve, and these objectives often conflict with one another. Even in the most successful of companies, there are limited resources that must be used to accomplish seemingly unlimited goals and objectives. Regardless of how well the company has performed in the past, management will always expect a little more in the future. Guests develop ever-increasing expectations for all aspects of the product–service mix. Owners want increased profits, and the employees want a little more each year. The manager's task is to balance the three objectives mentioned in the preceding paragraph. Managers often view profitability as the single most important objective of the firm, yet for the long-term financial well-being of the firm, profits may not be the most important objective. It is quite possible, as many shortsighted owners and managers have demonstrated, to achieve high levels of short-term profitability at the expense of long-term consumer satisfaction and long-term profits. After a period of time, however, consumers will perceive that they are not receiving a high level of value for their money, and the operation will develop a reputation for being overpriced and/or offering poor service. As a result, the number of patrons is likely to decline, and so will profitability.

On the other hand, if management establishes a consumer orientation and places customer satisfaction as the number one priority, the firm's products and services are more likely to meet customers' expectations. As a result, they will return more frequently to the hospitality operation, and this will have a positive influence on long-term sales and profits. In addition, by telling their friends and acquaintances about their positive experiences, satisfied consumers are likely to influence others to patronize the establishment. This **word-of-mouth** passed on by satisfied customers can become a very important part of a firm's promotional efforts. It doesn't cost anything, yet it can be a very powerful influence on sales, and as sales increase, so does profitability. Experience shows that when the marketing concept is understood, and applied by all of a firm's employees, substantial changes have often been made in the establishment's manner of operation, and the financial results have often been improved significantly.

▲ THE MARKETING MIX

The term *marketing mix* was first used in the mid-1900s. Since then, the concept of the marketing mix has gained universal acceptance. It is important for marketing students to understand this concept, both conceptually and strategically. This section outlines the major components of the traditional marketing mix, and the next section covers the hospitality marketing mix that was offered as an alternative for the industry. We will explain the similarities and differences between the two approaches.

A successful hospitality organization is one that focuses on the needs and wants of the consumers and markets the product–service mix of the operation. Management of this type of operation involves integrating the components of the marketing mix into a marketing program that will appeal to potential consumers and meet the goals and objectives of the firm. The following sections will introduce the components of the marketing mix, which will be discussed in more detail in Chapters 7–14.

Hospitality firms use the elements of the marketing mix to establish a competitve position in the market. *Courtesy of Red Lobster Restaurants, Orlando, Florida*

The Traditional Marketing Mix

The marketing mix, many believe, consists of four elements, sometimes called the *four Ps* of marketing:

Price. This component refers to the value placed by a firm on its products and services. Some of the decisions involve pricing the product line, discounting strategies, and positioning against competitors.

Product. This component refers to the unique combination of goods and services offered by a firm to consumers. The product includes both the tangible and intangible elements of the service offering. Product decisions involve product attributes such as quality, the breadth and mix of the product line (i.e., the number and type of products and services offered by a firm), and services such as warranties and guarantees.

Place. This component refers to the manner in which the products and services are being delivered to consumers. This component is sometimes referred to as **distribution**, and it involves decisions related to the location of facilities and the use of intermediaries. In addition, the marketing of services includes the decision regarding customer involvement in the production process.

Promotion. This component refers to the methods used to communicate with consumer markets. The **promotion mix** includes advertising, personal selling, sales promotions (e.g., coupons, rebates, and contests), and publicity. These are the vehicles that can be used to communicate the firm's intended messages to consumers. The decisions for promotion involve the amount to be spent on each component of the promotion mix, the strategies for each of the components, and the overall message to be sent.

To achieve success in marketing a hospitality operation, a manager must closely examine and understand all of the components of the marketing mix. To be successful, these components must be combined into well-conceived marketing programs and managed properly. There is no magical formula that will guarantee success. If there were, no hospitality operation would ever fail or go out of business. Yet each year, many hospitality operations fail because they are not able to combine the elements of the marketing mix into effective marketing programs, or they fail to implement them properly.

The Hospitality Marketing Mix

Just as researchers have demonstrated distinct differences between goods and services, some researchers believe that the traditional four Ps approach to the marketing mix does not apply to the hospitality industry. Rather, a modified marketing mix is more appropriate. This marketing mix consists of three components:[3]

Product–service mix. This is a combination of all the products and services offered by the hospitality operation, including both tangibles and intangibles. More will be discussed in Chapter 2 concerning the unique nature of services. Keep in mind that once a hospitality consumer leaves the hotel or restaurant, there is nothing tangible to show. Because the consumer has purchased and consumed the service, the largest part of the hospitality industry product–service mix is indeed service.

Presentation mix. This includes those elements that the marketing manager uses to increase the tangibility of the product–service mix as perceived by the consumer. This mix includes physical location, atmosphere (lighting, sound, and color), price, and personnel.

Communication mix. This involves all communication that takes place between the hospitality operation and the consumer. It includes advertising, marketing research, and feedback about consumer perceptions. The communications mix should be viewed as a two-way communications link, rather than as a simple one-way link with the hospitality operation communicating to the consumer. This two-way link allows for the traditional advertising and promotion that flow from the seller to the buyer, but it also allows for marketing research and other data collection vehicles. In these cases, the seller is seeking information and data from the consumer, thereby establishing open communication with the various market segments.

There are some similarities and differences between the traditional marketing mix and the hospitality marketing mix. In the hospitality version, the product component is expanded to include some aspects of distribution. People are part of the production process in services and distribution occurs in the presence of the consumer. The communication mix is almost identical with the promotion component in the traditional marketing mix, although it does include some additional communications such as marketing research. Finally, the presentation mix represents the largest departure from the traditional marketing mix. It includes price, some of the aspects of the place component like location, and it adds elements such as atmosphere and the personal contact between customers and employees.

It should be noted that some hospitality marketing researchers believe that a fourth element should be added to the hospitality marketing mix.[4] The **distribution mix** would include all channels available between the firm and the target market. As newer distribution channels, such as the Internet, have developed the distribution mix has increased in importance. However, this adapted version of the hospitality marketing mix strongly resembles the traditional marketing mix with some semantic differences.

distribution mix all channels available between the firm and the target market

The marketing mix, whether designed in the traditional or modified hospitality services format, is an important concept for managers of marketing functions. Initially, the marketing mix is used to formulate a marketing strategy and plan (see Chapter 5), but it pervades all aspects of marketing management. As a manager attempts to professionally manage the components of the hospitality marketing mix, several external factors can reduce the effectiveness of the manager's efforts. These factors, which either directly or indirectly influence the hospitality marketing mix, are consumer perceptions, attitudes, and behavior; industry practices and trends; local competition; broad national and international trends; and government policy and legislation.

▲ THE MARKETING ENVIRONMENT

During the past decade, many changes have had an impact on the hospitality industry in the United States. The industry has confronted and adapted to such diverse situations as economic recession, overbuilding, increased competition, increased emphasis on technology, increased foreign ownership of previously American brands, changes in dining habits, changes in food consumption patterns, and the ever-increasing globalization of the hospitality and tourism industry. Each of these external forces has brought with it changes that hospitality firms have had to make to remain competitive in a global marketplace.

When marketing managers examine change, they often look at changes in five major marketing environments: competitive, economic, political and legal, social, and technological. Firms cannot directly influence their external environments, but they can monitor changes and be somewhat proactive. It is critical for firms to engage in some level of **environmental scanning** so they can take advantage of marketing opportunities, while at the same time, anticipate any threats to their business. Environmental scanning can be a formal mechanism within a firm, or merely the result of salespeople and managers keeping up with the changes. The larger the firm, the more likely it will have a structured approach to scanning the environment and documenting trends. The following contains brief descriptions of each of the external environments.

environmental scanning used to monitor external factors that could affect an organization

Economic Environment

The goal of all marketing activity is to create and satisfy customers. Consumers' **purchasing power**, or ability to purchase products and services, is directly related to the economic health of the city, state, and country. As marketers study the economic environment, they are concerned about such things as inflation, unemployment, resource availability, personal income growth, business growth and performance, and consumers' confidence in the economy. There are some other key economic terms that relate to marketing and will used throughout the text. The **consumer price index (CPI)** is a measure of the relative level of prices for

purchasing power ability to purchase products and services

consumer price index measure of the relative level of prices for consumer goods in the economy

consumer goods in the economy. As this measure rises, there are more concerns about inflation and a poor economy. The term **disposable income** refers to that portion of an individual's income that is left for spending after required deductions such as taxes. **Discretionary income** is probably a more important measure for most marketers because it refers to the income that is available for spending after deducting taxes and necessary expenditures on housing, food, and basic clothing.

Some examples of issues related to the economic environment that affect the hospitality and travel industry include:

- The percentage of independently owned hospitality operations has declined, resulting in a concentration of power among large hospitality chains. In turn, these chains are becoming large, multinational firms based in the United States or abroad.
- An increase in the amount of discretionary income has resulted in an increase in the percentage of the household food budget spent outside the home. The hospitality industry today receives in excess of 50 percent of all consumer expenditures for food.[5]
- After a period of excess supply due to overbuilding in the 1980s, hotel occupancy percentages fell to the low 60 percent range. This trend has since reversed because of the strong economy and business growth. Following a recession in the early 1990s, occupancy and profitability have reached all-time highs for many lodging companies.
- Variations in consumer purchasing power have led the hospitality and travel industry to offer products and services at different price levels. For example, most of the major lodging chains now have established multiple brand names, ranging from economy to luxury based on prices and amenities.

Some of the issues in the economic environment are closely related to the trends in the social environment that will be discussed next.

Social Environment

There are constantly changes in the social environment as consumers evolve. The social environment is affected by all of the other environments. Changes in the economy, advances in technology, competitive actions, and government regulations all shape the way consumers view the world. These changes may be sudden, or they may take place over a number of years or even decades. First, there have been changes in **demographics**, or the characteristics that describe the population such as age, income, education, occupation, family size, marital status, and gender. Second, there have been changes in consumers' attitudes, interests, and opinions that determine their lifestyles.

Some examples of issues related to the social environment that affect the hospitality and travel industry include:

disposable income portion of an individual's income that is left for spending after required deductions such as taxes

discretionary income income that is available for spending after deducting taxes and necessary expenditures on housing, food, and basic clothing

demographics characteristics that describe a population, such as age, income, education, occupation, family size, marital status, and gender

- The proportion of two-income families and the impact that the increased discretionary income and time pressures have on their lodging, dining, and travel behaviors. These families take more vacations of shorter length to fit their busy lifestyles. Also, they are quality conscious and focus on brand names.

- The continual increase in the proportion of older Americans and their purchasing power. This is becoming a very important market segment because people are living longer, there is an improved quality of life among seniors, and their disposable income continues to increase. This segment has specific needs, and the American Association of Retired Persons (AARP) is one of the strongest political lobbying organizations in the nation.

- The dietary habits of the American people have also changed, as many individuals are showing an increased concern for their health. The trend has been toward healthier, more natural foods. In support of this, the United States Department of Agriculture publishes *Dietary Guidelines for Americans*, which outlines the dietary goals for the nation. The American Heart Association provides menu review and recipes that meet their dietary guidelines for good health. Many food service operations now feature menu items that have been approved by this organization. The National Restaurant Association has also been active in this area, especially in the form of education for its members.

Fast-food restaurants, extended-stay hotels, and the growth in the cruise industry are all the result of changes in the social environment. These changes can offer opportunities for new products and services, while posing a threat to existing companies. For example, the focus on brand names has resulted in tremendous growth in franchising theme restaurants like Outback Steak House, but it has come at the expense of many independent restaurants.

Competitive Environment

competitive structure combination of buyers and sellers in a market

monopoly one seller and many buyers

perfect competition many buyers and sellers of **homogeneous** products that are almost exactly the same

oligopolies a few sellers and many buyers

Within all markets, a variety of competitors seek to win the favor of the consumer. Each offers what they believe will be the best combination of products and services designed to result in maximum consumer satisfaction. The **competitive structure** in an industry can range from a **monopoly**, with one seller and many buyers, to **perfect competition**, with many buyers and sellers of homogeneous products that are almost exactly the same. In between, there are **oligopolies**, with a few sellers and many buyers, and the most common form of competitive structure, **monopolistic competition**, where there are many buyers and sellers with differentiated products. The **price elasticity of demand** is a measure of the percentage change in demand for a product resulting from a percentage change in price. The price elasticity of demand normally increases as the competitive structure changes from monopoly, to oligopoly, to monopolistic competition, and ends with perfect competition. The hospitality and travel industry is highly competitive, with new companies entering the industry every day.

monopolistic competition *many buyers and sellers with differentiated products*

In the business world, four levels of competition that must be considered in order for firms to be able to protect their positions in the market[6]:

- **Product form competition** exists among companies that provide similar products and services to the same customers at a similar price level. For example, McDonald's would compete with Burger King and Wendy's; Delta Airlines would compete with United Airlines and US Airways; Hertz would compete with Avis and National; and Four Seasons Hotels would compete with Ritz Carlton and other luxury hotels.

- **Product category competition** exists among companies that make the same class of products. In this case, McDonald's would compete with other fast-food restaurants such as Pizza Hut, Taco Bell, and Kentucky Fried Chicken. Similarly, Delta Airlines would compete with charter airlines and commuter airlines; Hertz would compete with all the local rental car companies; and Four Seasons Hotels would compete with nonluxury hotel chains such as Marriott and Sheraton.

- **General competition** exists among companies that offer the same basic service that fulfills the same basic consumer needs. For example, McDonald's would compete with all restaurants as well as with convenience stores and supermarkets. Similarly, Delta Airlines and Hertz would compete with all forms of transportation like bus and rail, and Four Seasons Hotels would compete with all forms of lodging such as bed and breakfasts and YMCAs.

- **Budget competition** exists among all companies that compete for consumers' disposable incomes. Most consumers have limited budgets that can be used for purchasing products and services, and all companies compete for these consumer dollars, especially the discretionary income. The hospitality and travel firms discussed earlier would compete with department stores, movie theaters, health clubs, and financial institutions for consumers' limited resources.

As companies examine the competitive environment, three important questions that need to be addressed. The questions may seem straightforward, but the answers are often difficult to determine, and many firms do not make the correct decision. The questions are:

1. Should we compete?
2. If we compete, in what markets should we compete?
3. What should our competitive strategy be?

The response to the first question should be based on such things as the firm's resources and objectives. They must examine the level of potential sales, potential profitability, and the overall feasibility of competing. A firm may decide that it should not compete if the risks outweigh the potential returns or if the projected returns are not as high as they would like to see.

The second question relates to the markets in which a firm wishes to compete. Most firms elect not to compete in all potential markets. For example, although many firms, such as Marriott International, have developed brands that compete in all price segments of the lodging industry (economy through luxury), others, such as Hyatt Hotel and Resorts, have chosen not to compete in all price segments. This firm believes that this strategy would not serve their best long-term interests. This area will be covered in more detail in Chapter 5.

The third question relates to marketing strategy. How should the firm attempt to gain a competitive advantage? These decisions, which will be explored in much greater depth throughout the text, are related to issues such as products and services, pricing, distribution, and promotion.

Political and Legal Environment

Understanding the political and legal environment means that you understand the rules by which the game is played. At all levels of government, local, state, national, and international, there are laws and regulations that businesses must follow. To compete successfully, a firm must understand not only the current laws and regulations, but any new ones might come into play in the future. Most professional hospitality and tourism managers belong to one or more professional associations. One of the goals of these associations is to help members not only understand developing laws and regulations, but to have influence in how they are written through lobbying efforts with politicians and government officials. Two examples of associations for the hospitality industry are the National Restaurant Association (NRA) and the American Hotel and Motel Association (AHMA).

Some examples of issues related to the political and legal environment that affect the hospitality and travel industry include:

- Changes in the federal tax codes have made hotel development less desirable than under previous tax codes. So-called passive investments, in which the investor is not an active participant in the daily management of the facility, are not treated as favorably under the new federal tax codes as they were in the past. As a result, future hotel development decisions will be based more on operational feasibility and less on the real estate investment aspects of the project.
- As a means to reduce the federal budget deficit, costs are being shifted to state and local governments. To raise tax revenues at the local level without incurring the disapproval of local voters, many localities have implemented or increased taxes on lodging and restaurant meals.

These use taxes serve to increase consumer perceptions of the prices for hospitality and travel products, and can have a major negative impact on operations.

- Another related tax issue that affects the hospitality industry is the reduction in the tax credit for business meals and expenses. The lobbyists for the NRA argued that this tax change would have a major negative impact on restaurant sales.

- National, state, and local governments also pass laws that can affect firms' operations without using taxes. For example, while the national government has chosen to stay on the sidelines, local and state governments are taking on the issue of smoking in public places like restaurants and arenas. This directly affects the competitive structure of the industry when regulations do not affect all firms equally. For instance, in some of areas with smoking bans, consumers can go to restaurants in nearby towns and smoke.

The idea of a level playing field is critical when governments evaluate new taxes and regulations. It is often difficult for firms to address social issues as a priority over profits, especially small firms with very limited resources. However, governments can make sure that their laws and regulations do not distort the balance of competition.

Technological Environment

We live in an increasingly technological society. With the advent of the personal computer in the late 1970s and the Internet in the early 1990s, our lives have changed in ways we only could have dreamed about. The power of computers doubles roughly every 18 to 24 months, with prices constantly dropping. Computers are being used for more and more applications every day. Although the hospitality and tourism industry remains a highly labor-intensive and personal-contact industry, computers and technology have had and will continue to have an impact. The area in which technology will have the greatest impact in the next ten years is in **direct marketing**. Through the use of database software technology, marketers have improved their ability to target their customers and track their behavior. We can monitor purchase behavior of guests and then tailor service offerings to meet their needs.

direct marketing
contacting consumers at home or work with promotions

Some examples of issues related to the technological environment that affect the hospitality and travel industry include:

- New technologies have helped to combat labor shortages and the high cost of labor by enabling hospitality and travel firms to shift some of these duties to consumers through self-service operations (e.g., automated checkout). This is occurring within all segments of the industry, from fast-food restaurants to luxury hotels and resorts.

- The increasing sophistication and decrease in price of computer technology has had a significant impact. Most of the larger firms maintain relational databases and use resource management systems that can provide managers with the potential to better serve customers. This technology is becoming more accessible to smaller firms through service contractors and consultants.

- The development and growth of the Internet has changed the competitive structure in the hospitality and travel industry. Even smaller firms can now market on a national or international basis. Selling on the Internet also reduces the costs associated with service delivery, thereby increasing the profit potential for service firms. Consumers are finding it possible to evaluate service alternatives and make reservations without leaving their homes.

Along with these changes, the hospitality industry has experienced dramatic growth, and the future looks very positive. Most of the leading hospitality experts are projecting continued industry growth, albeit somewhat slower than during the 1980s. Certainly, a few large obstacles loom on the horizon. Existing economic cycles will cause some upward and downward shifts in the hospitality industry, and further changes in the tax codes may have some negative impact on business travel and entertaining.

▲ THE MARKETING MANAGEMENT CYCLE

Marketing is an ongoing process. It needs constant attention to be successful. Management must constantly obtain feedback and use it to revise strategic plans. Management's role in the marketing effort is critical, for without diligent effort, the results will be less than satisfactory.

Large hospitality and travel organizations normally have a director of marketing who is responsible for the management of all marketing activities. However, in most hospitality and travel units, and especially in independent firms, the marketing function is the responsibility of an operations manager who must be concerned with other functions as well. This, together with the lack of a sizeable budget, results in a low priority for marketing in these situations. For the larger organizations, the units are all treated the same, which could lead to some missed opportunities and competitive disadvantages. For smaller organizations, it is difficult to compete with the larger chains that benefit from national marketing campaigns.

The successful marketing of a hospitality operation is not something that can be accomplished overnight, or with only a few hours of attention each week. Establishing and maintaining a successful marketing program requires significant management time and effort. The management activities in marketing a hospitality operation can be divided into three major areas that form a marketing management cycle: marketing planning, marketing execution, and marketing evaluation. Each of these areas will be discussed in more depth in later chapters; however, a brief overview of the major functions of each element of the marketing management cycle is presented in Figure 1.2.

Marketing Planning

The marketing planning process will be discussed in detail in Chapter 5. There are three basic questions that should be addressed during this process. The first question is "Where are we now?" A situation analysis should performed to determine the company's strengths and weaknesses. This information is based on past trends and historical performance, and it should include an analysis of the market and the competition. In addition, it is necessary to scan the environment to look for opportunities and threats that may present themselves. Once the company has a good grasp of the situation, it is time to move on to the next question.

The second question is "Where do we want to go?" It is at this point that a company must set its goals and objectives for operating in the future. These goals and objectives should be clear, concise, and measurable over a specific time frame. All employees and stakeholders should be made aware of the strategic direction of the firm. Also, these goals and objectives become targets for evaluating the performance of the company's employees. Finally, these goals and objectives should be consistent with the company's mission statement.

The third question is "How are we going to get there?" Once the company determines its direction for the future, it is necessary to devise strategies and action plans that can serve as a road map. Basically, marketing managers develop marketing programs that are consistent with the goals of the firm. The components of the marketing mix are under the direct control of managers, and they can be used to form strategies that will help the company to reach its goals. The actions taken with price, the

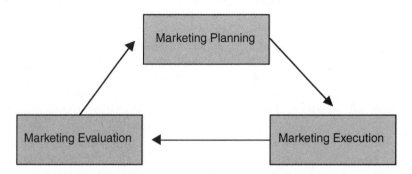

Figure 1.2   The Marketing Management Cycle

product–service mix, promotion, and distribution should be integrated and lead to a common end.

Marketing Execution

Once the objectives and strategies are determined, the next step is to implement the action plans developed during the planning process, using the specific timetable that was part of the marketing plan. This is accomplished using the promotional, advertising, personal selling, and direct marketing materials and methods that were devised in the planning stage. Employees should be informed about the company's plans for its service offerings and receive additional training, if necessary. Unit managers and franchisees should be made aware of the changes in the marketing plan so they can implement them in their respective units.

Marketing Evaluation

The final step in the marketing management cycle is to monitor and control the elements of the marketing plan. Data is collected and evaluated using marketing research and stored in marketing information systems for easy retrieval. Organizational performance needs to be analyzed in comparison with goals and objectives, looking for the underlying reasons for the difference between stated performance goals and actual performance.

Specifically, the company should analyze the effectiveness of its marketing programs, including its strategies for pricing, promoting, and distributing its products and services. The firm's performance can be evaluated relative to its competitors, using measures such as sales, market share, and customer satisfaction. Finally, at this point, firms can return to the planning stage of the marketing management cycle and make any desired changes in their objectives or their strategies.

▲ MARKETING WITHIN THE ORGANIZATION

Marketing management, as practiced today, differs tremendously from the techniques used in earlier decades. Marketing within the hospitality and travel industry is in a constant state of flux, as corporations plan, implement, and evaluate new marketing strategies and tactics. General marketing management practices and techniques should be analyzed and used as guidelines, but it is necessary for each hospitality organization to adjust and modify these general guidelines and techniques as dictated by the competitive environment. The competitive environment is ever changing, and this serves to attract management personnel who want to be continuously stimulated and who don't want to work in a repetitive environment.

It is also important to remember that marketing is but one of the key result areas with which management must be concerned. Within large hospitality organizations, specialists are hired to staff positions within each of the functional areas. In small organizations, however, managers must wear many hats and successfully perform all or some of these managerial functions. The following discussion places marketing in its proper place as a major part of the successful management of any hospitality organization. To fulfill an organization's potential, management must integrate its various key result areas in and manage them successfully. The key result areas are interdependent and must support each other, thereby increasing the overall strength of the organization.

Operations

Management is responsible for the day-to-day operation of the hospitality facility. This includes such diverse activities as purchasing, receiving, inventory control, production, service of guest rooms, and all of the other activities that take place each day within a successful hospitality or travel operation. Without a strong focus on operations, the quality of the product–service mix is likely to be poor or inconsistent. Problems in the operations area of a firm can lead to declining customer counts and possible business failure. People in operations are mainly concerned with efficiency and cost containment, which are best achieved by limiting product flexibility and standardizing production and delivery. Conversely, marketing personnel are concerned with pleasing customers by providing them with the types of products and services that they prefer. This requires a good deal of variety and customization that conflicts with the goals of production personnel. Management must balance the goals of the two areas with the goals of the firm in order to be successful.

Finance

A central and overriding goal of all businesses, including hospitality organizations, is to increase the wealth of the owners or stockholders. In periods of economic uncertainty, such as during high rates of inflation, high interest rates, or periods of recession, skilled management of the financial function becomes even more critical to the success of the hospitality organization. All hospitality organizations need to focus considerable attention on this function to manage the organization's assets and financial affairs successfully. Most areas within a firm have bottom-line responsibility, and managers need to understand the fundamentals of finance and accounting. All firms have limited resources, regardless of size, and it is important to invest in areas that demonstrate a high potential for meeting the targeted return. For example, financial considerations must be applied when developing new products and services, creating advertising campaigns, and setting pricing policies.

Human Resource Management

As a service industry, the hospitality industry places a heavy emphasis on customer service. The success of a hospitality venture depends greatly on the ability of its employees to provide a consistently high level of customer service. Management is responsible for establishing the overall direction, but it is left to each employee to implement management's strategies and action plans. The major activities of human resource management include recruitment, selection, orientation, training, professional development, and personnel relations. Historically, the turnover rate in the hospitality industry has been much higher than in other industries. Wages tend to be low in relation to responsibility, and in some cases, there is a lack of upward mobility unless the employee is willing to relocate. High rates of turnover for all positions adversely affect the entire organization. It is the responsibility of the human resources department to select employees who fit the profile of a dedicated service employee and then train them and provide support throughout their careers. In essence, the human resources department must market the firm to employees who will then be motivated to market the firm and its products to customers.

Research and Development

To compete successfully in the years ahead, hospitality firms must invest time and money in the key result area of research and development. These efforts typically focus on developing new market segments and new elements of the product–service mix. The growth of new concepts and new types of product–service mixes is an example of the outgrowth of research and development efforts. Lodging organizations such as Holiday Inn Worldwide, Choice Hotels International, Marriott International, and others developed all-suite hotels in response to research and development efforts that identified a substantial consumer market for small suites at affordable prices. Each year, they further refine their products and services offered to the traveling public with the goal of meeting and exceeding customer expectations. Because it is unlikely that a single hospitality concept will be successful indefinitely, management must be future oriented and must anticipate necessary changes. Research and development efforts must be attuned to what consumers will want in the future. Being ready and able to change to meet future consumer needs is the real challenge of research and development.

▲ MARKETING ACTION NOW!

If a firm does a good job of managing the marketing process for its products and services, it should be very evident to consumers, as well as to competitors, how they are positioned in the market. For example, it is not difficult to determine the target market(s) for McDonald's operations. McDonald's use of the marketing mix should provide important information concerning its positioning strategy. The main market segments being targeted by McDonald's are families with small children, and young adults. The firm's products are priced affordably, the product–service mix includes value meals and kids' meals with a toy, the outlets are located near shopping malls and high-traffic areas, and the promotions include child-friendly characters and celebrities that would appeal to young adults.

Choose another hospitality or travel firm and provide a similar analysis of its marketing program. First, determine the market segment(s) being targeted by the firm based on what you have observed. Second, discuss the various strategies used by the firm for the components in the marketing mix. Try to make some comparisons with other firms that would compete for different markets. Also, be as specific as possible. For example, where do you see advertisements, and what is the message being conveyed in the ads? Finally, discuss the different environments that have an impact on the firm's operations. What are the current trends and possible opportunities and threats that you can see over the intermediate- to long-term horizon?

▲ SUMMARY OF CHAPTER OBJECTIVES

This chapter serves a vital function in introducing many concepts that will be used throughout the text. First, it provides an introduction to marketing, including the definition of marketing, the marketing process, and the difference between marketing and selling. For the purposes of this book, marketing is defined as the process of determining consumer needs, creating a product–service mix that satisfies these needs, and promoting the product–service mix in order to attain the goals and objectives of the firm.

The marketing process starts with research to determine the wants and needs of consumers, so that products and services can be developed to fulfill those needs. Then, once the product–service mix is determined, the firm develops a marketing program using the other three elements of the marketing mix: price, place, and promotion. The strategies for each of the 4Ps are combined into a marketing program that is used to position the firm's products and services in the marketplace. The marketing management cycle consists of marketing planning, execution, and evaluation. Finally, the firm scans the environment throughout the marketing management cycle to identify any potential opportunities or threats that should be addressed. The external environment can be divided into five subenvironments: economic, social, competitive, political and legal, and technological.

Marketing is different from selling because marketing focuses on the needs of consumers, whereas selling focuses on the needs of the seller. In addition, the marketing concept advances the philosophy that the needs of the consumer should be given priority over any financial goals that the firm may have. The concept holds that if the consumer's needs and wants are totally satisfied, then financial success will follow.

Finally, it is management's responsibility to understand the role of marketing within the organization. It is important to understand how marketing interfaces with the other key result areas in the firm: operations, finance, human resources, and research and development. These key areas are normally well defined within large organizations. However, it may be difficult to separate these functions in smaller firms because the same employees are often responsible for more than one key area. One of the most critical issues is to balance the often conflicting goals of the operations area and the marketing area with the overall goals of the firm.

▲ KEY TERMS AND CONCEPTS

Barter

Competitive structure

Consumer price index (CPI)

Demographics

Direct marketing

Discretionary income

Disposable income

Distribution

Environmental scanning

External environments

Hospitality marketing mix

Market segmentation

Marketing

Marketing concept

Marketing information systems (MIS)

Marketing management cycle

Marketing mix

Marketing planning

Marketing program

Marketing research process

Monopolistic competition

Monopoly

Oligopoly

Perfect competition

Place

Price

Price elasticity of demand

Product

Product–service mix

Promotion

Purchasing power

Service

Word-of-mouth

▲ QUESTIONS FOR REVIEW AND DISCUSSION

1. Why has marketing assumed a position of increased importance in the management of hospitality organizations?

2. Explain the difference between selling and marketing. How are the two similar? Can you think of an example to illustrate each concept?

3. What is the marketing process? Briefly explain the process and its elements.

4. What is the marketing concept? What role should the marketing concept play in managing a hospitality or travel facility?

5. Discuss the components of the traditional and hospitality marketing mixes. What role does the hospitality manager play in managing the marketing mix? How is the marketing mix used?

6. What factors can affect the marketing mix? How might these factors affect the marketing mix? How might a manager anticipate the impact that these factors might have?

7. What is the marketing management cycle? Explain and discuss the major activities with which a manager must be concerned.

8. How does the marketing function interface with other areas in an organization?

▲ NOTES

[1]Barbara A. Worcester, "The People Problem," *Hotel and Motel Management*, Volume 214, Number 4 (March 1, 1999) pp. 38.

[2]"AMA Board Approves New Marketing Definition," *Marketing News* (March 1, 1985), p. 1.

[3]Leo Renaghan, "A New Marketing Mix for the Hospitality Industry," *The Cornell Hotel and Restaurant Administration Quarterly*, April 1981, pp. 31, 35.

[4]Robert C. Lewis, Richard E. Chambers, and Harsha E. Chacko, *Marketing Leadership in Hospitality: Foundations and Practices* (New York: John Wiley and Sons, Inc., 1994) pp. 394–395.

[5]William Fisher, President of the National Restaurant Association, Presentation at the Annual Conference of the Council on Hotel, Restaurant and Institutional Education, July 1994.

[6]Donald R. Lehman and Russell S. Winer, *Analysis for Marketing Planning,* 2nd edition (Homewood, IL: Richard D. Irwin, Inc., 1991).

2

Introduction to Hospitality Services Marketing

❖ Chapter Objectives

By the end of this chapter, you should understand:

1. The differences between the nature of products and the nature of services
2. The reasons behind the growth in services
3. The types of attributes that are used to evaluate services
4. The service quality process and the potential gaps in service
5. The important issues in managing services
6. The concept of customer satisfaction and how to assess it
7. Why service failures occur and what can be done to recover
8. The service trends that will continue to impact the industry

❖ Chapter Outline

I. Chapter Opening Profile
II. Introduction to Services Marketing
   A. Services defined

❖ Chapter Opening Profile

WORDS SUCH AS *SCUZZY* AREN'T WELCOME in the lodging industry, but that's the word Best Western International officials are using to launch a new campaign focusing on quality.[1] "It's not a pretty picture," said Jerry Manion, Best Western's chief operating officer. "The message is clear: Best Western's image is dropping." A study by PriceWaterhouseCoopers concluded that consumers and travel agents rate Best Western average to below average on meeting their expectations. Consumers cited inconsistency among the chain's properties as a major reason why they are decreasing their stays with Best Western.

Hotel officials were concerned with the potential impact after a national travel writer reported that she stayed at a "scuzzy" Best Western property. In response, Best Western's Global Research Steering Committee drafted strategic recommendations for consideration by the chain's board of directors to address the quality issue, including:

- Strict enforcement of the company's quality-assurance system
- Development of property scoring (quality assurance, design, services) based on consumer testing
- Reassessment of minimum standards to ensure alignment with consumer expectations

- Improvement or elimination of properties below minimum standards
- Focused development on properties at or above Best Western average

Mike Scholz, vice chairman of the company's board of directors, said the importance of taking care of substandard properties should not be underestimated. "An overwhelming majority [of Best Western properties] meet or exceed current standards," he said. "Best Western is only as good as a customer's last experience."

▲ INTRODUCTION TO SERVICES MARKETING

The growth in the services sector of the worldwide economy has been phenomenal in the last two decades. In the United States, services currently account for more than 75 percent of the gross domestic product (GDP), which is a popular measure of an economy's productivity. Similarly, on an international scale, services continue to account for an ever-increasing percentage of economic activity. Most new jobs are created in the service sector, and the growth in the hospitality industry is a major contributor.

Until very recently, the emphasis within the marketing community has been on products. Now services have surpassed products and have taken on a more important role in marketing. Services, such as those offered by providers in the hospitality industry, have developed marketing strategies and practices that are unique. It has been established that the strategies, tactics, and practices that have been used successfully for product marketers do not always work successfully for those who market services. With the distinct differences between products and services in mind, the field of services marketing has evolved.

Services Defined

Unlike products, which are tangible, services are, for the most part, intangible. A service is not a physical good; rather, it is the performance of an act or a deed. This performance often requires consumers to be present during the production or delivery of the service. Service industries, including hospitality and travel, are actually selling consumers an experience. Service employees such as front desk clerks, housekeeping staff, hostesses, waiters, car rental agents, flight attendants, and travel agents are responsible for creating positive experiences for customers. These frontline employees are critical to the success of service firms and play **boundary-spanning roles** because of their direct contact with customers. These roles are important because customers' perceptions of service firms are formed as a result of their dealings with the boundary-spanning employees. Several reasons underlie the remarkable growth in services.

boundary-spanning roles service employees such as front desk clerks, housekeeping staff, hostesses, waiters, car rental agents, flight attendants, and travel agents who are responsible for creating positive experiences for customers

One of the leading services marketing experts, Christopher Lovelock, cites the following nine reasons for this growth:[2]

1. **Changing patterns of government regulation.** The reduction in government regulation has spurred the growth of services. In recent years, there has been a very noticeable shift toward the government taking a much less active role in the regulation of business activities. The most noteworthy of these shifts have been in the airline, trucking, and telecommunication industries.

2. **Relaxation of professional association standards.** A new element of competition has been introduced into professions such as law and medicine as more of the practitioners in these areas advertise their services. Bans or restrictions on promotion have been largely removed. Within the hospitality industry, standards have also changed. We have seen an increase in advertising focusing on direct comparisons, or attacks, on competitors' products and services. This type of advertising strategy is used to create, or sustain, the perception of superiority in the mind of the consumer in favor of the brand being advertised.

3. **Privatization.** This term was first used in Great Britain when the government adopted the policy of returning national industries from government to private ownership. This transformation has resulted in a greater emphasis on cost containment and a clearer focus on customers' needs. In middle and Eastern Europe, with the fall of Communism, we have witnessed a continuing transformation from planned or government-run economies to market-driven economies fueled by private companies. Many of these countries' governments have released the control of airlines and travel agencies to private firms.

4. **Computerization and technological innovation.** Technology continues to alter the way firms do business with consumers. In all types of businesses, consumers are taking a more active role in the service delivery process. For example, we are starting to see machines in hotel lobbies that allow guests to check themselves in and out, which is similar to the way financial institutions allow consumers to make transactions using automated teller machines (ATMs). Computers with touch screens are used to collect feedback from guests, in much the same manner that comment cards have been used previously. The ease with which a company can maintain and access a database has permitted the development of sophisticated reservation systems and has led to the creation of frequent traveler programs. The use of more sophisticated reservations and property management systems has allowed hospitality and travel firms to improve the level of service provided to guests. Another example of how a hospitality organization can use technology to gain a competitive advantage is in the area of guest history data. If a hotel guest requests a specific type of pillow, this prefer-

ence could be noted in the individual's guest history file. When this guest checks into another hotel operated by the chain, the items that were previously requested could be waiting, without the guest even having to request them. Also, by using sophisticated data analysis techniques, companies can provide directing marketing incentives to customers based on past purchase behavior.

5. **Growth in franchising.** Much of the growth in service firms, including the hospitality industry, has been the direct result of franchising efforts by some of the major companies. **Franchising** is a contractual arrangement whereby one firm (the franchisor) licenses a number of other firms (the franchisees) to use the franchisor's name and business practices. Notable lodging organizations such as Choice Hotels and Hospitality Franchise Systems, as well as food service firms such as McDonald's, Burger King, Kentucky Fried Chicken, and Wendy's have all used franchising as a major vehicle for growth. The continued growth of the hospitality industry by means of franchising has put additional stress on independent owners and operators. In fact, each year the percentage of hospitality and tourism operations that are independent decreases.

   franchising contractual arrangement whereby one firm licenses a number of other firms to use the franchisor's name and business practices

6. **Expansion of leasing and rental businesses.** The expansion of businesses that lease equipment and personnel to firms has been a contributing factor in the growth of the service sector. More and more firms are looking to outsource some elements of their operation, and they often start with elements that are not part of the firm's core product or business. For example, many hotels lease the audiovisual equipment used by their groups in meetings because other firms can specialize in purchasing and maintaining this equipment. Also, many businesses and institutions lease their kitchen facilities to contract food service providers that specialize in quantity production, rather than try to operate their own food service.

7. **Manufacturers as service providers.** Some of the firms that traditionally manufactured and distributed tangible products have found it profitable to provide services as well. For example, most automobile manufacturers have consumer credit agencies to facilitate the purchase of automobiles. In the hospitality industry, the Pepsi-Cola Corporation decided to enter the restaurant industry and distribute its products through acquisitions such as Taco Bell and Kentucky Fried Chicken. In the computer industry, firms such as IBM provide services in addition to hardware and software. In many cases, the profit margins on services are higher than on products such as computer hardware.

8. **Market responses by nonbusiness organizations.** Increasing financial pressures are confronting nonprofit organizations. They are continually looking for ways to decrease costs and increase revenues, as well as paying greater attention to customers' wants and needs. For example, many state and local governments are expanding their services to

promote tourism. Convention and visitors' bureaus are offering more fee-based destination management services and governments are entering into arrangements with private companies to provide travel information services.

9. **Globalization.** It is easy to notice the trend in the services industry for firms to engage in more international commerce. This growth outside the United States increases the overall size of service firms and allows them to become larger and more efficient in their domestic operations. Many American hospitality and travel firms such as Marriott, McDonald's, and Hertz provide services in other countries around the world, and firms from other countries such as Four Seasons and Hotel Nikko offer services in the United States.

The Nature of Services

Along with the growth in services has come an appreciation for the ways in which services are different from products. The traditional ways of marketing tangible products are not always equally effective in marketing services. In many industries, marketing involves tangible manufactured products, such as automobiles, washing machines, and clothing, whereas services industries focus on intangible products such as travel and food-source. However, before we can explore how services can be marketed successfully, we need to examine the ways services differ from products. Lovelock has identified six key differences:[3]

1. **Greater involvement of customers in the production process.** Because consumers tend to be present when the service is provided within a hospitality operation, they are involved in the service production. In many instances, they are directly involved through the element of self-service. Examples of this can be seen in fast-food restaurants as well as in hotels that provide automated check-in and check-out by means of either a machine or a video connection through the television. In any case, customer's level of the satisfaction depends on the nature of the interaction with the service provider, the nature of the physical facilities in which the service is provided, and by the nature of the other guests present in the facility at the time the service is provided.

2. **People as part of the product.** People or firms that purchase services come in contact with other consumers as well as the service employees. For example, a hotel guest waits in line at the front desk or the concierge desk with other guests. In addition, the guests share facilities like the pool, the restaurant, and the fitness center. Therefore, service firms must also manage consumer interactions to the best of their abilities to ensure customer satisfaction. For example, a hotel's sales department would be ill advised to book a religious group the same time as a rock group. Similarly, restaurants separate smokers and

nonsmokers, and they should try to separate other patrons that show some potential for conflict.

3. **Difficulties in maintaining quality standards.** It is easy to standardize the manufacturing process for goods, or tangible products, by establishing an automated assembly line. However, the fact that services are intangible and people are part of the production and delivery process makes it difficult to provide a consistent product or experience on every occasion. Service firms can try to minimize the amount of variability between service encounters, but much of the final product is situational. There are many uncontrollable aspects of the delivery process such as weather, the number of consumers present, the attitudes of the consumers, and the attitudes of the employees. Therefore, it is impossible to consistently control the quality for services in the same manner as the quality of manufactured products. For example, many flights are cancelled due to inclement weather that is beyond the control of the airlines, but it still affects the satisfaction of passengers.

4. **Absence of inventories.** Due to the intangible nature of services, they cannot be inventoried for future use. Therefore, a lost sale can never be recaptured. If there is an empty seat on a flight, a vacant hotel room, or an empty table in a restaurant, the potential revenue for these services is lost forever. In other words, services are perishable much like produce in a supermarket or items in a bakery. It is critical for hospitality and travel firms to manage supply and demand in an attempt to minimize unused capacity. For example, restaurants offer early bird specials and airlines offer supersaver rates in an attempt to shift demand from peak periods to nonpeak periods, thereby increasing revenue and profits.

5. **Relative importance of the time factor.** Hospitality services are generally produced and consumed simultaneously, unlike tangible products, which are manufactured, inventoried, and then sold at a later date. Customers must be present to receive the service. There are real limits to the amount of time that customers are willing to wait to receive service. Service firms study the phenomenon of service queues, or the maximum amount of time a customer will wait for a service before it has a significant (negative) impact on the her perception of service quality. Airline companies offer curbside check-in for the most time-conscious passengers, and restaurants have devised practices such as providing guests with pagers and expanding the bar area in order to reduce the negative effect that results from waiting for service.

6. **The nature of service distribution channels.** The distribution channel for services is usually more direct than the traditional channel (manufacturer–wholesaler–retailer–consumer) used by many product firms. The simultaneous production and consumption normally associated with service delivery limits the use of intermediaries. The service firm is typically both the manufacturer and the retailer, with no need for a

wholesaler to inventory its products. Consumers are present to consume the meals prepared in a restaurant, to take advantage of the amenities in a hotel, and to travel between cities by plane.

Search, Experience, and Credence Qualities

Consumer behavior is covered in greater depth in Chapter 3, but a brief introduction to the subject as it relates to services will be useful at this point. When consumers make purchase decisions, they move through a series of steps that explain the thought process leading up to and following the purchase of a product or service. Prior to making a purchase decision, consumers look for information about the product or service, referred to as **search qualities**. Search qualities are attributes that the consumer can investigate prior to making a purchase. For hospitality and travel services, consumers rely heavily on word-of-mouth and promotional materials such as advertising and publicity. Since services are intangible, search qualities can be difficult to evaluate. However, advances in technology and the increase in consumer advocacy groups have resulted in more information being available to consumers prior to purchase.

search qualities attributes that the consumer can investigate prior to making a purchase

The second set of qualities consumers can use to evaluate services are **experience qualities**. These refer to the attributes that can be evaluated only after the purchase and consumption of a service. The intangible nature of services forces consumers to rely heavily on experience qualities in the final evaluation of services. Therefore, there is a high risk associated with the purchase of services. For example, consumers who want to purchase an automobile will test drive the car and read the consumer reports that are available on that model. Conversely, consumers who rent cars will not be able to evaluate their purchases until after they have committed their payment. Few consumers will take the time or make the effort to test drive potential rental cars at the respective agencies. Similarly, consumers are taking a risk when they choose a restaurant because they can't sample meals before they are purchased.

experience qualities attributes that can be evaluated only after the purchase and consumption of a service

Finally, **credence qualities** are those attributes that are difficult to evaluate even after the service is consumed. Even though you arrive safely at your destination, you can't evaluate the pilot's work in any real depth. In many cases, you know a service was not performed correctly only when an obvious mistake is made. For example, there are often bacteria present on food that is served in restaurants, but it is only brought to the public's attention when there are major ramifications such as food poisoning or deaths.

credence quality attributes that are difficult to evaluate even after the service is consumed

Purchase decisions related to services are more difficult to make because of the lack of search qualities and the difficulty in evaluating credence qualities. Consumers tend to rely on their own past experiences and that of others when making purchase decisions. Therefore, it is critical for service firms to obtain as much feedback from consumers as possible. If consumers don't return, the firm may not know why, and they will probably tell others about their experience. It is better to know if consumers are not satisfied so that appropriate actions can be taken to improve the quality of service and increase repeat business.

▲ SERVICE QUALITY

Firms can use two basic strategies to compete. One is to be a low-cost provider of a particular service and focus on price competition. The other strategy is to focus on quality and try to differentiate your service from those offered by your competitors. Firms that are able to obtain high-quality images are able to charge higher prices. Pricing strategies will be discussed in detail in Chapter 14, but the concept of quality will be introduced in this chapter.

Service quality is a perception resulting from attitudes formed by customers' long-term, overall evaluations of performance.[4] Maintaining high-quality service in the hospitality and travel industry is difficult because of the variability in service delivery mentioned earlier in this chapter. Service quality is affected by all of the individuals who have contact with customers. If one employee provides service that is below standard or fails to satisfy the customer, a negative experience could result. Therefore, it is important to understand the entire process of service delivery that leads to consumer perceptions of quality.

service quality perception resulting from attitudes formed by customers' long term overall evaluations of performance

The Service Quality Process

The service quality process is the product of the expectations and perceptions of a firm's management, its employees, and the customers it serves (see Figure 2.1).[5] Whenever there are differences in expectations or perceptions between the people involved in the delivery and consumption of services, there is a potential for a gap in service quality. It is important for firms to diagnose any service quality gaps because there is a direct relationship between service quality and customer satisfaction. The **service gap** is the final gap that exists when there is a difference between customers' expectations of a service and their perceptions of the actual service once it is consumed. When this difference occurs, it is the result of one or more gaps that occur earlier in the service quality process.

The first potential gap is referred to as the **knowledge gap**, which occurs when management's perception of what consumers expect is different from the consumers' actual expectations. This gap may lead to other gaps in the service quality process, and it is usually the result of a failure in the firm's research program or organizational structure. Firms need to obtain feedback from customers and employees that can be used to design services that will appeal to customers. If the current service offering is not satisfying customers, then the firm should know from its customer surveys or because its employees are willing, and able, to provide valu-

service gap final gap that exists when there is a difference between customers' expectations of a service and their perceptions of the actual service once it is consumed

knowledge gap occurs when management's perception of what consumers expect is different from the consumers' actual expectations

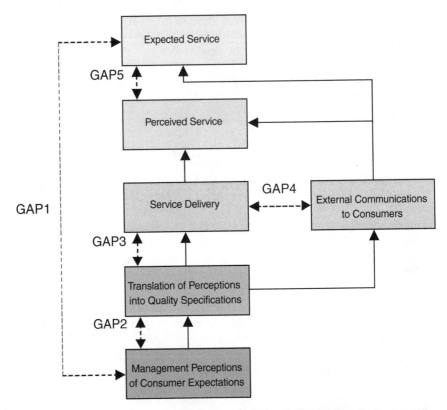

Figure 2.1. **Service Quality Process (Reprinted with permission from the *Journal of Marketing*, published by American Marketing Association[5]).**

able information that they obtain from customers, either voluntarily or involuntarily.

The second potential gap is referred to as the **standards gap**, which refers to the discrepancy that can occur between management's perception of what customers expect and how they design the service delivery process to meet those expectations. Management establishes the specifications to provide the desired service at the desired level of quality. Therefore, even if management is accurate in its perception of customer expectations, there could still be a gap in service because the delivery process does not accomplish the goals of the firm. For example, management may have correctly determined the amount of time that customers are willing to wait to check in to a hotel, but they may not schedule enough front desk clerks to meet the customers' expectations. This could be due to a lack of commitment on the part of management or the result of management trying to reduce the firm's operating costs. One of the techniques that can be used by management is to develop a **service blue-**

standards gap the discrepancy that can occur between management's perception of what customers expect and how they design the service delivery process to meet those exceptions

print, or a flowchart that details the delivery process, including the points of contact with customers. This will help to uncover any shortcomings in the delivery process that may lead to a gap in service quality.

The third potential gap is referred to as the **delivery gap**, which occurs when there is a difference between the service delivery specifications and the actual service delivery. Management may have correctly assessed customer expectations and developed specifications that will meet these expectations, but employees may not deliver the service properly. For example, a restaurant may specify that waiters should approach customers within two minutes of being seated. However, the waiters may be standing around discussing their plans for later in the evening and ignoring the specifications. Firms must find ways to create an atmosphere for employees that ensures their willingness to perform the job tasks as desired by management. Employee selection and training are critical in this process, as are the rewards and recognition provided for good performance.

The fourth potential gap is referred to as the **communications gap**, which occurs when there is a difference between the service delivered and the service promised through the firm's external communications with customers. Many firms have a tendency to promise more than they can deliver in an attempt to persuade customers. For instance, the advertisements for hospitality and travel firms would lead customers to believe that in the event of a problem or mishap the firms will do whatever they can to satisfy customers. Making promises to consumers that can't be delivered is a big mistake that service providers often make. It results in service performance levels that are below consumer expectations, leading to dissatisfaction.

Anyone who travels on a regular basis can provide horror stories related to their experiences with airlines, hotels, and restaurants. Ironically, firms that advertise 100 percent satisfaction guarantees are banking on the fact that most customers will not complain or force the issue. In other cases, firms simply neglect to inform customers about procedures or policies that would affect their expectations. For example, a good waitress will make sure that customers know that a dish is spicy or that a certain entrée will take longer to prepare properly so that customers can make informed decisions and are less likely to be dissatisfied.

If any of the first four gaps occur, then the service gap will occur because the actual service will not meet the customer's expectations. Comment cards and basic surveys will often uncover a service gap, but they may lack the detail needed to evaluate the other potential gaps. Therefore, firms should have a mechanism in place to obtain feedback from customers and employees that can be used to examine the entire service quality process. If services don't meet customers' expectations of quality, then they won't be satisfied, and it is unlikely they will return. Also, they will convey these negative experiences to their friends and acquaintances.

service blueprint flowchart that details the delivery points of contact with customers

delivery gap occurs when there is a difference between the service delivery specifications and the actual service delivery

communications gap occurs when there is a difference between the service delivered and the service promised

Managing Service Quality

To provide high-quality service, it is imperative that all members of the staff, from the highest to the lowest level of the organizational chart, view the guest as the highest priority. Delivering high-quality service is based on an attitude of serving customers. For example, the mission statement of the five-star Greenbrier resort states, "we are ladies and gentlemen serving ladies and gentlemen."[6]

Developing an attitude that places the customer as the very highest priority for the business is critical. Without satisfied customers and repeat patronage, the business will not succeed in the long term. To develop a service quality orientation, customers should be perceived in the following way:

- Each customer is the most important person in any business.
- Customers are not dependent on us, but we are dependent on them.
- Customers do not interrupt our work. They are the purpose for it.
- Customers do us a favor when they call. We are not doing them favors by providing them services.
- Customers are part of our business, not outsiders.
- Customers are human beings like us, with the same feelings and emotions.
- Customers bring us their wants, and it is our job to fulfill them.
- Customers deserve the most courteous and attentive service we can provide.
- Customers are the lifeblood of every business.

Firms that use a customer orientation will be more successful at providing products and services that meet customers' needs and expectations. In contrast, firms that assume they know what is best for the customer will be more likely to fail.

Relationship marketing. All progressive companies devote marketing resources to attract and retain new customers. Relationship marketing is based on the proposition that it is less expensive to keep the customers that you already have than to acquire new customers. It is shortsighted to think that merely attracting new customers will keep the business headed in a successful direction. Rather, an equal amount of attention and resources should be devoted to keeping the customer base that is already in place. In times of slow market growth and increasing competition, it will be less expensive to maintain an existing customer base than to seek new customers.

Relationship marketing involves attracting, developing, and retaining customer relationships.[7] This long-term view toward the customer must be seen as being equal in importance to attracting new customers. Many firms make the mistake of focusing on new customers at the expense of existing customers, and the level of service quality is diminished. For example, hotel salespeople are expected to develop new accounts with corporate and association groups. Sometimes they spend so much time trying to get these new accounts that they neglect some of their existing accounts. This lack of attention may cost the hotel the group's future business because they took the customer for granted. It is important for service firms to build relationships and maintain them.

A relationship marketing approach is highly desirable when the following conditions are met:

- A customer has an ongoing or periodic desire for the service.
- The service customer controls the selection of the service organization.
- Alternative service providers make it easy for customers to switch.

All three of these conditions are present in the hospitality and travel industry. Many firms offer special prices and additional services to good customers in an attempt to build long-term relationships. These practices are most commonly used with business accounts and frequent users. For example, hotels provide contract rates for corporations that supply a high volume of annual business. Airlines receive one of the lowest rates possible in hotels near airports because they have flight crews and passengers that need rooms on a daily basis. Also, airlines build relationships with frequent flyers by providing them with additional services such as preboarding, free upgrades, and airport clubs where they can rest or conduct business away from large crowds.

Internal Marketing.   In addition to focusing efforts on consumers, firms can achieve higher levels of service quality by marketing to their employees. Efforts should be made to communicate with all employees, especially those in boundary-spanning roles that come in contact with customers. The ability to deliver consistent, high-quality service depends on the organization's ability to recruit, train, retain, and motivate dedicated service personnel.

First, service firms need to select and hire employees who are willing and able to provide high-quality service. There are many people in the job market, and firms need to create attractive positions that appeal to highly motivated individuals. There is a range of potential service that an employee can provide from the minimum necessary to retain the position and not be penalized to the maximum possible service. This variability in the level of possible service is referred to as **discretionary effort**. For example, if an airline passenger leaves a carry-on item on a flight, the airline's personnel have some discretion as to the level of service they will provide. They can take their time and forward the item to the traveler's next destination, or they can try to deliver it to the traveler before he boards his next plane or leaves the airport.

Second, service firms should provide employees with adequate training so they possess the skills that are required in performing their job

discretionary effort employee effort beyond the minimum requirements for the job

tasks. In addition, the firm should communicate with employees so they are aware of changes within the organization as well as upcoming events. If service personnel are well trained and they understand what is expected of them, the environment is right for success. Firms can use internal communications such as newsletters and e-mail, and external communications such as advertising and public relations to convey their expectations to employees. An advertisement can be used to create and manage consumer perceptions and expectations, but at the same time, the ad can be used to educate employees as well. One of the major airlines aired a commercial on television that showed an athletic employee running through the airport to catch a traveler who left his briefcase at the check-in counter. This commercial served two purposes: (1) it let customers know that the airline provided high-quality service, and (2) it gave employees an idea of the firm's expectations for service.

Finally, firms need to provide employees with rewards and recognition when they perform at a high level of discretionary effort. This will motivate service personnel to continue to perform at high levels and remain loyal to the firm. Retaining good employees is important in providing high-quality service, and it reduces the costs associated with turnover. It takes a great deal of time and effort to hire and train good employees. Firms can use **extrinsic rewards** like pay raises and bonuses or **intrinsic rewards** like recognition and job satisfaction to motivate employees. Many firms recognize the "employees of the month" by honoring them with a plaque displayed where customers can see them or allowing them to use a special parking space close to the building.

extrinsic rewards pay raises and bonuses used to motivate employees

intrinsic rewards recognition and job satisfaction used to motivate employees

▲ CUSTOMER SATISFACTION

Most firms understand the importance of customer satisfaction and will at least provide basic training to their employees. The more sophisticated firms actually have instruments that they use to measure customer satisfaction and establish **benchmarks** for future comparisons. Unfortunately, many firms still only pay lip service to customer satisfaction and the complaints received from customers. The following information was collected through the efforts of the Technical Assistance Research Program more than a decade ago, but it is still thought to be accurate today[8]:

benchmarks base measurements used to evaluate performance

- The average business does not hear from 96 percent of its unhappy customers.
- For every complaint received, 26 other customers have the same problem.
- The average person with a problem tells 9 or 10 people, and 13 percent will tell more than 20.
- Customers who have their complaints resolved to their satisfaction tell an average of five people about the experience.

- Complainers are more likely to do business with you again than non-complainers who have a problem: 54–70 percent if resolved at all, and 95 percent if resolved quickly.

These statistics support the contention that it is more common for a dissatisfied customer to tell people about a bad experience than for a satisfied customer to tell people about a good experience. However, firms should take note that it is beneficial to have customers voice their complaints so that they can be resolved and increase the likelihood that the customers will return.

Improving Customer Service and Customer Satisfaction

Improving customer service should be a top priority of all managers working in the hospitality industry. **Customer satisfaction** occurs when a firm's service, as perceived by customers, meets or exceeds their expectations. Firms that can consistently meet or exceed customer expectations will develop good reputations and often good quality images. As each of us travels, we encounter service providers in hotels and restaurants who provide exceptional service. This type and consistency of service does not happen by accident; it begins with a commitment by management to make it that way. Conversely, when the opposite occurs, the finger should be pointed at management as well.

An excellent source for methods to improve service is *Quality Service: The Restaurant Manager's Bible* by William Martin.[9] Martin recommends the five-step process for improving customer service that is shown in Figure 2.2.

1. **Define your standards of quality service with measurable indicators.** Before you can evaluate the level of service provided by lay personnel within your organization, it is imperative that you establish the standards by which they will be judged. These standards, or benchmarks, should be observable and measurable. For example, it might be reasonable to expect front desk personnel in a hotel to answer the telephone within four rings or room service to deliver meals within 30 minutes. Once these standards are developed, it is important that they be communicated to all personnel. It is crucial that standards are clearly defined before any plans are developed to improve the level of service.

   Martin suggests two major dimensions to define quality service, the **procedural dimension** and the **convivial dimension.** The procedural dimension includes incremental flow of service, timeliness, accommodation to consumer needs, anticipation of consumer needs before they occur or are requested by the consumer, communication that is clear and concise, consumer feedback, and proper coordination through supervision. The convivial dimension includes displaying a positive attitude and body language, using the guest's name as a means of deliv-

customer satisfaction occurs when a firm's service, as perceived by customers, meets or exceeds their expectations

procedural dimension refers to the procedures used in the service delivery process

convivial dimension refers to the human element in service delivery

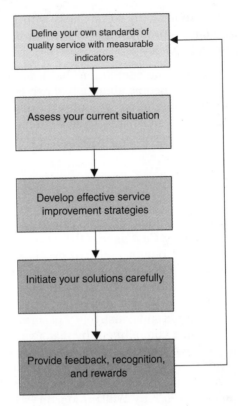

Figure 2.2. Martin's Five-Step Process for Improving Customer Service

ering personal attention, attending to the guest on a personal basis, providing guidance to guests who are indecisive, and solving problems that arise.

2. **Assess your current situation.** As in any continuous improvement program, before you move forward, you must determine your current position. This can be done by objectively assessing the level of service currently provided within the organization; this involves conducting an audit of the services provided by service personnel within the organization. As a result of the audit, the strengths and weaknesses of the firm can be determined; this will provide a means of building on the aspects of service that are positive and improving the areas that are deficient.

3. **Develop effective service improvement strategies.** This must be accomplished through well-planned and thorough training of service providers. Attention must be paid to identifying objectives for the training and providing specific instructions and clear descriptions of the expected outcome of the training.

4. **Initiate your solutions carefully.** As is the case with any plan, implementation is the most critical stage. It is best to proceed with caution, taking steps incrementally rather than all at once. It is best to build on small successes, rather than trying to accomplish too much too soon.

5. **Provide feedback, recognition, and rewards**. Positive feedback must be provided if the change in behavior is to continue. A reward structure must be provided that will maintain the level of interest and enthusiasm among the service providers throughout their careers. This represents a major challenge for management, but one that is well worth the effort.

Finally, management must continually evaluate the performance of its employees and make the appropriate changes. Over time, customers' expectations of service firms change, and competitive firms may increase the level of service that is considered the standard in an industry. Therefore, firms must constantly reassess their strategies and redefine their service standards. Service performance and customer satisfaction should be measured and evaluated using benchmarks established during previous periods. Also, direct comparisons with the performance of firms considered industry leaders are an excellent way to establish goals for future improvement.

Service Failures, Customer Complaints, and Recovery Strategies

Service failures occur at **critical incidents**, or "moments of truth," in the service encounter, when customers interact with a firm's employees. It is important to provide service personnel with the authority and the recovery tools necessary to correct service failures as they occur. This section will discuss the types of service failures, common consumer complaints, and recovery strategies that can be used to repair the service failures.

critical incidents "moments of truth" when customers interact with a firm's employees

Service Failures. The timeliness and form of response by service providers to service failures will have a direct impact on customer satisfaction and quality perceptions. Service failures are assigned to one of three major categories: (1) responses to service delivery system failures, (2) responses to customer needs and requests, and (3) unprompted and unsolicited employee actions.

The first category, **system failures**, refers to failures in the core service offering of the firm. These failures are the result of normally available services being unavailable, unreasonably slow service, or some other core service failure that will differ by industry. For example, a hotel's pool may have a leak and be closed, a customer may have to wait a long time for the shuttle to an airport rental car agency, or an airline might mishandle a passenger's luggage.

system failures failures in the core service offering of the firm

The second category, **customer needs failures**, are based on employee responses to customer needs or special requests. These failures come

customer needs failures based on employee responses to customer needs or special requests in the form of special needs, customer preferences, customer errors, and disruptive others (i.e., disputes between customers). For example, a hotel guest may want to have a pet in the room, a customer may want to be switched to a window seat on an airline, a customer at an event may lose his ticket, or a customer in a restaurant may be smoking in a non-smoking section.

The third category, **unsolicited employee actions**, refers to the actions, both good and bad, of employees that are not expected by customers. These actions can be related to the level of attention an employee gives to customers, to unusual actions that can be performed by employees, to an action's reinforcement of a customer's cultural norms, or an employee's actions under adverse conditions. For example, a hostess in a restaurant could anticipate the needs of a family with a small child, a hotel front desk clerk could give a free upgrade to a guest who waited in line too long, a flight attendant could ignore passengers with children, or a cruise employee could help to evacuate passengers during a crisis.

unsolicited employee actions actions, both good and bad, of employees that are not expected by customers

Customer Complaint Behavior. As mentioned earlier in this chapter, there are certain undesired outcomes are associated with dissatisfied customers. Two of the more common are to engage in negative word-of-mouth and to change service providers. A third, less common reaction is to engage in some form of retaliation. This retaliation can range from a negative word-of-mouth campaign to causing physical damage or launching a major protest. The way a firm approaches and handles complaints will determine its long-term performance. Some firms show a dislike for customers that complain, while other firms create an atmosphere that encourages customers to voice their concerns. For example, Bertucci's Brick-Oven Pizzerias, headquartered in Massachusetts, offers customers a toll-free number that they can call to register a complaint.

Most customers complain in an attempt to reverse an undesirable state. Other more complicated reasons for complaining are to release pressure, to regain some form of control over a situation, or to get the sympathy of others. Whatever the reason, the outcome is that customers are not completely satisfied, and it is in the firm's best interest to know when this occurs. There are many other dissatisfied customers who do not complain because they don't know what to do or they don't think it will do any good.

Recovery strategies. When customers complain, firms are presented with the opportunity to recover from service failures. Service recovery occurs when a firm's reaction to a service failure results in customer satisfaction and goodwill. In fact, customers who are involved in successful service recoveries often demonstrate higher levels of satisfaction than customers who do not report service failures or complain. The following is a list of popular service recovery strategies:

- *Cost/benefit analysis.* Service firms should compare the costs of losing customers and obtaining new customers with the benefits of keeping existing customers. Most firms place a high value on retaining customers. However, some guests take advantage of satisfaction guarantees and complain on every occasion. Many hotel chains, like Doubletree, maintain a database on complaints and will flag chronic complainers.

- *Actively encourage complaints.* It is better to know when customers are not satisfied so that action can be taken to rectify the situation. It is important to note that, while unhappy customers may not complain to service firms, they will often complain to their family and friends. Hospitality and travel firms use comment cards and toll-free numbers to encourage customers to provide feedback. Also, service personnel are trained to ask customer "if everything was okay."

- *Anticipate the need for recovery.* Service firms should "blueprint" the service delivery process and determine the moments of truth, or critical incidents, where customers interact with employees. The process can be designed to avoid failures, but recovery plans should be determined in the event a failure occurs.

- *Respond quickly.* The more timely the response in the event of a service failure, the more likely that recovery efforts will be successful. Once a customer leaves a service establishment, the likelihood of a successful recovery falls dramatically. Based on this principle, firms like Marriott Hotels and Resorts provide service hotlines at each hotel to help resolve problems quickly.

- *Train employees.* Employees should be made aware of the critical incidents and provided with potential strategies for recovery. For example, some hotel training programs use videotaped scenarios of service failures to show employees potential problems and the appropriate solutions.

- *Empower the front line.* In many cases, a successful recovery will hinge on a frontline employee's ability to take timely action and make a decision. Firms should empower employees to handle service failures at the time they occur, within certain limits. For example, Ritz-Carlton allows its employees to spend up to $1,000 to take care of dissatisfied customers.

Recently, Northwest Airlines had a service failure at the Detroit airport. The airline flew several of its planes into Detroit during a period of inclement weather. Unfortunately, many of the outbound flights were cancelled, and no gates were available for unloading passengers from the inbound flights. This traffic jam left many passengers stranded as the airplanes sat on the taxiways for as long as 8 hours. Northwest's inability to provide the passengers with information or a solution has resulted in a class action lawsuit. Having delayed flights and a shortage of gates is not a new phenomenon at airports in climates like Detroit, and Northwest

Airlines should have had a viable service recovery program in place that could have lessened the severity of the problem and avoided the impending lawsuit.

Techniques to Assess Customer Satisfaction

One of the critical components of a firm's commitment to customer satisfaction is to obtain feedback that will provide an assessment of the firm's performance. Then, benchmarks can be established and future progress can be evaluated. Also, these measures can be used to reward service personnel in a way that is consistent with a firm's customer satisfaction goals. The following is a discussion of the most common techniques used by firms to assess customer satisfaction.

Spoken Comments and Complaints.   Listening to consumer comments and complaints is the most straightforward way to evaluate customer satisfaction. Service firms should set up formal systems that encourage customer and employee feedback regarding service experiences. It is important not to overlook the value of the information obtained by boundary spanning personnel through their normal contact with customers. One of the most recent approaches is to provide toll-free numbers that customers can call to voice complaints.

Surveys and Comment Cards.   Many hospitality and travel firms leave comment cards in guests' rooms, on tables in restaurants, and at other points of contact so they can obtain feedback. One of the problems associated with this method is the lack of representation. The response rate is small, and it tends to be biased toward those who are most upset and chronic complainers. Larger operations will conduct surveys through the corporate offices either by telephone or mail. Surveys will normally be more representative than comment cards and provide more detailed information. These types of surveys also provide for a more representative sample of customers.

Number of Repeat Customers.   Service firms can gauge customer satisfaction by keeping track of repeat business. Higher levels of satisfaction would be associated with higher percentages of repeat customers. This is an unobtrusive method of assessing customer satisfaction, but it doesn't provide much detail.

Trends in Sales and Market Share.   Another way to evaluate customer satisfaction without direct contact with customers is to examine the firm's internal sales records. Comparisons can be made on a month-to-month basis and with the same period of the previous year. Higher levels of satisfaction would be associated with increases in sales. However, firms should be careful with this method because there are many possible explanations for increases in sales. For example, the firm may have launched a new advertising campaign, a competitor may be renovating or going out of business, or the firm may have decreased its prices. In addition to examining sales records, firms should also look at market share. This measure considers sales in relation to the competition, which is a more accurate assessment of improved market performance. However, there could also be other explanations for changes in market share besides customer satisfaction.

Shopping Reports.   Another approach used by hospitality and travel firms is to have someone consume a service just like any other customer. The "secret shopper" can be an employee of the firm, an outside person chosen by the firm, or an employee of an outside firm that specializes in this activity. These shoppers are normally equipped with detailed evaluation forms based on company guidelines that can be used to record the desired information. It is often recommended that someone outside the firm be used in an attempt to maintain some level objectivity. It is important to have a particular operation evaluated by more than one shopper on several occasions throughout the desired period. Doing so will result in a more representative sample of service experiences.

▲ TRENDS AFFECTING THE HOSPITALITY INDUSTRY

Identifying trends within any business is one of the keys to success. Being in a position to identify what is occurring and what is likely to occur in the future is very important. As discussed in Chapter 1, when studying trends in a macro or broad sense, one should examine five major areas: the competitive environment, the economic environment, the political and legal environment, the social environment, and the technological environment.

Several issues and trends are critical to understanding hospitality and tourism marketing. They help to put into proper perspective what is occurring in the competitive marketplace. Three trends that are having and will continue to have an impact on the hospitality industry are shrinking customer loyalty, increasing customer sophistication, and increased emphasis on the needs of individual customers.

Shrinking Customer Loyalty

Advertising and promotions for the hospitality and travel industry's product–service mix have traditionally focused on the product, the services provided, and the physical plant or atmosphere in which the customer enjoys the product–service mix. Today, many hospitality and travel firms focus their promotions on price; that is, there is heavy price competition and a good deal of discounting. Unfortunately, price discounting is a short-term strategy that seldom builds brand loyalty. Consumers often shop around for the best deal and are loyal only to organizations that give them a consistently superior deal. Recognizing this, companies have sought ways to increase brand loyalty, especially among heavy users of the product–service mix. The best examples of this approach are the frequent flyer programs promoted by the airlines, and the frequent traveler programs promoted by the lodging companies. The basic concept common to all of these programs is to:

- Identify individuals who frequently use your product,
- Recognize the contribution those individuals make to the success of your company,
- Reward those individuals with awards and incentives that will increase their loyalty to your company.

Tie-ins with other companies providing travel-related services are also frequently used. For example, it is common for airlines, hotels, and rental car companies to offer bonus points within their programs if the traveler uses the services offered by one of the companies participating in the tie-in. Both the airlines and hotel companies are constantly making minor alterations to their programs.

Increasing Consumer Sophistication

The budget segment of the lodging industry has undergone significant growth in the last several years. This growth has been fueled by the consumer demand for affordable accommodations that provide good value. In fact, consumers are focusing more on value and less on quality or price alone. Consumers have become more sophisticated and understand the concept of value at any price level. Companies have responded with brands that offer good quality at an affordable price (e.g., Hampton Inns, Comfort Inns, Holiday Inn Express, and Fairfield Inns). Each of these brands feature very nicely appointed guest rooms, limited or no public meeting space, limited or no food service provided on the hotel site, and a complimentary continental breakfast for guests. These limited service brands incur lower development and operating expenses, and thereby provide guests with a lower price and good value, something that all consumers are seeking.

Hotels in the upscale segment are also trying to increase the consumer's perception of value. They continually provide a broad assortment of amenities, such as health clubs on property, business centers, rooms that provide more work space for business travelers, and personalized concierge service. These properties are striving to become "one-stop" destinations, providing a complete product–service mix that includes a variety of food and beverage outlets, in-house office services, a wide variety of meeting room configurations, and other services, such as recreation, that will appeal to potential guests.

Within the fast-food service segment, companies often "bundle" their products in an attempt to increase sales and provide a better value for their customers. For example, they might combine a sandwich, a large order of french fries, and a large soft drink at a price lower than the normal price if the same items were purchased separately. Similarly, tour operators and travel agents attempt to provide customers with more value by "bundling" the various components of travel (e.g., airline ticket, hotel, rental car, and tickets for tourist attractions) at a price lower than the sum of the individual components.

Increased Emphasis on the Needs of Individual Customers

The markets within both food service and lodging segments have been segmented for a long time. However, during the 1980s and 1990s, this trend has become even more pronounced. Mass marketing has become a thing of the past, as more firms increase their product lines to meet the specific needs of smaller segments of travelers and diners. Nowhere is this phenomenon more apparent than in the lodging industry. During the last several years, most of the major lodging chains developed several new brands or types of lodging properties to appeal to market segments that they weren't currently serving. In addition, many hotel chains have merged with or acquired other hotel chains that focus on different market segments.

Improvements in technology have given firms the ability to maintain large databases that detail consumer purchasing behavior and preferences. This information can be used to direct marketing efforts toward individual customers or market segments. Instead of relying on the mass media for promotions, a marketer can target past customers through direct mail with special promotions and incentives that have a high probability of being successful. There is more customization of products and promotions and less wasted coverage with media campaigns.

▲ MARKETING ACTION NOW!

One of this book's authors attended a conference at a popular hotel in a southeastern city. The author was traveling with his wife and his son, who was then four years old. The author's connecting flight was delayed, so the family didn't arrive at their final destination until 10:00 PM. Fortunately, the hotel had an advertised check-in facility at the airport, and the author assumed he would be able to secure his room while waiting for the luggage. When he approached the employee at the hotel's airport facility, he was told that check-in service was not available at that time of the day. The author found this to be surprising since this was the very type of situation in which an airport facility would be beneficial.

Next, the family took a shuttle van from the airport to the hotel where they were given directions to the front desk. Two front-desk clerks were on duty when the passengers from the airport shuttle arrived a little before 11:00 PM. However, one of the front-desk clerks was apparently going off duty at 11:00 PM, and she proceeded to close her drawer at that exact moment. This left a line of approximately 10 or12 guests to be checked in by one clerk. Needless to say, it took some time to process all of the guests, and the author had to wait 20 or 30 minutes for his turn. The author was assigned to a room, but at this point he had a few bags and his son was fast asleep and had to be carried. When he asked for assistance with his luggage, he was told that no one was available at this time of night. The hotel was large, having over 2,000 rooms, and the rooms were spread out among several adjacent buildings. The author's room was two buildings away from the lobby area.

The author and his wife struggled to carry the luggage and their son to their room. They arrived there about 11:30 PM and attempted to enter the room. The key unlocked the door, but the door would not open. After a couple of attempts, the couple heard a woman's voice in the room. Obviously, the room had been double-booked and the woman was awoken from her sleep. The author used the house phone to call the front desk and explain the predicament. The front desk manager offered a quick apology and said that she would send someone with a key to a nearby room. About 10 minutes later, a housekeeper happened to be going through the hallway and she let the family into the room that the author had been given over the phone. However, the housekeeper had no idea what was going on and took the author's word. After another 10 minutes, the phone in the room rang and the author spoke with the front desk manager. She acted as though she had sent the housekeeper to open the room, but she still needed to send someone with the room keys. She apologized one last time and told the author to call the front desk if he had any other problems.

1. Discuss the gaps in the service quality process for this service encounter.
2. What kind of service failures occurred, and what recovery strategies were employed?
3. Did the hotel meet the author's expectations? What other actions could have been taken?

▲ SUMMARY OF CHAPTER OBJECTIVES

This chapter introduced you to the important area of hospitality services marketing. It started by defining services and explaining the characteristics that separate tangible products and services. Services are intangible and cannot be inventoried. This requires changes in the distribution process, and it makes it difficult to maintain consistent quality. It also requires more involvement on the part of customers, who actually become part of the product. The intangible nature of services results in more of an emphasis on experience qualities that are evaluated after a product is consumed, and less on search qualities that can be evaluated prior to purchase.

The concept of service quality is important because consumers form perceptions of a firm based on its ability to provide a consistent level of service. This chapter introduced the service quality process and the potential gaps that could occur throughout the process. These gaps in service will decrease the level of service quality and lead to a decrease in customer satisfaction. Firms learn to manage service operations and improve quality through employee selection and training. Once a firm focuses on the needs of consumers, it can build customer loyalty through relationship marketing. The overall performance of the firm can be improved through internal marketing efforts that attempt to communicate with employees and provide them with an environment for success.

Customer satisfaction is the ultimate goal for a firm because it leads to brand loyalty and repeat purchases. Firms must meet or exceed customer expectations on a consistent basis in order to satisfy them. This chapter discussed ways to improve customer service and increase customer satisfaction. There are critical incidents, or moments of truth, when customers interact with employees, and service failures can occur. Firms should encourage customers to voice their complaints so that they can anticipate and avoid possible failures. Also, firms can prepare service recovery strategies and train their employees to use them. The firm's progress concerning customer satisfaction can be assessed using the techniques provided in this chapter, and benchmarks can be set for future comparisons.

Finally, the chapter discussed some of the current trends in the hospitality and travel industry that affect service operations. First, there is shrinking customer loyalty. Customers have many alternatives for fulfilling their needs, and it is easy to compare these alternatives with all of the information that is available. The stronger the competition, the more incentives that customers are given to switch service providers. Second, consumers are becoming more sophisticated. Consumers have access to a proliferation of information about products and services. This information allows them to focus on overall value, rather than price or quality alone. Also, consumer advocacy organizations provide helpful tips for getting bargains and avoiding firms with poor reputations. Finally, there is an increased emphasis on the individual needs of customers. Improved technology has made database marketing possible, allowing more precise targeting of markets and less wasted coverage with promotions. Firms are able to service more market segments by introducing new brands or forming relationships with other firms (e.g., strategic alliances, mergers, and acquisitions).

▲ KEY WORDS AND CONCEPTS

Benchmarking

Boundary-spanning roles

Communications gap

Computerization and
technological innovation

Consumer complaint behavior

Consumer expectations

Convivial dimension

Core service strategy

Cost/benefit analysis

Credence qualities

Critical incidents

Customer satisfaction

Customer service

Delivery gap

Discretionary effort

Empowerment

Experience qualities

Extrinsic rewards

Franchising

Globalization

Gross domestic product (GDP)

Internal marketing

Intrinsic rewards

Knowledge gap

Moments of truth

Perceived value

Privitization

Procedural dimension

Product bundling

Recovery strategies

Relationship marketing

Search qualities

Service blueprint

Service failures

Service gap

Service quality

Services marketing

Standards gap

▲ QUESTIONS FOR REVIEW AND DISCUSSION

1. What are services? Do you believe that service marketing should be studied separately from product marketing? Why or why not?

2. List and discuss several of the reasons behind the growth in services. Which of these do you consider to be the most important? Why?

3. How do services differ from products?

4. What is service quality? Discuss the service quality process.

5. What are search and experience qualities? How are they used my consumers to evaluate services?

6. What is relationship marketing? How can it be applied to the hospitality industry?

7. What are the types of service failures? What recovery strategies can be used in the event of a service failure?

8. How would you define customer satisfaction? How can you improve customer satisfaction?

9. What are the techniques that can be used to assess customer satisfaction?

10. Discuss some of the current trends that affect hospitality and travel firms.

▲ NOTES

[1] Jeff Higley, "Quality Issue Concerns Best Western," *Hotel & Motel Management*, volume 213, number 21 (December 14, 1998), p. 4+.

[2] Christopher H. Lovelock, *Services Marketing*, second edition (Englewood Cliffs, NJ: Prentice-Hall, 1991), pp. 1–6.

[3] Christopher H. Lovelock, *Services Marketing*, second edition (Englewood Cliffs, NJ: Prentice-Hall, 1991), pp. 7–8.

[4] K. Douglas Hoffman and John E. G. Bateson, *Essentials of Services Marketing* (Fort Worth, TX: The Dryden Press, 1997).

[5] A. Parasuraman, Valerie Zeithaml, and Leonard Berry, "A Conceptual Model of Service Quality and Its Implications for Service Quality Research," *Journal of Marketing*, 49 (Fall 1985) pp. 41–50.

[6] Mission statement card, The Greenbrier, White Sulphur Springs, WV, 1994.

[7] Leonard L. Berry and A. Parasuraman, *Marketing Services: Competing Through Quality* (New York: The Free Press, 1991), p. 133.

[8] Karl Albrecht and Ron Zemke, *Service America! Doing Business in the New Economy* (Homewood, IL: Business One Irwin, 1985), p. 6.

[9] William B. Martin, *Quality Service: The Restaurant Manager's Bible* (Ithaca, NY: Cornell University, 1986).

Understanding and Targeting Hospitality Consumers

3

Understanding the Behavior of Hospitality Consumers

❖ Chapter Objectives

By the end of this chapter, you should understand:

1. The external and internal factors that influence consumer decision-making
2. The process used by consumers to make purchase decisions
3. The alternative problem-solving processes and techniques
4. Some basic models of consumer behavior
5. The differences between organizational and consumer buying processes

❖ Chapter Outline

❖ Chapter Opening Profile

THE DEMAND FOR SERVICES IN THE organizational market is derived from the demand in consumer markets. In addition, purchase decisions by organizations are affected by many outside factors. One of the best examples of organizational buying in hospitality and travel is the meetings market. Meeting planners make decisions regarding destinations and hotel facilities that can have a major impact on an area or hotel. However, meeting planners must consider the needs and desires of their groups. Association meeting planners often find themselves dealing with social and political issues that affect their organizations.[1]

For example, the American Library Association (ALA) has had a long history of "political correctness" in choosing destinations for its meetings, starting as far back as 1936 with issues regarding racial equality. In 1977, the ALA passed a resolution to hold meetings only in states that had ratified the Equal Rights Amendment. In 1992, the ALA's Association of College and Research Libraries pulled its national conference out of Arizona when the state failed to recognize Martin Luther King, Jr. holiday legislation. In 1995, the ALA cancelled a meeting in Cincinnati because of legislation barring enforcement of legal protection for lesbian and gay citizens. These decisions affect many people and businesses. For instance, the Greater Phoenix Visitors and Convention Bureau estimates the city lost 166 groups and $190 million in revenues, and that 4,700 jobs were affected during the period before the holiday was recognized (1987–1992).

▲ INTRODUCTION

Successful marketing managers focus on understanding their consumers' wants and needs as clearly as possible. Thorough marketing research has allowed marketing managers of tangible products such as automobiles, toothpaste, laundry detergent, and most other products to understand their customers. More recently, marketers have begun to better understand the subject of consumer behavior as it relates to the consumption of services. This knowledge enables marketing managers to develop sophisticated marketing programs aimed at very specifically targeted market segments.

One of the most perplexing problems confronting hospitality managers is to understand why hospitality consumers behave as they do. This chapter explores several important aspects of consumer behavior, including the internal and external factors that influence consumer behavior, the way in which consumers make purchase decisions, satisfaction of hospitality consumers, and how continuous quality improvement can be used as a marketing tool.

Understanding the behavior of hospitality and tourism consumers is among the most important challenges facing management. It is critical that managers be in constant communication with those who consume the products and services, and pay close attention to consumer needs so that they will be ready to change elements of the marketing mix when the consumer preferences, wants, or needs change. As an example, in recent years many consumers have demonstrated an increasing emphasis on healthier diets. This concern has led them to request and, in some cases, to demand menu choices that are healthier. Restaurants have responded by providing menu choices that are lower in fat and salt, and adding more fresh fruits, vegetables, and grains. The products and services made available to consumers must respond to the changing needs of the target market segments.

The study of consumer behavior focuses on understanding consumers as they purchase products or services. This behavior takes place within the larger context of the environment in which each individual operates. Therefore, consumer behavior examines the roles and influences that others have on the behavior of individual consumers.

The study of consumer behavior is based on two fundamental ideas: that consumer behavior is rational and predictable and that as marketers, we can influence this behavior. Contrary to what some may think, the behavior of consumers is not irrational or random. Consumer behavior that appears to be irrational to the outside observer is very rational to the individual making the purchase decisions. In an earlier example, we noted that restaurants were increasing the number of healthier menu choices because restaurant guests were demanding more healthy choices. Yet at the same time, the sale of desserts and other sweets has also increased. Is this rational? Does it make sense from a consumer's point of view? How can consumers appear to exhibit this conflicting, and perhaps irrational, behavior? Consider it from the restaurant guest's point of view and it is very rational. Suppose that a particular customer has made healthy menu choices all during the week. This individual has reduced the amount of calories, fat, and salt in his diet throughout the entire week. However, when dining out on Friday evening, he indulges in a high-caloric, fattening dessert, saying to his friends, "It's been a long hard week, and I'm going to treat myself to the mocha-swirl cheesecake." This is not irrational behavior in the mind of the consumer. He believes that he has cut back on calorie and fat consumption all week and in fact deserves a special treat at dinner on Friday. The challenge for restaurant marketers is to recognize the trends in consumer behavior and provide the products and services that consumers demand.

Consumer behavior can be described, and to some extent, it can be predicted. Certainly, the study of consumer behavior is based to a large extent on theory. However, this theory can be used to understand and predict the future behavior of consumers. McNeal advances the idea that human behavior is influenced by several factors:[2]

- **The social setting.** All consumers make decisions and take actions within the larger social setting and, in doing so, are influenced by their peers. In addition, the same consumers will, in turn, influence the actions of other consumers. Social settings will vary greatly. For example, the social setting of a consumer living in New York City is very different from that of someone living in Ames, Iowa; Paris, France; or an Eastern European country.

- **Social forces.** Forces within the society set the standards of acceptable behavior. These rules are both written and unwritten, and they are established by those within the society with the most influence. For example, the behavior that a college student exhibits at a party on campus is likely to be quite different than the behavior that is exhibited while at home during a Christmas vacation. Different social forces are at work in these two situations.

- **Roles.** A role is a pattern of behavior associated with a specific position within a social setting. Each of us assumes a variety of roles, some professional, others personal. Each role brings with it a set of expectations for behavior. For example, when an individual is in a position of authority, such as the manager of a hotel, employees look to the manger to provide direction, make decisions, and help the operation to run smoothly. However, when this manager leaves work and goes home, he or she may assume a less active decision-making role when interacting with his or her children. For example, at home, the manager may defer to the children the decision about what type of activity they will engage in during a day that they spend together.

- **Attitudes relative to roles.** Within each of the roles that we play are attitudes and knowledge that we gain about the setting. Attitudes are defined as favorable or unfavorable evaluation about objects or situations. Knowledge is defined as facts that we gain about objects or situations. Attitudes are directly tied to a consumer's needs. These needs, which are the cause for all consumer behavior, are linked to an individual's attitudes and knowledge.

Why should you study consumer behavior? Because it is critical to the future success of all hospitality managers. Every day, managers in the hospitality industry come into direct contact with many consumers. One of the primary goals for each of these managers is to create and maintain satisfied consumers. Without a working knowledge of their wants and needs, it will be much more difficult to satisfy them. Keep in mind that the fundamental reason for being in business is to create and satisfy consumers.

Second, if a company is to grow and prosper it must anticipate the needs and wants of consumers. For example, if a hospitality company is considering whether to build a new hotel, it must anticipate the demand for hotel rooms, meeting space, and food and beverage demand for a particular location. In doing so, they are likely to project demand for several years into the future. One of the ways to help make a better decision in this case is to more thoroughly understand the current and future behavior of consumers.

▲ FACTORS THAT INFLUENCE CONSUMER BEHAVIOR

Consumers do not make purchase decisions in a vacuum. Rather, they are subject to both internal and external factors that influence them.

External Influences on Consumer Behavior

Consumers are influenced by external and internal influences. The external influences include culture, socioeconomic level, reference groups, and household.

Culture. Culture is defined as the patterns of behavior and social relations that characterize a society and separate it from others. Culture com-

Consumer behavior is influenced by both internal and external factors. *Courtesy of Knott's Berry Farm:* © *Knott's Berry Farm*

municates values, ideals, and attitudes that help individuals communicate with each and evaluate situations. It is important in viewing culture to draw legitimate generalizations about a given culture or subculture without resorting to stereotyping. An individual's culture provides a frame of reference concerning acceptable behaviors, and as such, culture is a learned set of arbitrary values. The dominant culture in the United States today stresses equality, use of resources, materialism, individualism, and youth.

Difference in culture is most apparent when a hospitality and tourism firm attempts to expand into international markets. There are significant differences between, for example, the way that Europeans and Americans make purchase decisions and exhibit travel behavior. For example, in much of Europe, it is very common for a family to take an extended vacation that might last for two, three, or more weeks. In France, it is very common for businesses to shut down for much of the month of August while the entire country is on vacation. In the United States, the opposite trend is prevalent. Families are less likely to take a vacation of more than one week and are more likely to take a series of minivacations that extend over three-day weekends. In fact, in the early 1990s, Stouffer Renaissance Hotels went so far as to trademark the phrase "break-ation"™ to use in their promotion and advertising to describe the mini or get-away vacations that have become common in the United States.

In addition to the general culture of the United States, marketers must also be concerned with subcultures. Subcultures might include the African-American subculture, the Jewish subculture, the Hispanic subculture, the Asian subculture, and the youth subculture.

One example illustrates the importance of subcultures in marketing. Although families are one of the major markets for fast-food chains, and parents pay the bills for the family, much of the advertising for these chains is directed toward the youth subculture. Research has shown that it is often the children who influence the decision on where to dine, once the adults have decided to dine out.

Socioeconomic level. Socioeconomic level has a large influence in consumer decision-making. Marketing managers have long attempted to correlate socioeconomic level with dining-out habits and travel patterns. Hospitality managers must identify the relative socioeconomic levels to which the operation appeals and appeal directly to those groups with the marketing mix that they use. For example, an upscale and expensive four- or five-star resort property will target its promotional efforts at those in upper income groups. They are likely to advertise in publications read by professional and those who are in the top 25 percent of annual household income. That is their target market.

Reference groups. A reference group is a group with whom an individual identifies to the point where the group dictates a standard of behavior. Reference groups exert tremendous influence on consumers' hospitality and tourism purchase decisions. Every individual is influenced directly and indirectly. Marketing research has identified three types of reference groups: comparative, status, and normative.

Individual consumers use reference groups to compare their own feelings and thoughts with those of others. For example, an individual may have gone to dinner at a restaurant and felt that the food and service were excellent. Before these perceptions are internalized, however, a reference group is often consulted to validate the perceptions. An individual may check with friends who are members of a reference group, asking for their perceptions of the restaurant. They will then compare the perceptions of their friends against their own perceptions. In many cases, the perceptions of a reference group can influence purchase and repeat purchase behavior.

Reference groups also serve a status function. For example, when an individual seeks to become a member of a group, his or her actions are likely to emulate the group members' behaviors. If someone looks up to a reference group as a source of status, he or she is likely to model the behavior exhibited by the members of the reference group.

Finally, reference groups establish norms and values that regulate the behavior of individuals. For example, consider a high-school-age reference group dining out. The group norm may state that patronizing chain restaurant A is more desirable than going to locally owned restaurant B, yet objective analysis indicates that restaurant B's product–service mix is superior. The group's norms and values might still point toward the established chain restaurant. Simply put, dining at restaurant A is "cool" and dining at restaurant B is not. What is in favor within the reference group will change over time. For example, 10 to 15 years ago college students seeking the most exciting destination for a spring break getaway often went to Daytona Beach, Florida. In recent years, Cancun, Mexico, and cruises in the Caribbean have become more popular.

A hospitality manager can also influence consumer behavior through the use of opinion leaders. Opinion leaders include both formal and/or informal leaders of reference groups, and their opinions normally influence opinion formation in others. Common opinion leaders are leaders within the community, such as doctors, lawyers, and politicians, and those who are viewed as subject matter experts. For example, a travel agent is clearly an opinion leader for travel-related products. Potential travelers often seek advice from a travel agent because they believe that the agent has knowledge far superior to their own. Another example is the food critic who writes for a local newspaper. The opinions that the critic expresses in a newspaper column have direct and immediate influence on readers.

Hospitality managers often strive to create their own reference groups and opinion leaders. Frequent guests can be rewarded with complimentary samples of new menu items or perhaps a complimentary flavored coffee or bottle of champagne. The champagne creates excitement and is very likely to increase sales, as individuals sitting at other tables want to become part of the excitement and often order a bottle for their own table. The desired result is of course a snowball effect among many tables, which results in increased sales. Frequent guests can also be used for feedback about potential new menu items or new services. If they are favorably impressed with the new products or services, they will tell their friends and colleagues, and increased business can result.

Household. A household is defined as those individuals who occupy a single living unit. There are more than 80 million households in the United States, and within every household certain characteristics, leadership, and norms exist. Leadership is normally rotated among members of the household. For example, the children may decide which breakfast cereal to eat or which fast-food restaurant to patronize, while an adult selects the type of living accommodations. Hospitality marketing research points out that leadership is often shared. For example, the parents normally decide when the household will go out to eat, but it is the children who decide which restaurant will be patronized.

All external influences discussed can affect the decision-making process of a consumer whenever a decision about hospitality and tourism products and services is made. The culture, socioeconomic level, reference groups, and household members influence directly and indirectly, consciously and unconsciously, the dining habits of all consumers.

Internal Influences on Consumer Behavior

In addition to the external influences, consumers are influenced by internal items as well—personal needs and motives, experience, personality and self-image, and perceptions and attitudes. The exact influence of internal factors is less well known than the external factors. The internal factors are not as observable and therefore are not as well documented and understood.

Personal Needs and Motives.   The first of the internal influences are needs and motives. A need is defined as lacking something or the difference between someone's desired and actual states. Motives are defined as a person's inner state that directs the individual toward satisfying a felt need. For example, a consumer may have a need to dine out in order to enjoy a fine meal in a restaurant. They may be hungry and tired (their actual state) yet they desire to be well fed and rested (desired state). This felt need would therefore cause them to have the motivation to seek out a restaurant where this need could be satisfied.

Despite years of consumer behavior research, it is very difficult, if not impossible, to explain all of the needs which consumers feel fully. Figure 3.1 illustrates the role of needs in consumer behavior. Simply stated, needs lead to motivation, which leads to behavioral intentions, which ultimately leads to observable behavior. Following behavior, feedback affects and may change a consumer's motivation. To continue our earlier example, once the consumer had been to a particular restaurant, if the meal was satisfying and met prior expectations, then the feedback would be favorable and the consumer would likely plan to return to this particular restaurant. If, however, the meal was not satisfying or did not meet prior expectations, then the negative feelings that the individual felt would likely result in not returning to this particular restaurant. It is important to remember that successful marketing

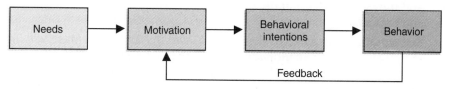

Figure 3.1   Needs Related to Consumer Behavior

is about identifying and then meeting or exceeding the expectations of consumers.

Maslow identified five classes of needs arranged in the following hierarchy: physiological needs, safety needs, social and belonging needs, esteem needs, and self-actualization needs.[3] Individuals are believed to satisfy the lower-level needs before they move to the higher-level needs.

- **Physiological needs.** Physiological needs are primary needs for food, shelter, and clothing that one must have before thinking about higher order needs. Nearly all products and services offered to consumers by hospitality and tourism firms address these needs. In the purest sense, a person's physiological needs are met by vending machines and low-cost providers of food and lodging products.

- **Safety needs.** These second-level needs include personal security and protection from physical harms. The movement toward greater security and safety within the hotel industry has addressed these needs. Electronic door locks, increased lighting, outside entrances that are locked after dark, and more sophisticated fire detection devices all are designed to meet safety needs.

- **Social and belonging needs.** Once needs at the lower two levels are satisfied, consumers look toward achieving social acceptance by others. From the hospitality and tourism perspective, we cater to consumers who want to join private clubs that offer a variety of social and recreational activities. We also make consumers feel like they belong by offering special products and services available for frequent guests. Hotels that target longer-term guests, such as Marriott's Residence Inns™, will often schedule social events for their guests in order to satisfy the social needs of guests who are away from family and friends for an extended period of time.

- **Esteem needs.** Once consumers feel accepted, they seek to enhance their self-esteem. Hospitality and tourism companies cater to these individuals by providing a higher level of personal service. For example, airlines provide first class and business class, in addition to coach service. Airlines also provide special lounges and waiting areas for frequent travelers and for individuals who purchase memberships to their "airline clubs." A second example that illustrates how hospitality and travel firms seek to satisfy esteem needs are expensive restaurants that offer only the finest food, beverages, and service. They provide a level of products and services that cater to the esteem needs of guests and they expend a good deal of effort to make guests feel very special and important.

- **Self-actualization needs.** The highest-level needs within Maslow's hierarchy focuses on an individual's need to reach their full potential. For the most part, these needs are often beyond the scope of what hospitality and travel marketers can expect to fulfill. However, there are examples from within the hospitality and travel industry regarding the consumer's attempt to satisfy self-actualization needs. For example, when guests are attracted to sports programs at five-star resorts focusing on how to play the best golf or tennis possible, they are seeking to reach a state of self-actualization with regard to the sport.

An alternative approach combines the work of Maslow with the work on personality development by Erik Erikson.[4] In this model, adults pass through three life stages and each stage will help to determine the kinds of experiences that they will seek as consumers (see Figure 3.2). Consumers purchase products either because they need them, they desire them, or both. Purchases based on need are considered nondiscretionary, while purchases based on desire are considered discretionary. Consumer satisfaction is achieved mainly through discretionary purchases.

In the first stage, young adults (aged 40 or younger) are seeking satisfaction through purchasing *possession experiences* in their early career development and family building years. Examples of products purchased during this stage are cars and houses. Then, as they grow older (aged 40 to 60), consumers focus more on purchasing *catered experiences* such as travel, restaurants, education, and sports. Finally, the third stage finds consumers shifting their focus toward *being experiences* associated with interpersonal relationships and simple pleasures. In this context, hospitality services would be purchased more in the second stage, although they would be purchased merely for survival throughout a consumer's lifespan. Some resorts, spas, and travel destinations target the third stage as well. For example, some destinations market religious experiences to older travelers who are seeking a more spiritual experience.

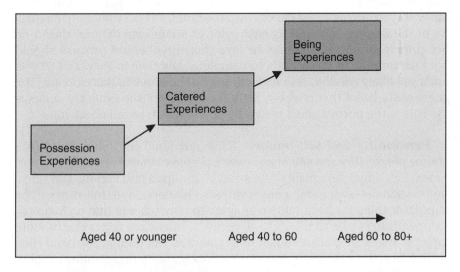

Figure 3.2   Consumer Discretionary Purchasing over a Lifespan

McClelland identified three social motives: achievement, affiliation, and power.[5] Achievement causes an individual to work harder to reach a goal. Affiliation causes individuals to belong to groups or to seek the approval of others. Each person has the need to belong and to be accepted. Finally, McClelland identified individuals' need for power. Individuals want to feel that they are in control and that they have some control over their immediate environment. Many individuals extend this need for power to others; that is, they want to be able to control others as well.

Experience. Experience is also a major internal influence on consumer behavior. As individuals encounter new situations, such as dining in a particular restaurant for the first time, they integrate their perceptions into an experience framework that influences future decisions. The old adage "first impressions are important" applies directly to the hospitality and travel industry. If consumers are turned off the first time that they walk up to the front desk in a hotel or are greeted by a host in a restaurant, they are unlikely to return. One of the factors that have lead to the success of Disneyworld™ is that the staff, called "cast members," focuses on the guests' needs, from the moment they arrive on site until they depart. In the morning when carloads of excited families arrive, they are greeted by smiling parking lot cast members who help to get everyone's day at Disneyworld off to a great start. These initial impressions are the start of a great day for the guests.

Hospitality managers must remember that people (consumers) are a product of their environments. Each new experience is integrated into a "frame of reference" against which new situations are evaluated. This frame of reference includes each individual's beliefs, values, norms, and assumptions. Consider the following example. A guest who travels more than 100 days each year checks into a hotel at which she has not previously stayed. As the guest checks into the hotel, she is evaluating the quality of the service received against prior check-in experiences. Based on her prior experience, she may believe that the check-in process should not take more than 60 seconds to complete. Any time in excess of 60 seconds will likely result in dissatisfaction with the hotel. In this example, the guest has a belief that check-in should be accomplished quickly and easily. This is the norm against which the guest will judge all check-ins.

Personality and Self-Image. Each individual consumer develops a unique personality and self-image over a period of time. For marketing purposes, individual personality types can be grouped into various classifications such as swingers, conservatives, leaders, and followers. The important thing for hospitality managers to remember is that no hospitality operation can be all things to all people. Firms must select one or more target markets that are a subset or segment of the total market and then appeal directly to these consumers. Many hospitality organizations experience difficulty when attempting to appeal to too wide a segment of the total market. The result is quite predictable—failure to satisfy any of the target markets, which leads to poor financial performance and often failure.

One example of this type of thinking involved a restaurant that featured a beef and seafood menu, with moderate to high prices and a semiformal atmosphere. This restaurant had been successful, but the owners and managers felt that more profits could and should be generated. In an attempt to broaden the target market, the atmosphere was made more informal, and the menu was changed to include hamburgers, snacks, sandwiches, and pizza, as well as steaks and seafood. Thirty days after the change was made, sales volume had increased by 15 percent. Within three months, however, volume had fallen by 38 percent, and what had once been a profitable operation was now running a deficit. Following careful examination of the performance of several hospitality organizations, one finds that it is normally those with well-defined target markets that are the most successful. Those attempting to be "all things to all people" often fail.

Perception and Attitude. Each day, consumers are exposed to thousands of stimuli. Some of these stimuli are consciously received, resulting in a thought process, while others are simply ignored. **Perception** is the process by which stimuli are recognized, received, and interpreted. Each individual consumer perceives the world differently. Perceptions are manifested in attitudes. **Attitudes** are learned predispositions to act in a consistently favorable or unfavorable manner. For example, some individuals' attitudes are that fast-food meals are very good because they are of high quality and low cost and offer fast and courteous service. Other individuals' attitudes are that fast-food meals are of low nutritional value and poor culinary quality and are not visually attractive. Both types of individuals hold attitudes based on their perceptions. Their perceptions may or may not be valid, but it is important for the marketing manager to remember that perceptions are the way an individual sees the world. In the mind of the individual consumer, the perceptions and resulting attitudes are correct and valid. It is very difficult to change the perceptions and resulting attitudes that individuals have developed over time.

perception process by which stimuli are recognized, received, and interpreted

attitude learned predisposition to act in a consistently favorable or unfavorable manner

Consumer Adoption Process

Hospitality consumers today are demanding more sophisticated dining and lodging experiences. Consumers are better educated, earn more money, and are more confident when they travel and dine outside the home. Today's hospitality consumer is seeking products and services tailored to meet their specific needs. They are more concerned about nutrition and safety, and they know more about value. Some of the following trends in individual behavior are affecting consumerism:

- Instant gratification rather than the Protestant concept of self-denial
- Feeling terrific rather than feeling responsible

- Improvising rather than planning
- Choosing simplicity over complexity
- Concern for status rather than egalitarianism

These trends shape the way firms develop and market their products and services. There are consumer models that aid marketers in understanding consumers and determining strategies.

Individuals have been classified according to willingness to change. Some are not upset by change, while others resist change in any form. Figure 3.3 illustrates the diffusion of consumers over a typical product life cycle. Consumers will adopt new products at different rates depending on their level of aversion to risk and change. When a new hospitality operation opens, it is very important that individuals representing the "innovators" and "early adaptors" are reached by marketing efforts. These individuals offer excellent potential as early customers, for if they are satisfied, they will tell friends and associates, and these people in turn may become customers. People falling into the "early" and "late majority" categories will not usually try a new hospitality operation until they have heard positive comments from others.

This process of influencing the innovators and early adopters is called *diffusion and adoption*. The key is to get the consumers who are most likely to try new products and services to make a trial purchase—that is, to dine at the restaurant, stay in the hotel, rent a car, or purchase a flight. If they are satisfied with the products and services received, they will then help to spread the positive word to others, and the number of customers will increase over time. How quickly consumers adopt a new product depends on the actual need for the product and the risk associated with the product's purchase.

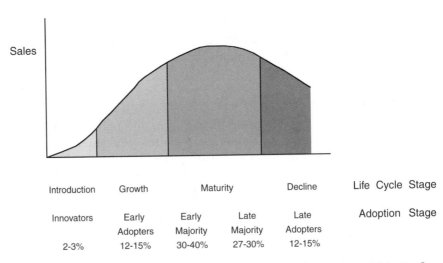

Figure 3.3 Diffusion and Adoption Across the Product Life Cycle

First, products that are necessary will be adopted more readily than products that are not essential. For example, a fine dining restaurant may take longer to build a clientele than a fast food restaurant in a growing suburb. Second, the more risk involved with a product's purchase, the slower the adoption process. Several types of risk are associated with the purchase of a product or service:

- *Financial risk* is the monetary loss that would result with a wrong decision,
- *Performance risk* is the chance that the product or service does not meet a consumer's expectations,
- *Physical risk* is any mental or physical harm that could occur, and
- *Social risk* is the likelihood that the product will meet the approval of one's peers.

For example, a cruise can be expensive, it carries a certain prestige, and consumers have high expectations. Also, there have been instances where passengers have been harmed or even killed, as the result of fires, taking on water, and terrorists.

▲ CONSUMER DECISION-MAKING MODEL

When consumers make decisions concerning the purchase of goods and services, a very complex decision-making process takes place. Numerous variables influence this decision-making process, as the many models of consumer behavior demonstrate. Figure 3.4 draws together several theories into a model that shows both external and internal influences we have

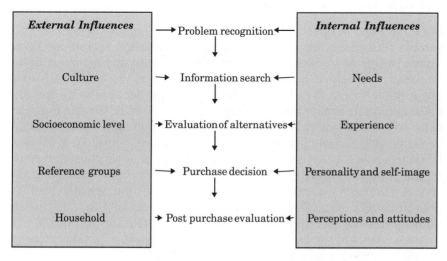

Figure 3.4   A Consumer Decision-Making Model

just discussed, as well as the process by which consumers make purchase decisions.

This model illustrates the major steps in the decision making process, as well as the role external and internal influences play as the individual makes purchase decisions. Because both external and internal variables influence the decision-making processes of consumers, hospitality managers need to develop awareness of the specific influences most important to their particular target market segments. Figure 3.4 shows five key elements in the decision-making model: problem recognition; information search; evaluation of alternatives; the purchase decision; and post-purchase evaluation. Each element is affected by external and internal influences.

Problem Recognition

The decision-making process begins with problem recognition. Thousands of different stimuli can trigger the awareness of a need or a problem. For example, if one feels hungry when driving down an interstate highway, this may trigger a need to search a restaurant to satisfy the hunger need. In another situation, the need to feel important and be treated with the utmost respect may lead a potential guest to search for an upscale hotel with a concierge floor when making a reservation. The need may not begin within a single individual. For example, if a couple comes home after both have worked all day, and one says to the other, "Let's go out tonight; I'm too tired to cook," this manifests a joint need that only one of the individuals may have felt. Hospitality marketing managers should recognize the wide variety of needs that consumers are attempting to satisfy when they dine out.

Information Search

Once the need is raised to a conscious level, the model holds that consumers seek to retrieve information. This information search can come from a variety of sources, including reference groups and members of the immediate household, as well as the mass media in the form of advertising. If the felt need is as basic as the need to eat because of hunger, the information-retrieval process is likely to be brief. That is, the restaurant facility selected in this case is likely to be chosen primarily because of convenience, and the number of sources of information consulted is likely to be quite small. In other situations, the number of sources consulted could be much larger. Consider the meeting planner who is coordinating the annual meeting for a professional association. This individual is likely to consult several sources of information before selecting an appropriate hotel for this important event. The important thing for the hospitality marketing manager to remember is that consumers rely to a certain extent on the mass media for information.

Evaluation of Alternatives

Once the consumer has gathered a sufficient amount of information, the third element in the decision-making process is to evaluate alternatives. Consumers who ask "At which one of several possible restaurants should I dine tonight?" go through a cognitive process in answering this question, whereby they weigh the positive and negative aspects of each alternative. They also examine the attributes of the product–service mix of each restaurant. Consumers consider the relative importance of each attribute of the product–service mix by making tradeoffs between the various attributes and their levels. The final result is an **evoked set**, or set of brands that will be considered in the final purchase decision.

evoked set   set of brands that will be considered in the final purchase decision

Marketing managers in other industries have long recognized this cognitive process and have used it to advantage in advertising and promoting their products and services. Rather than simply discussing their products or services as if they existed in a vacuum, firms make direct comparisons with the competition. This assists the consumer's cognitive process of evaluating alternatives. Of course, every advertiser makes certain that its product or service compares favorably with those of the competition based on the criteria selected.

Purchase Decision

The fourth stage in the consumer decision-making model is the purchase decision. It is at this point that the individual actually makes the decision. All external and internal variables come together to produce a decision. This decision is made based on the perceived risk associated with each alternative and the willingness of the individual to take risks. This risk factor offers a tremendous competitive advantage for hospitality chains. When consumers step through the front door of a McDonald's, Burger King, Red Lobster, or any other nationally recognized chain, they are taking a much smaller risk than if they entered an independent restaurant about which they knew very little. There is less risk with the chain operation because the product–service mix is well known to customers. Independent hospitality operations must work very hard to establish themselves and thereby reduce some of the risk consumers associate with patronizing a restaurant where the product–service mix is not well known.

Postpurchase Evaluation

Following the product–service mix consumption, the final stage is postpurchase evaluation. How did the actual experience compare with the expectations prior to purchase? Was the product–service mix better than or not quite up to the standards anticipated? Postconsumption feelings are based on two factors: the consumer's expectations and the actual performance by the hospitality operation. For this reason, it is very important for any hospitality operation to deliver the product–service mix promised in advertising promotion or personal selling. Failure to perform at or above the level anticipated by the consumer is likely to lead to negative postconsumption feelings. These negative feelings produce dissatisfaction and reduce the level of repeat patronage. From a management perspective, it is important to promise less and deliver more—underpromise and overdeliver. This is a key concept in producing satisfied customers.[6] Finally, there is a period of time between when hospitality or travel services are purchased and when they are consumed. During this period, consumer may have second thoughts or negative feelings about the purchase that are referred to as **cognitive dissonance.** That is why it is important for hospitality firms to run advertisements that depict satisfied customers.

Consumer decision-making is extremely complex. Marketing managers constantly strive to learn more about the way consumers reach decisions. As with other forms of human behavior, consumer behavior may never be totally understood.

cognitive dissonance
second thoughts or
negative feelings about a
purchase

▲ CONSUMER PROBLEM-SOLVING PROCESSES

Consumers, either consciously or subconsciously, use certain processes to integrate the information that they have obtained over time to evaluate and choose among the various alternatives. These formal integration strategies can be termed compensatory, noncompensatory, or a combination of the two.

Compensatory Strategies

When consumers use compensatory strategies, they use a product's strengths in one or more areas to compensate for deficiencies in other areas. In other words, consumers view products and services as bundles of attributes. The set of alternatives that a consumer is considering for purchase will contain products or services that have various combinations of these attributes and their levels. This multiattribute approach assumes that consumers are capable of evaluating each of a product's attributes and then arriving at an overall assessment, or score, for the product that can be compared to alternative products. It is believed that consumers can make these complicated comparisons and tradeoffs, and choose the product that achieves the highest rating.

Noncompensatory Strategies

When using noncompensatory strategies, consumers do not allow product strengths in one area to compensate for deficiencies, or weaknesses, in another area. Instead, consumers place more emphasis on individual attributes and, in some cases, develop minimum thresholds to use in evaluating products and services. Three main noncompensatory strategies are used by consumers: conjunctive, disjunctive, and lexicographic.

Conjunctive. A conjunctive approach involves setting minimum thresholds for each attribute and eliminating alternative brands that do not surpass this threshold on any one salient attribute. The consumer determines which attributes will be important in choosing between brands. For example, a certain individual might consider location, food quality, food variety, and price to be the salient attributes in choosing a restaurant while on vacation. Upon examining the menus that are posted in the windows of restaurants in a busy tourist area, the individual can quickly eliminate restaurants that are deficient on menu variety or have prices that exceed the minimum (maximum) threshold. In addition, restaurants with good reputations for food quality and menu variety, that are within the acceptable price range, will be eliminated if they are not within walking distance.

Disjunctive. Some consumers do not get as involved in the purchase process and may prefer to take a less complicated approach to making purchase decisions. With the disjunctive approach, consumers still establish minimum thresholds for their salient attributes. However, a brand will be acceptable if it exceeds the minimum standard on at least one attribute. Consumers applying this approach tend to have only one or two salient attributes, the products or services tend to be very similar (i.e., homogeneous), and they are not as highly involved in the decision-making process. For example, a truck driver might consider price, location, and basic quality in choosing a hotel or motel to stop for the night. However, it is not unusual for truck drivers to choose the closest hotel or motel when they are starting to get tired. Similarly, an international tourist might choose the first hotel that looks clean or fits his price range.

Lexicographic. The lexicographic approach falls somewhere between conjunctive and disjunctive choice processes in terms of complexity. Just as in the other two approaches, the consumer determines a set of salient attributes, or choice criteria. Next, the consumer places these choice criteria in rank order from most important to least important. Then, the consumer evaluates the alternative brands starting with the most important attribute. The brand that rates the highest on the most important attribute will be selected. If two or more brands tie or are closely rated, then those brands are evaluated using the second most important attribute. This continues until one brand remains or the list of attributes is exhausted—forcing a choice between the remaining brands. It is important to note that all brands are not evaluated on all criteria. For example, a business traveler might rank the most important attributes in airline travel to be convenience, comfort, food quality, and price, in that order. Depending on the airport where the flight is going to originate, the traveler might be able to narrow the choices down to two airlines that offer direct flights at the preferred time. The final choice might then be made based on the fact that one of the airlines is perceived by the traveler to provide better service or comfort.

Combination

One of the main questions regarding problem-solving strategies is the ability of consumers to obtain, integrate, and evaluate the information available on the myriad brands in most product categories. The compensatory approach is particularly cumbersome in this respect, as can be noncompensatory approaches like conjunctive or lexicographic. And, in many cases, the disjunctive approach would seem overly simplistic. Therefore, it could be argued that consumers actually use a combination of approaches in an attempt to adapt to the purchase situation and simplify the decision process. For example, a family might eliminate all restaurants that don't have children's menus using a conjunctive strategy. Then, the remaining restaurants could be evaluated using a more complicated compensatory strategy or a more simple disjunctive strategy.

▲ CONSUMER PROBLEM-SOLVING TECHNIQUES

The consumer decision-making process differs in the length of time and effort expended on each stage based on the consumer's level of involvement and experience with a product category. Also, the level of involvement may change depending on the purchase situation. For instance, a young man's choice process for a restaurant could differ greatly when it is for a date versus a dinner with his buddies. Table 3.1 provides a comparison of the three levels of problem solving: routine response behavior, limited problem solving, and extended problem solving.

Routine Response Behavior. For some products, consumers exert very little effort in the decision-making process. Some marketing professionals believe that consumers actually skip stages of the process, while others feel that consumers merely move through all of the stages very quickly. This routine, or habitual, response involves very little information search or cognitive processing because the decision is almost automatic. Routine response behavior is typical for low-priced, frequently purchased products where consumer involvement is low. The amount of effort that consumers exert in the problem-solving process tends to decrease over time as they learn more about a product category and gain experience through consumption. An example of this behavior would be workers choosing the employee cafeteria for lunch.

Table 3.1	Problem-Solving Techniques		
Characteristics	*Routine Response Behavior*	*Limited Problem-Solving*	*Extended Problem-Solving*
Amount of search	Minimal	Moderate	Substantial
Number of brands considered	One	Few	Many
Number of attributes evaluated	One or two	Few	Many
Cognitive processing	Minimal	Moderate	Substantial
Number of external information sources used	None	Few	Many
Level of involvement	Low	Medium	High
Total amount of effort	Low	Medium	High

Limited Problem Solving. Many consumers' purchase decisions involve limited problem solving because of some product differentiation and alternative brands. There is some information search, including external sources, unlike routine response behavior. Consumers have a low to moderate level of involvement and they consider a moderate number of attributes in making the purchase decision. At this point, the consumer usually has some knowledge and experience with regard to the product category. Consumers are willing to exert some time and effort to ensure a good choice. For example, choosing a restaurant for everyday dining is a limited problem-solving task for most consumers. Similarly, the choice of airline or rental car agency usually involves a few salient attributes and the choice of alternatives is easily reduced to two or three brands.

Extended Problem Solving. This type of problem solving is most often associated with high-priced products that are purchased infrequently. Consumers need to engage in an extensive search process to identify salient attributes and alternative brands. Consumers are highly involved because of the price and risk of making a bad choice, and they exert a good deal of time and effort. The cognitive process is substantial because consumers need to evaluate the alternative brands using many attributes. For example, a couple planning a cruise will talk to friends, as well as a travel agent, and take their time to evaluate the various cruise lines based on price, accommodations, destinations, cabin availability, service, and quality.

▲ ORGANIZATIONAL BUYER BEHAVIOR

Purchase decisions differ between organizations and individual buyers, but both types of buyers are trying to satisfy their particular needs. The buying process for organizations is much more structured and formal in comparison to the individual buying process. The most common organization markets in hospitality and travel are the meetings market for hotels and the tour market for travel. This section highlights some of the main characteristics of organizational buying.

Characteristics of Organizational Buying

The organizational buying process includes the stages used by organizations to determine needs (problem recognition), search for information, evaluate alternatives, make a purchase, and evaluate the purchase (post-consumption evaluation). In general, organizations go through the same decision-making process as individual consumers. However, there are some major differences between the activities within the stages.

- **Larger volume purchases.** Organizational buyers usually purchase in large volumes. For example, meeting planners book anywhere from 10 to 1,000 or more rooms, and tour operators package trips for groups of 10 or more.

- **Derived demand.** The demand for organization products is derived from the demand for consumer products. For example, when the demand for insurance increases, insurance companies have more sales meetings and sponsor more incentive trips. Corporations and associations tend to have larger travel budgets when their industries are doing well.

- **More emphasis on specifications and service.** The products in organization markets tend to be more technical in nature, and buyers are more concerned about specifications and service after the sale. For example, meeting planners are concerned about meeting room dimensions, audiovisual equipment, room temperature control, and conference service. Rarely do transient customers get into detail about the room dimensions and other specifications.

- **Professional buyers and more negotiation.** Organization buyers tend to be professionals with an extensive knowledge of the product. Therefore, the purchase process tends to be longer and more involved for organizations than for regular consumers. Also, when buying large volumes, organization buyers have more power and can negotiate. For example, hotels and tour operators are willing to make more concessions in the price and product–service mix to sell higher volume to one buyer.

- **Repeat business.** One of the benefits of selling to organizations is that they tend to become repeat purchasers. For example, corporations will use the same hotel throughout the year to amass higher volume and receive more concessions. Then, if the corporation is pleased with the service, it will use the hotel for meetings in subsequent years.

- **Multiple buyers.** Often, more than one individual is involved in the buying process and making the ultimate purchase decision for organizations. *Buying centers* are groups of people that influence buying decisions for organizations. For example, many associations have site selection committees that choose destinations and hotels for future meetings.

Table 3.2 provides a comparison of the stages in the buying process between consumers and organizations. The example involves the purchase of hotel services and provides a step-by-step summary of the possible activities at each stage.

Members of the Buying Unit

As mentioned earlier, organizations will normally have *buying centers* or *buying units* that influence their purchase decisions. Five specific roles have been identified for individuals constituting a buying unit: user, influencer, buyer, decider, and gatekeeper. In some instances, there is more than one person in each role, or the same person occupies more than one role.

- **Users.** These are the people in the firm who actually use the product. For example, front desk personnel will use a reservation system, waiters will use a point-of-sale system, and meeting attendees will use hotel facilities.

- **Influencers.** These are the people who have some expertise in the product area and help define the necessary specifications. For example, computer systems personnel would help choose a reservation system or a point-of-sale system, and human resources personnel often influence site selection for meetings.

- **Buyers.** These are the people who have the formal authority and responsibility for making the purchase decision. For example, an employee at the corporate office for a hotel or restaurant chain will purchase reservation systems or point-of-sale systems, and a meeting planner will sign a contract for hotel facilities.

- **Deciders.** These are the people who have the authority to select or approve a supplier. They are often top executives within the organization that have the formal power to make decisions, but they are normally only involved with high-dollar purchases. For example, general managers, CEOs, directors, and presidents usually have this type of authority.

- **Gatekeepers.** These individuals control the flow of information that is relevant to a purchase decision. For example, administrative assistants or receptionists have the ability to restrict the flow of information to buyers, and other members of the buying unit. Hotel salespeople must often rely on administrative assistants to get information to meeting planners.

| Table 3.2 | A Comparison of Consumer and Organizational Buying |

Stage in the Buying Process	Consumer purchase of a weekend hotel room	Organizational purchase of hotel facilities for an association meeting
Problem Recognition	A couple feels like getting away for a weekend	An association has to hold its annual meeting for members to elect officers
Information Search	Based on past experience, may contact a travel agent, or rely on word-of-mouth and other forms of promotion	Looks through information on file, contacts the local CVB and hotel salespeople, based on past experience, looks at Web sites, or looks at meeting magazines or other advertising materials.
Evaluation of Alternatives	Uses routine or limited problem-solving based on a few salient attributes.	Reviews hotel specifications, makes site visits, and talks to salespeople. Many attributes are important.
Purchase Decision	A specific hotel is chosen and the room is charged to a credit card	The meeting planner negotiates with a salesperson, the terms are determined, and a contract is signed.
Postpurchase Evaluation	There is some time before the actual visit for cognitive dissonance, but it is difficult to evaluate the service before it is consumed.	Association meetings are planned three to five years in advance, leaving time for cognitive dissonance. The hotel or the city could undergo some major changes within that period.

▲ MARKETING ACTION NOW!

The marketing of products and services is difficult because everything is based on perceptions, and consumers' decisions are affected by a number of factors, including the purchase situation. Think about all of the different types of occasions for which you would have to choose a restaurant. For example, when you are with a group of friends going out to have a good time, when you are going out on a date with someone for the first time, when your family is coming to visit, or when you are interviewing for a job.

1. What are some of the internal and external influences that would apply to the various situations?
2. How would you progress through the stages of the consumer decision-making process in each of these situations?
3. What are the likely processes and techniques that you would use for problem solving?

▲ SUMMARY OF CHAPTER OBJECTIVES

This chapter provides a broad overview of the complex subject of consumer behavior. Management must constantly strive to learn more about consumer behavior, for this will allow managers to better serve the needs of customers. In this way, sales and profits can be increased and a competitive advantage can be gained.

A variety of factors influence consumers' purchase decisions. External influences include culture, socioeconomic status, reference groups, and household. All of these entities have an influence on the way a consumer progresses through the five stages of the decision-making process: problem recognition, information search, evaluation of alternatives, purchase decision, and postpurchase evaluation. In addition, internal influences such as needs, experiences, personality, perceptions, and attitudes affect the decision-making process.

In theory, consumers are believed to apply certain processes, or strategies, when they evaluate alternatives. Compensatory strategies allow product strength's to compensate for weaknesses, while noncompensatory strategies reduce the number of salient attributes to streamline the process. However, it is possible that consumers use a combination of more than one approach or strategy. There are various problem-solving techniques that consider the consumer's level of involvement and explain how the decision-making process may differ across product categories. The level of problem solving ranges from routine response behavior, to limited problem solving, to extended problem solving, depending upon the situation.

▲ KEY TERMS AND CONCEPTS

Attitudes

Buying center or buying unit

Cognitive dissonance

Compensatory strategies

Consumer adoption process

Consumer decision-making model

Consumer problem-solving
   techniques

Cue

Culture

Drive

Evoked set

External Influences

Internal Influences

Maslow's hierarchy of needs

Motives

Needs

Noncompensatory strategies

Opinion leaders

Organizational buying

Perceptions

Personality

Reference groups

▲ QUESTIONS FOR REVIEW AND DISCUSSION

1. What are some of the internal and external influences on consumer purchases?

2. List and discuss the five stages in the consumer decision-making process.

3. What are the differences between compensatory strategies and non-compensatory strategies for problem solving?

4. Give an example of how a consumer would use a combination of problem-solving processes.

5. What are the three problem-solving techniques used by consumers? Explain how they differ using the stages of the consumer decision-making process.

6. How would a hospitality marketer use the consumer adoption process in planning a promotional strategy?

7. How does the decision-making process differ between consumers and organizations?

8. What are the five components of the buying unit? Give an example of a buying unit in hospitality or travel.

▲ NOTES

[1]Ginny Phillips, "Social Agendas Make Site Selection a Political Decision," *Convene*, vol. 14, no. 4, pp. 43–50.

[2]James U. McNeal, *Consumer Behavior* (Boston: Little, Brown, 1982, pp. 5–15).

[3]Maslow, Abraham H., *Motivation and Personality*, 2[nd]edition (New York: Harper and Row, 1970).

[4]David B. Wolfe, "The Ageless Market: The Key to the Older Market Is to Forget Age and Focus on Consumer Wants and Needs," *American Demographics*, Vol. 9, No. 7 (July 1987), pp. 26(6).

[5]David C. McClelland, "Toward a Theory of Motive Acquisition," *American Psychologist*, Vol. 20, pp. 321–333.

[6]Kenneth Blanchard and Sheldon M. Bowles, *Raving Fans: A Revolutionary Approach to Customer Service* (New York: William Morrow and Company, Inc., 1993, p. 101).

Chapter

4

Market Segmentation and Positioning

❖ Chapter Objectives

By the end of this chapter, you should understand:

1. What is meant by the term *market segmentation*
2. The variables that are commonly used to segment markets
3. How to identify the decisions that must be made when markets are segmented
4. The connection between market segmentation decisions and the development of marketing strategies
5. The basics of positioning and its use in gaining a competitive advantage
6. The relationship between market segmentation, targeting, and positioning

❖ Chapter Outline

I. Chapter Opening Profile
II. Introduction

A. The nature of market segmentation

B. Criteria for effective segmentation

III. Segmentation Variables

    A. Geographic

    B. Demographic

    C. Psychographic

    D. Behavioral

    E. Benefits sought

IV. Market Segmentation Decisions

    A. Identifying segmentation bases

    B. Developing profiles for each market segment

    C. Forecasting performance for each segment

    D. Selecting the best market segments

V. Market Segmentation Strategies

    A. Undifferentiated strategy

    B. Differentiated strategy

    C. Concentrated or focused strategy

VI. Positioning the Product–Service Mix

    A. Determine the ideal mix for consumers

    B. Measure consumer perceptions of available services

    C. Look for gaps in coverage and select a desired position

    D. Develop a strategy for obtaining the desired position

VII. Marketing Action Now!

VIII. Summary of Chapter Objectives

    A. Key terms and concepts

    B. Review and discussion questions

❖ Chapter Opening Profile

THE SENIOR MARKET, OFTEN REFERRED TO as the "gray market," is growing faster than any other market in America. By the year 2050, it is expected that one in three Americans will be 55 years or older.[1] The senior market has been expanding and is becoming more attractive because older Americans have a good deal of free time, they are healthier and living longer, and they have more discretionary income than ever before. These trends make the senior market particularly attractive to firms in the hospitality and travel industry. However, although the age of 55 is a common cutoff used for describing this market, the American Association for Retired Persons (AARP) accepts members starting at 50 years of age, and many firms use a figure in the range of 60 to 65 year old age when offering discounts to the senior market. For example, U.S. Airways offers a senior discount to those 62 and older, and American Airlines uses 65 as the qualifier. Regardless, this market is growing in size, as well as clout, when it comes to influencing the government and marketers. AARP is quite possibly the most influential association in Washington, D.C., and most hospitality and travel firms offer some type of discount to senior citizens.

If a firm chooses to target the senior market, it should determine the attributes that are important to this market segment in purchasing its types of products and services. Then, products and services can be designed and marketed specifically to seniors. For example, hotels should provide luggage carts or bell service so seniors can get help with heavy luggage. In addition, rooms should have wide aisles, telephones and remote controls with larger numbers, simple alarm clocks with large numbers, and easy-to-use facilities in the bathroom, including bars near the toilet and in the bathtub that can be used for getting up and down. Similarly, restaurants should provide menus with large print, meals that are healthy and have smaller portions, and adequate lighting so seniors can read the menus. Finally, hospitality and travel firms should realize that seniors like to travel in tour groups for the companionship and security, they are very value conscious, and they require frequent stops for resting, eating, and using restroom facilities.

▲ INTRODUCTION

Gaining and maintaining a competitive advantage in the broad consumer market for hospitality and travel products is a very difficult task. It is much easier to be successful if a firm tries to carve out a smaller niche or segment of the market, in which the firm can establish a competitive uniqueness, hence, the development of market segmentation. Marketing managers have long used market segmentation to separate the market into smaller homogeneous groups. Therefore, a simple definition for **market segmentation** is pursuing a marketing strategy whereby the total potential market is divided into homogeneous subsets of customers, each of which responds differently to the marketing mix of the organization.

For many years, most hospitality and travel organizations attempted to serve the needs of a fairly wide variety of markets. These groups included broad segments that cut across much of the spectrum of age, gender, income, geography, ethnicity, and education. Today, many hospitality chains serve the needs of markets in all 50 states and several foreign countries. Therefore, it is imperative that they use some type of segmentation strategy. These firms must take into consideration the sometimes subtle differences between various consumer groups that represent their target markets. For example, a national fast food chain should take into consideration the differences among individuals living in different regions of the United States. In addition to geographic location, firms must also consider differences in lifestyle and consumer behavior, all of which add special challenges to the marketing of the product–service mix for hospitality and travel organizations.

Segmentation can be used effectively in all facets of the hospitality and travel industry, even in areas that may appear to be less suitable for segmentation. For example, airline travel may not appear to be well suited to segmentation. Each year, millions of travelers will board an aircraft to take them to their destination. At first glance, one might assume that airline travel is a fairly homogeneous product serving the same basic need for most travelers. However, airlines have been successful at segmenting based on price sensitivity and frequency of use. Within many aircraft today, you will find three levels of price: first class, business class, and coach. Each level offers differences in seat size and comfort, the level of service, and the ratio of the number of flight attendants to passengers. The individual consumer is able to select the level of service desired and is charged a differing price for each level of service. Airlines also segment the market based on frequency of travel.

The Nature of Market Segmentation

Why is it desirable to segment markets? Many owners and managers of hospitality organizations ask this question. Often, they believe that they need to appeal to *all* potential customers and that by segmenting the market they will weaken their competitive position and profits. They believe that if they segment the market and target their marketing and promotional efforts squarely at a few segments, their sales volume will fall. This approach is short-sighted and fails to consider the reasons underlying a market segmentation approach. The basic premise to segmentation is to allocate limited resources so that the return on investment can be maximized.

Market segmentation, when done properly, can improve sales and profits because it allows the organization to target specific market segments that are much more likely to patronize the organization's facilities. This approach permits the organization to more effectively allocate scarce marketing resources aimed at those market segments with the highest probability of purchasing the organization's products and services. Using market segmentation, companies can identify those market segments that are heavy users of their products and services. At the same time, segments that hold little potential for using a company's products receive little or no attention so that the marketing resources that are available are not wasted chasing after market segments with little sales potential.

When the market is segmented, different product–service mixes can be promoted to meet the needs of the different segments. For example, a hotel's bar and restaurant can be used to attract a variety of market segments by varying the type of entertainment offered. Management could try to increase sales volume by establishing specific nights of the week such as "jazz night," "oldies night," "country night," and "blues night." Each of these events offers a specific type of entertainment that appeals to a specific clientele. Within the lodging segment of the industry, hotels that cater to the business traveler are usually busy on Monday through Thursday night and are often quite slow on the weekends. Therefore, one of the marketing communications and promotional goals is to target those market segments with the most potential for boosting weekend occupancy. Each hotel chain attempts to present the total package of amenities, room, and food and beverage in an appealing manner. By attempting to appeal to those target segments seeking a getaway weekend or a mini-vacation at a good price, the hotel is able to boost occupancy and total revenue during a time when the hotel would normally not be operating at full capacity (i.e., 100 percent occupancy).

Criteria for Effective Segmentation

As firms attempt to segment markets, they have many methods from which to choose. However, it is important to know when to segment and how far the segmentation efforts should go in targeting specific markets. There is a point where a market can be segmented too much, with the resulting subset being too small to be profitable. Or, it may not be efficient to develop several different marketing programs for the various market segments, when one or two could be used for the entire market. When any segmentation efforts are undertaken, three criteria should be used to evaluate the effectiveness of the market segmentation strategy:

- Substantiality
- Measurability
- Accessibility

First, the size of the segment must be reasonably *substantial*. As the market is segmented, a hospitality manager manipulates the elements of the marketing mix to meet the needs of the individual segments and to achieve the marketing objectives of the firm. The size of each of these segments must be large enough to warrant this special attention. For example, segmenting the market into target market segments based on age, income, marital status, and number of children seems logical because a substantial number of individuals would fall into each category. Segmenting a hospitality market into two segments for college graduates who had obtained master's degrees and those who had doctoral degrees would not be logical because the number of individuals in each of these categories would not be substantial.

Second, each of the segments should be *measurable*. This measurability should be assessed from two perspectives: the overall size of the target market segment and the projected total demand or purchasing power of the target market. Minimum cutoff points should be established relative to the size and projected demand of any target market segments. If the number of consumers or projected total demand within a given segment falls below these cutoff points, target market segments can simply be combined.

Third, the segments must be *accessible*. It must be possible to reach the large target market segments through a variety of marketing communications efforts. Marketing communication can include a wide variety of approaches, which include, but are not limited to, advertising, promotion, direct marketing, telemarketing, and personal selling. Without accessibility, there is very little point to segmenting the target market at all, as a major purpose for segmenting the market is to isolate viable segments of potential business and direct marketing communication efforts related to specific aspects of the product–service mix toward these segments. Without accessibility, this is not possible, and segmenting the target market is of little value.

▲ SEGMENTATION VARIABLES

Five basic types of variables used to segment consumer markets: **geographic, demographic, psychographic, behavioral,** and **benefits sought**

Marketing managers can use five basic types of variables when segmenting consumer markets: **geographic, demographic, psychographic, behavioral,** and **benefits sought.** These segmentation variables can be used alone or in combination with one another, depending on the level of segmentation that is desired. Figures 4.1a–4.1d illustrate the basic concept of market segmentation. Figure 4.1a illustrates a market that has not been segmented. In other words, no attempt has been made to divide the large, heterogeneous market into smaller, homogeneous subsets. Figures 4.1b and 4.1c illustrate markets that have been segmented using one variable, and Figure 4.1d illustrates a market that has been segmented using two variables. In practice, it is normally best to use at least two or more of the following types of variables to segment markets.

Geographic Variables

A geographic variable, as the name implies, relates to the consumer's geographic area of residence. Markets are often segmented by dividing the country into regions such as Northeast, Mid-Atlantic, North Central, Southwest, and Northwest. Segmentation is also often accomplished by examining the population of a given area. Within the United States, the total population is more than 250 million. However, this population is not evenly distributed; it is concentrated in major metropolitan areas. For example, in 1990, the fifteen largest cities had a total population of 60.4 million, or nearly 25 percent of the population of the entire country.[2]

Figure 4.1a   **A Nonsegmented Market**

Figure 4.1b   A Market Segmented by Age (A = 18–34, B = 35–49, C = above 49)

Figure 4.1c   A Market Segmented by Income (H = high, M = moderate, L = low)

Figure 4.1d   A Market Segmented by Age and Income

In addition to population density, there are differing patterns of population migration. During the last decade, the population of the Southeast and Southwest increased by 15 percent, and the West increased by 21 percent. Contrast this growth rate with a 4 percent increase in the Northeast and a 2 percent increase in the Midwest.[3]

Several different terms are used to describe cities and metropolitan areas, but the following designation is the most popular in marketing. The term **metropolitan statistical area (MSA)** refers to the smallest urban area with an urban center population of 50,000 and a total metropolitan population of more than 100,000. Metropolitan statistical areas are normally urban areas that are self-contained and surrounded by rural areas. Examples of MSAs include Roanoke, Virginia, and Peoria, Illinois. The next category of urban area is **primary metropolitan statistical area (PMSA)**. A PMSA is an urbanized county or multicounty area with a population of more than 1 million individuals. Examples of PMSAs include Cook County in Illinois and

metropolitan statistical area smallest urban area with an urban center population of 50,000 and a total metropolitan population of more than 100,000

primary metropolitan statistical area an urbanized county or multicounty area with a population of more than 1 million

consolidated metropolitan statistical areas the very largest cities such as New York, Chicago, and Los Angeles; a CMSA must include at least two PMSAs.

Nassau County in New York. Finally, the very largest cities such as New York, Chicago, and Los Angeles are known as **consolidated metropolitan statistical areas (CMA)**. A CMSA must include at least two PMSAs.

Geographic variables are used extensively by the print and broadcast media to define and describe their readers and audience. It is also vital to know from which geographic areas your business comes. For example, nearly 50 percent of all of the room nights in the hotel industry are generated by the top 25 CMSAs, PSMAs, and MSAs. Segmenting a hotel's market based on the origin of the guests by using their zip codes is an effective way to identify those areas that merit the heaviest concentration of advertising and promotion.

Demographic Variables

Markets are often segmented based on demographic variables such as age, gender, income and expenditure patterns, family size, stage in the family life cycle, educational level achieved, and occupation. When these variables are used in defining consumers within the hospitality and travel industry, certain trends emerge. For instance, as family size increases, the number of times per week that the families dine outside the home tends to decrease. Also, when families do dine out, their choice of restaurant changes as the family makeup changes. This is important because the size of the average family has decreased over the years. In 1970, the average family size was 5.8 persons. Today, the average family size is 2.7 persons.[4] There is also a growing trend toward an increased number of individuals living alone. This represents a market segment opportunity for the hospitality and tourism industry.

family life cycle segmentation scheme using age, marital status, and number of children

The **family life cycle** provides a good example of how variables can be combined to create categories that can be used for segmentation. The family life cycle uses age, marital status, and the number of children to create categories sharing common discretionary income levels and purchasing behaviors. The traditional family life cycle proposes that as individuals become adults and enter the workforce, they tend to be single and have lower incomes, resulting in lower levels of discretionary income. However, these young singles do not have many obligations or responsibilities, and are able to spend money on items that are not necessities. Individuals begin to increase their incomes as they age, and young married couples without children will have increasing amounts of discretionary income. However, once married couples have children, their discretionary incomes begin to decrease, until the children are older and move out. At this point the couples are said to have an "empty nest," and discretionary income begins to increase again. Finally, as individuals reach their "golden years," they retire and see their incomes start to decrease.

This traditional family life cycle has changed over time and it now includes several extensions. First, many people are waiting longer to get married and extending the bachelor stage. In addition, more people are choosing to not marry and some of them adopt children. Second, the increase in the divorce rate has resulted in more single parents and second marriages that involve older parents with younger children. Third, there are more same sex couples and organizations are beginning to recognize this partnership for benefits and adoptions. Finally, people are living longer, resulting in a higher percentage of solitary survivors, many of which form relationships later in life.

Segmentation using demographic variables is very common. In fact, firms should always collect demographic information on their customers so that they can construct a basic profile of heavy users. Demographic information is easy to collect and understand. Also, there is aggregate data collected by the government at all levels that can be used for comparisons in surveys and targeting potential markets. Finally, demographic classifications are widely used by various media to describe viewers, listeners, and readers. This allows firms to select media vehicles that will reach individuals fitting the profile of a typical customer.

Psychographic Variables

Psychographic variables are also commonly used to segment markets. Psychographics refer to segmentation based on lifestyle, attitudes, and personality. The development of psychographic segmentation is based on lifestyle profiles normally derived from survey responses to **AIO statements** that focus on an individual's activities, interests, and opinions.

AIO statements refer to activities (e.g., hobbies and sports), interests (e.g., family), and opinions (e.g., politics).

Psychographics have the following characteristics:

- Generally, psychographics may be viewed as the practical application of the behavioral and social sciences to marketing research.

- More specifically, psychographics make use of research procedures that are indicated when demographic, socioeconomic, and user–nonuser analyses are not sufficient to explain and predict consumer behavior.

- Most specifically, psychographics seek to describe the human characteristics of consumers that may have bearing on their response to products, packaging, advertising, promotion, and public relations efforts. Such variables may range from self-concept and lifestyle to attitudes, interests, and opinions, as well as perceptions of product attributes.

Psychographics are used primarily to segment markets, but they can be used for other purposes as well. Psychographics are useful when selecting the most effective advertising vehicles, in that the vehicle(s) selected can be matched with the interests, attitudes, opinions and personalities of the target market segment. Psychographics are also helpful when designing the advertising and promotion messages. Illustrations, pictures, and the actual copy can be designed with the needs of a specific market segment in mind. By pinpointing the target market in this manner, the advertising and promotional messages and images are likely to be more effective, resulting in increased sales and profits.

Synergy Consulting developed a segmentation scheme with seven social value groups based on consumers' attitudes and opinions. Table 4.1 contains the framework for the Social Value Groups™. The first column lists the group and the percentage of the population that it represents. The second column lists the types of needs that the group is seeking to fulfill. The third column lists the characteristics that can be used to describe each group.

Table 4.1	Social Value Groups	
Group	Needs	Characteristics
Self Explorers (18% of the population)	*Inner Directed Needs* Cognitive, Aesthetic, Integration	Ethical, tolerant, open understanding, introspective, nonmaterialistic, individualistic
Experimentalists (10% of the population)	*Inner Directed Needs* Cognitive, Aesthetic, Integration *Outer Directed Needs* Esteem, Achievement	Unconventional, technological, creative, self-confident, physically fit, risk-oriented
Conspicuous Consumers (18% of the population)	*Outer Directed Needs* Esteem, Achievement	Acquisitive, competitive, assertive, conscious of appearances, self-indulgent, materialistic
Belongers (18% of the population)	*Outer Directed Needs* Esteem, Achievement *Sustenance Driven* Physiological, Safety, Belonging	Conservative, pragmatic, traditionalist, conventional, self-sacrificing, tribal, pedantic
Social Resisters (8% of the population)	*Sustenance Driven* Physiological, Safety, Belonging	Altruistic, concerned with social views and supporters of standards but also doctrinaire, intolerant, and moralistic
Survivors (25% of the population)	*Sustenance Driven* Physiological, Safety, Belonging	Sustenance driven, class-conscious, community minded, traditionalist, cheerful, awkward if treated badly, but quietly hardworking if treated well
Aimless (6% of the population)	*Sustenance Driven* Physiological, Safety, Belonging	Either old, lonely, purposeless, and disinterested, or young, hostile, antiauthoritarian, and frequently violent

Source: reprinted with permission from Synergy Consulting, London, England.

The division of the markets into segments is not based solely on easily quantified demographic variables, such as age, sex, or income. Rather, the division is based on less easily defined psychographic factors, such as lifestyle, attitudes, opinions, and personality. Individual firms can define their target markets and address the needs of those markets with products and promotional campaigns. For instance, tour operators could design various overseas tour packages that would appeal to different social value groups.

Behavioral Variables

Another type of variable that can be used to segment markets is the behavioral variable. Behavioral segmentation focuses on the behaviors that consumers exhibit in the marketplace. For example, are consumers loyal or are they easily persuaded by competitors' marketing communications and promotional efforts? How frequently do they dine out? Would they be considered light, medium, or heavy users of various types of hospitality products? When they travel on business, at what types of lodging facilities do they stay? When they travel for pleasure, do they stay at the same types of lodging facilities as when they travel on business?

One of the best uses of the behavioral variables is to identify those individuals who are heavy users, meaning that they dine out frequently, stay in hotels many more nights per year than the average person, or account for a large percentage of air travel. If these individuals can be identified, then a marketing plan can be formulated to increase loyalty and increase frequency of use even further. For example, most airlines offer a frequent traveler membership program to encourage brand loyalty. Within each program are varying levels of membership. Anyone can join the **frequent traveler program**, but the rewards are commensurate with the level of use. Airline miles are accumulated and they can be redeemed for free flights or a variety of other travel services. Many hotels and restaurants offer similar programs, and often, hotels and airlines develop strategic alliances and combine their programs.

frequent traveler program awards commensurate with level of use

Each year, more and more research is undertaken to help companies to more fully understand consumer behavior. Behavioral variables represent an excellent segmentation tool, for as data are collected concerning the manner in which consumers actually behave in the marketplace, the information will allow hospitality managers to gain a better understanding of consumer behavior. As marketing managers gain a better understanding of what motivates consumers to buy, it will facilitate the development of product–service mixes that will better satisfy the needs of consumers.

Benefits Sought

Finally, market segmentation can be based on the benefits that consumers are seeking when they purchase a product. Once a firm has determined the benefits sought by consumers, it can use this information to design products and services and to create promotional materials that focus on these benefits. Market research can be used to identify the benefits that are important to various types of consumers. This marketing information allows management to segment the market based on benefits sought, as well as demographic, psychographic, or behavioral variables. For example, a ski resort may conclude that ski conditions are the most important attribute for most of its customers. However, the resort also realizes that most of its customers have annual household incomes greater than $60,000. Therefore, it is critical to consider both of these variables when targeting new markets and choosing media vehicles. Otherwise, the resort will be wasting valuable resources and effort marketing to customers who can't afford to stay at the resort or stressing benefits that aren't important.

▲ MARKET SEGMENTATION DECISIONS

When faced with market segmentation decisions, a hospitality and tourism marketing manager should use a systematic approach that em-

Travelers choose airport hotels because of convenience and location. *Courtesy of Wyndham Hotel at Los Angeles Airport.*

ploys critical thinking and careful analysis. Figure 4.2 presents a four-step process that can be used by marketing managers in segmenting potential markets. The four steps are: (1) identifying segmentation bases; (2) developing profiles for each segment; (3) forecasting projected demand; and (4) selecting specific target market segments.

Identify Segmentation Bases

The first thing a marketing manager must do is to identify one or more characteristics that can describe the target market segment. Any of the previously discussed segmentation criteria can be used to accomplish this. In almost all cases, several characteristics will be used. For example, a new restaurant might elect to target a consumer market consisting of the following individuals: 25 to 40 years of age, living in cities with a population greater than 500,000, who have annual incomes greater than $35,000.

The objective of identifying the segmentation bases is to develop a relatively homogenous market segment made up of individual consumers who will respond in a similar manner to the marketing strategies and marketing communications efforts of the firm. It is also important that the members of the selected target markets place a high value on the combination of attributes that the firm has used in the product–service mix. For example, the economy segment of the lodging industry has experienced exceptional growth in recent years by offering basic amenities at a relatively low price, resulting in a high level of perceived value to consumers. However, it would not make sense for this type of lodging chain to target the mid-level and senior-level executives of Fortune 500 companies. These individuals, for both business and personal reasons, normally elect to stay in and conduct business in full-service hotels.

Develop Profiles for Each Segment

Once the target market has been identified, it is very important to compile as much information about the target market consumers as possible. The overall goal is to match the stated wants and needs of the targeted segment with the product–service mix offerings and marketing communications that the firm uses. The importance of matching consumers' wants and needs with the marketing offerings and communication efforts of the firm cannot be overemphasized. It is also important to identify the similarities and differences among and between various target markets. People within the same market segment should share similar characteristics and react in

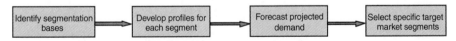

Figure 4.2   Market Segmentation Decision Process

a similar fashion to changes in marketing programs. When developing a profile of the target markets, it is necessary to use the various segmentation variables described earlier in this chapter. The Chapter Opening Profile provides a good example of profiling a target market segment.

Forecast Projected Demand

Determining the sales potential of a given market segment or an entire market for any given product–service mix is an extremely difficult task. Computer models and statistical approaches have facilitated the process somewhat, but it is still very difficult to account for all of the variables that can influence consumer demand. Even the best forecasts may be subject to a **margin of error** of several percentage points in either direction. However, marketing managers must have some knowledge of the level of market demand in order to plan for short- and long-term contingencies as well as day-to-day operations. Without reasonably accurate forecasts, management must operate by the seat of their pants. The demands of the competitive situation in the hospitality and tourism industry today will not permit this casual approach.

margin of error   difference between forecasted value and actual value

market demand potential consumers having both purchasing power and motivation

Market demand can be defined as potential consumers having both purchasing power and motivation. Many variables can affect the demand within any given segment. Variables such as consumer motivation are often difficult to quantify. Market demand for a product or service is the total volume that would be bought by a clearly specified customer group in a defined geographic area in a defined period. Only when clear definitions are available for each of these variables can market demand be calculated precisely. Determining total market demand is an important marketing function because so many other assumptions are based on its forecast. Hospitality managers should be able to examine forecasts for market demand and understand their uses and limitations.

projected demand total market demand multiplied by the market share

market share percentage of the market that the firm's product–service mix will capture

Projected demand for the product–service mix is calculated based on the total market demand multiplied by the **market share**, or the percentage of the market that the firm's product–service mix will capture. Market share is calculated by dividing the firm's sales by the total industry sales. Determining the projected market share is an imprecise science. It should be based on a thorough and objective assessment of the firm's capabilities, the relative competitiveness of those also targeting the same consumers, and marketing strategies used by all firms. Once decisions have been made about the specific marketing strategies and tactics that will be used, then resource needs can be determined to market the product–service mix to specific target market segments.

Select Specific Target Market Segments

Based on the steps previously discussed, those responsible for developing and implementing the marketing plans must decide on the specific target market segments that are selected. While the use of data and factual information is very important, the judgment, insight, and experience that a seasoned marketing manager brings to the decision are also valuable. The overall goal is to limit the uncertainty surrounding market segmentation decisions. Decisions should be based on a careful assessment of the data, the analysis of the data, and how the forecasts of projected demand and market share were determined. It is imperative that the marketing manager examines the projected **return on investment (ROI)** that the target market will provide. ROI is calculated by dividing return, or net profit, by the amount of the investment. Firms will normally have target ROIs for their investments, but the higher the ROI, the better the investment.

return on investment calculated by dividing return, or net profit, by the amount of the investment

▲ MARKET SEGMENTATION STRATEGIES

Once specific target markets have been identified, the marketing managers must begin to develop broad marketing strategies. In general, there are three segmentation strategies that can be applied: a **mass-market strategy**, a **differentiated strategy**, or a **concentrated strategy**.

mass-market strategy one product–service mix that is marketed to all potential consumers in the target markets

Mass-Market Strategy

A mass-market, or undifferentiated, strategy calls upon a firm to develop one product–service mix that is marketed to all potential consumers in the target markets. This approach considers the market to be one homogeneous market segment with similar wants and needs. There is no reason to develop more than one marketing program, since consumers are alike and react in a similar fashion to the components of the marketing program. For example, when McDonald's first opened, the firm offered a very limited menu that was consistent across the entire organization. It featured only a couple of hamburger choices, milkshakes, soft drinks, and french fries. No other choices were available, and all stores offered the identical menu. This strategy was also used by hotel chains (e.g., Holiday Inns), airlines (United Airlines), and tourism destinations (e.g., cities and countries) in the early stages of their life cycles.

differentiated strategy separate marketing program for each segment

concentrated strategy one or more product–service mixes that are marketed to one or relatively few market segments with limited changes in the marketing program

However, in reality, few products or services appeal to all segments of the market. Since its inception, McDonald's has changed this strategy in response to trends in the demographic and social environments. The fast-food restaurant now offers chicken sandwiches, salads, and other menu items that appeal to a more health-conscious market segment. Hotels, airlines, and other hospitality and travel firms have moved away from mass-marketing as well. The largest threat when using this strategy is that competitors will tailor their product–service mix and take away market share because they are better able to meet the needs of smaller target market segments of consumers.

Differentiated Strategy

When a firm elects to follow a differentiated strategy, it is following a strategy that calls for the firm to appeal to more than one market segment with a separate marketing program for each segment. The overall objective of this approach is to increase sales and market share by capturing sales from several smaller market segments. Each of the marketing programs, including the product–service mix, is tailored to the specific needs of a market segment.

Perhaps the best example within the hospitality and travel industry of this approach is the strategy followed by Choice Hotels, International. The hotel chain has developed numerous product–service mixes or brands, each targeting a different market. Among the brands offered by Choice Hotels are Clarion Hotel and Suites, Quality Inn and Suites, Comfort Inns and Suites, Sleep Inns, Econo-Lodge, and Travelodge. Each of the brands offers a different array of amenities at various price levels in an attempt to have at least one brand that will appeal to any consumer in the economy or midpriced market segments.

A differentiated strategy can also be used at the unit or property level. Consider a hotel that is targeting the following markets:

- Individual travelers, including those traveling for both pleasure and business during the week
- Group meetings, representing corporations, associations, social, and other smaller segments
- Tour and travel groups, including those traveling by motor coach

Each of these target markets has needs and wants that differ from the other markets. Those responsible for the marketing efforts of the hotels will, using a differentiated strategy, develop a product–service mix that meets the needs of the individual market segments.

Most successful firms use some type of a differentiated marketing strategy. While the marketing costs associated with a differentiated strategy are higher in most cases, the return on investment is also higher. By targeting the needs and wants of specific target markets and communicating directly to these target markets with separate marketing programs, overall sales usually increase.

Concentrated Strategy

A concentrated, or focused, strategy calls upon firms to develop modifications of one or more product–service mixes that are marketed to one or relatively few market segments with limited changes in the marketing program. This strategy is used successfully by smaller firms without the resources to compete in a broader market. Consider that many firms in the lodging industry have developed multiple product–service mixes and brands targeting many markets, while companies such as Hyatt Hotels and

Resorts and Renaissance Hotels have not taken this approach. Instead, these hotels have concentrated marketing efforts on business travelers and those who have the need for full-service lodging. It is not a question of which company is correct. Rather, it is a question of which strategy is the most appropriate in light of the firm's mission and long-term goals.

▲ POSITIONING THE PRODUCT–SERVICE MIX

Once market segments have been selected, management must develop a positioning strategy for its products and services in each target market. Put simply, **positioning** is the process of determining how to differentiate a firm's product offerings from those of its competitors in the minds of consumers. This requires the firm to know how important certain attributes are to consumers in purchasing the firm's product, and the consumers' perceptions of how well the firm and its competitors are doing with respect to these attributes.[5] Marketers want to position their products so consumers purchase them instead of competing products.

positioning determining how to differentiate a firm's product offerings from those of its competitors in the minds of consumers

This motor lodge uses a concentrated segmentation strategy to attract visitors to the local college. *Courtesy of Hampshire Hospitality Group, Northampton, Massachusetts*

Generally, firms have choices on the positioning of their products, and it is important to consider the alternatives. For example, rental car companies have chosen different bases to position their products. Hertz stresses the benefits of using the number-one rental car company to satisfy consumer needs, emphasizing the employee ownership of the company, while Avis positions itself against Hertz using the "we try harder" slogan. In addition, Enterprise Rent-A-Car stresses pick-up service, and Budget stresses a specific product feature—price. Other bases for positioning could be specific usage occasions or user category. For instance, Marriott positions its Residence Inns for extended stays and its Courtyard Hotels for business travelers. Finally, it is also possible to use more than one basis for positioning when targeting a specific market.

Several factors will affect a firm's decision regarding which positioning bases it should use. First, a firm's current market position and the positions of its competitors are important. Second, a firm should consider the compatibility of a desired position with the needs of consumers and the goals of the firm. Third, a firm must have the resources necessary to communicate and maintain the desired position. Figure 4.3 provides a four-step process that considers these factors and can be used in positioning a firm's products.

Determine the Ideal Mix for Consumers

salient attributes attributes that are the most important to consumers in evaluating the alternative products or service offerings

The first step in the process is to determine what consumers are looking for when they purchase a specific product or service. Once a firm establishes this *ideal mix* of attributes, it can begin to examine the ability of its product–service mix to meet the needs of consumers. Normally, there are a few **salient attributes** that are important to consumers in evaluating the alternative products or service offerings. These attributes will differ by product or service, but Table 4.2 provides some of the more important attributes for hospitality and travel products.

As you can see, many of the attributes are important for all products and services. Price is not always the most important attribute, but is almost always one of the top three. Service quality is another attribute that is important to consumers in choosing service providers, and it is commonly used to differentiate between brands. Other attributes are more specific to a particular type of firm. For example, food quality is very important to consumers in choosing a restaurant, and room quality is important to consumers in choosing a hotel.

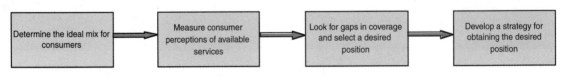

Figure 4.3 The Positioning Process

It is necessary for firms to obtain importance ratings from consumers using some type of research method. These methods will be discussed in more detail in Chapter 6, but the most common method is to conduct some type of survey. Normally, individuals are asked to rate a list of attributes using an importance scale. For example, a restaurant's comment card may ask a customer to rate the quality of food on a scale of 1 to 5, with 1 being "not important at all" and 5 being "very important." The answers to these ratings are combined to provide an average rating for each desired target market. The averages for all of the attributes can then be examined and used to construct an ideal mix for the product. In other words, what are consumers looking for?

Measure Consumer Perceptions of Available Services

Once the ideal mix is determined, the next step is to examine the current offerings of your firm and its competitors to evaluate their abilities to meet consumer needs. More important, it is necessary to obtain consumer perceptions of your service and your competitors' services. Even if a firm believes its product–service mix offers good value to consumers, it is only true if consumers believe it to be true. In marketing, *perceptions are everything*. It would be a critical mistake for a firm to assume that it knows what

Table 4.2	**Important Attributes for Hospitality and Travel Firms**
Type of Firm	*List of Attributes*
Restaurant	Price, value, quality of food, type of food, service quality, menu variety, employee friendliness, location, atmosphere, speed of service, cleanliness, parking
Hotel	Price, value, room quality, restaurant quality, location, number and types of restaurants, other facilities (e.g., pool and fitness center), cleanliness, atmosphere, employee friendliness, speed of check-in and check-out, amenities (e.g., valet parking and room service), service quality
Airline	Price, value, service quality, employee friendliness, on-time performance, baggage handling, direct routes, cities served, scheduled flights, frequent flyer programs
Rental Car Company	Price, value, service quality, convenience, location, types of cars, condition of cars, speed of service, pick-up and drop-off policies

consumers want and that its products are meeting consumers' wants and needs. Once again, it is essential for firms to evaluate consumer perceptions through the use of consumer surveys and other research methods. Table 4.3 provides an example of a competitive benefit matrix that can be used by restaurants to compile consumer perceptions for the firm and its closest competitors.

perceptual map
graphic representation of how consumers in a market perceive a competing set of products relative to each other

At this point, it may be helpful for a firm to be able to visualize the information in the competitive benefit matrix by using a **perceptual map**. Perceptual mapping is a technique used to construct a graphic representation of how consumers in a market perceive a competing set of products relative to each other. Because of the difficulties associated with graphing and understanding multidimensional presentations, managers must determine the two or three most important dimensions to consumers in evaluating competing products, and use these dimensions to construct the perceptual map. For example, Figure 4.4 provides a hypothetical perceptual map for hotel chains.

The perceptual map was constructed using perceived price and perceived quality as the two dimensions. Assuming the ratings for the hotel chains on these dimensions were collected using consumer research, the placement of the firms in the perceptual space depicts their relative positions in the market. The results of perceptual mapping can be used for the following purposes:

- To learn how consumers perceive the strengths, weaknesses, and similarities of the alternative product–service mixes being offered
- To learn about consumers' desires and how these are satisfied or not satisfied by the current products and services in the market
- To integrate these findings strategically to determine the greatest opportunities for new product–service mixes and how a product or service's image should be modified to produce the greatest sales gain.

Table 4.3	Competitve Benefit Matrix		
Potential Benefits	*Our Operation*	*Competitor A*	*Competitor B*
Value for price			
Quality of food			
Quality of service			
Atmosphere			
Location			
Menu variety			

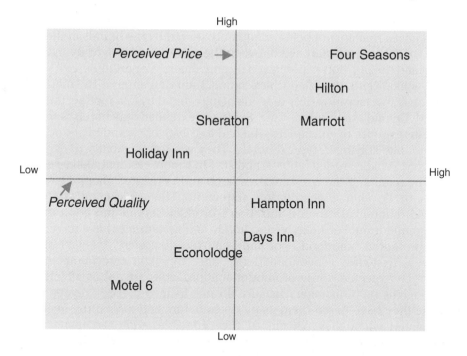

Figure 4.4. **Perceptual Map for Hotel Service**

Several methods can be used to construct a perceptual map. **Similarity–dissimilarity data** involves asking consumers to make direct comparisons between alternative brands. For example, consumers might be given the names of restaurants and asked to select the ones that are most similar or the ones that are least similar. **Preference data** involves asking consumers to indicate their preferences for a list of alternative brands. For example, consumers might be asked to rank-order a short list of restaurants or rate a specific restaurant on a 1 to 5 scale, with 1 being least preferred and 5 being most preferred. **Attribute data** involves asking consumers to rate the alternative brands on predetermined list of attributes. For example, consumers might be asked to rate a given restaurant based on a series of attributes.

After the data is collected, sophisticated statistical techniques are used to reduce the list of attributes into two or three dimensions for easier presentation and interpretation. Then, management can use these perceptual maps to fine-tune current product–service mixes, and uncover gaps in market coverage between the ideal mix and the alternative offerings.

similarity–dissimilarity data data obtained by asking consumers to make direct comparisons between alternative brands

preference data data obtained by asking consumers to indicate their preferences for a list of alternative brands

attribute data data obtained by asking consumers to rate the alternative brands on predetermined list of attributes

Look for Gaps in Coverage and Select a Desired Position

Once consumers' perceptions are obtained, measured, and plotted on a perceptual map, the third step in the process is to examine the map for gaps in coverage. In other words, are there any areas on the map depicting ideal mixes that are not being adequately served by the brands in the market? Or, is there a difference between the position as sought by management and the position as perceived by consumers? For example, restaurant chains like Kentucky Fried Chicken and Taco Bell entered the market in response to a lack in variety of foods being offered by fast-food restaurants like McDonald's and Burger King. Similarly, extended stay hotels were created in response to consumers who had to travel for extended periods and did not like staying in typical hotels. They wanted the ability to cook, do laundry, avoid crowded lobbies, and stay in a more residential-like setting.

positioning statement statement used to differentiate the organization's product–service mix from that of the competition

The results of the consumer research and perceptual mapping enable firms to develop a **positioning statement**. The positioning statement should differentiate the organization's product–service mix from that of the competition. For many years, hotels and restaurants have advertised and promoted "fine food," "prompt, courteous service," "elegant atmosphere," "first-class accommodations," and "top-flight entertainment." As might be expected, these promotional approaches are not as effective as they might be. Consumers usually do not believe these statements because they have heard them many times before and have often been disappointed when they patronized the properties that had made these promotional claims. Also, these statements do little to separate the organization's product–service mix from that of the competition. If other hospitality organizations are promoting "fine food" or similar benefits, then all the promotion and advertising is basically the same.

unique selling proposition promoting a unique element of the product–service mix

The key to success in positioning is to establish some unique element of the product–service mix and promote it. This allows management to differentiate the product–service mix from that of the competition and thereby gain a competitive advantage. This approach is known as establishing a **unique selling proposition (USP)**. With a USP, every effort should be made to link the benefits with tangible aspects of the product–service mix. In this way, consumers have something tangible with which to associate the hospitality operation.

Develop a Strategy for Obtaining the Desired Position

The final step in the positioning process is to develop strategies for obtaining the desired position that results from the analyses performed in the first three steps. As with any other discussions of strategy in this text, marketing managers must use the components of the marketing mix to develop marketing programs that can be used to achieve the firm's objectives. In this case, decisions regarding price, product–service mix, promotion, and distribution must be made to help the firm achieve its desired position. It should be noted that the easiest changes in the marketing mix involve price and promotion. Changes to the product–service mix and distribution are more complicated and often involve expensive changes in tangible elements.

One of the most effective ways to change consumer perceptions of the product–service mix is through promotion and advertising. There are many examples of how products have been positioned or repositioned using advertising and promotional campaigns. For instance, there are some classic examples of positioning within the fast-food industry. The first example involves Wendy's attempt to differentiate its product–service mix as superior to other hamburger restaurants in the fast-food industry. Wendy's used the now-famous spokesperson Clara Peller to bellow, "Where's the beef?" Wendy's standard burger was a 4-ounce patty, whereas other fast-food companies used a 1.6-ounce patty for their standard hamburgers. Clara Peller was a distinctive personality who helped to establish Wendy's superior position in the consumer's mind.

The second example of using product–service mix positioning is the manner in which Taco Bell used price and packaging to gain a competitive advantage. At a time when the typical meal at a fast-food restaurant cost between $3.50 and $4.00, Taco Bell took a very different positioning strategy. They introduced a line of value-priced products and meals. They introduced a line of products placed at price points between 59 cents and 99 cents. The focus of all promotions and point of purchase displays was on low price and value pricing. As a result of these promotions, Taco Bell was able to increase its market share, largely at the expense of other fast-food restaurants.

Al Ries and Jack Trout provide a useful set of guidelines to use in developing positioning strategies in their text entitled *Positioning: The Battle for Your Mind.*[6] The authors formulated six questions that can be used to guide one's thinking:

1. *What position do you own?* It is critical that you look at the marketplace and your image from the consumer's point of view. How do consumers view your product? What image does your product have in their minds? Keep in mind that you must be objective and look at your product from the consumer's perspective.

2. *What position do you want?* Remember that those who are most successful tend to carve out a niche of the broad market. Those who attempt to be all things to all people often are not successful. Don't think beyond your organization's capabilities. You must be able to "own" the position, even if that means displacing a competitor's brand. Not every firm can be the leader, but firms can be successful with other strategies.

3. *Who must you outgun?* No positioning statement is created in a vacuum. You must clearly visualize the positions held by the major competitors. Do they have a firm lock on their positions, or are they vulnerable? It is wise to avoid a direct frontal attack if they are strong; it's better to go around them.

4. *Do you have enough money?* Establishing and maintaining an image in the consumers' mind is no small task. Every day we are exposed to

hundreds of advertising images. If a change in positioning strategy is planned, then the necessary marketing resources must be appropriated for the change to be successful.

5. **Can you stick it out?** A key to successful positioning is the ability to defend that position. The most successful companies don't change their position, only the short-term tactics they use to communicate their position.

6. **Do you match your position?** It is critical that the exact positioning statement be communicated in the advertising and promotions that follow. The desired position should be consistent with the image of the firm and fit with the image of the firm's other products and services.

▲ MARKETING ACTION NOW!

The positioning of a firm and its products is one of the most important concepts in business. Positioning is the cornerstone of competition and, unless it is done correctly, the firm's employees will not have their jobs for long. Consider one of your favorite restaurants in your local area. Proceed through the positioning process for this restaurant.

- First, determine the ideal mix for a restaurant using the students in your class as a target market. Use the attributes discussed in this chapter for restaurants.
- Second, measure consumer perceptions of this restaurant and two of its closest competitors using the competitive benefit matrix in Table 4.3.
- Third, construct a perceptual map based on two of the most important attributes.

Once you have completed the perceptual map, it is time to evaluate the firm's position in the market.

1. Are there any gaps in coverage?
2. Do you see problems with any of the three restaurants' positioning strategies?
3. If so, what would you suggest to improve this situation?

▲ SUMMARY OF CHAPTER OBJECTIVES

Market segmentation is defined as pursuing a marketing strategy whereby the total potential market is divided into homogeneous subsets of customers, each of which responds differently to the marketing mix of the organization. Market segmentation involves considering several segmentation variables as well as segmentation criteria. Criteria for effective segmentation are substantiality, measurability, and accessibility to the selected target markets. Variables that can be used to segment markets include geographic, demographic, psychographic, behavioral, and benefits sought.

Once potential target markets have been identified, decisions must be made concerning which market segments offer the best opportunity to succeed; once determined, these should be pursued. A four-step process was introduced to accomplish this. Firms need to identify segmentation bases, develop profiles for each segment, forecast potential demand, and select specific target market segments.

The important link between target market segmentation and marketing strategy was also introduced. The vast majority of firms follow one of three broad strategies: a mass-market strategy, a differentiated strategy, or a concentrated strategy. The market segmentation strategies differ in the number and type of marketing programs and target markets.

Positioning is a very important aspect of the marketing efforts of any hospitality organization. The positioning statement, and thus the promotional messages, should clearly reflect image, benefit package and support, and differentiation of the product–service mix. Only when all three of these elements are reflected in the organization's advertising and promotion does the organization realize its full potential. The positioning statement should be supported with tangible clues, rather than the intangible and ineffective "fine food" or "excellent service" slogans used by many firms.

Firms should go through the positioning process by (1) determining the ideal mix for consumers; (2) measuring consumer perceptions of available services; (3) looking for gaps in coverage and selecting a desired position; and (4) developing a strategy for obtaining the desired position. Consumer research is vital in this process of collecting information on consumer perceptions regarding the brands in the market. Perceptual maps can be constructed that provide a graphical representation of the consumer preferences and resulting brand positions. Then, firms can select their desired positions and devise strategies for obtaining those positions.

▲ KEY TERMS AND CONCEPTS

Accessibility

AIO (attitudes, interests, and opinions) statements

Attribute data

Behavioral segmentation

Benefit segmentation

Competitive advantage

Consolidated metropolitan statistical area (CMSA)

Marketing communications

Measurability of market segments

Metropolitan statistical area (MSA)

Perceptual mapping

Point of purchase

Positioning

Positioning statement

Preference data

Demographic segmentation

Family life cycle

Forecasts

Frequent traveler programs

Geographic segmentation

Margin of error

Market demand

Market share

Market segmentation

Primary metropolitan statistical area (PMSA)

Projected demand

Psychographic segmentation

Return on investment (ROI)

Similarity–dissimilarity data

Substantiality

Unique selling proposition (USP)

▲ QUESTIONS FOR REVIEW AND DISCUSSION

1. What is market segmentation?
2. Of what value is market segmentation to marketing managers?
3. What variables are used to segment target markets?
4. Which of these variables from question 3 do you see as most and least useful to a manager working in the hospitality and tourism industry?
5. Cite and discuss the criteria for effective segmentation.
6. Is it possible to oversegment a market? If so, can you give an example?
7. What are the four steps in the market segmentation decision process?
8. Explain and give examples of each of the three market segmentation strategies.
9. What is positioning? Why is it important?
10. Describe the four steps in the positioning process.
11. What is perceptual mapping?

▲ NOTES

[1]Anthony Marshall, "Common Complaints Often Arise from 'Mature' Travelers," *Hotel & Motel Management*, Vol. 24, No. 5 (March 15, 1999), p. 10.

[2]Diane Crispell, Thomas Exter and Judith Waltrop, "Census '90," *The Wall Street Journal Reports* (March 9, 1990), p. R13.

[3]Diane Crispell, Thomas Exter and Judith Waltrop, "Snapshots of the Nation," *The Wall Street Journal Reports* (March 9, 1990), p. R12.

[4]"Average Household Slips to Record Low of About 2½ People," *The Wall Street Journal* (May 5, 1989), p. B5.

[5]James H. Martin and James M. Daley, "How to Develop a Customer-Driven Positioning Strategy," *Business*, 39 (October–December 1989), p. 11.

[6]Al Ries and Jack Trout. *Positioning: The Battle for Your Mind* (New York: McGraw-Hill, 1981).

Marketing Planning and Information

5

Developing a Marketing Plan

❖ Chapter Objectives

By the end of this chapter, you should understand:

1. The need for marketing plans
2. The difference between plans that have a strategic and tactical orientation
3. The advantages and disadvantages of planning
4. The operational definitions of terms such as mission, goals and objectives, organizational resources, market risks and opportunities, evaluation plans, marketing strategies, and action plans
5. The steps of the marketing planning process and
6. The qualitative and quantitative techniques for developing sales forecasts

❖ Chapter Outline

  I. Chapter Opening Profile
  II. Introduction

❖ Chapter Opening Profile

ALL TYPES OF FIRMS ENGAGE IN marketing planning so they can determine the future direction of the firm and develop strategies to guide them. Even nonprofit organizations like convention and visitors bureaus (CVBs) find it beneficial to prepare marketing plans to act as blueprints for conducting business. A typical mission statement for a CVB may be:

To enhance the economic fabric of the region through the promotion, advertising, and marketing of the region, its facilities and resources, as a site for conventions, meetings, trade shows, special events, and leisure travel.

As you can see, there is no mention of profit or other financial objectives. Instead, the goal of the organization is to promote the area for its members that include hotels, restaurants, shopping centers, transportation firms, and tourist attractions. CVBs must compete with other destinations for meetings and conventions, and for business and leisure travel. Therefore, these nonprofit organizations must target markets with the greatest potential, much like profit organizations that sell various products and services.

All organizations, profit and nonprofit, must have a mission that is communicated to its stakeholders so they can pursue common goals and objectives. All cities and regions compete for a share of the travel market, and they use organizations like convention and visitors bureaus to help them promote their destinations in an attempt to gain some type of competitive advantage. The goals for a CVB could be:

1. To promote the region as a visitor and convention destination
2. To coordinate a joint marketing program encompassing the entire region and involving promotional agencies and allied business organizations
3. To promote efforts toward increasing the level of tourism, meetings, conferences, and related business, and to improve hospitality services
4. To cooperate closely with state agencies involved in visitor and convention promotion

The challenge for these nonprofit organizations is to raise enough money through government and private sources to be effective in promoting their regions. To accomplish this, CVBs must establish specific objectives and develop strategies that will help the firm achieve its objectives. Aside from the lack of a profit goal, the planning process is very similar for profit and nonprofit organizations.

▲ INTRODUCTION

Planning focuses on the future. It involves assessing the current environmental trends and determining what is most likely to occur in the future. People who are responsible for developing business plans chart a course of action that they believe will allow the firm to achieve its stated objectives. Planners can never be 100 percent certain that they will be successful in achieving their stated objectives, but well-developed plans have a much higher probability of achieving the desired results.

In general, a marketing plan can be defined as "a written document containing the guidelines for the business center's marketing programs and allocations over the planning period."[1] Some key parts of this definition should be discussed. First, the fact that marketing plans are written documents requires managers to analyze the company, its products, and the environment so they can prepare well-organized documents to guide their companies. Second, marketing plans are written for the appropriate business center as defined by the organization. These business centers are often referred to as strategic business units (SBUs) because they consist of products that share common characteristics and have the same competitors. Finally, there is a relevant planning period that varies from product to product or unit to unit based on the scope or breadth of the planning activity. For example, strategic plans are broad, have far-reaching implications and often extend three or more years into future. Conversely, tactical plans are more short-term in focus with an emphasis on implementation.

Strategic marketing plans are based on a careful examination of a firm's core business strategy and primary marketing objectives. When in-

strategic marketing plan based on a careful examination of a firm's core business strategy and primary marketing objectives

tactical marketing plan focus on implementing the broad strategies that are established in the strategic plan

volved in this type of planning, firms should focus on some key areas starting with the type of business the firms is in, or wishes to be in. Next, the firm should ask where are we now, where would we like to be, and what should we do to get there? Questions such as these are not easy to answer, but they are the foundation on which strategic plans are based. Strategic planning is the process of determining the firm's primary goals and objectives, and initiating actions that will allow it to achieve these stated goals and objectives. Strategic marketing planning is should be performed by all types of hospitality and travel firms, but it is an absolute necessity for multiunit firms or chains.

Tactical marketing plans focus on implementing the broad strategies that are established in the strategic plan. Tactical plans typically cover a period of one year and focus on specific activities that must be implemented if the firm is to achieve the goals and objectives stated in the more long-range, strategic plan. One of the focal points for tactical plans is the allocation of resources to achieve the stated objectives. Tactical plans are sometimes modified, based on the actions of the primary competitors and the availability of resources, but strategic plans are normally not modified without considerable reflection.

Within small chains and independent operations, the unit management is often granted great autonomy. Within larger chain organizations, most aspects of the marketing function are tightly controlled, and the manager of an individual unit is more involved in implementation rather than planning. Planning is conducted at a higher level within the organization to ensure coordination of marketing efforts and consistency throughout the chain. Corporate-level marketing managers will normally work with the managers of the unit level to help them formulate and implement tactical plans that will allow the unit to be successful, while at the same time supporting the overall corporate marketing strategic plan.

Tactical plans prepared for a one-year time horizon might be based on the answers to questions similar to those listed below.

- What is our market share? Is it increasing or decreasing?
- How have the strengths and weaknesses of our firm changed in the last year?
- How has our mix of guests changed in the last year?
- What advertising and promotions were the most and least successful during the last year?
- What types of promotions and sales efforts should be undertaken to build business during our slow periods?
- What types of promotion and advertising schedules should be planned?
- What in-house promotions should we schedule?

Advantages and Disadvantages of Planning

Formulating an organized and well-conceived marketing plan can have a tremendously positive impact on a hospitality firm. Some of the main *advantages* of marketing planning are:

1. It helps the firm cope with change more effectively. If the competitive environment changes rapidly, a firm that has developed strategic plans with several contingency options is in a better position to effectively deal with the change.

2. Planning related to the marketing function helps ensure that the firm's objectives are either achieved or modified. The plans formulated serve as guides to help the firm achieve the objectives. If, in some unforeseen circumstances, the objectives are not attainable, revised objectives and plans can be formulated. This is done after a very careful analysis of the situation investigating why the original objectives could not be achieved.

3. Establishing a marketing plan aids management in decision-making. The established plans can easily serve as a point of reference for management to consult when confronted with a difficult decision. Given the alternative choices, managers can decide which ones will contribute the most to the achievement of their objectives.

4. Planning forces managers to carefully examine the firm's operations. Marketing plans make it necessary for managers to relate employee tasks and resources allocation to the firm's objectives. There must be a clear delineation of how the use of resources and employee time will help the firm achieve its objectives.

5. Developing both strategic and tactical marketing plans aids management in the evaluation of the marketing efforts. Results of marketing efforts can be compared with projected results, thereby giving management a control process for the marketing function.

While establishing a marketing plan has many advantages, there are also some disadvantages associated with marketing planning. Some of the main *disadvantages* of marketing planning are:

1. Establishing objectives and formulating a marketing plan is very time-consuming. The time that management invests in planning can be expensive, and the results of planning must be cost effective. The overall benefits of these efforts, however, normally far exceed the cost to the firm.

2. If planning is to be successful and have the desired impact on an organization, it must have the support and commitment of the top management. If those involved in the planning process perceive that they

are merely "going through the motions" and that their activities will not have any impact, they will have a negative opinion of planning. Under these circumstances, the planning process will be viewed as an extra duty and will be given a low priority, resulting in an inferior plan.

3. If plans are poorly conceived or are based on false assumptions, they may be inaccurate or ineffective. For this reason, some managers feel that planning is of little value. Additionally, unplanned scenarios can develop rapidly, rendering marketing plans much less effective.

4. Since plans often need to be prepared within a short period of time, it may not be possible to conduct as much background work as necessary for a high-quality plan. Also, the planning task is often assigned to a manager that has other duties and responsibilities, limiting the amount of time the manager has for planning. The development of a plan should be viewed as a means to an end, such as increased sales and profits, not as an end unto itself.

5. Many firms do not have the personnel with the required knowledge and expertise in planning. Many aspects are involved in marketing planning and the employee responsible for planning should have some level of formal training.

Why Some Plans Fail

Despite the best efforts of marketing planners and all those involved in the planning process, some plans fail to fully achieve the desired results because of tactical shortcomings. The following are the most common reasons that some plans fail, based on the findings of several research studies:

- ***Strategic planning is not integrated into the day-to-day activities of the firm.*** In these cases, the plan is seen as an end in itself, and is not made operational. Often, plans are carefully prepared, but they remain unused as employees are either unable, or unwilling, to implement them. The planning process is a dynamic, ongoing process. Plans should be implemented, evaluated, revised, and implemented again. Only when this cycle is continual can planning truly succeed.

- ***Those responsible for planning do not understand the planning process.*** It is important that when a plan is being designed, the planners must make sure to work through all of the steps of the planning process. Sometimes managers want to jump ahead and draw conclusions before all environmental variables are considered and before a clear consensus has been reached. This tendency should be avoided, for the results are usually unreliable. Every member of the planning team must fully understand the steps involved in the planning process and should actively contribute during each step.

- ***There is a lack of input from nonmarketing managers.*** For a marketing plan to succeed, it must be implemented in part by managers who have major responsibilities in areas other than marketing. In some cases, the planning process is assigned to professional planners, while implementation is left to line managers who are concerned mainly with normal operations. These managers did not participate in the planning process and do not see the advantages or importance of planning. Also, the planners did not benefit from the operational knowledge possessed by the line managers.

- *Financial projections are treated as marketing plans.* Some hospitality firms make projections or forecasts for sales and call this activity "marketing planning." Projections by themselves are not plans. Only when clearly defined tactics are identified for achieving the desired objectives does planning take place.
- *There is inadequate input and insufficient consideration of all environmental variables.* Although it is impossible to consider all the variables, the real danger is basing decisions and plans on an insufficient amount of information. Managers often want to rush to a conclusion rather than gather information that is readily available and make informed decisions. This type of information is available through environmental scanning and the use of marketing information systems.
- *Planning is based too heavily on short-term results.* The emphasis should be placed on formulating plans that will allow the firm to move toward the successful achievement of long-term goals. Too frequently, the emphasis is placed on short-term profits at the expense of long-term objectives and profits.
- *No procedures established to monitor and control the planning process.* It is important to establish procedures to monitor the planning process from the time it is started through implementation and beyond. This will allow the firm to make changes as necessary based on new information or problems that may arise.

There are many other reasons why plans sometimes fail to achieve the desired results. However, if the members of the planning group focus their attention clearly on the initial stages of the planning process, the later stages will become much easier to complete, and the probability of success will also increase. It is important to avoid the temptation to rush through the initial steps in order to produce quick results.

An old saying that still holds true today indicates that there are three types of companies: companies that make things happen, companies that watch things happen, and companies that wonder what happened. Companies that make things happen are generally engaged in planning. They have established a mission statement as well as goals and objectives, leading to the formation of overall strategies that result in success. Becoming overly concerned with day-to-day operations causes the downfall of many hospitality organizations. The result is that managers become so engrossed in meeting the daily demands of their positions that they fail to see the big picture—they can't see the forest through the trees. Because of this myopic perspective, they are not aware of trends, and when the competitive environment does change, they are not prepared for it.

Successful planning is a key element in the financial success of all firms. Hospitality firms that allocate human and monetary resources for planning are much more likely to reach their financial goals than firms who do not engage in planning.

▲ THE MARKETING PLANNING PROCESS

No magic formula will guarantee success for a firm in the hospitality and travel industry. Even well-managed firms may fail to achieve the desired level of success. However, there are steps that can be taken to increase the probability of success. Figure 5.1 illustrates the basic steps in the marketing planning process. If managers focus on these elements, they are more likely to lead the firm in a direction that will accomplish its goals.

Before actually beginning the marketing planning process, it is necessary for a firm to establish a **mission statement**. Mission statements define

mission statement
defines the purpose of a firm and how it attempts to differentiate itself from its competitors

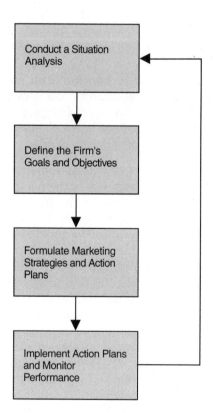

FIGURE 5.1 The Marketing Planning Process

the purpose of the firm and how it attempts to differentiate itself from its competitors. It should provide managers with the general guidelines for decision-making. Typically, mission statements are brief, usually less than two paragraphs, they define the scope of business for the corporation, and they answer the question "What business are we in?" For example, if a corporation defined its mission as providing outstanding hospitality services in the budget-priced segment of the market, this would be the primary focus for the corporation. This is the message that is conveyed to the firm's internal stakeholders such as owners/investors, managers, and employees. Then a **position statement** is created to describe this mission to the firm's external stakeholders (e.g., customers, suppliers, and the general community) in terms of the public's perceptions of the benefits you are offering.

position statement describes the mission to the firm's external stakeholders

This idea of focus, or purpose, is important in proceeding with the marketing planning process. A firm's mission is a function of its available resources and capabilities. It is difficult to operate outside these parameters and still be successful. For example, the budget hotel mentioned earlier would not be able to compete for customers with full-service hotels that offer a wide array of amenities and services that are not available at budget properties. Budget hotels know that they appeal to price-sensitive customers who want a nice room that is clean and safe. If the hotel adheres to its mission, there will be no confusion among the stakeholders, and there is a better chance for success. Once the mission statement is established, the firm can begin the planning process.

Conducting a Situation Analysis

The first step in the marketing planning process requires a firm to perform a situation analysis. This begins by looking at the history of the firm, followed an objective assessment of the firm's strengths and weaknesses relative to competitors, including an analysis of the potential opportunities and threats posed by the changes in the firm's external environment. The situation analysis provides the background information necessary to make decisions regarding the future direction of the firm. Basically, it answers the questions "Where are we now" and "How did we get here"? A good deal can be gained by studying the history of an organization.

Historical Appraisal. The historical appraisal starts by examining the market, looking at its size, its scope, and the market shares of the competitors. It is important to look at the trends in the market to better understand how the firm arrived at its present position. The firm should examine internal data regarding its sales history, including costs and profits. It is helpful to see the trends in sales, costs, and profit margins that resulted from changes in marketing programs and the environment. This provides insight into possible future directions based on the current position of products in the market. Many of the trends can be attributed to changes in the external environment. For example, changes in technology and government regulations will force firms to rethink their strategies and react appropriately. Travel agents are competing with online reservations, and hotels and airlines are benefiting from customers having access to their Web sites on the Internet. Restaurants are faced with changes in tax laws and smoking regulations, and must adapt their strategies in response to these changes in government regulations.

Firms must also examine sales histories for changes in consumer purchasing patterns. Consumers are likely to change their buying procedures and practices over time. For instance, there may be changes in frequency, the quantity, or timing of their purchases. Understanding these changes is crucial for firms that want to be competitive at getting products to consumers in the form, and at the time, they want them. Firms will undoubtedly use this information to gain competitive advantages through pricing and product design. These advantages will then be communicated to consumers through the firms' promotions. For example, restaurants may notice that a larger percentage of customers are dining earlier as a result of the aging population and the increase in families with small children. Similarly, resorts may find that consumers are taking more vacations of shorter duration. All types of hospitality and travel firms will benefit from conducting a formal situation analysis, beginning with a historical appraisal.

Consumer analysis should be conducted to identify the buyers and users of the product to make sure they are the same. In some cases, the person who purchases the product is not the user (e.g., meeting planners, travel agents). Also, it is important to identify the individuals who may influence a purchase (e.g., family members, buying centers). Next, firms must identify other factors that could influence the purchase (e.g., demographics, socioeconomics, lifestyles) and any variations in purchase behavior (e.g., seasonal or cyclical variations). A related area is to determine what motivates consumers to purchase this type of product, how they can be segmented, and who are the most frequent purchasers. Once a firm identifies the salient (important) attributes and the end-benefit that consumers are seeking, it can be determined if there are any unmet needs that can be targeted.

Industry analysis should be conducted to determine the actual and potential industry size, the historical growth rate and future predictions, the industry structure (including costs and distribution), industry trends, and key success factors. It may be useful to rank competitors by market share and identify both direct and indirect competition. For example, restaurants are facing competition from supermarkets, convenience stores, and delivery services. The next section will elaborate on the process of assessing the internal strengths and weaknesses of firms, relative to the competition, and the opportunities and threats posed by the environment.

SWOT Analysis. The next part of the situation analysis involves a detailed examination of the firm's internal strengths and weaknesses, and the external opportunities and threats. This analysis is often referred to as a SWOT analysis. Figure 5.2 illustrates the various components of a SWOT analysis and their relationships with one another.

The strengths and weaknesses components reflect an evaluation of the firm's internal situation. What are the things that the firm does well, and where are they below standard? The opportunities and threats reflect an assessment of the external environment that the firm faces. Strengths and opportunities represent positive attributes that the firm can use to gain a competitive advantage. If items that appear as strengths and opportunities for the firm are similar to weaknesses and threats for the competitors, then the firm has a distinct competitive advantage that can be leveraged for gains in sales and market share. Similarly, weaknesses and threats should be viewed as problem areas. Firms need to compensate for weaknesses until they can be eliminated, if possible, and threats need to be anticipated so strategies can be developed to minimize their impact.

As shown in Figure 5.2, strengths and opportunities are items that can be leveraged to gain a competitive advantage. For example, if a food service operation found that there would be minimal competition for an off-premise catering business in addition to its existing restaurant operation, this would represent an opportunity or an area for potential growth. Using the same example, a food service operation might find that if it decided to enter the off-premise catering business, competition might follow. This potential competition represents an external threat.

Inherent in this analysis is the need to critically examine what the business does well and what could be improved upon. At the same time, a critical assessment of the market is needed to determine, as specifically as possible, the threats and potential opportunities that exist outside firm. Management must ask "What do we have or offer that is different, unique, or superior to what the competition offers consumers?" Management must also examine the organization's shortcomings by asking "What do we provide that is below average?"

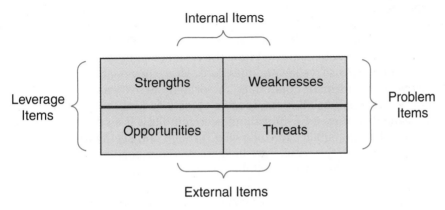

FIGURE 5.2 SWOT Analysis

The process of identifying internal strengths and weaknesses or external threats and opportunities is similar to examining a balance sheet with assets and liabilities. The strengths and opportunities should be used to promote the business and to make decisions about new directions that should be taken. At the same time, management must make every effort to correct or neutralize the weaknesses and threats. Many managers find it difficult to identify an organization's weaknesses or threats clearly, tending to overlook or downplay negative factors.

Successful managers seem to be able to predict the future and adapt to meet the changes that are occurring in the marketplace. Although this may not be entirely true, those who are successful seem to know what will occur in the market place before it actually happens. Is it luck or successful planning? Luck has been defined as "preparation meeting opportunity." Successful managers are students of trends. They carefully watch the broad marketing environment discussed in Chapter 1, looking for subtle changes in the economic, political and legal, social, and technological environments that may potentially impact their businesses. They carefully study the moves made by their competitors, and do everything they can to stay close to their customers. In doing so, they attempt to match their product–service mix to the everchanging needs and wants of their customers and potential customers.

Defining the Firm's Goals and Objectives

A firm's goals and objectives should evolve from the mission statement. Some firms use both goals and objectives, others prefer to use one or the other. In fact, the two terms are often used synonymously. **Goals** are broad statements of what the firm seeks to accomplish. For example, a firm may develop a goal that states, "We are seeking to achieve the number one market share in the mid-Atlantic region." The goal does not tell how the results are to be achieved; rather it states, in broad terms, the desired end result. An **objective** is a more detailed statement, or refinement, of what the firm intends to accomplish. A good objective will include: (1) what will be accomplished in measurable terms, (2) within what specific time frame it will be accomplished, (3) which individual or group will be responsible for achieving the objective, and (4) how the results will be evaluated.

The objectives serve several functions. First, they enable management to arrive at a consensus concerning the primary activities of the organization. Second, responsibility for specific objectives can be assigned to specific managers, thereby establishing accountability. If a specific manager is assigned responsibility for following through and seeing that an objective is completed, the results are likely to be more positive than if no one individual is assigned responsibility. Third, establishing objectives with the input of all managers serves as a brainstorming and motivational tool. When individuals have input into formulating the organizational marketing objectives, they develop a sense of ownership and allegiance toward the

goals broad statements of what the firm seeks to accomplish

objective more detailed statement of what the firm intends to accomplish

objectives. As a result, employees are likely to work more diligently to achieve stated objectives.

The formulation of well-written and measurable objectives will take time, and care should be taken to assure that the objectives are feasible. Several characteristics of good objectives follow:

- *Objectives should be specific and easy to understand.* They should not be too broad and difficult to define. Everyone involved in formulating the objectives should clearly understand the precise objectives toward which the organization seeks to move.
- *Objectives should identify expected results.* If at all possible, they should be quantitative so that no gray area will exist for purposes of evaluation. When the objective is stated in quantitative terms, the expected results are more readily understood.
- *Objectives must be within the power of the organization to achieve.* When establishing objectives, management must keep in mind the relative abilities of the organization.
- *Objectives must be acceptable to the individuals within the organization.* Management must come to a consensus concerning the objectives. It is extremely difficult for a firm to successfully achieve the stated objectives if the managers, who have input into the formation of the objectives, do not agree.

Table 5.1 provides some examples of good objectives that are well stated, and some that are poorly stated. It is easy to see how the two types

Table 5.1	**Examples of Objectives**
Good (Well-Stated) Objectives	*Bad (Poorly Stated) Objectives*
Our objective is to increase occupancy rate from 70% to 75% within one year by decreasing group rates by 5%.	Our objective is to increase occupancy rate.
Our objective is to increase our awareness rating from 60% to 70% within one year by allocating $200,000 to advertising for an awareness campaign.	Our objective is to increase awareness over the next year.
Our objective is to increase the average check by 10% within six months by providing waiters with a 2-hour suggestive selling training program.	Our objective is to increase the average check by training waiters.

differ in their abilities to steer firms and allow for the measurement of performance. The good objectives are clear and concise, they provide a specific time frame for completion, and they contain quantified targets. In addition to the stated objectives, it is necessary for firms to provide an explanation of how the results will be evaluated, and who has the actual responsibility for attaining the objective. Finally, adequate resources must be committed to achieving the objective, including personnel, facilities, and financial resources.

Types of Objectives.   Objectives can be grouped into four main categories: financial objectives, sales objectives, competitive objectives, and customer objectives. Table 5.2 contains a list of some specific objectives that can be used under each of the four categories. *Financial objectives* are concerned with the firm's ability to generate enough money to pay its bills, offer investors an adequate return, and retain some of the earnings for investing in the firm. *Sales objectives* are concerned with the level of sales in units or dollars, and the firm's sales relative to its competitors (i.e., market share). *Competitive objectives* are concerned with the firm's ability to compete in the marketplace. The firm positions itself against the competition, determines the best strategies for survival, or tries to keep pace with the competition in terms of sales growth, market share, and/or marketing expenditures. Finally, *customer objectives* are concerned with the firm's ability to make consumers aware of its products, provide them

Table 5.2	**Types of Objectives**
Main Category	*Specific Objectives*
Financial	Maximize profit Target rate of return Increase cash flow
Sales	Increase or maximize sales/revenues Increase volume (number of units sold) Increase or maximize market share
Competitive	Position against competitors Long-term survival Maintain competitive parity (market share or marketing expenditures
Customer	Increase market awareness Increase customer satisfaction Improve or change image Create goodwill

with a product–service mix that meets their expectations, and create a level of goodwill among customers and other stakeholders.

Firms can use a combination of objectives such as a desire to maximize profit and increase customer satisfaction. These objectives do not conflict, so the firm can work at attaining both. However, it is necessary to prioritize multiple objectives and allocate resources appropriately. One potential problem with multiple objectives is that there could be a conflict between them. For example, consider the case of a firm that wants to increase market share and maximize profit. In the short-run, increases in market share are normally accomplished by lowering price and/or increasing marketing expenditures on changes in the product–service mix and promotion. Decreasing price or increasing marketing expenditures will both result in a decrease in short-term profits. The firm must rethink its objectives or make a distinction between short-term and long-term profits.

Formulating Marketing Strategies and Action Plans

A strategy is the manner by which an organization attempts to link with, respond to, integrate with, and exploit its environment. In other words, a firm's strategies integrate its mission, goals, objectives, and action plans. When they are well formulated, strategies help firms maximize the use of their resources. This, in turn, puts them in a viable position within the competitive environment.

It has been said that, timing is everything. This is true when developing marketing strategies. Managers must always look for **strategic windows**, or limited periods of time when marketing opportunities present themselves and the firm is in a position to take advantage of those opportunities. These are the periods when the firm can act to gain a competitive advantage. Suppose, for example, that your firm had stockpiled a large supply of frozen beef tenderloins and your major competitor had not. Due to weather conditions in the major growing areas, a beef shortage occurred. Prices escalated rapidly and supplies of beef tenderloins were low. This occurrence would offer your firm a strategic window in which to gain a competitive advantage. You could undercut the price of the product and run a promotion for a product that your competition was unable to match.

When developing a marketing strategy, a manager first selects the markets the firm will target and then blends the elements of the marketing mix, which includes the product–service mix, price, promotion, and distribution. Strategic options for each of the marketing mix areas will be covered in detail in later chapters. However, there are various frameworks that can be used by firms to aid in general strategy formulation. One of the more popular frameworks provides four basic strategies for achieving growth based on whether the products are new or they currently exist, and whether the markets are new or they are currently being served. These growth strategies appear in Table 5.3.

strategic windows
limited periods of time when marketing opportunities present themselves and the firm is in a position to take advantage of those opportunities

Table 5.3	**Product Development Strategy Options**	
	Existing Product	*New Product*
Existing Market	Market Penetration	Product Development
New Market	Market Development	Product Diversification

market penetration strategy selling the existing product–service mix to existing target markets

A **market penetration** strategy focuses on selling the existing product–service mix to the existing target markets. Most firms will attempt to increase the quality and consistency of the product–service mix as a means of increasing customer satisfaction, promoting brand loyalty, and increasing sales and market share. Kentucky Fried Chicken continues to focus primarily on selling chicken to fast food customers, with only minor modifications in its menu to retain customers who have become somewhat more health conscious.

In an effort to increase sales, management attempts to increase the rate of repeat patronage, building on a solid base of clientele. Another part of this strategy is to increase initial patronage among those members of existing markets who have not previously patronized the hospitality operation. This is accomplished by attracting patrons from competing operations, thereby increasing the market share. The overall goal is twofold: to increase sales and to increase market share. This strategy is commonly used during periods of economic uncertainty, such as when the inflation rate is high. As it becomes more expensive to borrow capital for physical expansion, one of the best ways to grow is to increase sales within existing units. In this manner, a larger percentage of the increased sales will eventually become profits.

product development strategy developing new products for existing markets

A **product development strategy** is founded on the idea of developing new products for existing markets. As new elements of the product–service mix are introduced, sales increase and the long-term financial viability of the firm is assured. Examples of this strategy are common within the hospitality and tourism industry. For instance, noncommercial foodservice firms such as ARAMARK and Sodexho-Marriott have long managed the foodservice operations for host firms, or companies whose primary business is not providing a final food product (i.e., businesses, hospitals, colleges and universities, and other government and nonprofit organizations). Building on the successful relationship that has been established through running the foodservice aspects of the business, ARAMARK and Sodexho-Marriott have expanded into facilities management (e.g., managing all aspects of stadiums and arenas for events). Another possible product development strategy for contract foodservice firms is to manage university housing and dining service.

No hospitality or travel firm can remain unchanged for too long and expect to prosper. Markets change, consumer needs and wants change, and so too must the product–service mix of any hospitality and tourism firm. Consider, for example, the product development of any of the fast-food chains. New menu items have been added continually over the years to increase unit sales and expand the total market. McDonald's was the first to add breakfast items to its menu, adding significantly to total sales of the individual units and the total corporation. Finally, the addition of drive-through service also increased total sales significantly.

A **market development** strategy focuses on developing new markets for existing products and services. In the case of hotels and restaurants, this normally involves building new units and expanding into new markets. One of the most lucrative growth areas within the hospitality and tourism industry is outside the United States. As growth rates slow within the domestic market, large hospitality and tourism marketers look to grow internationally. Hyatt Hotels has targeted many Asian countries for its expansion, while other hotel chains have focused on European countries. Foreign markets offer attractive growth prospects because many are virtually untapped. However, this potential for high return is ac-

market development strategy developing new markets for existing products and services

Many hotels sell memberships to pools and fitness clubs to local residents to earn additional revenue using a market development strategy. *Courtesy of Hampshire Hospitality Group, Northampton, Massachusetts*

diversification strategy introducing new products and services into new markets

companied by risks associated with the political and economic environments in foreign countries. Most local and regional hospitality firms still choose to add units in other regions within the U.S. before attempting overseas expansion.

A **diversification strategy** involves introducing new products and services into new markets. This strategy offers the most long-term potential, but it is also the strategy with the greatest degree of risk. The upside potential is important because any sales that are generated will be new sales. They will not take sales away from existing products and services. When existing customers buy new products and services rather than existing products and services, it is referred to as *cannibalization*. When new products and services are introduced into new markets, there is no potential for cannibalization. However, the risk, and potential downside, is that actual sales will lag the company's forecasted sales and not meet profit projections. In this case, success will not be achieved.

Other popular frameworks offer baseline strategies based on the firm's competitive position, or business strengths, and the growth rate in the market, or industry attractiveness.[2] In general, firms with weak competitive positions should look for ways to improve their current status either by concentrating on a single business, or through mergers and acquisitions. Firms in markets with slow growth rates should look for new markets or form alliances with other firms to strengthen their positions. This will allow them to survive and prosper, while other firms find it necessary to divest or liquidate.

Many hospitality and tourism firms, particularly small organizations, often do not devote the human and monetary resources necessary to develop adequate strategic marketing plans. Without such plans, the marketing strategy can easily become reactionary; the organization merely reacts to each new competitive force and lacks an overall sense of direction and purpose. Conversely, an organization that develops well-defined strategic marketing plans has laid the groundwork necessary for a proactive marketing effort that takes the initiative instead of allowing competitors to control the environment.

Implementing Action Plans and Evaluating Performance

Once the best strategic alternatives are selected, management must develop action plans and a timetable for implementation. The best action plans are detailed, spelling out the specifics of what will happen, when it will be done, and how the marketing plan should be implemented. This does not mean that it is inflexible, but a clear implementation plan is important. Action plans should contain the following information:

- Who will assume primary responsibility for each part of the action plan?
- How they will proceed to implement the action plan?

- When should they have it completed?
- What resources will be needed to fully implement the action plan?
- What methods and measures will be used to evaluate the plan?

Following the development of the action plans and before implementing them, two activities should be completed. First, an implementation schedule should be developed. Since not all the action plans can be implemented at the same time, an orderly timetable or schedule will help determine when the various actions should be conducted. Next, a set of performance criteria should be established for evaluating the relative success of the action plans. Performance criteria should be precise, so that the marketing plan can be carefully evaluated. It is important to note that marketing planning is a continuous process that must be monitored and adapted based on actual performance. There are four key control areas that can be used to evaluate performance: sales, costs, profits, and consumers.[3] These control areas relate closely with the types of objectives discussed earlier in this section.

Sales control data should focus on the firm's sales by market segment, its market share, and its sales inputs. The quantified targets in the sales objectives should be broken down on a quarterly basis, by market segment, and used as a standard against which actual sales results can be compared. Differences can be evaluated in terms of absolute dollar amount as well as percentages that allow for easier comparisons. Firms should determine why there are variances between the targeted sales figures and the actual sales figures, even if the actual figures are better than expected. Then, the elements of the marketing plan can be adjusted to reflect the changes that are deemed necessary.

Another measure of a firm's performance in terms of sales is market share. Market share data provides the firm with a comparison of its performance relative to its competitors (i.e., firm sales/total industry sales). The first step in performing market share analysis is to define the market. For example, a hotel chain could calculate its market share based on sales in the entire lodging industry or calculate market share based on sales in its key segment(s) such as economy, luxury, extended stay, or all suites. The firm's sales figures would remain the same, but the denominator, which reflects the basis for comparison, would change. Therefore, the definition of the market is critical in the overall analysis.

The final type of sales control data involves the firm's sales inputs. In other words, what resources are being used to obtain sales, and how efficient is the firm in its use of these resources? Mainly, sales input data deals with the various components of the promotion mix—advertising, personal selling, sales promotions, and publicity. First, firms need to examine the amount of time and money spent by its sales force. How much time is spent in selling and nonselling activities, how many calls are they making per day, what are their expenses, and what is their conversion rate with customers? For example, hotels can determine averages, or benchmarks,

sales control data
firm's sales by market segment, market share, and sales inputs

that can be used to evaluate the performance of their salespeople. Salespeople are given annual quotas that can be evaluated on a quarterly basis to determine their progress.

Next, the firm can look at the effectiveness of its advertising and sales promotions (publicity is difficult to assess because it is free and not easy to control). How many consumers in their target markets are reached, and with what frequency? What is the cost per thousand of reaching those consumers, and how many inquiries are made in response to the promotion? For example, a restaurant may have put a discount coupon in the area's Val-Pak that is mailed to all local residents. It is important to keep track of the redemption rate to determine the net impact of the promotion.

cost control data compare forecasted budgets with actual budgets and examine large deviations

Cost control data represents another form of data that can be used to evaluate performance. Firms should compare their forecasted budgets with actual budgets to determine where there are large deviations. Normally, sales forecasts are used to set budgets for various expense items as a percentage of sales. This cost information is determined on an annual basis, but it should be evaluated either monthly or quarterly. Any large discrepancies should be examined to determine the cause, and adjustments made. Some of the more common expense ratios are profit margins, selling expense ratio, cost per sales call, and advertising expense ratio. In most cases, the various expense items are simply divided by total sales. However, as with sales control data, it is important to analyze the data by market segment. This will help the firm identify the profitability of its products and market segments. The standards for some of these cost items are based on the historical performance of firms in the industry. For example, a common rule of thumb in the restaurant industry is to keep food costs between 30 and 35 percent of the total costs of operation. When the actual percentage exceeds this range, it should alert the management to a potential problem that should be examined closely.

profit control data function of sales and costs; should be broken down by market segment as well

Profit control data is a function of sales and costs, and should be broken down by market segment as well. To perform this type of analysis, it is important to understand basic accounting and income statement. Here is a typical income statement:

$$
\begin{array}{rl}
 & \text{Sales revenue} \\
- & \text{Cost of goods sold} \\
\hline
= & \text{Gross profit} \\
\\
- & \text{Selling expenses} \\
- & \text{Depreciation} \\
- & \text{Administrative overhead} \\
\hline
= & \text{Operating profit} \\
\\
- & \text{Interest expense} \\
\hline
= & \text{Pretax profit}
\end{array}
$$

It is crucial that firms examine the statement to determine why net profit is negative or does not meet the target set in the marketing plan. Often, firms approach profitability from a cost perspective without having a good understanding of pricing strategy. Pricing will be discussed in detail in Chapter 14, but it is important to know the price sensitivity of consumers in regard to the firm's products and services. There is no simple solution for obtaining desired profit levels. It isn't easy to maximize sales revenue and minimize costs simultaneously. Decreases in costs can lead to lower quality and decreased sales and profits. In some cases, sales revenue can increase by incurring additional costs to improve the product–service mix and by raising prices. However, if profits are negative, the source of the problem can be determined by tracing it back through the sections of the income statement.

Consumer feedback is the final area of performance evaluation, and it is a key element in understanding the results of the financial analyses discussed earlier. Consumer feedback provides firms with information regarding awareness, knowledge, attitudes, purchasing behavior, and customer satisfaction. Chapter 3 discussed consumer behavior and Chapter 6 discusses the research methods that can be used to obtain this information. In many cases, the financial data merely represents the symptoms of problems within the firm. It is often necessary to obtain consumer feedback to gain a true understanding of the problem.

consumer feedback provides firms with information such as consumer awareness, knowledge, attitudes, purchasing behavior, and satisfaction

It can be detrimental if managers focus too much on numbers and not enough on consumer needs. For example, a hotel in Boston was experiencing a decrease in occupancy rate in relation to other hotels in the area. Management tried to approach the issue by discounting prices, but it had very little effect. After speaking with customers, the hotel realized that the business travelers found the rooms to be too small. Business travelers are not as price sensitive as other travelers, but they are quality conscious, which explained the ineffectiveness of the price discounting strategy. As a result, the hotel decided to focus on the government market because of the hotel's location. The government market is price sensitive (there is an allowable per diem), not as quality conscious, and the hotel could selectively discount to this large-volume market.

Once again, it is important to point out that marketing planning is a continuous process that must be evaluated and adapted according to changes that may occur. Evaluating the success of the marketing plan is the moment of truth. Planning is done to increase the probability of success and, once the plan is implemented, it is important for management to monitor the results. Any variance from the predicted results should be noted and evaluated.

As the environment changes or the results vary, management may need to return to the appropriate step to reformulate marketing strategy or the action plans. The marketing planning process is best viewed as a dynamic procedure, with sufficient flexibility to allow for changes in strategies, action plan, or implementation schedules.

▲ SALES FORECASTING

One of the most critical components of a marketing plan is the forecast for sales. Sales forecasting is the process for determining current sales and estimating future sales for a product or service. The success of the firm is often based on the accuracy of forecasts. The decisions about the elements of the marketing mix—product–service mix, price, promotion, and distribution—that are made during the situation analysis are based on sales forecasts.

Sales Forecasting Techniques

Sales forecasting techniques can be separated into two broad categories: quantitative techniques and qualitative techniques. Quantitative techniques use past data values and employ a set of rules to obtain estimates of future sales. Qualitative techniques tend to be used when data is not readily available and rely on judgment or intuition. Quantitative methods can be classified further as either causal or time series. Both types of quantitative methods use trends in historical data to predict future sales, however, causal techniques model the relationships between sales and other variables that can help predict changes in sales. Time series techniques extrapolate future sales estimates based on the trend in historical sales. In other words, past sales are used to predict future sales, assuming all other factors that affect sales will continue to have a similar affect in the future.

Qualitative forecasting techniques. The goal of qualitative forecasting techniques is to forecast changes in the basic sales pattern as well as the pattern itself. Qualitative techniques are often difficult to apply, and they tend to be very time-consuming and costly. Therefore, these techniques are used mainly for long-term forecasts and in situations that are of major importance to the firm. It is important for firms to be able to predict changes in sales patterns so they can take advantages of opportunities and minimize the impact of threats. To predict these changes, firms enlist the aid of experts, or individuals with an intimate knowledge of the product and its markets. Four basic approaches can be classified as qualitative forecasting techniques:

- ***Expert opinion.*** Marketers look to a panel of experts with knowledge of the industry and the marketplace to provide a forecast. Often, a variety of sources are consulted, and the results are combined to form a consensus forecast. These experts can be individuals from within the firm or individuals from outside the firm. Often, secondary sources, such as forecasts published in major trade journals or business journals, are used. The resulting forecast can be obtained by simply averaging the individual forecasts, or a more complicated weighting system can be used based on the experience and knowledge of the panel member.

- *Delphi technique.* This technique involves several rounds of forecasting and review by a panel of experts. It can be very time-consuming, but it is often quite accurate. The Delphi technique involves collecting forecasts, developing composites, and sending the data to those participating several times until a consensus is reached. The Delphi technique is normally used when the decision is an important one and there are no time constraints. Panel members are able to adjust their forecasts after seeing the forecasts of others on the panel.

- *Sales force forecast.* This technique aggregates the sales forecast of each salesperson or unit, depending on the level of the forecast. For example, a hotel may have each of its salespeople provide a forecast for his or her territory and then combine the forecasts to obtain an overall estimate. Or, a hotel or restaurant chain may have each unit provide a forecast and then combine the forecasts to obtain an overall estimate for the chain. The rationale for using this technique is that it may be more accurate to forecast the sales for each territory or unit rather than obtain a higher-level forecast and break it down for operational purposes. Each salesperson, or unit, is more in touch with the customers and changes in the environment.

- *Survey of buying intentions.* Firms can use marketing research to ask potential customers about their future purchase intentions and then estimate future sales. This type of forecast is very subjective because there is not a clear relationship between purchase intentions and actual purchase behavior. However, this kind of information can be obtained from published sources such as *Sales & Marketing Management*.

The experts employed in these methods may base their judgment based on prior experience, or they may use sophisticated quantitative techniques to model the effects of other factors that influence the level of sales. However, the ultimate outcome is to predict changes in sales patterns.

Quantitative Forecasting Techniques. The common element in quantitative forecasting techniques is that they are based almost exclusively on historical data. These forecasting techniques tend to be quicker and less costly because the data is readily available through existing sources. Quantitative forecasting techniques are also gaining in popularity due to their level of proven accuracy and the improvements in computer technology. Most spreadsheet programs have statistical applications that can be used for quantitative forecasting, and other statistical programs and forecasting packages are available at a reasonable price. Also, these programs are easy to use and many are compatible with computer software for preparing reports and charts. The two basic quantitative forecasting techniques are time series analysis and causal methods.

TIME SERIES ANALYSIS. This method uses statistical techniques to fit a trend line to the pattern of historical sales. The trend line is expressed in terms of a mathematical equation that can be used to project the trend forward into future periods and predict sales. The trend line can be linear (a straight line) or nonlinear (a curved line) depending upon the pattern of the historical data. Four major components of a time series should be considered in choosing a technique: (1) trend, the long-term pattern; (2) cycle, medium-term changes due to business and economic changes; (3) seasonal, short-term movements based on buying patterns; and (4) residual, unpredictable influences or disturbances. The most common methods of time series analysis are:

- *Trend extrapolation.* The simplest method for forecasting sales is the linear projection of past sales. It assumes that the factors that influenced sales in the past will have the same effect on future sales, and all data points are weighted equally. This is somewhat naïve, but firms' basic marketing programs and competitive situations normally don't change drastically from year to year. This method is very simple, the data requirements are minimal, and it can be very accurate for products in industries with low growth rates.

- *Moving average.* This technique is used for short-term forecasts (e.g., monthly) and takes the average of the most recent periods to predict future sales. For example, next month's sales could be forecast using the average of the monthly sales for the last 3 or 4 months. This method is simple and can be used when sales are fairly stable throughout the year, with only small fluctuations.

- *Exponential smoothing.* This technique uses the trend line to predict future sales, however, it places more weight on the most recent periods. This method is better at picking up trends than the previous time series methods, and there are more sophisticated formulas that allow for cycles and seasonal effects.

There are some more sophisticated time series techniques, but they are beyond the scope of this text. For example, there is a group of methods referred to as autoregressive moving averages (ARMA) that express forecasts as a linear combination of past actual values and/or past errors. These methods are becoming more widespread, but they require more than a rudimentary knowledge of forecasting.

CAUSAL METHODS. These are often referred to as explanatory methods because they used historical data to establish the relationship between sales and other factors that are believed to influence sales. The other factors, or causal factors, can differ based on the level of the forecast. The higher the level or the more macro-oriented the forecast, the more likely they are to be economic variables, such as disposable income, unemployment, and consumer prices. As the forecast becomes more specific, or micro-oriented, the causal factors become more specific, such as price, advertising expenditures, and competitors' prices and advertising. However, to forecast sales based on these causal factors, one must be able to forecast the causal variables as well. Also, the data requirements for causal methods are more extensive than for qualitative or time-series forecasting techniques. The two most common causal methods are:

- **Regression analysis.** This technique identifies the causal factors, or independent variables, that can be used to predict the level of sales, or the dependent variable. Single regression analysis uses one independent variable, and multiple regression analysis uses more than one independent variable. Trend extrapolation is actually a simplified form of regression analysis that uses time, or the period, as the independent variable and sales as the dependent variable.

- **Econometric models.** These models use statistical techniques to solve a simultaneous set of multiple regression equations. In this case, a causal factor may be predicted as a dependent variable from several other causal factors, and then used as an independent variable in an equation to predict sales. This method is more complicated and requires some expertise in statistical modeling. Also, this technique requires the largest amount of data because of the number of variables being used in the various equations.

Selecting a Forecasting Technique

All of the sales forecasting techniques discussed earlier have advantages and disadvantages based on the situation. Therefore, it is important to apply a set of selection criteria in choosing the appropriate technique. The following criteria can be used in forecasting to evaluate the situation and choose the technique that is best suited to the firm's needs.

- *The time horizon.* The period of time over which a decision will have an impact will clearly affect the selection of the most appropriate technique. Time series methods perform best for short-term (1 to 3 months) and medium-term (3 months to 2 years) forecasts, whereas qualitative techniques are best for long-term (more than 2 years) new product forecasts. Causal methods perform best in the short term, but they can also be used quite effectively for medium-term forecasts.

- *The availability of data.* The type and amount of data available can have a major effect on the choice of technique. If historical sales is the only data that is available, then time series methods would be most appropriate. However, if very little data available (e.g., new products), then the qualitative techniques would be most appropriate. If data is available for a large range of variables, then causal methods can be employed, providing a good deal of information regarding relationships between variables.

- *The pattern of the data.* The majority of quantitative forecasting techniques assume a particular pattern in the data to be forecast. Time-series methods work best when there are defined patterns (trends), including cycles and seasonal changes. However, causal methods and qualitative methods work best in high-growth markets and when there may be turning points in the pattern.

- *The desired level of accuracy.* The desired level of accuracy will vary based on the use of the forecast. Forecasts for control purposes tend to be more short-term and need to be more precise, whereas forecasts for planning tend to be longer term and are able to be less precise. Causal methods will normally be the most accurate in the short-term under various conditions. However, time series methods can be very accurate when there is a strong trend in the data. Qualitative methods will tend to be most accurate for long-term forecasts because they use the combined forecasts of experts.

- *Cost.* It is necessary to trade off the benefits of the various methods based on the other criteria with the cost involved in using the technique. Cost will be a function of data collection, storage, and analysis. The time-series methods require the least amount of data and expertise, resulting in the lowest cost. Causal methods can be costly because they require the most data and expertise, while qualitative methods incur a large expense for data collection.

- *Ease of application.* The ease with which the various forecasting techniques can be employed depends on factors such as the firm's computer capabilities, the expertise of its employees, and the availability of data. Time-series methods are the easiest to employ, while causal methods and qualitative methods are somewhat more complicated.

All of these criteria must be used in selecting the appropriate forecasting technique. Certain interrelationships among the criteria may help simplify the selection task. Fore example, when good historical data is available, time series methods provide good accuracy for short-term forecasts. Choosing the best forecasting technique is important because many of the elements of the marketing plan are based on the sales forecasts.

▲ MARKETING ACTION NOW!

When conducting a situation analysis in the marketing planning process, firms perform a historical appraisal and a SWOT analysis. This enables the firm to understand how it came to be where it is in the marketplace. The historical appraisal will give an indication of the market and its consumers, and the SWOT analysis will aid the firm in determining its internal strengths and weaknesses, and the potential opportunities and threats that exist in the external environment.

Choose a local hospitality or travel firm and conduct a situation analysis, including a historical appraisal and a SWOT analysis. Describe the market, including trends, and list the firm's strengths and weaknesses relative to competitors. Also, try to be creative when you list the potential opportunities and threats in the external environment.

1. What items can the firm leverage to gain a competitive advantage?
2. What are the problem areas that the firm needs to address?

▲ SUMMARY OF CHAPTER OBJECTIVES

This chapter focused on the essential process for formulating marketing plans. Strategic marketing planning focuses on the firm's broad and long-range goals and objectives, whereas tactical planning is more short-term and implementation oriented. Effective marketing planning includes both strategic and tactical components. Although there are numerous advantages and disadvantages to planning, several research studies have clearly demonstrated that firms that engage in marketing planning hold a decisive advantage over the competition and exhibit improved financial performance.

The marketing planning process includes four important stages: (1) conducting a situation analysis; (2) defining the firm's goals and objectives; (3) formulating marketing strategies and action plans; and (4) implementing action plans and evaluating performance. The situation analysis includes a historical appraisal and a SWOT analysis to determine where the firm is in terms of internal strengths and weaknesses, and external opportunities and threats. The objectives determine where the firm wants to go and should be concise and measurable and should include a time frame for completion. The firm's marketing strategies will guide the firm to achieve its objectives, and the entire process should be monitored and performance evaluated so that necessary changes can be made throughout.

The last section of the chapter reviewed sales forecasting, including both qualitative and quantitative techniques. Sales forecasts are crucial in establishing objectives and strategies, and are used to set budgets for marketing planning. Firms must understand the advantages and disadvantages of the various forecasting techniques so they can select the appropriate technique for a given situation. The selection of a forecasting technique is based on the time horizon, availability of data, pattern of data, desired level of accuracy, cost, and ease of application.

▲ KEY TERMS AND CONCEPTS

Causal analysis

Delphi technique

Diversification

Econometric models

Product development

Regression analysis

Sales force forecast

Sales forecasting

Expert opinion

Exponential smoothing

Goals

Historical appraisal

Market development

Market penetration

Mission statement

Moving average

Objectives

Position statement

Strategic business unit (SBU)

Strategic marketing plan

Strategic window

Survey of buying intentions

SWOT analysis

Tactical marketing plan

Time series analysis

Trend extrapolation

Vertical integration

▲ QUESTIONS FOR REVIEW AND DISCUSSION

1. What is the difference between strategic and tactical marketing plans?
2. What are the advantages and disadvantages associated with planning?
3. What are some of the reasons why marketing plans fail?
4. Illustrate and discuss the steps in the marketing planning process.
5. What are the criteria for good objectives?
6. What are the types of control data that are used to evaluate performance?
7. What is sales forecasting? Why is it important?
8. Explain the difference between qualitative and quantitative forecasting techniques.
9. Describe the criteria used in selecting a forecasting technique.

▲ NOTES

[1]Donald R. Lehmann and Russell S. Winer, *Analysis for Marketing Planning*, 2nd edition (Homewood, IL: Richard D. Irwin, Inc., 1991) p. 1.

[2]Arthur A. Thompson, Jr. and A. J. Strickland, *Strategy Formulation and Implementation* (Homewood, IL: BPI/Richard D. Irwin, 1989) p. 214.

[3]Robert E. Stevens, David L. Loudon, and William E. Warren, *Marketing Planning Guide* (New York: The Haworth Press, 1981) pp. 244–251.

6

Information for Marketing Decisions

❖ Chapter Objectives

By the end of this chapter, you should understand:

1. The components of a good marketing information system
2. The alternative sources of marketing information
3. The marketing research process and its role in collecting information
4. The ethical issues surrounding marketing research and information systems

❖ Chapter Outline

❖ Chapter Opening Profile

ZAGAT IS A POPULAR RESEARCH FIRM that is well known for its restaurant guides for major cities. The firm surveys thousands of customers in each city to obtain information about their attitudes and preferences in regard to various restaurants. This information is compiled and sold to consumers in the form of a restaurant guide that can be consulted when choosing a restaurant. These guides are popular among business travelers when they find themselves in unfamiliar cities. However, consumer awareness of the guides has grown over the years, and now consumers buy the guide for the cities where they live.

In addition to the restaurant guide, Zagat also conducts surveys to determine industry trends and changes in dining behavior. The 1999 Zagat Survey of New York City gathered input from 18,320 diners.[1] In general, the survey found that New Yorkers dined out less frequently in 1998 and spent about the same amount of money per meal as they did the previous year. On average, the respondents reported eating out 3.27 times a week and spending $31.48 per meal, the highest average tab for all cities that Zagat covers in the United States. As for industry trends, 117 restaurants closed and 277 new restaurants opened in 1998. The major trends were a declining interest in theme restaurants and an increase in "better alternative to home" restaurants. Most of the new openings were local, neighborhood restaurants.

The information provided by Zagat is useful to restaurants, but it would be very difficult for an individual restaurant or restaurant chain to perform the same type of research on its own. Zagat is able to survey a large number of people because the firm can sell the guide to business travelers and local patrons. In addition, the firm can sell the survey results to the restaurants at a fraction of the cost that would be incurred if they conducted their own surveys. This is a good example of why the use of syndicated services has grown in recent years.

▲ INTRODUCTION

Since the advent of personal computers, the United States has experienced an information explosion, and all industries have made substantial advances in information collection, analysis, storage, and retrieval. The hospitality industry was very much a part of this trend. As the external environment becomes more complex and more competitive, informational needs become more complex. Organizations that employ a systematic approach to collecting, analyzing, storing, retrieving, and using information effectively and efficiently are likely to be the most successful in the future. Without the proper types of information available on a timely basis, management is more likely to make decisions that will adversely affect the performance of the organization.

A simple example will illustrate this point. Suppose that the management of a small restaurant chain must make a decision concerning the allocation of the advertising budget among the available media for the upcoming quarter. The advertising objectives of this restaurant are to increase the rate of repeat patronage by 10 percent by reinforcing the chain's high level of perceived value among current customers, and to increase the number of customers who are patronizing one of the chain's restaurants for the first time by 10 percent. To make an effective decision about media allocation, the management of this chain has specific informational needs. Management needs access to the following types of information:

- The characteristics of the current clientele
- The characteristics of the target market segments most likely to patronize the chain's restaurants for the first time
- The media habits of both of these groups
- The profile of the consumers of all available media (e.g., television, radio, print) and the individual media vehicles (e.g., individual radio stations)

Without all of this information, the management of this restaurant chain will increase the uncertainty surrounding the decision. The results of a less-informed decision could adversely affect the advertising effectiveness of the organization and directly affect its financial performance.

All too often, management is forced to make critical decisions without the necessary marketing information. On many occasions, managers must work with information that is not complete, or information that is not in the desired form.

Definition of a Marketing Information System

marketing information system is the structure of people, equipment, and procedures used to gather, analyze, and distribute information needed by an organization

A **marketing information system (MIS)** is the structure of people, equipment, and procedures used to gather, analyze, and distribute information needed by an organization. These are the data to be used as a basis for marketing decisions. *Marketing information system* is a broader and more encompassing term than *market research*. Marketing research indicates that information is collected for a specific reason or project; the major objective is a one-time use. For example, a potential restaurant owner may undertake a feasibility study and use market research to determine whether to build a new restaurant. Such an information-gathering study is designed to answer a very specific question: "Should we open a restaurant in this area?"

A marketing information system, on the other hand, is part of an ongoing data-gathering process involving initial data collection as well as routine and systematic data collection procedures. For example, a hotel manager may choose to collect data by means of a zip code analysis of guest registration information to determine the geographic profile of the guests of a hotel. This systematic and routine information gathering is not intended to address one specific question but is instead part of an overall system designed to monitor the degree of marketing success that the operation is able to achieve.

A well-designed marketing information system satisfies four basic criteria:

1. It must include a structured organization or established system of people and information-gathering procedures.
2. The system should be designed to generate a continuous flow of information to provide accurate and current marketing information for management.
3. Information should be gathered from inside and outside the organization, involving external information gathering methods, such as consumer surveys; and internal information gathering methods, such as employee meetings, guest comment cards, analysis of point-of-sale data, all guest registration information, and in-house guest surveys.
4. Information should be compiled so that management can use it as a basis for marketing decisions.

It would be extremely difficult and quite hazardous for the management of a hospitality organization to make decisions without accurate and up-to-date marketing information. Professional management demands that decisions be based on sound information. Managers can reduce the uncertainty surrounding marketing decisions when valuable information is available. Marriott International serves as a good example. For many years this corporation has relied upon a widely based decision-making process. The resulting decisions have consistently been very good and have allowed Marriott to establish and maintain a leadership position in the hospitality industry. This is not to say that a very good marketing information system alone will allow an organization to achieve financial success, but it will be of tremendous benefit to management.

Components of a Marketing Information System

A key component of an effective marketing information system is having accurate information about the environment. The foundation for this data collection is environmental scanning, which refers to a process whereby external factors that could affect an organization are continually evaluated. Based on an initial evaluation, those with the greatest potential impact, either positive or negative, are examined in greater detail. From a theoretical standpoint, if management is to make rational decisions, all information that could affect the hospitality organization should be examined and evaluated. Realistically, however, this is not possible because of the finite limits on the valuable resources of time, money, and personnel. Instead, only those environmental variables that appear to he the most important or most critical are examined in greater detail.

In short, a marketing information system that uses environmental scanning provides an overview of the entire environment as well as further detail concerning those variables within the environment that are most critical to the successful operation of the hospitality organization. The firm's overall environment can be divided into three subenvironments: the macroenvironment, the competitive environment, and the organizational environment.

A conceptual model of the components of a marketing information system is shown in Figure 6.1. Data are generated for each of the three subenvironments through an environmental-scanning process. The data are then compiled, summarized, and stored until needed by management. At the appropriate time, management can readily retrieve data summaries, evaluate marketing trends, and formulate marketing plans and strategies. The overriding objectives of a marketing information system are (1) to collect relevant data concerning each of these subenvironments; (2) to compile, summarize, and store the data; and (3) to have data readily available for management on a timely basis.

The microenvironment concerns the broadest possible effects. Macroenvironmental effects are those that the individual hospitality organization is almost powerless to control and include economic, social, political, and technological aspects of the environment. As conditions change within the macroenvironment, the management of hospitality organizations should collect data concerning these changes. Knowledge of

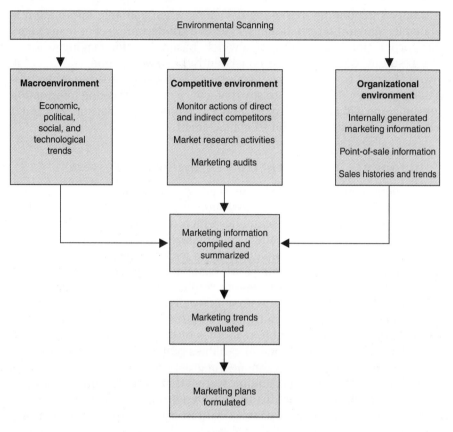

FIGURE 6.1 Components of a Marketing Information System

existing conditions will provide a basis for calculating the impact that these variables will have on the operation of a hospitality organization. For example, if the federal tax deductibility of business meals is further reduced or if the annual inflation rate rises by 3 to 4 percent, what impact is this likely to have on sales volume? Nearly 20 percent of the population moves each year—how will these demographic changes affect a hospitality organization? These are influences that the management of a hospitality organization is virtually powerless to control. At best, management can monitor the variables of the macroenvironment and can gauge the effects that they might have on business.

The competitive environment immediately surrounds the hospitality organization. The organization exerts some degree of control over this environment but can never control it totally. The major concern for management is to monitor closely the marketing and operational actions taken by direct and indirect competitors. Attention should be focused initially on changes made in the marketing mix, guest profile, room and menu prices, and sales volume as measured in both dollars and in guest counts. Management should also be concerned with the degree of concentration of competition, entries and exits among competitors, and changes in market share among competitors. Exact figures are not likely to be available, but all competitors should be monitored closely so that management can be prepared for changes before or when they occur, rather than weeks or months later. By monitoring competition in this way, management can prepare an appropriate competitive response, thereby gaining a differential competitive advantage.

The two other aspects of the competitive environment for a marketing information system are market research activities and marketing audits. Market research encompasses a wide range of activities undertaken to generate information about a firm's products, customers, and external environment. Marketing audits are evaluations of the effectiveness of current marketing practices. In particular, marketing audits are used to monitor marketing plans on an annual basis.

The third subenvironment that is a part of a marketing information system is the organizational environment. Data collection in this subenvironment involves examining all relevant information sources within the hospitality organization. The basis for data collection in this subenvironment is guest histories, although information can be generated from other sources as well. Guest histories are records that a hotel maintains for all types of guests, both individual and groups. In addition, histories should be maintained within all retail outlets, especially food and beverage. Within the food and beverage area, all sales should be recorded, broken down by menu group and menu item. Only when managers have access to records of previous sales are they able to make informed decisions concerning the product–service mix for the organization.

Requirements for a Successful Marketing Information System

The basic task of gathering data is important to an organization, but an effective marketing information system is one that is able to organize this task and supply the firm with useful information. To generate data that is useful for managers and decision-makers, a marketing information system should fulfill three requirements:

1. *It should be objective.* Management should be able to quantify and analyze the information gathered. Management needs as much purely objective data as possible to make sound decisions. For example, which of these two statements seems to provide better information for decision-making purposes?
   - *Statement A:* "As the owner of this restaurant, I think we should modify our menu so that we can appeal to more family business."
   - *Statement B:* "A recent study has indicated a 10 percent increase in the number of families with children under the age of 10 in our area."

Statement B would appear to be more objective and offer quantitative data on which to base a decision. Statement A is, on the other hand, merely an opinion and is not supported by any quantitative data.

Too many hospitality managers rely heavily on subjective opinions for decision-making purposes, and their decisions are often incorrect. Decisions based on purely personal opinion are often less than successful when implemented. Decisions based on a combination of data and managerial insight and experience generally yield higher-quality decisions.

2. *It should be systematic.* The marketing information system is not an on-off process; it is a system that should be designed to provide a continuing information source for management. When information is collected in a systematic and continuous manner, the quality and quantity of data improves.

3. *It should be useful.* Many studies produce information that is of little value. This is obviously not the purpose of a marketing information system. One rule of thumb to follow is this: Collect, compile, and store information only if it is used actively; do not collect information and then file it away without using it. This is a needless and expensive waste of time and effort, yet many hospitality operators, in attempts to gather any quantitative information, maintain data that are never used and are truly useless. The advent of low-cost and increased capacity hard disk storage within personal computers has partially encouraged this storage of little-used data. Every effort should be made to collect and store only information that is useful.

Sources of Marketing Information

A variety of sources can be used to obtain the information necessary to fuel a marketing information system. These information sources can be grouped into two main categories: secondary data and primary data. Secondary data refers to information that was previously collected for another purpose. Primary data is information generated for a specific purpose when the information is not available elsewhere. It is normally advisable to search for secondary data before engaging in a primary data collection process. The secondary data may provide the information necessary to make a decision, and even if it doesn't, it may be useful in developing the collection process for primary data. Figure 6.2 illustrates the possible sources of information for marketing decisions.

Secondary Data

As mentioned before, this type of data is already available from other sources and summarizes information about operations, marketing, human resource management, financial performance, and other topics of interest to management. A shrewd manager will make a thorough check of all avail-

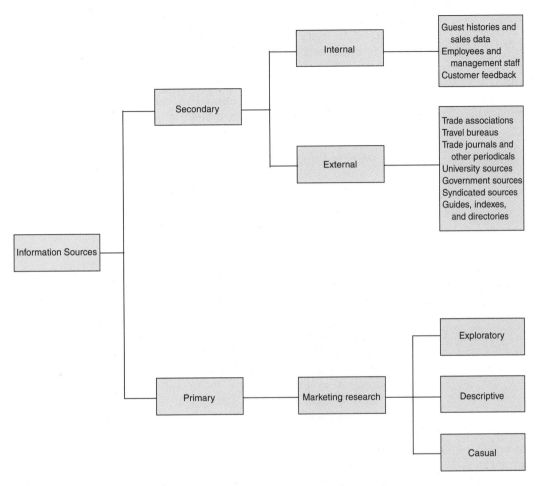

FIGURE 6.2 **Information Sources**

able secondary data sources before undertaking primary data collection. Secondary data can save many personnel hours and a great deal of money. The major advantages of using secondary data are:

1. *Cost.* It is much less expensive to obtain information from existing sources than to develop entirely new data. These existing sources may require a nominal charge for the information, but it will be much less than the cost of undertaking primary data collection.

2. *Timeliness.* Secondary data are available almost instantaneously. A manager can have access to data very quickly and therefore does not have to wait weeks or perhaps months for primary data to be collected, analyzed, and summarized.

By using secondary data whenever possible, a manager saves the frustration of developing the research methodology design, designing the data collection instrument, pretesting the instrument, devising a sampling plan, gathering the data, checking all data for accuracy and omissions, analyzing the data, and summarizing and reporting the results. Instead, a manager can merely locate the appropriate source and access the information desired. This process can be completed in a few hours or days, whereas primary data collection can take weeks or months to complete. However, secondary data collection does have the following disadvantages.

1. *Limited applicability.* A manager has no assurance that information gathered by others will be applicable to a particular hospitality operation. For example, information obtained in New York about the popularity of a specific menu item is not necessarily useful to a manager operating in another part of the country. Information that pertains to one operation may apply only to that operation and be of limited value to anyone else.

2. *Information may be outdated.* Managers need current and accurate information on which to base decisions. All too often, secondary data are not as useful as they might be merely because they are not current. For example, the results of a consumer attitude survey conducted by a restaurant four years ago would be of limited value to a manager making plans today. During the four years, a number of changes in consumer attitudes are likely to have taken place. These changes in attitudes will make the original data outdated and useful only in a historical sense. If a hospitality manager were to make use of less-than-timely data, the results are likely to be less than satisfactory.

3. *Reliability.* Whenever a hospitality operator uses secondary data as the basis for a decision, the manager runs the risk that the information may not be reliable and accurate. A manager would do well to determine, who collected the data and what method of data collection was used. Information is only as good as the individuals who collect it and the methods they use. If a study is administered in a haphazard manner, the results and conclusions should be viewed with caution.

Internal Data. The component of a marketing information system that is the simplest to design and implement is an internal system, or the component designed to collect data from within the organizational environment. When considering the organizational environment, management needs to be concerned only with information available from within the physical confines of the organization's units, whether they are hotels or restaurants. This component of a marketing information system requires less time and money than does the competitive environment or externally generated marketing information. The internal component of a marketing information system is very valuable to management because it provides a wealth of information.

Management has three main sources of internal marketing information: guest histories and sales data, employees and management staff, and customer feedback.

- *Guest histories and sales data.* No rules can tell a manager exactly what records should or should not be maintained. The management of every hospitality organization must make this decision based on individual needs. Within a hotel operation, the minimum records that should be maintained are both individual and group guest histories. These will permit management to have knowledge and monitor changes in zip code origin of guests, length of stay, guest expenditure per day, and other pertinent data concerning guests. Within a restaurant operation, the records maintained should include customer counts for each meal period, and sales for each menu item over a specified period of time. Many larger organizations have a sophisticated management information system in place. However, for the smaller organization, the design of a management information system is much easier than it has been in the past. Many point-of-sale terminals interface with personal computers, making the transfer of data to off-the-shelf data base management and accounting software relatively easy. By using a personal computer, a manager is better able to manage the data. The quality and ease of use of off-the-shelf business software such as Microsoft™ Office makes it far easier for a manager to capture and analyze large databases. It is more common for managers to conduct more sophisticated statistical analysis of the database of customers and to mine the database for keys to increasing the volume of business from current customers. It is obvious that, with accurate information readily available, a manager is more likely to consult such marketing information prior to making a marketing decision.

- *Employees and management staff.* All too often hospitality management ignores the wealth of information that is informally gathered by hourly employees, such as front desk personnel, telephone operators, restaurant service people, hosts, and hostesses. These individuals are in constant contact with guests, yet they are rarely asked to relay customer comments and reactions to operational changes, such as new menu items or guestroom decor changes. These employees represent an excellent source of information, although the information they provide may not be totally objective. It is a good idea for management to meet with employees on a regular basis to discuss problems and opportunities. Employees crave recognition from their supervisors; this recognition increases the employee's satisfaction and commitment to the organization. All employees need to be exposed to some motivational techniques, although managers often ignore the simple and basic needs of employees as individuals.

- *Customer feedback.* The focus of the marketing concept is the hospitality operation's clientele. All aspects of the entire operation should be aimed at satisfying these individuals. The purpose of using an internal marketing information system is to solicit opinions and comments from the current clientele. This can be done in a number of ways, such as having the manager talk with a few of the customers or having service personnel check with the customers. One method used frequently is the comment card. These cards are placed in guestrooms or are provided to the guest upon checkout or when they have finished a meal in a restaurant. The purpose is to solicit their opinions and comments concerning the operation's quality.

All three internal sources of marketing information are very valuable. Together they can provide a great deal of useful information with which to make decisions. Historically, hospitality managers have failed to use these sources to maximum advantage, but the current competitive situation in the hospitality industry dictates that all sources of information be used to gain a competitive advantage and to earn maximum financial rewards.

External Data.   Although externally generated marketing information is extremely valuable, it is normally not collected on a daily basis, as is the case with internally generated marketing information. This is due to a much larger investment of time, money, and other scarce resources required for externally generated information. Management should consider using a wide variety of sources of external marketing information. Literally thousands of sources are available, and these sources are limited only by management's own efforts to locate them. A few typical sources of external marketing information are:

- *Trade associations.* Many industries form trade groups that provide data for their members. These trade associations collect information from their members and then provide industry averages that can be used to measure a firm's relative performance. Some of the popular trade associations for the hospitality industry are the National Restaurant Association, the American Hotel and Motel Association, and the Hospitality Sales and Marketing Association International.

- *Travel bureaus.* Cities, states, and countries usually form organizations that are responsible for promoting travel to the area. Most cities have a chamber of commerce that is responsible for promoting business in the city and, in some cases, travel as well. Larger cities and regions form convention and visitors bureaus for the sole purpose of promoting business and leisure travel to the region. A chamber of commerce has member firms from all types of industries, whereas convention and visitors bureaus tend to have member firms from travel-related industries like lodging, restaurants, and tourism attractions. Finally, most states and countries have government travel and tourism bureaus that are responsible for promoting travel to that state or country.

- *Trade journals and periodicals.* Many industry, or trade, journals are available to firms. Trade associations often publish their own journals, but many other organizations publish periodicals covering certain industries. Some of the more popular hospitality publications are *Restaurants & Institutions, Restaurant Hospitality, Nation's Restaurant News, Restaurant Business, Lodging Hospitality, Lodging Magazine,* and *Hotel & Motel Management.* The articles in these publications provide information on new products and advertising campaigns, as well as current trends in the industry. These articles also provide a valuable resource for case studies involving successes and failures of industry firms.

- *Other Periodicals.* In addition to trade journals that specialize in a certain industry, other publications cover business in a variety of industries. Some of the more popular business publications that cover the hospitality industry are *Business Week, The Wall Street Journal, Fortune, Barron's,* and *Forbes.*

- *Internet.* The growth in both quantity and quality of information available on the Internet is well documented. Using one or more of the available Internet search engines will uncover information, some of which will be highly valuable for managers. A key consideration for managers is being able to determine the accuracy and usefulness of information gathered from the Internet.

- *University sources.* Universities and colleges have well-stocked libraries that can be a valuable resource for firms in the area. These institutions often have access to many of the other sources of external data. In addition, universities and colleges form centers to research specific areas such as hospitality. This information is often free to the public or available for a reasonable fee.

- *Government sources.* Local, state, and federal governments maintain detailed data on all aspects of the economy; it is free or available for a nominal fee. The *United States Census* contains detailed information about the population and retail business, and the *Statistical Abstract of the United States* contains similar information in abbreviated form. These documents are now available in electronic form enabling quicker searches and data retrieval. The federal government also contains information about foreign countries, and provides specialists to answer specific questions and address inquiries.

- *Syndicated services.* Syndicated services such as Harris or Gallup Polls, Target Group Index, Nielsen, or W.R. Simmons specialize in collecting and distributing marketing information for a fee. These sources provide information about consumer profiles and shopping behaviors, consumer responses to sales promotions and advertising, and consumer attitudes and preferences. This information is useful in focusing on market segments using aggregate data. These services often advertise in trade publications and marketing periodicals.

- *Guides, indexes, and directories.* Other valuable sources of external information include guides, indexes, and directories that are available at most university libraries and larger public libraries. Guides such as the *Business Periodicals Index* provide references by subject matter for articles in major journals and trade publications. Also, most major publications such as the *Wall Street Journal* and the *New York Times* have indexes that provide references by subject matter for articles that appeared in those particular sources. Finally, Lexis-Nexis is an excellent on-line resource for data about the performance of publicly traded companies.

A number of guidelines should be followed when collecting external information. If they are not followed, much time, effort, and money are likely to be wasted.

1. ***State known facts.*** Before undertaking an external study, make an inventory of all data currently available. It makes little sense to conduct an extensive study or pay to have one conducted only to produce information that is available from existing sources. By stating all known facts, management establishes a base from which to work. This base may easily be established by looking at all internal sources previously discussed and collecting all data available internally before proceeding with more expensive, external information-gathering techniques.

2. ***List specific goals and objectives.*** Once a base of information has been established, a plan must be formulated. Goals and objectives are the basis for this plan. Without goals and objectives, an external study could easily go astray and would not yield the information needed by a hospitality manager. The manager needs to ask, "What do I want to learn? What types of information about my clientele, my competition, or my own operation would be most useful?" Having answered such questions, a manager can begin to formulate potential questions for a survey to provide the desired information.

3. ***Collect all relevant data.*** At this point the actual legwork must be done to ensure an adequate sample. The information gathered must be both valid and reliable. Validity is the degree to which the data gathered measure what they are supposed to measure. Reliability is the degree with which data consistently measure whatever they measure. Data collection is extremely important and not a process to be treated lightly. The information generated will only be as accurate and valid as the procedures used to generate the information. For this reason, great care must be taken to assure that the information is gathered correctly.

4. ***Summarize the data and analyze the situation.*** No matter which data collection methods are used, some type of summary and analysis must be done to reduce the data into a manageable package. Then, management can access the organized information and use it for a wide variety of decisions.

Primary Data

Primary data consist of original research done to answer current questions regarding a specific operation. For example, a food service manager may attempt to ascertain consumer attitudes toward new menu offerings or to solicit consumer perceptions of increased menu prices or different portion sizes. This type of data is very pertinent to an individual operation but may not be applicable to other situations.

The advantages of using primary data include the following:

1. **Specificity.** These data are tailored to one operation and can provide excellent information for decision-making purposes.
2. **Practicality.** Just as the data are geared toward one operation, they can provide solid real-life information and a practical foundation to be used in the decision-making process.

The disadvantages of using primary data include the following:

1. **Cost.** For an individual manager, gathering primary data is extremely expensive. To gather primary data even from a city of 100,000 people may prove to be a monumental task for an operator and may cost too much in time and money.
2. **Time lag.** Marketing decisions often must be made quickly, yet it requires a good deal of time to conduct a thorough information-gathering study. While a manager is collecting the data, the competition may be driving the hospitality operation into bankruptcy.
3. **Duplication.** While primary data are geared toward a specific operation, other sources of existing data may closely duplicate the information collected and would therefore be appropriate for decision-making purposes. This duplication of effort is very expensive, and primary data collection should therefore be undertaken only after all secondary data sources have been exhausted.

In general, the advantages of using secondary data tend to be the disadvantages of using primary data, and vice versa. As mentioned earlier, before collecting primary data, it is advisable to perform secondary data search to determine the necessity and scope of a primary data collection effort. The next section covers the marketing research process that is followed when collecting primary data.

▲ THE MARKETING RESEARCH PROCESS

Market research efforts are undertaken to answer a wide variety of questions, which might include, "Where do our guests come from? How frequently do people dine out in this area? In what types of restaurants do they most frequently dine? If the seating capacity of a restaurant is expanded by 20 percent, what impact will this have on sales and profits? If the city builds a new convention center, how many additional room nights is that likely to bring to the city?"

Conducting market research is not an inexpensive proposition, and when research is undertaken, care must be taken to ensure that proper methods are used. This is true whether the hospitality organization conducts its own market research or relies on external consultants. Market research data are only as good as the methodology used. If poor methodology is used, the results are not likely to describe the situation accurately, and marketing decisions based on this information are not likely to be very appropriate. Figure 6.3 contains the six steps involved in the marketing research process.

Step 1. Define the Problem

Before initiating any marketing research effort, a firm must first decide whether marketing research is necessary. In general, marketing research should be undertaken if it clarifies a problem that could impact your business, if it helps in selecting between alternatives for achieving marketing objectives, if it can help in gaining a competitive advantage, or if it provides useful information on your markets.[2] Marketing research may not be needed if the information is already available, there is insufficient time for marketing research, resources are not available, or costs of conducting the research outweigh the potential benefits of having the information.

If the decision is made to proceed with the marketing research, the research problem should be clearly defined. What does the research effort propose to do? What types of questions need to be asked? What solutions are sought? A strong tendency among all researchers, especially novice researchers, is to rush into data collection without giving adequate thought to defining the problem. This tendency should be vigorously avoided. A small amount of time spent in defining and refining the problem will save many hours later on.

First, it is necessary to view the problem from the marketing manager's perspective. Normally, a problem is brought to the attention of a manager when there is a decrease in a performance measure such as sales volume, profit, or market share. It is important not to mistake this for the problem and recognize it as a symptom of an underlying problem. For example, if a hotel's occupancy rate has suddenly fallen, there could be a number of causes. A new competitor may have opened, current competitors may be discounting prices or increasing advertising expenditures, consumers may be dissatisfied with the hotel, there may be construction in the immediate area, or there may be a downturn in the economy. Regardless, one of these factors, or a combination of them, could be the cause of the decrease in performance.

Once the marketing manager has pinpointed the problem, it is time to formulate the marketing research problem. In other words, what informa-

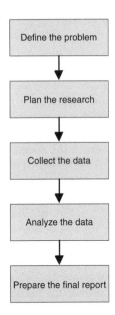

FIGURE 6.3   The Marketing Research Process

tion does the marketing manager need to solve the problem? This involves taking constructs (marketing terms or concepts) such as brand loyalty and customer satisfaction and establishing an operational definition that can be used to measure these constructs. For example, brand loyalty could be measured by asking travelers for the percentage of their flights that are on a particular airline. The researcher must also identify the relationships between constructs. One could assume that as customer satisfaction increases, so does brand loyalty. There may even be prior research to support this relationship.

Step 2. Plan the Research

The second step in the marketing research process involves planning the research design for obtaining the desired information to address the research problem. The **research design** is basically a master plan specifying the methods and procedures for collecting and analyzing the needed information. There are three main categories of research designs from which to choose, based on the objectives of the research.

research design   master plan for specifying the methods and procedures for collecting and analyzing the needed information

Exploratory Research.   This type of research is used to gain background information when a firm doesn't have a good understanding of the nature of the problem. Exploratory research can be used to obtain addi-

hypotheses in research, a conjecture about the relationships between two or more variables

secondary data analysis process of reviewing existing information that is related to the research problem

focus group 8 to 12 people who are representative of the population being studied brought together in an informal setting to discuss the issues surrounding a research problem

cross-sectional studies measure of a population at one point in time; provides a snapshot of a larger population

tional information about a topic and to generate **hypotheses** stating the relationships between two or more variables. This research tends to be informal, and unstructured, and it is mainly used to gain background information, define terms, and clarify problems. The hypotheses that are generated using exploratory research can be tested in future research efforts.

Some of the more common methods for conducting exploratory research are secondary data analysis, experience surveys, case analysis, and focus groups. **Secondary data analysis** is the process of reviewing existing information that is related to the research problem. The sources for secondary data analysis were discussed previously in this chapter, along with the advantages and disadvantages associated with using this method. Experience surveys are similar to the qualitative methods discussed in the sales forecasting section of Chapter 5. Basically, information is gathered from individuals that are believed to be knowledgeable about the research topic. Case analysis refers to the use of information about a situation that resembles the current situation surrounding the current research problem. Hospitality firms could benefit from the experiences of other firms in their industry, or firms in other industries that faced similar circumstances.

One of the most common methods of exploratory research is the **focus group**. Focus groups consist of 8 to 12 people who are representative of the population being studied that are brought together in an informal setting to discuss the issues surrounding the research problem. The sessions generally last from 1 to 2 hours and are guided by a *moderator*, who ensures that all the group's members give input and that all of the pertinent topics are covered. Focus groups are valuable for testing new product designs and service concepts, advertising campaigns, and gaining insight into the market's basic needs and attitudes. The use of focus groups has gained in popularity because the respondents can interact as the research client watches through a two-way mirror. Many focus group sessions are videotaped so they can be examined in more detail at a later date by a number of different people. The potential weaknesses of focus groups are that, given the small number of participants, the group may not represent the population of interest, and, being unstructured, the information provided during the session is often very subjective and open to interpretation. Finally, it may be difficult and expensive to obtain the participants, the moderator, and a facility for a focus group.

Descriptive Research. The second category of research design is concerned with answering the basic questions of who buys the product, what customers do with the product, where they buy, when they buy, why they buy, and how they buy. Primarily, the researcher is trying to profile the customer base in terms of demographics, psychographics, attitudes, and purchasing behavior. **Cross-sectional studies** measure the population at one point in time; they provide a snapshot of the population. This type of study is normally used to address a particular problem when it arises.

For example, one hotel surveyed customers in its atrium restaurant over a one-week period to obtain information that could be used to redesign the restaurant and its menu. **Longitudinal studies** are used to measure the same population over an extended period. Generally, these studies use the same sample, referred to as a *panel*, and collect the same information over time (e.g., once a year). Longitudinal data is useful in depicting trends and changes in consumer needs and attitudes. For example, many firms offering syndicated services will track the trends in an industry by constructing and maintaining a panel of consumers who complete an annual survey.

longitudinal studies used to measure a population over an extended period

Causal Research. The third category of research design focuses on cause and effect relationships that are pertinent to a research problem. A series of if-then statements can be used to model certain elements of the hospitality service. For example, a hospitality firm may want to examine how a particular change in the marketing mix affects sales, market share, and/or customer satisfaction. The following relationships could be tested. If the quality of food is improved, customer satisfaction will increase. If on-time performance improves, market share will increase. If an additional salesperson is hired, occupancy rate will increase. The potential benefits of understanding causal relationships are great. Firms could design better products, create effective advertising campaigns, and set prices that will maximize revenue. Unfortunately, many factors affect the consumer decision-making process, either alone or in combination, and it is almost impossible to understand them completely. In fact, many researchers argue that there is no such thing as true causality. Regardless, as managers' understanding of consumer behavior increases, the firm's performance will improve.

Step 3. Collect the Data

Three major decisions must be made during this stage in the marketing research process. They involve choosing a data collection method, designing data collection forms, and determining the sampling plan. Weaknesses in any of these areas can have a profound impact on the reliability and validity of the results. *Reliability* refers to the consistency of responses to questions, and *validity* refers to the accuracy of the measure. It is possible to have reliability without validity, but for a measure to be valid, it must also be reliable. For example, a poorly written question can solicit consistent responses, but it may not be a valid measure of the construct that is being studied. Even with the best sample, a poorly designed collection form will result in inaccurate data. Similarly, a well-designed collection form is useless if the sample does not represent the population.

Data Collection Methods. Once the research design has been planned, it is necessary to determine the best method for collecting the data. The three possible methods for obtaining primary data are observation, surveys, and experiments. The appropriate method will depend on the research objectives and the research design. Exploratory research is most often accomplished using observation and surveys. Descriptive research uses all of the data collection methods, but it relies very heavily on information received from surveys. Finally, experiments are used almost exclusively for causal research. However, observation and surveys are also used to obtain information to study causal relationships.

observation watching consumers and making organized notes to document or record observed behavior

Observation involves watching consumers and making organized notes to document or record the observed behavior. When doing this type of research, it is important that all individuals acting as observers record their observations in the same manner. *Direct observation* refers to the process of observing behavior as it actually occurs, either by a person or a mechanical device. For example, many hotels place mirrors near elevators in an attempt to relieve the boredom and agitation observed in guests while they were waiting. *Indirect observation* refers to the process of observing behavior after the fact. For example, airlines search the trash to determine the eating behaviors of their passengers. This *physical trace evidence* is useful in deciding which meal items to include and which ones to eliminate. In most cases, the observation is disguised so as not to affect the consumer's behavior. However, there are instances, such as food testing, when subjects know they are being observed. The observation method is useful because subjects are usually unaware that they are being observed and they behave in a normal fashion. Unfortunately, the subject's behavior is difficult to interpret, especially the attitudes and motivation behind it.

surveys asking consumers to provide information

Surveys involve asking consumers to provide information regarding the issues surrounding the research problem on a questionnaire or comment card. The survey can be filled in by the researcher, completed with the aid of a computer, or completed by the respondent (self-administered). When used properly, the survey method can gather a great deal of useful information. The survey method is adaptable to a variety of situations and is relatively inexpensive. Surveys may be accomplished using a number of different methods, including telephone surveys, direct mail surveys, or personal interviews. A summary of the advantages and disadvantages of these methods is provided in Table 6.1.

Telephone surveys are the most common method of survey data collection because they are the easiest to implement and produce very quick results. Another major advantage to this type of survey is the cost. No travel is involved, and a single individual may contact and solicit answers from a large number of people in a fairly short period of time. On the other hand, there is no face-to-face contact, and people are often not inclined to answer questions over the phone, especially if they are complicated. The reliability of the answers received over the telephone is also in question.

Direct mail surveys offer ease of completion, respondent anonymity, and a low cost per response. However, there are a few major drawbacks. First, the response rate is normally quite low, and the collection process is slow. Often, less than 25 percent of the surveys are properly completed

Table 6.1	**Comparison of Survey Data Collection Methods**		
Characteristics	*Direct Mail Surveys*	*Telephone Surveys*	*Personal Interviews*
Cost per respondent	Low	Medium	High
Speed of response	Low	High	Medium
Response rate	Low	Medium	High
Interviewer bias	Low	Medium	High
Allows feedback	Low	Medium	High
Ability to handle sensitive topics	High	Medium	Low
Ability to handle complex questions	Medium	Low	High

and returned, and it may take up to three months, and two or three mailings, to obtain an adequate sample. With such a low response rate, there is a risk that the individuals who returned the surveys do not represent the population and any decisions based on the results could be biased. Second, direct mail surveys do not allow any in-depth questioning, and they do not allow for follow-up questions. The respondent merely sees the written questions and has no opportunity for clarification. This may make it more difficult to generate answers that reflect the complexity of opinion within the targeted market segments.

Personal interviews allow more in-depth questioning. An interviewer normally uses a guide sheet to direct the interview and may adjust the questioning to focus on a point of special interest or to follow-up an answer given by the respondent. There are two drawbacks to personal interviews as a surveying technique. First, the major drawback is cost per interview. It is extremely expensive to have an interviewer spend a long period of time with each individual in order to gather information. An in-depth interview can last as long as an hour; hence the number of individuals that can be interviewed is limited, and the cost per interview is quite high. The cost of travel also makes this type of survey expensive. Second, a good deal of training must be done for interviewers to be effective. In addition, supervision is required in order to have control over the interviewers. *Intercept interviews* are a form of personal interview conducted in major traffic areas such as shopping malls, in an attempt to eliminate some of the drawbacks associated with cost and speed of response.

When conducting **experiments,** a researcher divides the sample of people into groups and exposes each group to a different treatment while try-

experiments examines the effect of a treatment on a test subject in a controlled setting

ing to control for other extraneous factors that may affect the outcome. The treatment variable is referred to as the *independent variable*, and the outcome of the treatment is measured using a *dependent variable* because changes in the variable are dependent on changes in the treatment. In other words, there is a cause and effect relationship in which the independent variable is the cause and the dependent variable is the effect. Experiments can be conducted in the *field* under normal conditions or in a *laboratory* setting where extraneous factors can be more easily controlled.

Test marketing is a common form of field experiment consisting of manipulations in the marketing mix at certain locations that represent the competitive environment and consumer profile of the overall population. For example, all of the national fast-food companies use cities across the country as test market centers. In each of these cities, the companies will introduce, or test market new products, or marketing mix changes, to obtain customer reactions and to project future sales. Sales may then be compared with those at other test market centers to determine the popularity of new and old items and to decide which products will be introduced systemwide. It is quite expensive to conduct this type of study, and it is also quite difficult to control all external variables that may affect the outcome of the experiment. For instance, extraneous variables such as the weather or the advertising efforts of competitive hospitality operations could easily have an effect on the sales volume of new products.

Designing Data Collection Forms. Data collection forms are necessary whether the research plan involves observation, surveys, or experiments. Surveys are most commonly used because much of the research being conducted is descriptive. Therefore, this section will focus on designing questionnaires to be used in surveys.

Questionnaires are comprised of questions designed to address the research objectives. The goal of the questionnaire is to standardize data collection by using questions that will elicit a consistent response from respondents. This is accomplished through the use of open-ended and closed-ended questions. An **open-ended question** does not provide the respondent with any options, categories, or scales to use in answering the question. These questions are valuable for obtaining information for exploratory research, or in instances when the researcher is not sure what the response might be. Conversely, a **closed-ended question** provides the respondent with options from which to select a response. It is much easier to collect and analyze information that is in the form of closed-ended questions. The respondents' answers are consistent and the data is in a form that is simple to record.

While open-ended questions are in the form of a basic question, closed-ended questions can be in three different forms. The simplest form of closed-ended question is a **dichotomous question**, which contains two possible options. Examples of a dichotomous question would be questions with "yes" or "no" answers, or a categorical question such as gender

open-ended question has no options, categories, or scales to use in responding

closed-ended question has options from which to select a response

dichotomous question contains two options

with two possible responses, like "male" and "female." Another type of closed-ended question is the **multiple category question**, which contains more than two options for the respondent. Demographic information like education and income is often obtained using multiple category questions. When framing the options for multiple category questions, it is important for the researcher to make sure the options are *mutually exclusive* and *collectively exhaustive*. Options are said to be *mutually exclusive* if there is only one possible option for each respondent, and *collectively exhaustive* if there is at least one option that pertains to each respondent. The final form of closed-ended question is the **scaled-response question**. This type of question involves a statement or question followed by a rating scale. One of the more popular scaled-response questions is the *Likert scale* which has respondents indicate their level of agreement with a statement on a five-point scale, with 1 being "strongly disagree" and 5 being "strongly agree."

> **multiple-category question** contains more than two options for the respondent

> **scaled-response question** statement or question followed by a rating scale

Surveys are used for a multitude of reasons, and it is difficult to establish rules that will apply in all situations. However, the following general guidelines apply to the construction of all survey instruments:

- Avoid talking down to the respondent or using technical language. Ask the questions using language the respondent understands and is familiar with.

- Avoid long and wordy questions. These will tend to discourage the respondent and may reduce the number of respondents to a written survey.

- Avoid questions that are vague and general in nature.

- Avoid including more than one idea per question.

- Avoid personal questions that might embarrass the respondent. Make certain that there is a legitimate reason for asking each question.

- Avoid putting any personal bias into the questions.

- Make sure that you fully understand the purpose of the question, for if you do not, the respondent is not likely to understand the question.

- In closed-ended questions, provide a "don't know" or "no opinion" response where appropriate.

- All responses in a closed-ended question should be mutually exclusive.

- The number of choices in a closed-ended question need not be limited to five or six responses; a larger number of responses can be used where appropriate.

- Indicate very clearly in the directions the number of choices a respondent should check.

- Watch for words and phrases that have more than one meaning, as this can confuse the respondent.

- Questions of a personal nature, such as income, are generally less threatening if they are placed toward the end of the survey.

To ensure good flow and a high response rate, it is necessary for researchers to follow some basic guidelines in organizing questionnaires. The following format is recommended to improve the probability that respondents will participate in the survey and complete the questionnaire. First, the questionnaire should start with some easy questions to screen respondents based on their purchasing behaviors. Respondents that fit the desired profile proceed to the next section, and those who do not are thanked for their time and cut loose. Second, more detailed information is obtained regarding respondents' purchase and usage behaviors so they can be categorized. This section focuses on basic information that is easy to provide, and it serves to warm-up the respondent for later sections. Third, respondents are asked to answer a series of complicated questions, including ratings and rankings. The fourth, and final, section of the questionnaire is used to obtain background information on the respondent. This demographic and psychographic information is used to classify individuals for statistical analysis.

The goal of questionnaire organization is to select respondents who represent the target population and ease them into the questionnaire so they become involved. Then, they are less likely to cut off in the middle of the questionnaire when they are confronted with more difficult questions and sensitive questions dealing with topics such as age and income. Therefore, it is important to *pretest* the questionnaire on a small sample to check the question wording and organization. Any problems can be identified and corrected before attempting to use the data collection form on the final sample.

Determining the Sampling Plan. Sampling is the process of using a small subset of the population to obtain information that can be used to make inferences about the total population. A **population** is the entire group, or target market, that is being studied for the purpose of answering the research questions. A **sample** is the subset of the population that is drawn is such a way so as to represent the overall population. A **sample unit** is the basic level of investigation. The sample unit could be an individual, a household, or a firm or organization. For example, studies in the hospitality industry could look at a hotel's guest, a specific hotel property, or a hotel chain. Normally, a **census**, or the investigation of the entire population, is cost prohibitive and would take too much time to complete. Therefore, a sample is used in hopes that the results can be applied to the overall population. Whenever a sample is used instead of a census, there is some difference between the sample results and actual population measures. This difference is referred to as **sampling error**.

There are two basic types of samples, probability and nonprobability. **Probability samples** are more scientific, and a population member's chance of being selected can be calculated. This type of sample tends to be favored when the firm has some understanding of the problem, sampling errors are larger, and there is a high degree of variability in the pop-

population the entire group that is being studied for the purpose of answering the research questions

sample subset of the population that is drawn in such a way so as to represent the overall population

sample unit basic level of investigation

census investigation of an entire population

sampling error difference between the sample results and actual population measures

probability samples each population member has a known, nonzero, chance of being selected

ulation (i.e., it is heterogeneous). The most common probability sampling method is the **simple random sample** where the process is totally random and each population member has an equal chance of being selected. With this method, there is little chance of selection bias or sampling error. Another popular probability method is the **systematic sample**, where a starting point is chosen arbitrarily and then every *n*th member is selected for the sample. This method is easier than random sampling and it is often used with lists containing addresses and/or telephone numbers (i.e., the telephone directory). Normally, there is no reason to believe that any bias would occur due to the ordering of members in the list. For example, it would be unusual for every 100th name on a list to share common characteristics like age and income. A **stratified sample** is one in which the population is separated into different strata based on an important population characteristic and a sample is taken from each stratum using a random or systematic process. For example, many firms want to include both "customers" and "noncustomers" in their samples, but place more weight on "customers" responses.

Nonprobability samples are based on judgment and the selection process is very subjective. You cannot calculate the chance of a member being selected, but that does not mean that the sample won't be representative of the population. The representativeness of the sample will depend greatly on the judgment of the researcher. Nonprobability samples tend to be favored when the research is exploratory, there is more potential for nonsampling errors, and the population is homogeneous. The most basic method of nonprobability sampling is the **convenience sample** because the researcher chooses a sample of population members that, in his or her opinion, represent the target population. Often, professors use a class of students, or research firms intercept people at shopping malls. A **judgment sample** is slightly different in that the researcher makes a determination as to a subset of population members that will represent the population. This process is similar to the one used in choosing the members for a focus group. A **quota sample** is one of the most popular sampling methods. The sample is chosen to fill certain quotas that are predetermined by the researcher. This method is similar to stratified sampling, except that a convenience sample is used to fill the quotas and a probability technique is used to fill each stratum.

For any of those methods, the first requirement is to define the population from which to gather information. (The population is simply a definition of the group of individuals from which to gather information.) For example, two specific populations might be (1) all males and females between the ages of 20 to 26 who are not married; and (2) all males and females who earn more than $25,000 per year and work within 1 mile of our restaurant.

The next step is to determine the number of individuals to survey. This is known as the **sample size**. The determination of sample size can be based on financial, statistical, and/or managerial issues. From a financial

---

simple random sample totally random process in which each population member has an equal chance of being selected

systematic sample a starting point is chosen randomly and from there every *n*th member is selected for the sample

stratified sample the population is separated into different strata based on an important population characteristic and a sample is taken from each using a random or systematic process

nonprobability sample based on judgment; the selection process is very subjective

convenience sample a sample of a population is chosen by the researcher based on convenience

judgment sample similar to a focus group, members are selected by a researcher to represent a population

quota sample sample is chosen to fill certain quotas

sample size the number of individuals to be surveyed

standpoint, the size of the sample depends on the available budget, or what the client can afford. As shown in Table 6.1, the cost of obtaining a completed questionnaire increases as you go from mail surveys, to telephone surveys, to personal interviews. Each method has its own particular set of costs. For example, mail surveys require postage (including return postage), two sets of envelopes, and printing costs. Depending on the quality of the components, this can range from $1.00 to $2.00 for each sample unit, regardless of whether the recipient chooses to participate. This is in addition to the cost of data input and analysis.

From a managerial standpoint, the size of the sample can be a function of an arbitrary judgment or based on similar studies. Managers may have a certain number that they feel is adequate for whatever reason. Sometimes, this decision is based on some rule of thumb that may or may not be based on some consideration of sampling error. A manager may just feel that a sample of 200 is a good size. Another common approach for managers is to base the decision on similar studies conducted by the firm or other firms that they are familiar with. For example, it may be what the manager did at another firm, or it may be the size of a sample used in a study published in a trade magazine.

From a statistical standpoint, the size of the sample may depend on the type of analysis that will be used. In general, more sophisticated statistical techniques tend to require a certain number of observations to be valid. Another consideration is the number of subgroups to be analyzed. For example, as the number of variables used in segmenting and cross-tabulating increases, the number of cells to be analyzed increases. Many researchers prefer to have a minimum number of observations in each cell (i.e., 50 or 100). Traditionally, there are three main factors to consider when determining the appropriate sample size using a statistical approach: (1) the acceptable level of sampling error; (2) the amount of variability in the population; and (3) the desired level of confidence. The sample size would increase as the desired accuracy increases, the desired level of confidence increases, and/or the amount of variability in the population increases. Sampling error decreases at a diminishing rate as sample size increases. Table 6.2 provides the figures for sampling error at the 95 percent confidence level.

Step 4. Analyze the Data

descriptive analysis uses aggregate data to describe the average or typical respondent and the degree to which respondents vary from this profile

Two basic forms of statistical analysis are used in marketing research: descriptive analysis and inferential analysis. **Descriptive analysis** uses aggregate data to describe the "average" or "typical" respondent, and to what degree respondents vary from this profile. The measures used for central tendency are the mode, median, and mean. As you may recall from your basic statistics course, the *mode* refers to the value that occurs most often. The *median* refers to the value that represents the middle of an ordered set of responses. In other words, the responses are ordered from high to low, or

Table 6.2	**Sampling Error by Sample Size**
Sample Size	*Allowance for Sampling Error (95% confidence level)*
200	5–8%
400	4–6%
600	3–5%
800	3–4%
1,000	2–4%
1,500	2–3%

low to high, and then the middle value is determined. The *mean* refers to the arithmetic average, or the sum of all responses divided by the number of responses. The measures of variability are the frequency distribution, range, and standard deviation. The *frequency distribution* provides the counts for each value in the set of responses. The *range* is calculated by taking the difference between the highest value and the lowest value of the ordered set of responses. The *standard deviation* is a measure of variance between the observed values and the mean for the set of responses.

The second form of statistical analysis is **inferential analysis**, which is used to test hypotheses and estimate population parameters using sample statistics. Statistics like the *t-statistic* and the *z-statistic* are used to test for differences between the sample mean and a hypothesized mean. These test statistics can also be used to test for differences between two groups, and *analysis of variance (ANOVA)* is used to test for differences between more than two groups based on their respective means and variances. *Correlations* and *cross-tabulations* are used to determine if an association exists between two variables. If so, the two variables will vary together either directly or inversely. Finally, *multivariate statistics* can be used to test for relationships between more than two variables. These forms of statistical analysis are beyond the scope of this text, and interested readers should refer to a marketing research text for more details.

inferential analysis used to test hypotheses and estimate population parameters using sample statistics

Step 5. Prepare the Final Report

Once the research is completed and the data is analyzed, it is necessary to prepare a final report that provides a detailed outline of the research design, summarizes the results, and provides some conclusions or recommendations. The researcher should consider the audience for the presentation when preparing the final report. Both written and oral reports have been criticized for things such as excessive length, impractical recommendations, and the use of complex terms. These mistakes can be avoided if the researcher determines the personality and requirements of the audience and takes them into consideration when preparing the report. For example, many clients prefer to be shown the results summarized in tables and charts rather than read detailed discussions including statistics.

There are some guidelines that can be followed when preparing the final report that will improve the probability of client satisfaction, and success. First, the research team should plan to devote an adequate amount of time to prepare the report. In fact, the time for report preparation should be included in the time frame outlined in the proposal. Second, the original proposal should be examined and the research objectives should be addressed in the final report. Third, the research team must understand the needs of the audience and determine the content and length that is appropriate for the report. Fourth, it is important to anticipate possible objections or concerns and to address them in the report or presentation.

Most written reports follow a standard outline. The report normally begins with an executive or management summary that clearly and concisely states the project's objectives, methods, conclusions, and recommendations. Next, the actual body of the report begins with a detailed discussion of the research objectives, followed by an explanation of the research methodology, including its advantages and limitations. The research methodology section contains the elements of the research plan, including questionnaire design, sampling, data collection, and type of analysis. The next section contains a detailed description of the results, with references to charts, figures, and tables that summarize the results. Finally, the report ends with the conclusions, implications, and recommendations of the research team. Any tables, charts, figures, or other supplemental materials will appear in an appendix at the end of the report. Examples of supplemental materials would be an *annotated questionnaire* containing the results for each question, or a list of responses to open-ended questions.

▲ ETHICAL ISSUES IN MARKETING RESEARCH

research ethics codes of behavior that are set by society and the research industry to define appropriate behavior for firms and individuals

As with most other areas in marketing, there is potential for unethical behavior in marketing research. **Research ethics** are the codes of behavior that are set by society and the research industry to define appropriate behavior for firms and individuals. Three parties are involved in the marketing research process, and each has its own set of rights and obligations concerning ethics. The following is a brief description of the rights and obligations for respondents, researchers, and clients:

Rights and Obligations of the Respondent. Research clients make major decisions based on the information that they obtain through surveys and other research methods. Therefore, it is incumbent upon respondents to be truthful in their responses and their behavior when they choose to participate. Research suppliers count on this honesty, but the suppliers must be honest with respondents as well. Respondents have the right to privacy and should be allowed to refuse to participate. Also, research suppliers should honor any confidentiality agreements that they may make with respondents. Finally, respondents have the right to be informed about the true nature of the research. Respondents are often contacted under the guise of research, when in reality, it is merely a sales pitch. This type of deception is not acceptable behavior under normal ethical standards.

Rights and Obligations of the Researcher. As mentioned before, research suppliers have an obligation to maintain the privacy and confidentiality of both their respondents and their clients. Research suppliers should not perform research for the sake of selling, and they should not sell their lists to other firms. Research suppliers have an obligation to remain impartial and objective in performing their research. Also, the results should be presented accurately, without any attempt to misrepresent them. Similarly, conclusions should be based on the actual results, not misrepresented, or tailored, to meet the needs of the client.

Rights and Obligations of the Client. Clients have an obligation to be open and forthright with research suppliers regarding the actual nature of the research. If clients send out a request for proposals, it should be for an actual project, not to obtain information for conducting their own research or for negotiating with other research suppliers. Clients should not misrepresent the research project as a pilot study that could lead to more projects in an attempt to decrease the cost. Finally, clients should have a real commitment to research and plan to use it properly. They should not put undue pressure on the research supplier to misrepresent results to suit the client's wishes.

In some cases, the client firm conducts research through an in-house research department. In this situation, the client and the research supplier are one in the same, and the firm is subject to the rights and obligations of both parties. This discussion is not meant to be complete, but instead, it provides a list of the most common areas for unethical behavior.

▲ MARKETING ACTION NOW!

You are the general manager of a restaurant in a small college town. Recently, you have seen your sales revenues decreasing by 5% to 10% on any given day. In the past, the restaurant has enjoyed a stable flow of customers and revenue, without having to make any major changes in the operation. You are concerned by this new trend, and you need to take some type of action, but you aren't quite sure how to approach the situation.

Fortunately, the local university has a marketing research class that will conduct a study for free as part of a class project.

1. What are some of the potential causes or problems associated with the decrease in sales?
2. Pick one of these problems and discuss the type of research that would be necessary.
3. What method of data collection would you use, and what are some of the questions you would ask?
4. How would this information be analyzed?

▲ SUMMARY OF CHAPTER OBJECTIVES

Marketing information systems should be designed to produce data that are useful to a hospitality manager. This information can be used as a basis for decisions. This information should not, however, be used as the sole determining factor when making any decision. Two other factors also come into play when making a decision—experience and intuition. If all decisions could be based solely on information produced by marketing information systems, there would be no need for managers. Instead, machines could be used to tabulate the information and predict the correct answer. Managers, however, have far too many uncontrollable variables to contend with in gathering marketing information. For this reason a hospitality manager must view the situation by considering marketing information, previous experience in similar situations, and intuition as to what the future holds. Based on these three factors, a decision must be made, and the hospitality manager must accept the final responsibility for the decision.

A hospitality marketing information system is a structured organization of people and procedures designed to generate a flow of data from inside and outside the operation. It is used as a basis for marketing decisions. A marketing information system scans three subenvironments: the macroenvironment, the competitive environment, and the organizational environment. Marketing information systems involve both internally and externally generated marketing information, each with its own set of sources for information and its own methodology for obtaining necessary information.

The marketing research process is used to collect data to store in marketing information systems to be used in making marketing decisions. The basics of conducting marketing research are not difficult, but the specifics of designing, implementing, analyzing, and interpreting the results of a marketing research project are very demanding. It requires great skill to successfully manage a marketing research project. This chapter provided an overview of the research process, which involves five steps: (1) define the problem, (2) plan the research, (3) collect the data, (4) analyze the data, and (5) prepare the final report.

Management problems must be defined and converted to research problems that can be evaluated. Once the research problems are defined, research objectives are established. Researchers can then choose the type of research to be performed: exploratory, descriptive, or causal. This decision is based on many factors, including the client's understanding of the nature of the problem, past research and experience, and the overall goal of the research. Next, the decision is made as to the method of data collection and data collection forms are designed. Then, a sampling plan is devised and implemented to ensure the reliability and validity of the research results. Finally, the data is analyzed using predetermined statistical methods, and the results are summarized in a final report.

The goal of marketing information systems is to collect information that can be useful in improving the quality of marketing decisions. The marketing research process is critical in this endeavor. Therefore, it is imperative that all parties involved in the research process adhere to the ethical standards set forth by society and the research industry. Each party to the process has certain rights and obligations that are crucial to the overall success of the marketing research process.

▲ KEY TERMS AND CONCEPTS

Causal research

Census

Closed-ended question

Cross-sectional study

Descriptive research

Experiments

Exploratory research

Focus group

Hypothesis

Longitudinal study

Marketing information system (MIS)

Marketing research process

Nonprobability sample

Observation

Open-ended question

Population

Primary data

Probability sample

Research design

Research ethics

Sample

Sample unit

Secondary data

Surveys

Syndicated services

Test marketing

▲ QUESTIONS FOR REVIEW AND DISCUSSION

1. Why would it be useful for a hospitality organization to implement a marketing information system?

2. Cite sources for internal and external marketing information that you consider the best. Discuss the advantages and disadvantages of each.

3. Differentiate between primary and secondary data, including their advantages and disadvantages.

4. What role should a marketing information system play in the management of a hospitality establishment?

5. Discuss the three types of research. Give an example of a situation in which you would use each one? Can you use more than one at a time?

6. What are the three methods of collecting data? Can you give an example of how each one would be used in the hospitality and travel industry?

7. Compare and contrast the three types of surveys.

8. How are questionnaires organized? What are some of the guidelines that should be followed in developing questions?

9. What is the difference between a probability sample and a nonprobability sample? Which one is best? Explain your answer.

10. What are the two major types of data analysis? When should the decision be made as to which methods will be used for analyzing the data?

11. Who are the parties involved in the marketing research process? What are the rights and obligations of each party?

▲ NOTES

[1]Milford Prewitt, "New Zagat Survey Cites NYC Dining-out Slowdown," *Nation's Restaurant News* (November 23, 1998), p. 8.

[2]Alvin C. Burns and Ronald F. Bush, *Marketing Research*, 2nd edition (Englewood Cliffs, NJ: Prentice Hall 1998).

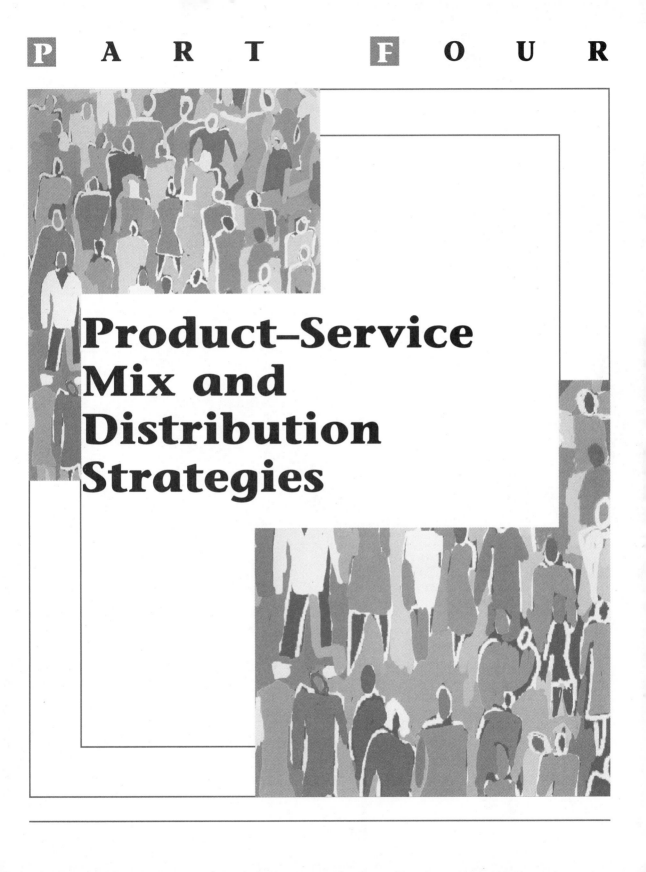

PART FOUR

Product–Service Mix and Distribution Strategies

7

Developing New Products and Services

❖ Chapter Objectives

By the end of this chapter, you should understand:

1. The importance of developing product lines
2. The process that many firms use to develop new products and services
3. The various organizational structures that firms use to develop new products and services
4. The importance of brands, brand names, and trademarks
5. The characteristics of effective branding

❖ Chapter Outline

I. Chapter Opening Profile

II. Introduction

   A. The importance of product lines

III. Planning for New Products

   A. Reactive strategies for new product development

❖ Chapter Opening Profile

BURGER KING IS COUNTING ON BETTER-TASTING products—and more of them—to keep sales sizzling.[1] At Burger King restaurants in Florida, consumers are enjoying thick-and-juicy steak sandwiches. In the Midwest they're trying pork tenderloin sandwiches on five-inch buns, and in Texas they have Mustard Whoppers without mayonnaise. Burger King is testing new sandwiches, breakfast items, and even drinks, such as the Icee, a slushy cola concoction much like the Slurpees sold at 7-Eleven convenience stores.

Amazingly, not one new product was launched by Burger King between 1990 and 1997. Now, the Miami-based chain, which had systemwide sales in 1997 of $9.8 billion, is doubling the budget of its research and development division and has hired a respected packaged-foods veteran to expand its staff and develop new menu items. Some of the recent additions to the menu: include the Big King (which resembles a Big Mac), new crispier french fries, and Cini-minis (with partner Pillsbury). The fast food chain has also created a Great Tastes Menu with eight items each costing 99 cents. This pricing strategy combined with the "it just tastes great" slogan is the basis for competition against rival firms.

▲ INTRODUCTION

No matter how successful a hospitality or tourism concept is, if the company associated with the concept doesn't evolve and change, it will be left behind. If we were to consider the top 100 companies in the lodging and food service segments, we would find that each year, some companies drop off the list and are replaced by new ones. Corporations such as McDonald's, Disney, and Marriott continue to lead the industry because they have been very successful in developing products that enhance their market position. However, it has become increasingly difficult for hospitality firms to expand sales and market share simply by adding new units. Today, growth must be accomplished within existing units by developing and implementing a superior product–service mix or by opening new units in untapped markets that may require a good deal of research and effort (e.g., international markets).

To illustrate this point, let's consider three examples. In recent years, as the number of truly great potential locations for restaurants has been reduced through market saturation, the leading companies have taken two steps to increase sales and grow their respective companies. First, they have sought new locations and venues to sell their product–service mix. For example, Pizza Hut, through an agreement with Marriott International, began selling a scaled-down version of their product–service mix in selected Marriott Hotels. This scaled-down version offers a limited menu in a facility with a relatively small seating capacity. In addition, Pizza Hut participates in some of the noncommercial foodservice accounts operated by contract foodservice companies like ARAMARK. This allowed Pizza Hut to reach new markets, ones that they had not previously reached. The result has been increased sales and increased consumer satisfaction. This is a **win–win relationship** for both Pizza Hut and their partners.

win–win situation
results when both parties are satisfied at end of negotiations

A second example of using product–service mix development to increase sales would be fast-food restaurants that introduce new products on a regular basis. Each of these companies routinely introduces new products or a bundle of products that will be available for a limited time. The goal is to induce patronage that will increase market share by taking customers away from the competition. A second goal is to increase brand loyalty, or the repeated purchasing of a firm's brand over time. These limited-time offerings are often a bundling of several products with a reduced price and/or increased portion size to convey a high level of perceived value to the consumer.

The third example is best illustrated by the manner in which theme parks extend the life of their product–service mix life cycle by engaging in product–service mix development. Each year, thrill seekers want to ride the newest and greatest rides at the many theme parks around the country. Among the leaders in this market are Disney, Six Flags, and Paramount. Each of these companies develops new rides each year in an effort to attract consumers to their respective parks. Having the largest or greatest of these thrill type rides can have a very positive impact on theme park attendance, sales, and profitability.

Product development takes two forms: **innovation** and **follow the leader**. Innovators are the risk-takers, always seeking to be the first in the market with a new product or service. The leader, or innovator, will benefit from being the first to market with a new product or concept. Customers may associate the innovation with the leader, or become loyal to that brand. For example, it is not unusual to hear customers at Burger King order a "value meal" (a McDonald's product). However, given the ease with which hospitality products and services can be duplicated, those who subscribe to the follow-the-leader approach can introduce their competing products and services soon after the market leader introduces its own products and services.

innovation approach seeking to be first to market with a new product or concept

follow-the-leader approach introduce competing products and services soon after the-market leader introduces its products and services

The Importance of Product Lines

For the continued success of a hospitality or travel firm, it is important to have a portfolio of products and services. Few firms can survive and sustain long-term growth with only one or two products or services because of the high risk associated with the lack of diversification. In addition to diversifying a firm's operating risk, there are several other reasons for developing new product lines. They include:

Growth Opportunities for the Business. When a company limits itself to one product or a limited number of products, it limits the firm's growth potential. Consider a firm like Baskin-Robbins. It was quite successful selling ice cream, but when consumer tastes shifted toward more low-fat or healthier items, the firm developed and offered new products such as frozen yogurt that met this demand.[2] This allowed Baskin-Robbins to appeal to more consumers and increase sales.

Efficient and Effective Use of Company Resources. As more products are developed or as a firm develops additional brands, it can make better use of corporate resources. For example, Choice International operates and franchises several brands of lodging products—Clarion Hotels and Suites, Quality Inns and Suites, Comfort Inns and Suites, and Sleep Inns and Suites. Marriott International uses a similar strategy offering traditional Marriott Hotels and Resorts, as well as Courtyards, Residence Inns, and Fairfield Inns. Operating multiple brands allows Choice International and Marriott International to make better use of corporate resources by segmenting the market and tailoring their offerings to the various segments using separate marketing programs.

Increasing Company Market Share and Importance of the Company Within the Overall Market. When multiple products or brands are made available to the public, sales will increase and overall market share will also increase. This affords the firm a stronger position in the market and increases the importance of the firm.

Diversifying a Firm's Business Risk. Without a steady flow of new products and services, a hospitality or travel firm could have serious problems if the sales of existing products start to decline. However, increased sales from new products and services can counteract poor sales from the current products. The larger the portfolio of products and product lines, the smaller the firm's business risk, especially when some of the products are in different industries.

▲ PLANNING FOR NEW PRODUCTS

It is critical for firms to take a systematic approach to developing and marketing new products and services. The potential rewards are high for successful new products or services, but the potential risks of failure are equally high. Firms must do a thorough analysis of a new product idea to determine if it is compatible with its goals, if it has the necessary resources, and if the environment is favorable. Marketing plans should contain information regarding new product development, as well as the goals and strategies for existing products. As with strategies for existing products, strategies for new products can be either **reactive** or **proactive**.[3]

Reactive Strategies for New Product Development

A **defensive** strategy is used to counter the effects on an existing product from a competitor's new product. Initially, this strategy involves minor changes in a firm's marketing mix such as advertising, packaging, and/or pricing. This will negate some of the impact from the competitive product until more information can be obtained and substantive changes made, if necessary. These changes could involve the development of a new product or service, or some major modifications to the current product–service mix. Normally, when new restaurants are being opened, the other local restaurants counter with increased promotions and/or discounts. Similarly, when small airlines have tried to start a new service in niche markets, the larger airlines have retaliated with price cuts and promotions for their routes in those markets.

reactive **strategy** respond to changes in the marketplace: **defensive, imitative, second but better, responsive**

An **imitative** strategy involves copying a new product or service before it can have a large impact in the market. This strategy is particularly appealing when the product or service is not unique or when it can be easily duplicated. This strategy is heavily relied upon in the fast-food industry. Every time McDonald's launches a successful new product, Burger King and some of the other competitors are quick to respond with similar offerings that tend to be very homogeneous.

An adapted version of the imitative strategy is the **second but better** strategy. Once again, firms are responding to competitors' new products, however, the firm's primary goal in this case is to improve upon the initial product. Marriott's introduction of its Courtyard division and extended-stay properties was eventually followed by competitors with similar products. For example, Wyndham Hotels recently introduced a line of garden hotels that are targeted at business travelers with modest budgets and a dislike for large hotels. This new product line will compete directly with the Marriott's Courtyard division, but the ultimate goal is to be better. This strategy is more common for products or services that require a large investment and a longer period of time to develop.

The final reactive strategy is referred to as a **responsive** strategy. Firms are responsive in that they react to the demands of customers. These new products are truly market driven. Hotels often modify their offerings and design new properties based on the observed behavior of their guests. The way guests rearrange a room, popular complaints, and frequency of use of amenities and services are all factors that affect the design of hotel products.

Proactive Strategies for New Product Development

proactive **strategy** anticipate changes in the marketplace: **research and development, marketing, entrepreneurial, acquisition, alliances**

Another approach to developing new products is to be proactive and initiate change, rather than reacting to it. A popular proactive strategy used by manufacturing firms is **research and development**. Service firms also do research in an attempt to design and develop new service concepts. Hospitality and travel firms are continually searching for new ways to improve facility designs and computer systems for reservations and resource management. Marriott has developed proprietary computer systems for conducting business, whereas many other firms choose to subscribe to systems developed by outside vendors.

Another proactive strategy used by service firms is **marketing**. This strategy embraces the marketing concept and the notion that it is important to determine customer wants and needs and then design products and services to meet those needs. Most hotels and restaurants use comment cards to gather information from consumers. However, firms like the Ritz-Carlton Hotels take a more comprehensive approach to gather information on service quality and satisfaction. The Ritz-Carlton received the Malcolm Baldridge Award for Quality as a result of its efforts to meet customer needs. The hotel firm obtained feedback from customers, employees, and suppliers in an attempt to completely understand the process of delivering high-quality service to its customers.

Firms that are innovative and tend to be leaders in their respective industries try to create an **entrepreneurial** environment for their employees. These firms are looking for new ideas that are generated internally through means other than research and development. Employees are a great source for ideas on improving existing products and services, and developing new products and services. After all, what employee doesn't have an opinion about how to improve his or her firm's products or services? Rather than have this be a negative influence on the organization, some firms choose to encourage employees to share their ideas and opinions. As a result, some of the new service concepts become separate operating divisions or separate components of current operations.

Another way to add products or services to a firm's portfolio is through mergers or **acquisitions**. A firm can acquire the rights to new products or services by entering into a legal arrangement with another firm, thereby combining the two firms' products and services. Acquisitions are plentiful in the hospitality and travel industry. Pepsi-Cola has developed a major presence in the hospitality industry through its acquisitions of firms like Taco Bell and Kentucky Fried Chicken. The advantage is that the individual firms do not have to diversify their offerings because the diversification has occurred at the corporate level.

acquisitions firm acquires a right to new products or services by entering into a legal arrangement with another firm

Finally, some firms choose to form **alliances** for a specific goal or purpose instead of combining ownership. Alliances are designed to take advantage of synergies that exist between companies by pooling resources such as marketing, research, and distribution. Many airlines, hotels, and rental car agencies have formed strategic alliances to help promote and sell their products and services. The firms benefit from cooperative advertising and shared databases, among many other areas. For example, Delta Airlines rewards SkyMiles members with free miles when they stay at a Holiday Inn, rent a car from Alamo, use MCI for long distance calls, or charge purchases on American Express.

alliances firms pool resources for a specific goal or purpose instead of combining ownership

Product development is a highly complex issue. It requires critical thinking and careful planning. The remainder of this section will address issues related to how companies organize for product development and how it is conducted.

▲ ORGANIZING FOR NEW PRODUCT PLANNING

Firms use a variety of organizational structures to develop new products and services. No one way is best and each has inherent advantages and disadvantages. The primary organizational structures are new product committees, new product departments, product managers, and venture teams. Each of these structures is explained in more detail in the following paragraphs.

New Product Committees

New product committees consist of individuals representing cross-functional areas of the firm. Usually, representatives provide input from operations, marketing, finance, and accounting. Committee members are charged with the responsibility of reviewing new product ideas and with determining the impact that new products will have on each of their respective areas. The process of using new product committees is often slow and members normally have their own day-to-day responsibilities within their respective functional areas of the firm. Although these committees typically make decisions about which new products or services to offer, they do not develop the actual products or services.

New Product Departments

Some firms establish full-time new product departments. This addresses the problem of product development being a part-time responsibility of members of the product development department. It is still very important for members of the product development department to solicit input from all cross-functional areas of the firm.

Product Managers

Some firms appoint product managers or brand managers to assume complete responsibility for determining marketing objectives and marketing strategies for a specific brand. Included in these responsibilities is product development as it relates to that brand. For example, suppose that someone was responsible for the brand Holiday Inn Express. In the role of a marketing manager, the individual would be responsible for all elements of the marketing mix: the product–service mix, the presentation mix, the communications mix, and the distribution mix. The marketing manager would also have the responsibility of establishing and implementing marketing strategies for the brand. Among the additional responsibilities of this role is being involved in product development.

Venture Teams

Venture teams are similar to new product committees, but they are formed to complete a specific product assignment. Venture teams bring together expertise from operations, marketing, accounting and finance, and, if necessary, architecture and construction. The venture team is charged with new product planning, development, and implementation. Unlike new product committees, which normally only review and make decisions about whether new products should be developed further, the venture team is expected to stay on the project through the entire new product development process.

▲ NEW PRODUCT DEVELOPMENT PROCESS

Developing new products and services is very time-consuming and very risky, but it is essential to the continued long-term success of a firm. Many methodologies can be used to develop products and services. In this section, we will explore the steps in a process that are often used within the hospitality and tourism industry. Many firms, especially food service firms, use this process when developing new products and services. The examples used in this section relate to how new menu items are developed by food service firms. Comparable product development processes are used in the development of lodging products and other types of products and services within the hospitality and tourism industry.

The stages of the product development process are: (1) idea generation, (2) product screening, (3) concept testing, (4) business analysis and test marketing, and (5) market introduction.

Idea Generation

New product ideas should take advantage of opportunities and trends in the dynamic marketplace, while matching the firm's strengths and overall mission. Ideas for new products can be generated internally as an assigned function for research and development groups or result from brainstorming by the other structures covered in the previous section. Other internal sources for ideas include salespeople and other employees. Many of the employees in a service firm are in customer contact positions. This enables them to get direct feedback concerning problems and detect prob-

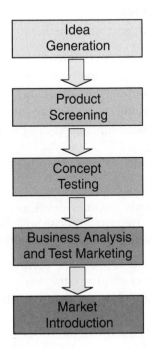

FIGURE 7.1 **New Product Development Process**

lem areas as they perform their normal job functions. This type of information is invaluable in improving customer satisfaction with service improvements and new services.

Some of the external sources for new product ideas are competitors, suppliers, trade shows, and trade magazines. A firm can produce new product ideas from following the actions of competitors and reading about new developments in trade magazines. These new developments are also the focus of companies attending trade shows, whether they are direct competitors or simply similar firms in other markets. Finally, suppliers can sometimes have a keen insight into a firm's operations. They deal with many different firms and often generate ideas for improvement based on their own developments.

Ideas should be sought from all potential sources. For example, menu items should be sought which expand, extend, or enhance the current food service menu. Currently, new menu item development appears to be most active in breakfast foods, light and healthy menu items, new tastes in foods such as regional cuisine, foods that cannot be prepared easily at home, foods that lend themselves to take-out, and food that is delivered.

Product Screening

Once ideas have been generated, the focus should turn toward screening the list of potential products to select the ones with the greatest potential for success. Both qualitative and quantitative analyses should be performed to evaluate new product ideas.

The qualitative standards involve answering the following questions:

- To what extent will the product increase sales and profits?
- Will the product attract new customers, and to what extent will it cannibalize from the sales of current products?
- What price would consumers pay for the product?
- Do we have the expertise and capacity to produce this product within our units?
- Does the competition offer a similar product? If so, how can we differentiate our product?

The quantitative analysis involves developing a weighted scoring for each new product idea to determine those with the greatest potential for success. The scoring is normally based on criteria such as the following:

- How the potential product or service contributes in a positive way to the image of the product and the company
- How the potential product contributes to the achieving the overall company goals
- The strengths, weaknesses, opportunities, and threats (SWOT) that the firm faces

Hotel location can provide unique value for new products. *Courtesy of Central Park Inter-Continental Hotel New York*

- Impact on current and potential customers
- Voids in the current product–service mix
- Equipment necessary to produce the new item
- Potential sources of supply for the new product or the necessary ingredients

Once the two types of analysis are completed, those new product ideas with the most potential are selected for further development.

Concept Testing

After new product ideas are screened, the ones that show signs of promise are subjected to concept testing. At this stage, a written or oral description and/or a visual representation is shown to consumers in the target market. The consumers are asked a series of questions regarding the concept and its value in relation to competitors' products. The results of this analysis are used to refine the new product's design and assess its market potential. At this point, only products with a high probability of success are moved forward because the resources necessary to proceed begin to escalate.

At this stage in the menu design process, the products are typically tested further in corporate test kitchens. The emphasis at this stage is on recipe development to refine the product so that it can be produced consistently. Standards are established for portions, preparation, holding times, and presentation. If the development plan proceeds according to schedule, the product is tested in a few units. At this stage of development, the product will likely be evaluated by focus groups made up of representatives of the target markets. The focus groups, led by a skilled facilitator, will assess the products potential impact by conducting taste tests and soliciting consumer feedback about the product, price, appearance, and other attributes. If this process continues to be successful, the product is then ready to undergo limited test marketing in more units.

Business Analysis and Test Marketing

The information obtained from potential consumers in the concept testing stage is used to analyze the business potential of the new product. Consumer responses are used to estimate potential sales and market share so that costs can be allocated and profits assessed. It is important to run more than one scenario (e.g., best case, worst case, and most likely case) for different market conditions. If the figures are promising, then the new product is prepared for test marketing.

Test marketing is the limited introduction on a new product in selected locations. It is necessary to extend the testing period long enough to view consumers' true purchase patterns, including repurchase (i.e., approximately 3 to 12 months). During the test market period, the product is evaluated based on: (1) consumer feedback concerning quality, price, and various forms of sales promotion and advertising; (2) sales figures during various days of the week and times during the day; and (3) the financial contribution that the new item has made.

Locations chosen for test markets should possess some common characteristics. First, the city or location should be similar to the planned market for the final product. It should have the same forms of media, the same demographic and psychographic backgrounds for potential customers, and the same competitors or similar competitors. Second, the city or location should be somewhat isolated and of manageable size. There shouldn't be any influence by competitors or media from neighboring locations. The most important point to remember when conducting test marketing is to make sure the test market locations are representative of the planned market to ensure the reliability and validity of the results.

Market Introduction

The final stage in the new product development process is to introduce the new product to the entire market, or to roll it out market-by-market. New products that demonstrate favorable business projections and test market results are given the green light by management. It is very costly to launch a new product because of the advertising campaigns and sales promotions, the employee training, and any required changes to the facility. At first, there are negative profits due to fixed start-up costs and inventories, and little revenue. It may take a good deal of time for the new product to be accepted and build market share. During this period, the firm must monitor the results and make any necessary changes in marketing strategy. Once the product is successfully launched, it is monitored and managed through the rest of its product life cycle.

▲ IDENTIFYING PRODUCTS AND SERVICES

Hospitality and travel firms may offer more than one service or product line that can be targeted at different market segments. It is often necessary to distinguish these offerings from one another if they are to hold different positions in the marketplace. Therefore, branding is a critical component of the marketing strategy for hospitality and tourism firms. The following section defines the terms related to branding and their use in the positioning of products.

The Importance of Branding

Brands are a very powerful marketing tool and, if properly managed, they have the potential of increasing sales, increasing profitability, and increasing customer satisfaction.

Before we proceed, let's define some important terms:

- *Brand.* This is the name, sign, symbol, design, or any combination of these items that is used to identify the product and establish an identity that is separate and unique from those competing. Consider the impact that various brands have within the hospitality and tourism industry. Is any brand more recognizable than the golden arches of McDonald's?

- *Brand name.* This is the part of the brand consisting of the words or letters that can be used to identify the firm.

- *Brand mark.* This is the symbol or logo design that is used to identify the product. Consider the stylized M and H that represents Marriott and Hilton respectively. When we see this brand symbol on the side of the hotel, we know instantly which brand the hotel represents. When Holiday Inn was in the early stages of its product–service mix life cycle, the Holiday Inn Great Sign was a very recognizable symbol of the Holiday Inn brand.

- *Trademark.* A trademark is the brand that has been given legal protection and is protected for exclusive use by the owner of the trademark.

The following example illustrates the importance of branding and its impact on sales and customer satisfaction.

In a university dining services operation, one of the venues that was available on campus was an unbranded pizza operation. It was successful and turned a reasonable profit for dining services and the university. Students could purchase pizzas from the operation á la carte or use part of their meal plan as a credit toward the cost of a pizza. As any professional manager would do, the dining service director of the university was seeking ways to increase student satisfaction with the dining service operations and also increase profitability for the university. One of the options considered was replacing the unbranded pizza operation with a regional or national brand pizza operation. After surveying the student body to determine preference, it was determined that Pizza Hut was the most popular choice among the students. Working with the corporate office of the contract foodservice company, who had previously negotiated with Pizza Hut for franchises at other universities, they were able to secure a franchise and open the Pizza Hut. In the first year that the Pizza Hut was in operation, sales increased nearly 30 percent. This increased revenue more than offset the franchise fee and other types of royalties that the management services company paid to Pizza Hut, Inc. The results of surveys administered to the students indicated that customer satisfaction had also increased. This is but one illustration of the impact that brands can have.

Characteristics of Effective Branding

Marketers, especially in other fields, have long studied the use of brand names and have established criteria that are believed to make brand names more effective. Within the hospitality and tourism industry, these criteria are not always followed closely. Instead, the names of families are often used as the basis for the brand name. Consider that McDonald was the family name of the two brothers that first opened a restaurant in California. J.W. Marriott Sr. opened the first restaurant, a Hot Shoppe in Washington, D.C. Conrad Hilton opened his first hotel in Texas.

Marketing managers recommend that the following criteria be used to establish brand names:

- *Easy to pronounce, recognize, and remember.* Some of the leading brands on the market are the ones that are easiest to remember. Some examples are USAir, Red Lobster, and National Car Rental.

- *Describes the benefits of the product or service.* It is a bonus for advertising and promoting a brand if the name describes the product's benefits. Some examples are Comfort Inns and Friendly's Restaurants.

- *Can be translated into foreign languages.* Many firms have been shortsighted in choosing brand names and overlooked problems that could occur if they expand into foreign markets. Some examples of good brand names are Marriott, Hertz, McDonald's, and United Airlines.

- *Distinctive and capable of legal protection.* Some brands are easy to remember and distinctive. It is also important to consider the possibility of becoming a chain or franchise and choose a brand name that can be registered. Some examples are Wyndham Hotels, Avis, and Delta Airlines.

▲ MARKETING ACTION NOW!

You are employed as the vice president of marketing for Jiffy Foods, Inc., a regional food service company that operates 40 restaurants in the fast-food or quick-service segment. In the quick-service market, Jiffy Foods is a small player, competing against the national chain companies such as McDonald's, Burger King, and Wendy's, as well as many other regional chains. During the last 18 months, sales at Jiffy Foods have been flat—there has been no increase in sales, despite the fact that prices were increased 2.5 percent a few months ago.

Earlier today, the president of the company dropped by your office in a very frustrated mood. The two of you had a very intense and animated conversation about how the products and services that Jiffy Foods offered on the menu were very traditional and not exciting to the targeted consumers. The national chains were always offering new products and services or modified products and services that were promoted for a limited period of time at a special price. The president felt that the competitors' promotions were hurting Jiffy Foods and wanted you to do something about it. You were quick to point out that the marketing strategy of "staying the course" had been very successful in the past. Ideas for new products generally came from the managers of the 40 restaurants or the customers who patronized the restaurants. Jiffy Foods did not maintain any product development structure or organization. As the vice president of marketing, your primary responsibilities centered around developing, implementing, and evaluating promotional campaigns, selecting sites for new stores, and working with the advertising agency to develop and evaluate campaigns.

As your meeting with the president concluded, she said, "It's Friday. I want you to think over the weekend about the way we develop new products and services. We need to do a better job. Maybe we should think about a different way of doing things. What we're doing is not producing the results we want, and we need to increase our sales. Let's meet on Monday to talk further. I want to see your preliminary plan first thing on Monday."

▲ SUMMARY OF CHAPTER OBJECTIVES

This chapter introduced the concept of product lines and how companies attempt to manage these product lines to achieve long-term customer satisfaction and financial success. We explored the strategies that companies use to develop new products and services, including the actual development process, branding, and the organizing of employees. Without a consistent flow of new products and services, few companies will achieve long-term success. New products are important to companies for the following reasons: (1) growth opportunities for the business; (2) efficient and effective use of company resources; (3) increasing market share and importance of the company within the market; and (4) exploiting and extending the product–service mix life cycle.

New product development strategies can be either reactive or proactive. The strategy employed depends on a firm's resources and market position. Some firms have chosen to be innovators and leaders in the market, whereas other firms are more comfortable in the follower role and tend to be more reactive than proactive. It is important to note that there are many success stories to support the use of both strategies.

Firms use many organizational structures to develop new products and services, the most common of which are new product committees, new product departments, product managers, and venture teams. The firm should provide an atmosphere conducive to the development of new ideas and support their progression through the development process.

The process used by many firms to develop new products includes the following steps: (1) idea generation; (2) product screening; (3) concept testing; (4) business analysis and test marketing; and (5) market introduction. Ideas can be generated through formal channels within the firm or through external sources such as competitors and customers. Ideas with good potential are screened, tested, and analyzed until management feels that they are ready for market introduction.

The importance of brands within the hospitality and tourism industry was explored. The important concepts of brands, brand names, brand marks, and trademarks were defined and discussed. Finally, the characteristics of effective branding were presented.

▲ KEY TERMS AND CONCEPTS

Acquisitions strategy

Alliances strategy

Brand marks

Brand names

Brands

Business analysis

Concept testing

Defensive strategy

Entrepreneurial strategy

Follow the leader

Idea generation

Imitative strategy

Innovation

Market introduction

Marketing strategy

New product committees

New product development

New product departments

Proactive strategies

Product line

Product managers

Product screening

Reactive strategies

Research and development
strategy

Second but better strategy

Trademarks

Venture teams

Win–win relationship

▲ QUESTIONS FOR REVIEW AND DISCUSSION

1. What is a product line?

2. What is the best type of new product development strategy: reactive or proactive? Explain your answer.

3. What are the four reasons it is important to develop and extend product lines within a business?

4. What is cannibalization, and how can it be reduced?

5. What steps are used to develop new products and services?

6. How are qualitative and quantitative analysis used in assessing potential new products and services?

7. Define and cite two examples for each of the following: brand; brand name; brand mark; and trade mark.

8. What are the characteristics of effective branding? Do you agree or disagree with these criteria? Can you cite examples of successful brands that do not meet these criteria? Why do you believe these brands are successful?

▲ NOTES

[1] Jennifer Waters, "R & I Special Report—Burger King," *Restaurants and Institutions*, October 1, 1998, pp. 54.

[2] Michola Zaklin, "Baskin-Robbins Scoops Up Healthier Fare." *Adweek's Marketing Week*, June 4, 1990, pp. 30–31.

[3] Glen L. Urban and John R. Hauser, *Design and Marketing of New Products*, 2nd edition (Englewood Cliffs, NJ: Prentice Hall, 1993).

8

Product–Service Mix Strategy

❖ Chapter Objectives

By the end of this chapter, you should understand:

1. The four levels comprising the product–service mix
2. The product life cycle and the role it plays in marketing strategy
3. The wheel of retailing concept
4. How to use a resource allocation model
5. The issues surrounding managing services

❖ Chapter Outline

❖ Chapter Opening Profile

TRYING TO REPOSITION A PRODUCT BY changing a brand's name or identity isn't easy. SBG Enterprises, which develops brand identities, helped Milwaukee-based Marcus Corp. turn its Budgetel brand into Baymont Inn and Suites.[1] Apparently, the Budgetel name was dated, and it created some confusion among consumers. Even though consumers recognized the name, they weren't clear on the brand's image. Hotel firms are replacing terms like *economy* and *budget* with terms like *suites* and *inns*. Consumers still want a bargain but they do not want to present themselves as cheap. Also, terms like *economy* and *budget* have been overused and they put constraints on a brand's pricing strategy.

Marcus Corp.'s decision to change the name was not a hasty one. The Budgetel name had been used for 25 years, a large investment in building brand equity. Unfortunately, the brand name locked the product into a price point, and it was often confused for a telecommunications company. SBG worked with Lexicon, a firm that specializes in naming brands, to compile a list of 3,000 possible names. However, only 20 of those names were available for legal reasons. The name Baymont was chosen because is suggests a pleasant place and a quality image. Few, if any, Baymont properties overlook a mountain or a bay, but the firm is interested in projecting a relaxing image.

▲ INTRODUCTION

Developing a sound marketing strategy is a cornerstone of successful marketing. When a company is successful and its marketing programs are the benchmarks among their competitors, it is often the result of a sound and well-developed marketing strategy. This chapter examines the key aspects of managing the product–service mix. The first area concerns the **product levels** and their importance in differentiating the product. The second area is the **product life cycle**. This advances the concept that all products and services progress through a life cycle, much as people do. The concept of the product life cycle is that alternative marketing strategies are best used at different stages in the life cycle. The third area involves the **resource allocation models** used by firms to determine the most effective use of company resources within their product portfolios. Most firms have a limited amount of resources, and it is necessary to prioritize their expenditures based on potential returns and company goals. Finally, this chapter examines the various issues surrounding managing services. The characteristics that differentiate services from goods create different challenges for managers. It is important to manage supply and demand in service industries because of the inability to maintain inventories for intangible products.

There are basically four product levels: the core product, the facilitating products, the supporting products, and the augmented product. The **core product** is the basic form of the product. In other words, it is the main benefit sought by customers in an attempt to satisfy their needs as recognized by the gap between the ideal state and actual state. For example, in the context of a restaurant, the core service is the food that will resolve the consumer's state of hunger. As one can see, there are many ways that this need can be satisfied. Similarly, consumers in the lodging industry are looking for guestrooms with a shower.

Two of the other product levels can be referred to as **peripheral services**. The peripheral services expand the core offering and can be used to obtain a competitive advantage. The peripheral services must meet or exceed customer expectations if customers are to be satisfied. The **facilitating products** are services that enable the customer to consume the core product. They must be present to make the product available where and when the customer wants it. Hotels have front desks and reservations departments, and restaurants have hostesses and waiters. **Supporting products** are additional goods and services that can be bundled with the core service in an attempt to increase the overall utility or value for consumers. Examples of supporting products within the hotel industry include concierge service, multilingual staff, 24-hour room service, and complimentary newspapers for business travelers.

The **augmented product** is the core product and peripheral services that combine to form the package of benefits offered by a product

product level position of a firm in an industry

product life cycle four stages of a product or service: introduction, growth, maturity, decline

resource allocation models used by firms to determine the most effective use of company resources within their product portfolios

core product basic form of the product

peripheral services additional goods and services that expand the core offering and can be used to obtain competitive advantage

facilitating products additional goods and services that enable the customer to consume the core product

supporting products additional goods and services that can be bundled with the core service in an attempt to increase the overall utility or value for customers

augmented product core product and peripheral services that combine to form the package of benefits offered by a product or service or service. In addition, the augmented product considers how a service is delivered. In other words, the augmented product encompasses everything surrounding the service and its delivery, including intangible attributes such as accessibility and atmosphere. For example, Planet Hollywood restaurants seek a competitive advantage by offering an atmosphere that is unrivaled by other casual restaurants. All of the restaurants in this segment offer similar food products and accept credit cards, but few provide the level of atmosphere and entertainment available at Planet Hollywood.

▲ PRODUCT LIFE CYCLE

The product life cycle theory describes how a product progresses from its infancy as a new product in development, through a growth phase, to a maturity phase, and then, eventually into decline. Each stage of the product life cycle will be discussed in detail, followed by a discussion of the uses of the theory. Figure 8.1 illustrates the general shape of a typical product life cycle and its four stages.

Introduction Stage

The first stage of the product life cycle is called the introduction stage. At this point, the product has been through the new product development process presented in Chapter 7. It has survived analysis and testing, and it was deemed worthy of market introduction. The product represents a new concept, so there are no competitors offering the same product and, if the product is unique, there aren't even similar products in the market. Therefore, the goals for the firm are to develop product awareness and stimulate trial and adoption. To accomplish these goals, the firm must make a sizeable investment with low sales, leading to negative profits. The investment is in the form of capital expenditures on facilities and inventories, and a

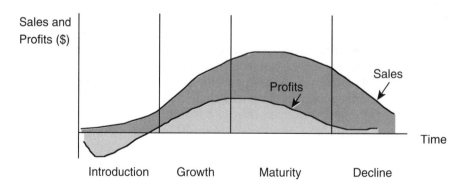

FIGURE 8.1 The Product Life Cycle

promotional campaign to attract customers. However, even though the cost per unit of manufacturing the product or providing the service is high, it is often necessary to offer discounts and other promotions to induce trial. The pricing decision is usually based on the estimated costs and demand for the product because there are no direct competitors.

During the introductory phase, customers tend to be innovators who are willing to take risks to try new products and services. The distribution of the product is selective in an attempt to build a customer base before adding new units or distributors. Many of the large hotel and restaurant chains started with one unit and eventually grew to become a large chain or franchise. McDonald's was started as a single restaurant in Illinois, and Holiday Inn started with a single property in Tennessee. Some hotels may start with a test market property, but many recent concepts were started with more than one property. For instance, Wyndham's Garden Hotels were opened with multiple units in an attempt to generate more awareness and interest than could have been attained with a single property. It is more common for restaurants to begin as single-unit operations and add more units as they become successful and generate cash flow. This is due to the fact that repeat business can be generated from the local market, whereas hotels are dependent on a more transient market.

Growth Stage

If the firm is able to accomplish its goals in the introductory stage and the product builds an adequate customer base, the product will move into a growth stage. The growth stage is evidenced by rapidly rising sales and profits, and a decreasing cost per unit for providing the product or service. This positive outlook attracts competitors who are willing to take the risk because of the customer acceptance and the increasing profit margins. In this stage, the profits being generated by the product allow the firm to consider product extensions, new markets, and organizational expansion in the form of additional properties or units. Minor changes may be made in the unit design and concept, but normally the owners attempt to standardize the physical plant, thereby reducing developmental costs. The owners' rationalization is that if the original unit is successful, additional units will also be successful.

During the growth stage, the organization typically expands its distribution by adding new units. These units are often located in clusters within geographic regions. The development of the Courtyard brand of hotels by Marriott International is an illustration of this approach. Following a period of test marketing and research and development in the Atlanta area, the Courtyard brand was developed in clusters around major cities. This clustering allows the consolidation of staff-support services in a central location, where it can be provided to several hotel properties, thereby reducing the operating cost of each hotel.

It is during the growth stage that the second group of consumers, known as early adopters, begins to enter the market as they obtain feedback from the innovators. The increase in competitors during this stage and the need to build market share put downward pressure on price. The use of the intensive distribution strategy helps the firm build its customer base and market share by creating more awareness and interest in the product. Hopefully, as the firm penetrates the market and develops loyal customers, it is possible to reduce the amount of sales promotions and discounts. Instead, more emphasis can be placed on other forms of promotion such as personal selling and advertising.

Maturity Stage

If an organization is able to achieve the desired success in the growth stage, it will eventually move to the maturity stage. At this point, the organization has expanded as much as the market will allow, and volume, measured in annual gross sales, will level off. Companies in this stage of the product life cycle find that the market is often saturated and competition is increasing from alternative options. Industry profits tend to peak near the end of the growth stage as the product moves into maturity. However, there are still high profits due to the large volume and the beginning decline in the number of competitors. In other words, the weaker competitors leave as the market reaches equilibrium and stronger competitors battle for market share. A common strategy is for firms to standardize products and remove some of the less-valued attributes. This streamlining will enable the firm to take advantage of the **economies of scale** associated with higher volume, thereby widening the profit margin. For example, Delta Airlines introduced box lunches that passengers received as they boarded the plane. A couple of years later, it was announced that the airline will no longer include sandwiches in the box lunches, a move that is expected to save tens of millions of dollars.

economies of scale
cost efficiencies derived from operating at high volumes

There may also be changes in consumer preference, as the consumer turns toward newer and more innovative concepts. For example, the original pizza restaurants have seen competition in the form of gourmet products and "make-your-own" concepts. The advertising and promotions during this stage focus on differentiating the product, although it can be difficult because the core products tend to be very similar. This product homogeneity increases the consumer's price sensitivity and firms are forced to price at the market. At this point, the market may fragment into more segments with different needs and price sensitivities. Most hotel chains offer more than one brand in an attempt to attract consumers from various market segments.

In this stage, the distribution of the product becomes even more intensive to ensure consumer convenience and accessibility. This expansion can be developed internally, or it can be the result of mergers and acquisitions. Weaker competitors may be acquired by stronger—and often larger—competitors who wish to gain access to new markets. Most of the products in the United States are in the maturity phase, which can last indefinitely. Most consumers have been added to the innovators and early adopters, leaving little room for growth in the sales for the product category. As a result, individual brands can only increase sales at the expense of their competitors, rather than rely on new consumers in the market. The fast-food industry is notorious for its fierce competition in advertising and pricing. McDonald's and Burger King have been involved in the burger wars for two decades, as the battle for market share continues.

Decline Stage

The last stage in the product life cycle is decline. During this stage, industry sales and profits are declining more rapidly, and the number of competitors is reduced to those with very strong positions. The only new consumers entering the market are the laggards, and prices are often cut even further. Firms have progressed through the experience curve and the cost per unit has been driven down with accumulated volume. At this point, firms have phased out the weaker brands and focus more on the strong brands. The product consists of the core product and only those peripheral services that are of real value to the consumer. Distribution is selective as weaker outlets are closed. Hospitality firms will sell or close their properties in markets that aren't performing well in an attempt to free up resources for the more successful properties.

The major objective during the decline stage is to reduce overall marketing expenditures and increase cash flow. This strategy is referred to as "milking the brand" because you are trying to get as much profit from it as possible. The decrease in marketing expenditures comes in the form of reduced customer service, reduced quality and variety, reduced distribution, and reduced promotion and advertising. Firms are left with a group of loyal customers that may or may not be large enough to continue with a profitable operation. It is critical that firms are relatively certain about the product's status in the product life cycle because these actions may force the product into decline prematurely. Many independent hospitality and travel firms are finding themselves in the decline stage as large chains and franchises take advantage of their lower costs and engage in price wars that force the weaker firms out of the market.

▲ APPLYING THE PRODUCT LIFE CYCLE

McDonald's Corporation serves as an excellent illustration of the way a corporation progresses through the organizational life cycle. McDonald's Corporation, under the direction of Ray Kroc, began with a few units in the mid-1950s. The corporation quickly achieved a sound financial base and rapidly moved into the growth stage of the life cycle. New units were continually being constructed, and soon the familiar red and white buildings with the golden arches could be found throughout the country. However, an important decision was made as McDonald's was nearing the end of the maturity stage. The upper-level management felt that the red and white buildings with the golden arches had lived out their useful life and that a new image was needed.

With this in mind, the corporation began to rethink the design and decor of both new units and the vast majority of existing units. They determined that a more subdued appeal was needed to attract different target markets. The term *fast food* was not used in any promotional or corporate literature. Instead, emphasis was placed on the image of McDonald's as a restaurant. Instead of leveling off sales, McDonald's was able to inject new life into its concept and therefore continued to expand and increase the number of units, total sales, and bottom-line profits. Later in McDonald's history, when sales growth had begun to slow, the corporation's leaders launched a breakfast program. Before McDonald's had served meals only during lunch and dinner. By serving breakfast, the company was able to increase sales without adding new units or franchisees. Later, they added another feature that is very common today—the drive-through window. More recently, McDonald's has developed units in nontraditional locations as a means of increasing sales. These new locations include gas stations and convenience stores, as well as retail locations such as Wal-Mart.

Developing Strategies for the Product Life Cycle

A number of strategies have been used for the various stages in the product life cycle. To develop strategies, however, management must first analyze the life cycle. This can be done in a seven-step process:

1. Compile Historical Data.   It is imperative that hospitality firms compile historical sales data. Ideally, these data should be available for the entire history of the organization. The specific type of data needed include sales volume (in units), prices, total sales revenue, costs, and profits.

2. Identify Competitive Trends.   Recent activities of major competitors should be monitored closely to determine changes in market share and position, as well as changes in quality of the product–service mix. Additionally, the other elements of the marketing mix should be monitored for significant changes.

3. Determine Changes in Product–Service Mix.   The marketplace must be monitored to learn about new products and services that other hospitality organizations are introducing and anticipate the potential effects on your operation.

4. Study the Product Life Cycles of Similar Products.   It is helpful to study the product life cycle of similar products or services to determine whether a pattern exists. Rarely is a product or service so new and unusual that it is not possible to compare it with a previous one.

5. ***Project Sales.*** Based on the data collected, sales for a two-to-three year period should be projected. Applying computerized statistical techniques may be particularly beneficial at this stage. Specialized software packages are available that will allow a marketing manager to develop sophisticated sales forecasts. However, for many business decisions, the statistical procedures and techniques that are part of spreadsheet software, such as Microsoft Excel, will suffice. The software will permit the development of multiple scenarios, or what-if scenarios by altering the levels of the decision variables. In addition to projecting sales, management should examine key financial ratios and other indicators of financial performance.

6. ***Locate Current Position on the Life Cycle.*** Based on the historical data, as well as the projections, it should now be possible to locate the position on the product life cycle. This position is used to determine the most appropriate baseline marketing strategies.

7. ***Develop Strategies.*** Once the position is located on the product life cycle, strategy formulation begins. Table 8.1 illustrates the characteristics and strategies that apply to different stages in the product life cycle. These strategies should not be viewed as being absolutely firm, but they do represent the most widely accepted ideas in the marketing community.

Ways to Extend the Product Life Cycle

One of the marketing manager's goals is to extend the product life cycle as long as possible. By doing this, cash flow can be extended and greater long-term profitability will result. There are several techniques that can be used to accomplish this.

Increasing Sales to Existing Customers. During the maturity stage of the product life cycle, the rate of sales growth begins to decrease and eventually levels off because most of the potential users of the product have either been converted or left the market. Under normal circumstances, it becomes very difficult and expensive to identify potential new customers and convert them into buyers. One way to increase sales and market share under these circumstances is to sell more to existing customers. There are basically two alternatives: encourage the customers to purchase more on each occasion or encourage the customers to purchase more frequently. Hospitality and travel firms accomplish this with frequent traveler programs that reward heavy users with free products and services. Another common method of increasing sales to existing customers is the use of product bundling. Fast-food companies such as McDonald's and Taco Bell introduced the concepts of "value meals" and "super sizing," which encourage the consumer to purchase larger quantities than normal because of a higher perceived value. Disney has also bundled its offerings in an attempt to increase consumer spending. Travelers enjoy the convenience of one-stop shopping and the lure of a price incentive for purchasing

Table 8.1	Characteristics and Strategies for Stages of the Product–Service Mix Life Cycle			
	Stage I *Introduction*	*Stage II* *Growth*	*Stage III* *Maturity*	*Stage IV* *Decline*
Characteristics				
Sales	Low	Rapidly rising	Peak	Declining
Profits	Negative	Positive and increasing	High, starting to decline	Declining
Cash flow	Negligible	Moderate	High	Low
Customers	Innovators and some early adopters	Remaining early adopters and some early majority	Remaining early majority and late majority	Laggards
Competitors	Few	Increasing in number and strength	Many	Declining in number
Strategies				
Marketing objective	Create trial and awareness	Increase sales and maximize market share	Increase profits and maintain market share	Decrease market expenditures and maximize short term profits
Product	Core product with some basic peripheral services	Minor product changes and extensions	Add attributes with positive differentiation	Core product and key attributes
Distribution	Selective	Becoming intensive	Intensive	Selective
Price	Set initial price based on costs and estimated demand	Price to penetrate market based on actual demand	Price low to increase market share	Reduce price to maintain volume
Promotion	Create trial and awareness through sales promotions	Build awareness and interest and reduce sales promotions	Used to differentiate among major competitors	Reduce expenditures and focus on loyal customers

the bundle rather than each component separately. Disney has expanded beyond the product–service offerings of theme parks and hotels to include a line of cruise ships. This affords them the opportunity to sell travel packages that include several days at the theme parks while staying in a Disney hotel, followed by a cruise on one of its Disney cruise ships.

Increasing the Number of Users. Another strategy used to extend the product life cycle is to seek new users of the product. The goal is to increase the size of the overall market by identifying those who have not previously purchased the products or services. Several of the fast-food companies have used this strategy very successfully. As the number of primary locations for new stores decreased, these companies have sought additional locations where they might attract new customers. For example, these companies have developed kiosk locations within stores, shopping malls, and gas stations along the highways. By expanding the definition of suitable location, they have been able to increase the number of purchasers, increase sales, and extend the product life cycle.

Finding New Uses. Within the realm of product marketing, one of the ways product life cycles can be extended is to find new uses for products. For example, aspirin is being used to prevent heart attacks in addition to its use for headaches, and baking soda is being use to deodorize refrigerators in addition to its use in baking. In some cases, new uses for products are discovered and marketed by the firm. However, in other instances, they are the result of market feedback. For example, many restaurants realize that it is relatively easy to run a catering operation out of the same facility that is used to serve regular customers. The catering operation uses the same equipment and adds little to the fixed costs of operating the restaurant, but it brings in additional revenue that can enhance the firm's overall financial condition. Interestingly, a lot of restaurants that didn't explore this avenue until they received repeated inquiries regarding catering services.

Pros and Cons of the Product Life Cycle

As with most concepts or theories, the product life cycle has its supporters and its opponents. There has been a good deal of debate over the applicability and usefulness of the concept in the real world. The following discussion presents the pros and cons.

Pros. Supporters argue that firms that apply the concept correctly are able to identify the stage in which the organization or an individual product finds itself and then use this knowledge to formulate better marketing plans. Once a product's position in the product life cycle is determined, firms are able to consider the characteristics associated with the respective stage and use the aforementioned strategies. This would lead to the correct mix of products and services to improve the performance of the entire organization and allow the firm to analyze trends in the product–service mix as well as the impact this mix will have on short-term and long-term financial performance.

In addition, proponents argue that this will encourage firms to be more proactive in recognizing changes in the environment and taking advantage of opportunities. It will also help them recognize potential threats and implement strategies to avoid or minimize any negative impacts. Many products that are currently in the maturity stage of the product life cycle have been there for some time and have managed to stay profitable through product changes and extensions. Successful marketing managers have learned the art of extending the product life cycle by adapting to changes in the market and implementing timely growth strategies.

Cons.   The opponents of the product life cycle concept state their case with equal vigor. They contend that few products or services actually conform to the shape of the curve illustrated in Figure 8.1. Rather, the curve may rise and fall in any number of patterns, each unique to the product or service itself. If managers believe that a product follows the normal life cycle curve, the product's demise may become a self-fulfilling prophecy. As industry sales begin to decline, a firm may decide to reduce distribution and marketing expenditures in conformance with the recommendations for decline stage strategy. This may lead to the premature decline of the product with substantial consequences.

Opponents of the concept also claim that it is often difficult to determine the exact stage in which a product lies. There are clearly no indicators to mark the transition from one stage to another. It is possible that changes in industry sales or firm sales could be the result of temporary conditions, and it may be possible to rejuvenate the product and extend the product life cycle. A product could remain in the maturity stage indefinitely if management is able to continually reinvent it. The product life cycle is more of a descriptive tool, than a prescriptive tool. It cannot be used to forecast changes because of the various shapes and timeframes associated with different products and industries.

Finally, opponents of the product life cycle concept indicate that some marketing managers place too much faith in it. These individuals focus too much attention on the product life cycle and forget about all the other environmental factors that can influence the success of a product or service. This marketing myopia, or narrow-mindedness, can cause firms to miss opportunities and not take risks that could be advantageous in the long run. Finally, the product life cycle can put too much emphasis on the development of new products to the detriment of existing products. Managers are painfully aware that as products reach decline, they will be responsible for finding ways to replace the lost revenues.

Whether you agree or disagree with the use of the product life cycle, it is important to view it solely as a tool. Complete reliance on the product life cycle as the basis for marketing management decisions would be unwise. Equally unwise would be to totally ignore the sales trends that are the foundation of the product life cycle. The product life cycle is best characterized as a valuable tool for a marketing manager to use in analyzing past market behaviors and future marketing strategies.

▲ OTHER PRODUCT CONCEPTS

This section presents two other concepts that should be discussed to provide a thorough understanding of product management. These concepts are all interrelated in that they are based on the management of the marketing mix and the positioning of products in the marketplace. Firms change their product–service mixes over time to reflect changes in consumers' tastes and lifestyles. The two concepts in this section address the question of resource allocation as it relates to the firm's image and its mix of products and services.

Wheel of Retailing

The **wheel of retailing** is a concept that was originally used to describe the evolution of department stores and other retail outlets. However, it can be applied very easily to the hospitality and tourism industry. It is founded on the notion that there is some type of impetus for retail firms that enter the low end of the market with basic products and low prices, to gravitate toward the high end of the market (see Figure 8.2). This is accomplished by adding value through new features and amenities, and raising prices. Firms also look to move to locations with more traffic and higher rents or real estate values. Eventually, this continual upward movement of firms and their products provides an opportunity for new competitors to enter the market at the lower end of the market. This repositioning can backfire and cause a firm to lose sales and market share.

wheel of retailing
evolution of an organization from a low end provider to a high end provider

    The retailing world and the hospitality industry are filled with examples of how the wheel of retailing works. Sears was the original low-end department store serving rural areas throughout the United States. Over time, Sears increased its inventories of popular brand names and moved to shopping malls and strip malls on major roads. As Sears' prices continued to increase, Kmart decided to start a new low-end operation. Sears

High End

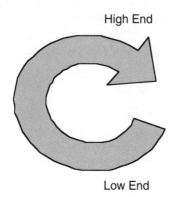

Low End

FIGURE 8.2   The Wheel of Retailing

lost a good deal of market share and even attempted to roll back prices to return to its original position, but it was too late. Surprisingly, Kmart followed in Sears' footsteps and added brand names and moved to more expensive locations. This opened the door for Wal-Mart to occupy the low-end position and the firm has attained the highest market share in the industry, leaving both Sears and Kmart to question their strategies. Wal-Mart has not made the mistake of moving up the wheel of retailing toward the high end and away from their strengths.

The hotel industry has demonstrated a similar pattern. Holiday Inn and Howard Johnson's were the original economy hotel chains. However, both of these chains attempted to become more like the Marriott and Sheraton chains that occupied positions in the middle to upper-end of the market with more amenities and higher prices. This vacated the low-end position that was eventually filled by other firms like Red Roof Inns and Days Inn. The economy segment has become one of the fastest-growing segments, attracting more and more competitors. Unfortunately, very few firms are successful at recapturing a market once they abandon it.

One might wonder what compels companies to leave their comfortable positions for the risk of new markets. One of the reasons responsible for this phenomenon is the allure of high prices and high profit margins. In the hotel industry the daily cost of servicing a room between guests ranges from around $15 to $50. At the same time, the **average daily rate** (ADR) paid for most hotel rooms ranges from around $40 to $300. The additional amenities offered at higher-priced properties do not substantially increase the variable costs of providing the service. This potential for increasing the profit margin is difficult to ignore. However, hotel chains may underestimate the investment necessary to obtain the expensive real estate and add restaurants and indoor pools. Also, once a brand is identified in the minds of consumers, it is almost impossible to change their perceptions.

average daily rate average rate paid for occupied hotel rooms on a daily basis

The other reason that has been used to explain this phenomenon is the prestige, or lack thereof, associated with a hotel chain. Most managers and college graduates want to work for prestigious hotels like the Four Seasons or the Ritz-Carlton. Managers either consciously or subconsciously adapt the hotel to be more like the chains that they aspire to, rather than exercise sound marketing strategies and planning. Similarly, most people would rather work for Bloomingdale's or Macy's than Sears or Kmart.

Resource Allocation Models

It is important for firms to view themselves as a portfolio of products that both provide funds and need funds. Within the portfolio some brands or items are in industries or categories that show strong potential for future growth, whereas others don't show the same potential. In addition, some of the brands or items have strong positions in their industries or categories while others do not. These brands or items can be referred to as **strategic business units** (SBUs) because each is viewed as a separate en-

strategic business units brands or units that have their own sets of market conditions and competitors

tity with its own set of market conditions and competitors. All of a firm's SBUs will affect a firm's cash flow by providing a source of funds through revenues and using funds in the form of expenses to produce the product and compete in the marketplace.

A few variations of **resource allocation models** are similar in their matrix approaches. The cells within the matrix are classified using the SBU's ability to act as a source of funds (e.g., relative market share or competitive position) and its need for funds based on future growth potential (e.g., market growth rate or industry attractiveness). This process of plotting SBUs and determining the best sources and uses for funds will aid an organization in allocating its finite resources. The resource allocation process will be explained using the **Boston Consulting Group (BCG) matrix** because it is the most common, straightforward resource allocation model in marketing.

The BCG matrix is illustrated in Figure 8.3 with four cells based on two axes. The horizontal axis is labeled *relative market share* and can be viewed as a proxy for competitive position. Relative market share refers to a firm's market share relative to its largest competitor. The vertical axis is labeled *market growth rate* and can be viewed as a proxy for industry attractiveness, or future growth potential. The market growth rate is usually based on average annual growth rate over the last few years, depending

resource allocation models used by firms to determine the most effective use of company resources within their product portfolios

Boston Consulting Group (BCG) matrix commonly used resource allocation model

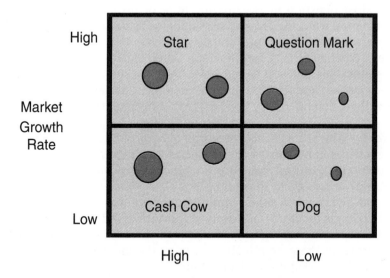

FIGURE 8.3 The Boston Consulting Group Matrix. *Source: Reprinted from Long Range Planning, B. Hedley, "Strategy and the Business Portfolio," p. 12, February 1977, with permission from Elsevier Science.*

on the age of the industry, or category. There are two levels, high and low, for each axis, resulting in four cells.

Two other factors are important in evaluating SBUs: the size of the circle and the placement within the cell. The size of the circle representing each SBU gives an indication as to the actual size of the unit measured in sales or volume. This is important because some SBUs may generate a good deal of revenue based on sheer volume but not look as attractive in terms of relative market share and market growth rate. The SBU's placement within the cell is also important because the axes represent a continuous scale even though there are only two labels. Two SBUs could be on opposite sides of the same cell and should be viewed differently. The ensuing discussion will explain the characteristics and marketing objectives associated with each of the four cells.

Question Marks. The SBUs in this category contain products and services that have low relative market shares in industries or categories with high market growth rates. This is a critical category for managers because question marks can either improve their market shares or the growth rate in the industry could decline. At this point, these SBUs require a good deal of cash to increase sales and build market share. However, with limited available resources, not all question marks can be completely funded, and choices have to be made. If a question mark does not receive adequate funding, it is almost certain that its business position will not improve. Most question marks provide little or no positive cash flow and must be supported for growth or eliminated from the portfolio. SBUs in this category are often represented with relatively new products in new markets, creating a risky environment. When Marriott introduced its Residence Inns, this division would have been considered a question mark. The properties were trying to build a customer base among business travelers with an extended stay concept that showed potential for growth.

Stars. The SBUs in this category contain products with high relative market shares in industries or categories with high market growth rates. This is the second best category for producing positive cash flows, and the objective is to build these products. The SBUs' strong business positions and high market shares provide good returns and become a good source of funds for the firm. However, they are in industries or categories that are experiencing high market growth rates. This will attract many competitors and require a high level of marketing expenditures in order for the SBU to compete and maintain its business position. Therefore, these SBUs are normally self-sustaining in that they don't require funds from other sources, but they aren't able to supply much in the way of excess funds for other SBUs.

Cash Cows. The SBUs in this category contain products with high relative market shares in industries or categories with low market growth rates. Products or divisions that are cash cows are the best source for positive cash flows because they have strong sales in established markets. There is not much growth potential, and the risk of new competitors is low. Cash cows are used as sources of funds for the SBUs in the other categories, especially question marks. However, it is important that as much of the cash flow as necessary to maintain or hold the market shares for cash cows is kept within the division or SBU. They are the foundation of the firm's portfolio, making it possible to develop new products and take chances with other existing products.

Dogs. The SBUs in this category contain products with low relative market shares in industries or categories with low market growth rates. Dogs are the least attractive category in the matrix. They generate low or negative cash flows because of their poor business positions and the low rate of growth in their markets. These SBUs are drains on the firm's resources and should be phased out or divested. Marketing expenditures should be decreased unless there is some potential for repositioning the product. Most firms will try to sell these divisions and products to companies that are better equipped to market them while they are still viable.

Resource Allocation Models and the Product Life Cycle

There is a relationship between resource allocation models like the BCG matrix and the product life cycle. The two dimensions in the product life cycle are time and annual sales. The stages are based on the rate of sales growth over time. The two dimensions in resource allocation models are competitive position or market share and industry attractiveness or market growth rate. The underlying premise of the resource allocation models is that products evolve from question marks into stars and then into cash cows. When the market stops growing and/or the product loses market share, it will move into the dog category, where it is eventually divested. This is similar to a product's movement from introduction (question mark), through a growth stage (star), to maturity (cash cow), and eventually into decline (dog).

In addition to the similarities in evolution or movement through the matrix, the two concepts share similar characteristics and strategies. Question marks are often new products, like those found in the introduction stage having negative cash flows, but good growth potential. Stars experience rapid growth and start to realize positive cash flows, like products in the growth stage. Cash cows have large sales volumes and market shares, resulting in large cash flows, like the products that survive the maturity stage. Finally, dogs have low market shares and decreasing cash flows, just like products in the decline stage.

Marketing strategies are also similar. Marketing expenditures are greatest for question marks and stars, like products in the introduction and growth stages. Money is spent selectively to hold market share during the maturity phase and for cash cows, whereas marketing expenditures are very low for dogs and products in decline. Finally, both concepts can overemphasize the importance of new product development to the detriment of existing products. Many companies have survived with cash cows and products in the maturity stage over a long period of time. Many local or regional food chains, airlines, and large hotel chains like Sheraton and Holiday Inn have survived with minor product extensions over their respective life cycles.

▲ MANAGING IN THE SERVICE ENVIRONMENT

As discussed in Chapter 2, certain characteristics are associated with services that distinguish them from tangible products. Most of these characteristics stem from the fact that services are intangible. In other words, services cannot be held, inspected before purchase, or inventoried. As a result, the consumer is actually part of the production process, making it difficult to maintain the consistency and efficiency that a firm can experience in the manufacture of tangible products.

Conflicts between Operations and Marketing

Within any service organization there are bound to be conflicts between those responsible for sales and marketing and those with operational responsibilities. In virtually every hotel, those working in operating departments could share stories of how sales and marketing personnel have made promises to clients that were impossible to fulfill to the satisfaction of the client. For example, hotel salespeople will sometimes price meals for a banquet below the benchmark set by the catering department in order to book a group into the hotel. Similarly, sales and marketing personnel could share stories of how the operating personnel were inflexible and cost them business. One of the best ways to keep the conflicts to a minimum is to try to look at things from the other person's perspective.

Sales and marketing personnel tend to view the world from a revenue perspective. That is, everything that they attempt to do is targeted toward increasing revenue. Every new group that is booked into the hotel is seen as additional revenue. If a promotion is developed to increase the number of covers served in the dining room, the goal is to increase revenue. From this perspective, it is best to have many options and flexibility in providing a service.

Operations personnel, on the other hand, tend to view the world from a cost containment perspective. All efforts are focused on increasing efficiency and reducing costs to the lowest level that will keep the operation running smoothly. The main objective of production and operations is to standardize as much as possible and lower the cost per unit of providing a service. Both sales and marketing and operations want to increase profits, but they focus on different components of the profit equation.

When it comes to offering expanded products and services as a means of gaining a competitive advantage, the sales and marketing staff will be eager to offer many alternatives. However, they may not stop to think how the new products and services will integrate with those that already exist. Operations personnel will tend to take a very conservative point of view, trying to keep the operation as simple and straightforward as possible.

Some of the conflict between the two functions stems from the way each is evaluated. A salesperson's performance is based on generating revenue and meeting quotas, whereas people in operations are rewarded for lowering costs and maintaining quality control. There isn't much incentive for the two departments to work together, even though a joint effort would benefit the company as a whole.

Lovelock[2] recommends several ways that managers can be persuaded to build bridges between the functional areas:

1. *Transfer Managers Across Functional Areas.* In other words, have them work in the different departments so they gain an understanding of the nuances of each area.

2. *Create Cross-Functional Teams.* Top management's goal should be to build on the energy of managers who have been working in different departments instead of letting their energies evolve into internal disputes.

3. *Cross-Train Associates to Perform a Broader Variety of Tasks.* Moving hourly associates across departmental lines can serve to break down the barriers and build relationships that can help the departments work together more effectively.

4. *Delegate Authority to Individual Units.* Historically, operational managers in the hospitality industry have focused on cost containment. By transforming cost centers into profit centers and empowering managers and associates to take greater responsibility for both revenue generation and spending decisions, managers and associates focus more on the "big picture."

5. *Institute Gain-Sharing Programs.* Allowing managers and associates to share in the results from improved profits provides an incentive to continue to seek better ways to operate the business.

Managing Supply and Demand

Managing supply and demand in a service organization such as a hotel or restaurant is very difficult. Demand for services comes in waves and often is not as consistent as one would like. The demand may be seasonal, as with a resort hotel, or it may fluctuate by time of day, as with restaurants. It might also fluctuate by day of the week, as is the case with business-oriented hotels that are busy Monday through Thursday but quite slow on

Friday through Sunday. Managing the fluctuations in demand and the corresponding supply is perhaps one of management's greatest challenges.

Two calculations can be used to evaluate the extent to which the supply and demand is being successfully managed: **asset revenue generating efficiency** (ARGE) and **revenue per available room** (REVPAR). ARGE evaluates the relationship between actual revenue and maximum potential revenue. For example, within a hotel operation, the ARGE will examine the occupancy percentage and the average daily rate to determine the extent to which the revenue potential is being realized. Suppose that a hotel has 400 available rooms each day with a rack rate of $100. If all of the rooms were sold each day at this maximum rate, the maximum daily revenue would be $40,000. However, it is rare that a hotel would be able to do this consistently. Assume that over a period of time, say, a month, the hotel achieved a 68 percent occupancy rate and had an average daily rate of $75. This means that on average, 272 rooms were sold each day at an average daily room rate of $75, resulting in total revenue of $20,400. This figure is then divided by the maximum potential daily revenue of $40,000, and the ARGE is calculated to be 51 percent (20,400/40,000 × 100). The ARGE is useful as an evaluation tool for sales and marketing personnel because it measures performance against the potential revenue at full capacity.

REVPAR, or revenue per available room, is calculated by multiplying the average daily rate by the occupancy percentage. For example, if a hotel has an average daily rate of $85 and is running an occupancy percentage of 75 percent, then the REVPAR would be $85 × 75 percent = $63.75. This figure, like ARGE, accounts for the amount of unused capacity. An alternative calculation would be to multiply the average daily rate by the number of occupied rooms to get the total room revenue, and then divide total room revenue by the total number of rooms in the hotel to get the REVPAR. The main difference between ARGE and REVPAR is that REVPAR does not compare actual revenue to maximum potential revenue. However, REVPAR does give a measure that can be tracked over time to assess the hotel's performance. Higher values of REVPAR would denote more effective use of available resources.

One of the major issues facing service industries like hospitality and travel is the inability to inventory the product. Unused capacity is lost forever when there are empty hotel rooms, tables in restaurants, or seats on airplanes. The following strategies can be used to manage supply and demand.

Modify Price. Prices can be used to transfer demand from peak periods to nonpeak periods. Many restaurants in tourist areas use "early bird" prices to encourage price-sensitive consumers, like families and senior citizens, to eat earlier. Restaurants are able to offer a limited selection of meals at lower prices, enabling them to purchase and prepare in larger, more efficient volumes. This shifts the demand to a period when there are

---

asset revenue generating efficiency (ARGE) evaluates the relationship between actual revenue and maximum potential revenue

revenue per available room (REVPAR) calculated by multiplying the average daily rate by the occupancy percentage

empty tables and the customers can be easily accommodated. This results in less waiting and turning people away during the peak period between 7:00 PM and 10:00 PM. Firms can also raise prices during peak demand periods in an effort to shift demand to nonpeak periods. Hotels and fine dining restaurants use this practice to maximize the potential revenue from limited capacity.

Develop Programs to Boost Nonpeak Demand Periods. When the fast-food companies first began operation they were open only for lunch and dinner. They did not offer breakfast. After many years of operation, most began to develop breakfast programs, which resulted in a very significant increase in total revenue. This represents an example of how fast-food restaurants stimulated demand during a nonpeak period. In the case of fast-food companies that did not have any type of breakfast menu, they were stimulating business during a zero-volume period. Business-oriented hotels adopt the same sort of strategy when they offer special weekend rates and packages to boost occupancy during low-demand weekends.

Shift Demand through Reservations. All of the major hotel chains maintain toll-free telephone reservation services. If demand for a particular location exceeds capacity rather than losing the business, they will simply offer to make a reservation at a hotel that is closest to the desired location. If a hotel company operates multiple brands and the hotel at which the guest is seeking a reservation is full, the reservations agent will offer to make a reservation at a nearby hotel that is owned, franchised, or operated by the same company. For example, if a customer wants to make a reservation at a Quality Inn and all of the rooms are reserved, the reservations agent would try to make a reservation at a nearby Comfort Inn or a Sleep Inn because they are part of the same organization. In this way, the company still realizes the revenue, while providing a valuable service to the guest.

Increase Personnel Efficiency. By using part-time employees and cross-training employees to perform two or more jobs, management can improve employee productivity. Restaurants can decrease the time it takes to take orders and prepare meals, enabling them to serve more customers in the same time period.

Increase Consumer Involvement in Self-Service Aspects of the Service Delivery System. Service firms are able to decrease labor costs and increase supply by having consumers become more involved in the service delivery process. A common trend in restaurants is to offer buffet-style service. In fact, this is one of the methods used by many of the food service operations at Epcot Center in Disneyworld to increase capacity, revenues, and profits.

▲ MARKETING ACTION NOW!

This chapter discusses the use of resource allocation models for a firm's product portfolio. The original models were based on large companies with multiple divisions that were designated as strategic business units (SBUs). Also, the models were designed for use by firms offering a mix of tangible products. However, these models have been used successfully in smaller firms as well as service firms of all sizes. One of the potential uses for the BCG matrix is by restaurants in evaluating their menus.

McDonald's offers a variety of sandwiches and meals on its menus. Some of these items generate high revenues with little advertising, while others require larger marketing expenditures and more attention. However, some of the items receiving more attention generate higher revenues, while others have little or no positive cash flow. It is important to consider consumer trends that have affected the fast-food industry, and the growth potential in each of the markets. Also, remember that there are different competitors and levels of competition for some of the menu items.

1. Plot McDonald's menu items on a BCG matrix and explain your decisions.
2. Can this approach be used in fine dining restaurants? Explain your answer.

▲ SUMMARY OF CHAPTER OBJECTIVES

The product–service mix is an important component of a firm's marketing program. The other strategies (price, promotion, and distribution) are used to provide further assistance in positioning the brand in conjunction with the product–service mix. All of the strategies are based on the customers' wants and needs and the tradeoffs that are necessary to offer a competitive product. When managing a product or service, it is necessary to consider all of the product levels: the core product, the facilitating products, the supporting products, and the augmented product.

The product life cycle can be used to develop marketing strategies that are appropriate for the product or service throughout its useful life. Products evolve from introduction, through growth, into maturity, and eventually decline. History shows us that certain marketing strategies or actions are more appropriate in certain stages in the life cycle. The pros and cons of the product life cycle were presented, as well as the ways to extend the product life cycle. The wheel of retailing concept was introduced to explain why firms change their product–service mixes over time and make room for new competitors at the low end.

Some issues are unique to the managing of services that were discussed in this chapter. Most of the problems stem from the fact that services are intangible and cannot be inventoried. Therefore, it is crucial that firms concentrate on managing supply and demand so they can maximize potential revenue. Customers are an integral part of the service delivery process and should be included in the product–service mix strategy.

Finally, resource allocation models were introduced, and the Boston Consulting Group (BCG) matrix was presented in some detail. These types of models are useful to firms in establishing marketing budgets and developing marketing strategies in an attempt to achieve the firms' overall goals. Each strategic business unit has a unique set of conditions and competitors that must be monitored so the firm can analyze cash flow.

▲ KEY TERMS AND CONCEPTS

Asset revenue generating efficiency (ARGE)

Augmented product

Average daily rate (ADR)

Boston Consulting Group (BCG) matrix

Cash cows

Core product

Dogs

Economies of scale

Facilitating products

Market growth rate

Marketing strategy

Peripheral services

Product levels

Product life cycle

Product–service mix

Product–service mix differentiation

Question marks

Relative market share

Resource allocation models

Revenue per available room (REVPAR)

Stars

Strategic business units

Supporting products

Wheel of retailing

▲ QUESTIONS FOR REVIEW AND DISCUSSION

1. What are the four levels of a product? How can peripheral services be used to gain a competitive advantage?

2. What are the stages of the product life cycle? What are the characteristics of each stage?

3. What do you see as the advantages and disadvantages of using the product life cycle as a marketing tool?

4. How should a business go about developing a strategy for various stages in the product life cycle? What techniques are most appropriate for the various stages?

5. What are some of the ways to extend the product life cycle? Of these techniques, which one do you think is most useful? Why?

6. What is the wheel of retailing? Does it apply to the hospitality industry?

7. What are Lovelock's recommendations for reducing the conflicts between sales and operations?

8. What are the methods for managing supply and demand? Which methods are capable of increasing capacity for hospitality firms?

9. What are resource allocation models? How are they related to the product life cycle?

▲ NOTES

[1] Jeff Higley, "The Name Game," *Hotel & Motel Management*, February 1, 1999, pp. 36.

[2] Christopher H. Lovelock, *Product Plus: How Product + Service = Competitive Advantage* (New York: McGraw-Hill, Inc., 1994) pp. 351–352.

Chapter

9

Distribution, Intermediaries, and Electronic Commerce

❖ Chapter Objectives

By the end of this chapter, you should understand:

1. The role of distribution in hospitality and travel services
2. The issues surrounding channel organization and management
3. The types of intermediaries in the hospitality and travel industry
4. Electronic commerce and its role in distribution

❖ Chapter Outline

❖ Chapter Opening Profile

HOLIDAY INN EXPRESS STARTED OFFERING ITS customers complete on-line booking capabilities for Express hotels worldwide through the brand's new Web site. The Web site is intended to help both current and potential guests "stay smart" about Express hotels. According to John Sweetwood, president of Holiday Inn Express, "guests can make reservations by simply logging onto www. hiexpress.com. And, the brand's Internet presence also will introduce potential guests to Express hotels."[1]

In addition to the booking features, the user-friendly site features graphics that make it both visually appealing and easy to navigate. Visitors to the site can also obtain information about the Holiday Inn Express brand, which features a complimentary breakfast bar, free local phone calls, and travel tips from Randy Petersen, travel industry expert and editor of *InsideFlyer* magazine. The Holiday Inn Express Web site also enables consumers to enroll on-line in Priority Club Worldwide, the brand's frequent guest program. Finally, the site has plans to have select articles and information from the hotel's in-room magazine, *Navigator*, available on-line for consumers to sample.

▲ INTRODUCTION

Distribution is an important element of the marketing mix, but it is often difficult to understand its role in services marketing. Service channels are usually not traditional in the sense that there is a manufacturer, a whole-saler, and a retailer. Often, one firm performs all of the channel functions because there is no physical transportation of a product, and the production and consumption of the service occurs simultaneously. However, service firms in industries like hospitality and travel must still make decisions regarding **channel organization** and **channel management**.

One of the decisions that must be made by hotel and travel firms concerns the use of **intermediaries**. Intermediaries, like wholesalers and retailers, may be valuable to service firms because of their expertise and ability to specialize in certain channel functions. Also, government organizations such as travel bureaus exist to help promote and distribute travel services to individuals and groups for its constituents.

The fastest growing distribution alternative involves **electronic commerce** over the Internet. Hospitality and travel firms use this outlet to promote their services and offer a direct channel to consumers. This form of commerce is efficient and provides other advantages that will be discussed in this chapter.

▲ DISTRIBUTION MANAGEMENT

A firm's distribution strategy must be consistent with the other elements of its marketing mix in order to be successful. The overall position of the firm in the marketplace is established by many factors, including price levels, product–service mix characteristics, and distribution. The promotion strategy is used to convey this positioning strategy to potential users of the firm's product or service. The delivery of products or services is intertwined with these other decisions. For instance, consumers would not associate gourmet quality food with an establishment that is part of a food court in a shopping mall. Similarly, consumers would not expect to pay high prices for food purchased through this type of outlet.

The main objective of the distribution function is to get products and services to consumers where, when, and how they prefer them. A good distribution system will result in a smooth flow of products and services to consumers, while at the same time, achieving the firm's goals concerning market coverage, sales, and profitability. Firms have limited resources and must determine the most efficient and effective way to distribute their

channel organization the relationships between suppliers and sellers

channel management direction of participants in a channel organization

intermediaries organizations or individuals with expertise or the ability to specialize in certain channel functions (e.g. wholesalers and retailers)

electronic commerce business activity using a Web site as the primary means of providing information about and selling products and services products and services. Some of the necessary activities associated with distribution include: (1) communication and negotiation, (2) facilitating transactions, (3) storing and moving physical goods, and (4) installation and service.

Channel Organization

Channel design decisions must be made with regard to channel width (desired market coverage) and channel length (number of intermediaries). It is also possible to use a single channel to distribute a firm's products and services or multiple channels of various widths and lengths. Channel decisions are affected by product–service mix characteristics, market characteristics, and environmental characteristics. Obviously, the intangible nature of services tends to minimize the length of the channel of distribution. As discussed earlier, the service delivery process often requires consumers to be present during the production process. This eliminates the need for the storage and movement of a physical product. However, distribution is still an important consideration in the delivery of services. Some firms use a variety of channels depending upon the desired market coverage, the positioning of different services or brands, and the existence of different markets.

Channel Width. The channel-width decision is based on the desired amount of market coverage. In other words, larger widths would be associated with more market coverage. Basically, three channel-width strategies are employed by firms: (1) exclusive distribution, (2) selective distribution, and (3) intensive distribution. The width of the channel ranges from exclusive distribution (one outlet) to intensive distribution (as many outlets as possible). As mentioned earlier, this decision must be consistent with the firm's other marketing mix strategies.

The narrowest channel width is **exclusive distribution**, where a firm limits the availability of its products or services to a particular outlet. This is common among independent operators in the hospitality industry. Le Cirque 2000 restaurant in New York City is a single-unit operation, and it is the only place consumers can purchase and experience this firm's product. This is also true of independent hotels such as The Palace Hotel in New York City and resorts such as The Greenbrier in West Virginia or The Homestead in Virginia. Many single-unit restaurants and lodging facilities offer a personal touch and a one-of-a-kind experience. However, this individual attention comes at the expense of market coverage and the cost economies associated with high-volume business.

The middle channel width is referred to as **selective distribution**, where a firm uses more than one outlet but restricts availability of the product or service to a limited number of outlets. In the hospitality industry, many firms limit market coverage based on geographic segmentation. Some multiunit operations are strictly local, but some are regional or

exclusive distribution
where a firm limits the availability of its products or services to a particular outlet

selective distribution
where a firm uses more than one outlet but restricts availability of the product or service to a limited number of outlets

national with a limited number of outlets. Restaurant chains such as Hard Rock Cafe and Planet Hollywood limit themselves to large cities. In contrast, Bertucci's Brick Oven Pizzeria, based in Somerville, Massachusetts, limits itself to the Northeast and recently expanded to the mid-Atlantic region. Many other multiunit restaurant operations are family owned and stay within a very confined area. Some hotel chains such as Omni Hotels and Four Seasons have a limited number of hotels that are found in large cities, while others operate in limited regions. This distribution strategy is also popular among many travel agents, noncommercial foodservice firms, and certain airlines.

Finally, the widest channel strategy is **intensive distribution**, where firms attempt to make products and services available through as many outlets as possible. This is a common approach among franchise operations that use mass advertising and realize economies of scale. These firms, like McDonald's and Marriott Hotels, try to standardize their services so that consumers can expect a consistent experience at any of the firms' outlets. Consumers are more concerned with familiarity and consistency than with a one-of-a-kind experience. However, these firms do their best to provide consumers with a personal touch. Most airlines and rental car agencies use this distribution strategy as well.

intensive distribution firms attempt to make products and services available through as many outlets as possible

Channel Length. The channel-length decision is based on the number of intermediaries between the manufacturer and the final consumer. In the case of services, the channel is usually very short because of simultaneous production and consumption. In other words, consumers must be present to consume a service such as airline transportation, a meal, or an overnight stay in a hotel. A channel can either be direct from the manufacturer to the consumer or indirect with intermediaries performing some of the necessary channel functions.

Direct channels are the most popular for hospitality and travel firms, as well as for most other service industries. The manufacturer sells directly to the consumer, and the manufacturer performs all of the channel functions. In product firms, this choice is made either because there are no qualified intermediaries or because the manufacturer feels it can do a better job. In service firms, there is often no choice because the service must be performed while the consumer is present. The direct channel enables the firm to have close contact with the final consumer and the ability to react quickly to changes in the market.

direct channel hospitality or travel firm sells directly to the consumer and performs all of the channel functions

An **indirect channel** involves at least one intermediary that is responsible for one or more channel functions. This type of channel can exist in many forms, but it is not very common in service industries. Service firms are normally both producers and retailers. There are a few indirect channels in the hospitality and travel industries, but they seem to be more prevalent in the travel industry or in business markets that involve large volume purchases. For example, tour operators work directly with travel service firms like hotels and airlines to combine services to market as a

indirect channel involves at least one intermediary that is responsible for one or more channel functions

package to travel agents who, in turn, market to the final consumers. Another example of an indirect channel is the meetings market. Hotel salespeople market their properties to meeting planners who purchase the hotel product on behalf of a group of final consumers. The various intermediaries will be discussed in more detail in a later section.

Channel Management

Once a channel is developed, it becomes an ongoing task to manage it over time. Many conflicts and problems can occur that will require the cooperation of the members of the channel. It is also important to note that the same company can be a part of more than one channel and occupy a different position in each channel. For example, a restaurant would be a consumer in the channel for bulk food items and napkins, but a producer in the market for meals and dining. Similarly, hotels purchase many products and services ranging from items like pens and soap, to items such as linens and chlorine for swimming pools. Therefore, a problem in one channel will affect the performance of the other channels in which the firm is a member. The Ritz-Carlton chain, a past recipient of the Malcolm Baldridge Award for Quality, recognizes the critical nature of these relationships and makes a special effort to recruit suppliers who understand and agree with its philosophy of customer service and quality.

There will always be conflicts between parties engaged in some form of negotiations over issues such as price, quantity, quality, and availability. Rather than attempt to eliminate these conflicts, it is better to find ways to manage conflict. In competitive markets, it is necessary to create fair exchanges so that both parties are mutually satisfied. This mutual satisfaction can be the cornerstone of a loyal relationship that will benefit both parties in the future. Otherwise, it is in a firm's best interest to find a more equitable arrangement with other suppliers or retailers. Approaches to managing channel conflict can be behavioral (channel power and channel leadership) or contractual (vertical marketing systems).

reward power ability of one channel member to influence the behavior of another member through the use of incentives

coercive power the ability to influence a channel member's behavior through the use of threats (e.g., restricted availability or access to products)

Channel Power.   Channel power can be defined as the ability of one channel member to influence the behavior of other channel members in such a way as to get them to do things that they normally would not do. The most common forms of power are reward, coercive, expert, legitimate, and referent.[2] The balance of power depends on which channel member uses the bases of power most effectively. Any one of the channel members could conceivably have access to any of the forms of power.

Reward power is the ability of one channel member to influence the behavior of another member through the use of incentives. These incentives can be in the form of discounts, trade promotions, or some other form of promotional support. Airlines often reward travel agents by offering special commissions on certain flights. A related form of power is **coercive power**, or the ability to influence a channel member's behavior through the use of threats. These threats could be in the form of restricted availability or products, or other unfavorable terms such as price or discounts. In this case, a travel agent may limit its association with an airline because the commission is too low.

Expert power is the result of the superior knowledge of one channel member relative to another. Some hotels agree to pay commissions and employ independent hotel representatives because of their expertise in dealing with certain market segments. **Legitimate power** is obtained through contractual arrangements that specify the members' expected behaviors. The most common form of legitimate power in the hospitality industry is franchising, which will be discussed in detail in a later section. Finally, **referent power** occurs when a channel member has a certain prestige or image that would benefit another member as a result of their association.

Channel Leadership. At some point, one of the channel members should take a leadership role. The leader can then organize the other channel members and strive toward common goals and objectives. The channel leader can be a manufacturer, an intermediary, or a retailer. However, the leader will normally be large and have a sustainable, competitive advantage in its industry because of financial resources, marketing skills, or some other factor. These competitive advantages will enable firms to obtain channel power and leadership. It is often beneficial for other channel members to associate themselves with successful companies.

Manufacturers can obtain a power base and take on a leadership role if it has have ample resources or controls a product that is in short supply and in great demand among consumers. For example, a popular resort such as Disneyworld can exercise power and leadership over travel agents, rental car companies, and airlines. Intermediaries such as wholesalers and retailers can gain control over a channel if they have the ability to group components from various manufacturers and create an attractive product or if they have access to important markets. Tour wholesalers combine travel products into packages that are marketed to travel agents, who are retailers that have access to important markets and specialize in dealing with the various market segments.

Vertical Marketing Systems. One approach to reducing channel conflict and uncertainty is the vertical marketing system. In a vertical marketing system, channel members work together as if they were one organization. Channel members work together to achieve a higher degree of efficiency, thereby reducing the overall costs of providing products and services. Vertical marketing systems offer a unified approach to channel management and can be corporate, administered, or contractual.

In a **corporate system** all of the participants are actually members of the same organization. In this case, the original firm either develops or purchases other firms at the various levels in the channel. McDonald's

expert power result of the superior knowledge of one channel member relative to another

legitimate power obtained through contractual arrangements that specify the members' expected behaviors

referent power occurs when a channel member has a certain prestige or image that would benefit another member as a result of their association

operates its own food distributors in an effort to control price fluctuations and availability of its food supplies. A corporate system can be developed through backward integration (toward the manufacturer or supplier) or forward integration (toward the retailer or distributor). An example of forward integration would be a food distributor that decides to start a catering operation.

administered system
a manufacturer or supplier attempts to control the flow of goods or services through the channel by exerting some form of power

An **administered system** is one in which a manufacturer or supplier attempts to control the flow of goods or services through the channel. This is usually associated with expert power in that distributors and retailers are willing to relinquish some of their control in order to benefit from the producer's knowledge and background. Event management companies may have this type of arrangement with ticket agents who market and sell their events. This arrangement is similar to a conventional channel, but a greater degree of cooperation and sharing of information is necessary for a successful operation.

contractual system
unifies the channel members by means of a legal and binding contract

A **contractual system** unifies the channel members by means of a legal and binding contract. The firms agree to abide by the terms of the agreement, the goal of which is to realize cost economies that would not be possible if the firms operated independently. This approach is similar to a corporate system, but it may be preferable when firms do not have the resources or expertise to develop operations at all channel levels. The firms benefit from pooling resources for functions such as advertising and research. Franchising is one example of a contractual distribution system.

Channel Member Selection and Retention. It is important that firms exercise good judgment when choosing channel members. Intermediaries must demonstrate the ability and willingness to perform the desired tasks. In addition, prospective channel members must "buy in" to the philosophy of the service provider. The service provider should determine the characteristics that it feels are critical in a channel member and then evaluate potential members on the basis of these characteristics. Once a firm is selected, it is necessary to retain the firm through the use of financial and nonfinancial motivators.

Financial motivators are aimed at improving the channel member's profit. A service provider can improve a channel member's profit by offering more discounts or promotions related to desired outcomes, reducing prices, or increasing promotional support. While financial motivators are effective motivators, nonfinancial motivators should also be considered. Some nonfinancial motivators that could be used are training or improving products and services.

Franchising

Franchising is a contractual arrangement whereby one firm (the franchisor) licenses a number of other firms (the franchisees) to use the franchisor's name and business practices. As a method of distribution, franchising provides many opportunities for growth and profitability. However, when considering a franchising relationship, both parties should carefully evaluate the alternative forms of ownership and operation. The individual goals and objectives of each party have to be weighed against the trade-offs that are required from a franchisor–franchisee relationship. Table 9.1 summarizes the advantages and disadvantages associated with franchising.

Franchisee. There are many advantages to joining an existing operation rather than starting from the beginning. First, there is an established product or service with a brand name and an identity in the marketplace. It is normally very costly and time-consuming to build a brand image. Trying to start a new pizza business would be much more cumbersome than opening a Domino's. Second, franchisees receive technical and managerial assistance from the franchisor. This assistance could be in the form of recruitment and training of employees, or in the design of the facility. Franchisors transfer the knowledge they have accumulated as they progressed through the learning curve, thereby accelerating the process for franchisees. Third, the franchisee benefits from the quality standards that are already in place for the franchise. There is a system of controls that guide the operations and provide for a certain level of quality and consistency. Fourth, there is often less of a capital requirement for opening a franchise unit relative to the start-up costs for an independent operation. Franchises have a track record that can be used to estimate demand, design the facility, schedule employees, and order inventory. Fifth, there are opportunities to expand the business within the operating region. Franchisees are usually given some form of territorial rights to add units based on demand. Finally, the sixth advantage is that the franchisee benefits

Table 9.1	Franchising Advantages and Disadvantages	
	Advantages	*Disadvantages*
Franchisee	Established product/service Technical/managerial assistance Quality standards Less operating capital Opportunities for growth Cooperative advertising	Additional fees/expenses Loss of control Difficult to terminate Pooled performance
Franchisor	Rapid expansion Diversified risk Cost economics Cooperative advertising Employee issues	Loss of control Reduced profits Legal issues Recruitment

from the pooled resources of the many participants in advertising and promoting the product. The use of cooperative advertising results in a more efficient and effective means of communicating with customers. An independent restaurant would not be able to afford to place advertisements in major magazines or during prime time television.

There are also some disadvantages to becoming a franchisee. First, there are franchise fees and royalties that must be borne by the franchisee in return for the benefits just described. These expenses are normally a percentage of sales and result in a decrease in the profit margin. Second, the franchisee must adhere to the standards and procedures as set forth in the agreement. This restricts the franchisee's ability to control the entire operation in that certain requirements regarding products, price ranges, and expansion are imposed by the franchisor. Third, it may be difficult to terminate the agreement if the franchisee would like to change brands or sell the business. Finally, the brand image is the result of the pooled performance of all corporate owned and franchised units. The franchise's reputation and image can be negatively affected by the performance of individual units.

Franchisor.   Many companies are choosing to expand their operations using the franchise approach because of its advantages. Companies can experience more rapid expansion since franchisees provide additional investment capital and access to untapped markets. By limiting the investment and adding "partners," the franchisor is able to diversify the risk of doing business. A byproduct of this rapid expansion is the realization of cost economies from operating at a higher level of volume. The organization will get better prices on supplies and be able to allocate fixed costs over a larger number of units, bringing down the cost per unit. A related issue is the use of cooperative advertising. As mentioned before, this is an advantage for both the franchisor and the franchisees. Finally, certain human resources and management tasks are simplified by franchising. The franchisees play an important role in the selection and retention of employees. Plus, owners are very careful to monitor the performance of the franchise because they benefit directly from the profitability of the unit.

There are also a few disadvantages associated with being a franchisor. First, there is a reduction in control of the operation. Many owners or managers will have an affect on the overall performance of the franchise. Even though operating standards and procedures are written in the agreement, they are not always followed. Second, there is a trade-off between risk and return. The sharing of risk and ownership results in the sharing of profits as well. Third, the size and visibility of franchises exposes them to more potential litigation. They are easy targets for legal actions such as antitrust suits and class action suits. Also, injury claims are prevalent in many service industries. One of the most highly publicized cases in recent history was the lawsuit involving McDonald's brought by an elderly woman who spilled coffee in her lap while driving her car. Finally, it is difficult to find qualified prospects to be franchisees. While many investors have the necessary capital, they may lack the necessary knowledge and experience to run a successful franchise unit in the product or service category.

▲ INTERMEDIARIES

Many of the distribution channels in service industries tend to be direct in nature, eliminating the need for intermediaries. However, the hospitality and travel industries do have their share of valuable intermediaries that are responsible for volume business for hotels, airlines, and cruise ships. Intermediaries specialize in certain functions in the service delivery process and they can add value to the service with their knowledge and expertise. This specialization results in more efficient production and distribution of services, and lower prices for consumers. Table 9.2 contains a list of the most common intermediaries in hospitality and travel distribution channels.

Travel Agents

Travel agents are responsible for a large volume of bookings for airlines, hotels, and cruises. In addition, travel agents sell admissions to tourist attractions and special events. Although most of this volume comes from leisure travelers, a sizeable amount is also generated by corporate travelers. Some firms choose to use travel agents who specialize in corporate business rather than operate their own corporate travel departments. The benefit of using a travel agent is that agents specialize in finding and securing good rates for their customers. Another reason that travelers use travel agents is because of their extensive knowledge regarding travel products. Most agents have traveled to many popular cities and destinations, and they have access to informative promotional materials.

The travel agent's expertise and access to valuable markets can be useful to hotels, rental car agencies, airlines, and cruise operators. It is virtually impossible for any of these firms to operate its normal business while

Table 9.2	**Most Common Intermediaries**
Travel agents	
Tour wholesalers and operators	
Meeting planners	
Hotel representatives	
Travel bureaus	

keeping abreast of the many market segments and having access to all of their preferred methods for purchasing travel products. Travel agents and hospitality and travel firms seek to form relationships that will be mutually beneficial. Hospitality and travel firms are looking for more volume, but they want consumers that will fit their overall customer mix. Travel agents send their customers to hospitality and travel firms expecting them to have a good experience so that they tell their friends and colleagues and use the travel agent in the future. As long as this exchange satisfies both entities, they will continue the relationship to the benefit of both parties.

Tour Wholesalers and Operators

Tour wholesalers and operators contract with hospitality and travel firms to obtain services that can be combined in a package and offered to the leisure market. These packages can contain any combination of lodging, transportation, event or attraction tickets, and meals. These packages are marketed to travel agents and sometimes to consumers via the Internet or some other direct source. Tour wholesalers exist because they have access to the various suppliers and they specialize in packaging travel products, but they rely on travel agents to get the product to the mass market. This packaging concept appeals to consumers because of the convenience and the idea that the package can be purchased for a lower price than the components purchased individually. Once again, there is some value added to the services.

The package concept is particularly appealing to people engaged in international travel, senior citizens, groups, and novice travelers. There is some degree of risk associated with traveling to a new or foreign destination that is reduced by intermediaries such as tour wholesalers and travel agents. Tour wholesalers are able to sort services from suppliers into like grade and quality, package them, and offer them to retailers. This is a more efficient way to sell travel products to large volumes of leisure customers. Each of the channel members has a specialty that improves the service delivery process as well as the overall value of the final product.

Meeting Planners

Large organizations like corporations and trade associations have individuals or departments that are responsible for the travel plans of its members. These meeting planners negotiate with hotels, airlines, and other travel firms on behalf of their members for guest rooms and meeting space. There are also independent meeting planners and event planners that will work for organizations on a contract basis. As organizations seek to reduce overhead, outsourcing services such as meeting planning will become more common. Meeting planners are similar to travel agents in that they are familiar with many popular destinations. They have some expertise in areas such as negotiating, site selection, budgeting, and promotion, but it varies depending on whether they plan meetings for corporations, associations, or incentive groups. Each of these markets will be explained in more detail in the sales chapter later in the text.

Hotel Representatives

Large hotels have sales staffs that are responsible for selling guest rooms and meeting space to groups. These salespeople negotiate with meeting planners, tour operators, and travel agents in an effort to fill the hotel. Unfortunately, smaller hotels may not be able to justify the hiring of full-time salespeople, either because they are very small or they cannot afford to hire them. In this case, it may be in the hotel's best interest to hire an independent hotel representative to market the hotel to chosen market segments. Even large hotels may hire these independent representatives to take advantage of their access to certain markets. Much like travel agents, hotel representatives are able to deal with a wide array of consumers. Hotel representatives may not be as familiar with the hotel product as an in-house sales staff, but they may have more knowledge regarding the consumers that the hotel is targeting. Also, the hotel representatives may have better access to the targeted consumers.

Travel Bureaus

Each state in the United States has its own office for travel and tourism. These agencies, or bureaus, are responsible for promoting the state as a travel destination and securing major events. They are funded by the government and work in cooperation with the state's hospitality and travel firms. Each major city or region within a state will have a **convention and visitors' bureau (CVB)** that is responsible for promoting that city or region. Convention and visitors' bureaus work with local hospitality and travel firms to secure conventions, meetings, and special events for the region. Convention and visitors' bureaus can receive funding from various sources such as the government, membership fees, hotel taxes, and fees for services. CVBs also promote leisure travel to tour operators and travel agents, as well as the mass market of potential travelers. One of the services that CVBs will provide is to contact hotels with requests for proposals (RFPs) on behalf of interested groups. In essence, the CVB acts as a clearinghouse for information regarding large meetings, conferences, and conventions. Finally, most developed countries (and some developing countries) have tourism bureaus that are responsible for promoting international travel. These tourism bureaus also act as clearinghouses for information regarding tourism and group business.

▲ ELECTRONIC COMMERCE

Electronic commerce refers to the practice of carrying out business transactions over computer networks in an effort to improve organizational performance. Previous forms of electronic business included electronic data interchange (EDI) by businesses and the use of automated teller machines (ATMs) by consumers. These applications were limited to one-to-one or one-to-many, whereas the new form of electronic business application (the **Internet**) allows many-to-many communications. The number of companies engaging in electronic commerce on the Internet's **World Wide Web** (the Web) has been growing at a rapid rate since its global introduction in 1994. Organizations can communicate with all of their stakeholders through this new form of electronic commerce. Investors can obtain information about the company, consumers can obtain information about products or complain about customer service, and suppliers can communicate with their business partners. In addition, firms can gather information about their customers with on-line surveys and sales promotions.

World Wide Web primary venue for electronic commerce

One of the major reasons for the popularity of electronic commerce is the ability of manufacturers and service providers to sell direct to consumers at retail or near-retail margins without sharing the revenue with other channel members. Firms are able to increase profitability, gain market share, improve customer service, and deliver products quicker as a result of this direct channel to the consumer. Before discussing the details of electronic commerce, it is necessary to provide some background on the Internet and the World Wide Web.

What Is the Internet?[3]

The Internet was first introduced by the Rand Corporation in 1964 as a method for secure contact between the Pentagon and units of the U.S. armed forces. It was a decentralized computer communications network with no central computer or governing authority. In the event that one or more computers on the network were destroyed, it would still be possible to send information between the remaining computers. In other words, the Internet is simply a network of networks. Its use was expanded to university faculty and other researchers in the early 1970s, and improved with the National Science Foundation's (NSF) creation of a high-speed long-distance telecommunications network in the mid-1980s. The government restricted the use of the Internet to nonprofit, educational, and government organizations until 1991, at which time, commercial sites were allowed to participate.

Since 1991, the Internet has become an avenue for sharing information, obtaining software, and selling products and services. There is a file transfer protocol (FTP) for retrieving data, e-mail for exchanging messages, Telnet for accessing the Internet from a remote computer, Usenet for interactive discussion groups, and the World Wide Web for all of these operations plus the transfer of video and audio files. The Web was first developed in 1989 at the European Laboratory for Particle Physics known as (CERN) in Geneva, Switzerland, as a means of communication that could occur simultaneously while working on another project. This was made possible by the use of **hypertext**, which is a method of linking related information without a hierarchy or menu system. An example of this concept is the use of help screens in software applications. The software that is used to access the documents stored on servers located throughout the world is called a **browser**. The two most popular Web browsers are Netscape Navigator and Microsoft Explorer. The actual link to the Internet is made through a commercial service like America Online or some other Internet service provider (ISP) that specializes in linking individuals and organizations to the network.

hypertext a method of linking related information without a hierarchy or menu system

browser software that is used to access documents stored on servers located throughout the world

The Cyberspace Community. *Cyberspace* is a term coined by William Gibson in his novel *Neuromancer* to describe the electronic communities that are forming on the Internet. These communities are similar to normal communities in that members do not like being bothered by salespeople, and they have formed their own rules of "netiquette" concerning such actions. Therefore, most of the marketing of products and services has been restricted to the World Wide Web. The Web offers the most flexibility regarding the use of graphics and interactive communication, and it is the easiest area of the Internet to navigate. Also, as mentioned before, the ability to use many-to-many communication allows firms to mass-market their products and services within these electronic communities.

Security Issues. One of the appealing features of the Internet is the fact that there is open access without a governing body. In other words, Internet users are left to police themselves. This lack of governance or authority has left many to question the security and safety of the Internet. Many potential applications have been slow to develop because of the hysteria surrounding Internet security. On-line banking, investing, and travel reservations have all been slow to gain volume due to consumers' concerns about security. Initially, firms promoted products and services on-line, but provided a toll-free number consumers could call to place orders. Currently, more consumers are placing their orders on-line, but companies still provide toll-free numbers for those who are hesitant to provide confidential information, such as credit card numbers, on-line.

Concerns about Internet security have been blown out of proportion. Although on-line business transactions are not perfectly secure, they are no more risky than ordering via telephone or fax. Computer hackers are similar to everyday criminals that try to find ways to circumvent security systems and procedures, although there are some additional security issues associated with electronic commerce. First, the Internet is an open network without any physical barriers to prevent theft (e.g., hidden cameras, safes, security guards). Second, the same technologies that are being used for commerce can be used to breach security (e.g., computer programs used to search for passwords).

authentication use of some combination of account numbers, passwords, and IP addresses to verify a customer's identity

firewall electronic barrier used to restrict access to certain IP addresses or applications

coding or encryption techniques used to transform data to protect it from being used by unauthorized parties

Several methods can be used to restrict access and improve security in electronic commerce. First, a form of **authentication** can be required through the use of some combination of account numbers, passwords, and IP (Internet Protocol) addresses. Second, a **firewall** can be used to monitor traffic between an organization's network and the Internet. This barrier can restrict access to certain IP addresses or applications. A third method is to use **coding** or **encryption** techniques to transform data to protect their meaning. These security methods can be used individually or together depending on the level of security desired. For instance, firms that are transmitting payment information will be more inclined to use all three levels of defense.

Internet Strategies

Not all firms use the Internet for the same purpose. Some firms take orders through their Web sites, while others simply use them to provide information to consumers and other stakeholders. The following is a list of some of the more popular uses of Web sites:

- Providing customer service
- Selling products or services
- Educating and informing potential customers
- Offering discounts
- Promoting products and improving brand image
- Obtaining customer information and building a database

It is incumbent upon the firm to determine how its Web site will fit into the overall marketing plan. Strategies can then be formulated to attain the firm's goals and objectives.

Customer service has played an important role in the quest for product or service quality. The Ritz-Carlton introduced the concept of total quality management to the hotel industry, and a main component of the quality formula was customer service. As the number of Internet users continues to grow, Web sites become more attractive as outlets for customer service. This approach has proven to be more efficient than the telephone. Firms can list answers to commonly asked questions and guide inquiries or complaints through the proper channels. Customers are exposed to the different nuances of the Web site rather than waiting for a voice at each stage in the telephone answering system. Customers' concerns can be expressed via e-mail, and they can check later for a response.

Another reason for having a Web site would be to sell products and services. Most hotel and resort sites have a link to reservations so consumers can easily purchase the product after browsing the site. Airlines and rental car agencies provide similar services as well. The easier it is to find your products and complete a transaction, the more successful you will be in selling your product. Many Internet users value the convenience associated with electronic commerce. For example, consumers have 24-hour, 7-day-a-week (24/7) access to the Web site. They are not bound by the normal hours of operation that a firm chooses and can shop whenever they choose.

Web sites can be used to educate and inform consumers about a firm's products or services. Information search is the step after problem recognition in the consumer decision-making process. In the past, this information was obtained through word-of-mouth, past experience, an on-site visit, or speaking with salespeople over the telephone. Now it is possible to provide basic information regarding a hotel or restaurant over the Internet. Consumers can get the prices, availability, hours of operation, directions, and menus for hospitality and travel destinations. Hotels can provide materials for meeting planners at a fraction of the cost of producing and mailing brochures, planning guides, and videos. Travel agents also find Web sites to be valuable resources that can be accessed easily, are more convenient than maintaining large inventories of brochures and pamphlets that become outdated.

The Internet has become a useful outlet for reaching price-sensitive consumers. Firms offer reduced prices to attract bargain hunters who are familiar with normal price ranges for products and services. These consumers are aware that many firms offer discount prices through their Internet sites and they take the time and effort to search for deals. For example, airlines use the Internet to sell unused capacity to consumers that are willing to make their arrangements on short notice. The participating airports and routes are announced midweek for travel originating Friday or Saturday and returning on Monday or Tuesday. International flights are even included in this service, as well as hotel rooms and rental cars from the airline's partners. The discounts are normally for periods of slow demand or packages of services and are often accompanied by certain restrictions involving time or quantity.

Some firms categorize their use of the Internet as a component of the promotion mix. In some ways, it is a form of advertising, but it can also be used for sales promotions. Therefore, the firm's Web site should be integrated with the other components of the promotion mix in an effort to position the firm in the marketplace and improve its brand image. Sales promotions such as contests and sweepstakes can be used to attract customers and create an awareness and interest in the brand. These promotions should be creative and entertaining so consumers become involved with the brand while trying to win free services and merchandise. Hotels and resorts give away free vacations, and many hospitality firms give away free tee shirts and hats with corporate logos.

Finally, most of the aforementioned Internet uses have the added advantage of gaining access to customer information. Firms can build databases filled customers' names, addresses (including e-mail addresses), telephone numbers, and purchasing histories. These databases can be used for future mailings and promotions. One popular use of these databases is to survey customers and prospects about their behaviors, perceptions, and backgrounds. This information can be used to design products and services, promotions, and competitive strategies. In fact, surveys can be placed on the Web site, resulting in an efficient data collection process.

Site Design and Layout. A firm's Web site needs be creative and catch the attention of the visitors to the site. However, it is important to avoid overly complex layouts with hard-to-find links that slow movement between areas of the site. There should be a balance reached regarding the use of graphics and the speed of movement. The following are some useful tips regarding page layout:

- Include the corporate logo at the top of every page as if it were letterhead.
- Use graphic links for effect, but make sure there are also text links.
- Code pages so that the text displays before graphics are downloaded.
- Use a common style on every page and provide a link to the home page (and other pages if possible) through the use of frames, which can keep important links constantly available throughout a Web site.

The rest of the content included on the site depends on the type of product or service that is being marketed. There aren't many graphics that would need to accompany an airline's product information. However, hotels can give visitors a "tour" of the facility using snapshots or a video file. To conserve space, the hotel could use a thumbnail gallery with small pictures visitors can click on if they want to see a larger version. It is important to remember that consumers will access Web sites using a wide array of Internet connections, some of which are quite fast, while others will be quite slow. At present, the fastest Internet connection is 15 to 20 times faster than the slowest connection used commonly today. It is important to design the content of the Web site in such a way that an individual with a slower connection will not become discouraged and disconnect due to the long download waiting times.

Tourism bureaus and convention and visitors' bureaus provide users with many useful links to related sites. A traveler can go to a state's Web site and find general information regarding that state. From there, they can narrow their search to a city or region where they can find more detailed information. Finally, they can follow links to hospitality and travel firms

Holiday Inns of Greater Boston

Click on any of the locations on the map below to view that hotel's website & make online reservations.

HOME

HOTEL
INFO

COUPON

WEEKEND
GETAWAY
CONTEST

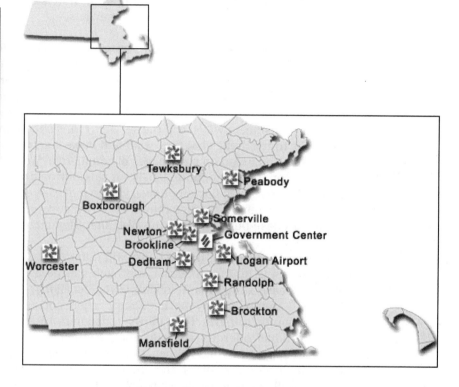

Print this page and present this coupon upon check-in
to receive $10.00 off your room rate.

$10 Off

Great Rates™

Valid 11/1/99 - 5/1/00. Not for use in combination with other
promotions or group rates. No cash surrender value

Click here to enter to win a weekend getaway
at the Holiday Inn of your choice!

FIGURE 9.1 **Web Pages Should Be Easy to Navigate for Consumers.** *Courtesy of Holiday Inns of Greater Boston*

such as hotels, restaurants, and tourist attractions and obtain very detailed information on a specific firm. Similarly, most of the search engines have links to travel reservations systems and tourism destinations. Therefore, it is crucial that hospitality and travel firms register their sites with these important directories so that their sites are easily accessed through a basic search. Also, firms should provide links to related pages that may benefit consumers. For example, restaurant or hotels can provide a link to a city map or the tourism bureau's list of events.

Taking Orders and Accepting Payment.   After a Web site is developed, it is necessary to determine the methods and procedures that will be used for completing transactions. One of the most important considerations is to make sure the process is fast, simple, and secure. The more complicated the process or the longer it takes to complete a purchase, the less likely consumers will use of the service. Firms should make it easy for customers to tell them what they want and make it secure and convenient to pay. A button found on most pages of commercial Web sites is the "purchase" button. Other common labels for this button are "place order" or "submit." Placing this button on every page makes it convenient for consumers make a purchase when they are ready. If consumers have to search for the purchase button within the Web site, they may give up and move on.

The order section of the Web site will differ based on the complexity of the shopping task. A checklist approach can be used for less complicated purchase situations involving fewer decisions. However, a "shopping cart" approach may be necessary when consumers are likely to purchase multiple items. This allows consumers to browse through the various product offerings and add items to their shopping carts as they decide to purchase them. When they are finished shopping, they can place one order for all of the items in the cart. Regardless of the approach, all commercial Web sites should:

- Itemize costs, provide totals for each line item (quantities purchased multiplied by price), and the overall total for the order
- Explain the delivery process, including alternatives methods and prices; let them know when to expect delivery
- Offer a special discount for Internet purchases and use reference prices so that consumers are aware of the savings

Sometimes, consumers become confused while shopping. They may not be sure how to proceed, or they may have questions about a product or service. This can be addressed by either providing a link to an on-line customer service representative via e-mail or by providing a toll-free number to call. As mentioned earlier, a toll-free number may also be necessary for consumers who are not comfortable with the security of the Internet for placing orders and giving confidential information.

The next step is to determine the method of payment. A firm's first line of defense in ensuring a secure transaction is to avoid having its internal records connected to the Web server while the server is connected to the Internet. The firm can store the electronic transactions in temporary files and transfer the data to the internal records later. Once again, there really isn't any more risk of fraud with Internet transactions than there would be with telephone or fax transactions. The following are the basic options for accepting payment:

- Having customers apply for credit accounts before they make any purchases. The personal information such as name, address, phone number and credit card is provided on-line, by telephone, by mail, or by fax. Customers are assigned an account name or number and a password or personal identification number (PIN). Orders can be billed to the credit card and delivered to the address in the preexisting account. The major drawback of this option is that consumers must take the time to establish accounts before they can make a purchase.

- Using encryption techniques with electronic transactions. The confidential information provided by customers is encrypted before it is sent, and then decrypted by the firm. Browsers like Netscape Navigator provide this service for Internet users. It would take a great deal of effort on the part of a hacker to break the code, and consumers could make purchases without any delay.

- Using a digital cash intermediary. Individuals open accounts with a third party that operates like a bank and are provided with a PIN (similar to a debit card account). The intermediary completes the transactions with the merchant off-line, but it is necessary for both the individual and the vendor to be affiliated with the intermediary.

None of the methods discussed is without its drawbacks. However, the popularity of the Internet has attracted many firms that specialize in computer security and the environment for electronic commerce is constantly improving.

▲ MARKETING ACTION NOW!

A student from a hospitality management program decided to start his own restaurant upon graduation. It started as a single unit restaurant in a college town that made calzones for pick-up and delivery. The menu consists of 30 to 40 different types of calzone and is marketed as "the pizza alternative." All of the calzones are the same price ($4.50) and the only other items on the menu are beverages (soft drink, ice tea, lemonade, and juice). The business has done well and the owner now has several units in college towns. However, as the business continues to grow, some important decisions need to be addressed.

The owner has expanded the number of units using the earnings from the operation. He chooses other towns with large colleges or universities that tend to be self-contained. His strategy is not to deviate from his formula for success. Lately, he has been giving serious thought to the idea of franchising the operation and advertising for franchisees. However, before he makes the decision to franchise, he wants to consider the implications.

1. What are the advantages and disadvantages associated with franchising?
2. What would you recommend based on your knowledge?
3. Is there anything else that you would need to consider?

▲ SUMMARY OF CHAPTER OBJECTIVES

This chapter discussed the role of distribution in planning the marketing strategy for hospitality and travel services. Decisions must be made regarding channel width (how many outlets) and channel length (number and type of intermediaries). If the decision is made to use an indirect channel (at least one intermediary), then the firm must examine channel management issues such as channel leadership and channel power. Finally, the extent of the relationships with other channel members will need to be considered. Some type of vertical marketing system can be used to provide more certainty in the relationships. Franchising is probably the most common form of vertical marketing system.

Intermediaries exist in channels because they perform certain channel functions more effectively than the other channel members. One advantage of using an intermediary is the fact that they often have access to markets that are desired by a manufacturer, or producer. Travel agents and tour operators specialize in packaging trips and selling them to groups and individuals for pleasure travel, and meeting planners and travel bureaus work more with business groups for conferences and conventions.

The newest form of distribution in the hospitality and travel industry is electronic commerce. Firms are promoting themselves on the Internet and providing customers with on-line access to reservations. On-line reservations account for a small portion of overall travel reservations, but this direct channel allows firms to charge lower prices to attract price sensitive consumers. As more households become connected, on-line reservations should experience strong growth.

▲ KEY TERMS AND CONCEPTS

Administered vertical marketing system
Authentication
Browser

Channel length
Channel width
Channel power
Coding

Coercive power

Contractural vertical marketing
   system

Convention and visitors bureau
   (CVB)

Corporate vertical marketing
   system

Cyberspace

Direct channel

Encryption

Expert power

Extensive distribution

Firewall

Franchisee

Franchising

Franchisor

Hypertext

Indirect channel

Intensive distribution

Intermediaries

Internet (the Net)

Legitimate power

Referent power

Reward power

Selective distribution

Vertical marketing system

World Wide Web (the Web)

▲ QUESTIONS FOR REVIEW AND DISCUSSION

1. What factors are considered in determining a firm's channel width and channel length?
2. List and describe the five forms of channel power.
3. Explain the three types of vertical marketing systems.
4. What is franchising? Why would firms or individuals choose to enter this type of arrangement?
5. List and give examples of the intermediaries that exist in the hospitality and travel industry.
6. What is the Internet? What is the difference between the Internet and the World Wide Web?
7. What are some of the possible strategies used by firms on the Internet?
8. What are the important considerations in site design and layout?
9. How do firms take orders and accept payment over the Internet?

▲ NOTES

[1]"Holiday Inn Express Launches New Web Site With Booking Capability," *Hotel Business*, Vol. 7, No. 24 (December 21–January 6, 1999), *Technology Trends*.

[2]Jack J. Kasulis and Robert E. Spekman, "A Framework for the Use of Power," *European Journal of Marketing*, 14 (1980), p. 183.

[3]Herschell Gordon Lewis and Robert D. Lewis, *Selling on the Net: The Complete Guide* (Lincolnwood, IL: NTC Publishing Group, 1997).

Promotional Strategy

10

Promotion and Advertising

❖ Chapter Objectives

By the end of this chapter, you should understand:

1. The difference between promotion and advertising
2. The elements of the promotional mix and how they are managed
3. How to establish promotional budgets
4. The planning, creation, and evaluation of advertising campaigns
5. The social consequences and economic effects of advertising

❖ Chapter Outline

I. Chapter Opening Profile
II. Introduction
  A. The promotional mix
  B. The functions of promotions and advertising
III. Managing the Promotional Mix
  A. Promoting over the product life cycle

❖ Chapter Opening Profile

HOSPITALITY AND TRAVEL FIRMS ENGAGE IN a good deal of advertising and promotion. In fact, these firms are often at the forefront in terms of creativity and spending. For example, national restaurants are at the top of the list in terms of dollars spent in all forms of television advertising based on figures from Competitive Media Reporting.[1] A good example of advertising creativity would be the recent campaign launched by Virgin Atlantic Airways that includes a tie-in with the movie *Austin Powers: The Spy Who Shagged Me.*

The goal of the campaign was to create a link between the movie and the airline prior to the movie's June 11, 1999 opening. Then, the airline could sit back and benefit from the advertising dollars spent by New Line Cinema promoting its movie. In addition to the advertising promoting the movie, Virgin Atlantic Airways also benefited from the advertising dollars spent by other corporate partners and the free publicity surrounding the movie. As early as May 11, 1999, ads were placed on billboards, buses, and phone booths in Los Angeles, New York, and Miami. Ads were also placed in the four U.S. cities where Virgin Atlantic Airways flies: Boston, Orlando, San Francisco, and Washington, D.C. Finally, the campaign, which cost between $8 million and $10 million, included product placements in the movie.

▲ INTRODUCTION

As the marketing environment in which hospitality and travel organizations function becomes more competitive, the importance of advertising and other forms of promotion increases. This chapter focuses on advertising management and lays the foundation for the next chapter, which focuses on advertising media. Emphasis here is on defining commonly used advertising terms, relations with an advertising agency, advertising budgets, positioning and strategy, and planning and evaluating advertising campaigns.

The Promotional Mix

The more visible forms of advertising are often used to help increase sales and profits. However, all of the elements of the promotional mix are equally important. The basic elements include advertising, personal selling, sales promotion, and public relations. This chapter will focus on the last two. All four are defined here:

- *Advertising* is any paid form of nonpersonal presentation of ideas and promotion of ideas, goods, or services by an identified sponsor.
- *Personal selling* is an oral presentation in a conversation with prospective consumers for the purpose of making a sale.
- *Sales promotion* includes marketing activities other than advertising, personal selling, and public relations that attempt to stimulate consumer demand and increase sales. Commonly, sales promotion is a direct inducement offering an extra incentive to take action, be it to buy the product or service or to inquire about further information.
- *Public relations* is a nonpersonal stimulation of demand for a product or service by providing commercially significant news about the product or service in a published medium or obtaining favorable presentation in a medium that is not paid for by the sponsor.

In all forms of the promotional mix, it is critical that the intended message be delivered to the potential target markets. A model of communication is shown in Figure 10.1 to illustrate how this process takes place.

Remember that both the sender and the receiver are humans and are subject to the failings common to all of us. No one communicates as well as he or she would like. We simply do not speak as clearly and understandably as we would like. Also, we do not listen as well as we should. With this in mind, all communication attempts with target markets should be kept as clear and concise as possible. In addition to the human failings, there are potential difficulties with the message, the channels that are used, and the noise level in the environment, and efforts should be made to overcome these difficulties. When management designs a new form of promotion, it is sometimes expected that the entire target market can be

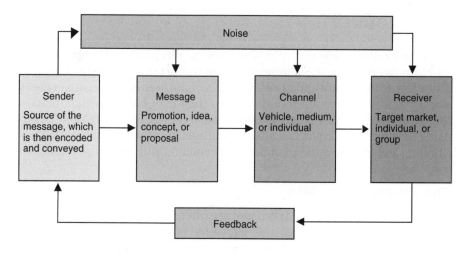

FIGURE 10.1 **Communications Model**

reached with a limited number of contacts. This is simply not possible, because the target market is being bombarded with other messages and as a result, sometimes your message is not received and retained above the noise in the environment. It is important to keep this communications model in mind when designing any type of communications with target markets. It will serve as a reminder of how great the challenge really is. It is also critical to review the feedback received, studying it carefully and looking for ways to improve.

The Functions of Promotion and Advertising

The terms *promotion* and *advertising* evoke many different responses from hospitality managers. Some smile, remembering a successful advertising campaign from the past. Others simply view advertising as a waste of time. They claim that advertising and promotion are things that should be used to sell automobiles or laundry detergent but not hospitality operations. Those individuals usually champion word of-mouth advertising, claiming that good food and service will produce satisfied consumers, who in turn will produce more consumers. Although this argument has some truth to it, managers who fail to engage in a significant advertising program may be missing a unique opportunity to increase both customer counts and total sales. Advertising is not something to be limited to the chain operations, such as McDonald's and Wendy's, nor is it only something a manager does when business is poor and needs a shot in the arm.

Advertising and promotion are marketing functions that need to be managed along with other functions. They demand management's time and attention if they are to be successful, for advertising must be planned, implemented, coordinated, and evaluated with care if it is to achieve increased sales. What can advertising and promotion do? First, advertising and promotion present information to the consumer about new products, new services, new decor, and other items of interest. Second, they reinforce consumer behavior by communicating with individuals who have patronized a particular hotel or restaurant in the past. Exposing these consumers to a continuous flow of advertising is likely to induce repeat patronage by reinforcing their positive experiences. Brand loyalty is very difficult to establish, but advertising is one weapon to use in this effort.

Third, advertising induces first-time patronage. If consumers are exposed to a continual flow of advertising, their curiosity is aroused and this often results in patronage. If a first-time guest is rewarded with a pleasant experience, the foundation for repeat patronage has been successfully established. At first a portion of the advertising must be directed toward individuals who have not already patronized the operation. Some managers believe that the key to success is to build a steady group of repeat guests, and although this is one aim of an advertising and promotional strategy, other efforts must be directed at those who have not previously been guests. Fourth, advertising enhances the image of hospitality operations. Advertising does not always seek to promote a specific product or service; it can instead seek to create and reinforce an image for the consuming public. Words and phrases often contribute to this image building; for example, Westin Hotels and Resorts, "Caring, Comfortable, Civilized" seeks to establish and maintain a specific image that has been created in the mind of the consumer.

Still, a significant number of hospitality owners and managers do not believe in advertising. Some argue that the only good form of promotion is by word-of-mouth: "Let our guests speak good words about us, and we'll succeed," they claim. Some operators refer to this as word-of-mouth advertising, but it is not advertising; rather, it is a form of public relations. Unfortunately for these individuals, this point of view does not always hold true. Many independent operations, especially those in the food service segment, are simply being squeezed by larger national and regional chain advertising, while many managers withdraw from all advertising, rationalizing that they cannot compete with the big chains. This often leads to decline and the eventual demise of the operation.

Advertising and promotion are necessarily a vital part of the marketing program of all types of hospitality operations. But just what should advertising do? What should it accomplish? Generally speaking, advertising should set out to accomplish three goals: (1) to establish awareness in the minds of consumers; (2) to establish positive value in the minds of consumers; and (3) to promote repeat patronage and brand loyalty among consumers.

Awareness must be created among consumers who have not heard of a particular hotel or restaurant establishment. This awareness should create sufficient interest so that patronage results. Next, to induce both first time and repeat patronage, a positive perceived value must be established and reinforced in the minds of consumers. All consumers have limited resources chasing after unlimited wants; hence, only products and services that offer a high level of perceived value will be rewarded with patronage. A hospitality operation might have the very finest to offer in rooms, food, and service in a given market segment, but if it has a low perceived value, the number of consumers served is likely to be small. Finally, advertising should strive to promote brand loyalty and repeat patronage among the highest possible percentage of consumers. Very few hospitality operations can survive on one-time patronage only. Repeat business must be encouraged and promoted. Even better than repeat patronage is brand loyalty, wherein consumers begin to prefer one brand of hotel or restaurant over and above the direct competition. However, the current competitiveness in the marketplace makes it very difficult to create brand loyalty.

▲ MANAGING THE PROMOTIONAL MIX

It is important for firms to create promotional mixes that will lead to a strong position in the marketplace. Each firm must choose its own mix of advertising, publicity, personal selling, and sales promotions, depending on the firm's positioning and image. However, one marketing tool that is helpful in determining baseline strategies for promotion is the product life cycle.

Promoting over the Product Life Cycle

As discussed in chapter 7, all hospitality organizations progress through a distinct life cycle (see Figure 10.2). As an organization moves through the stages of the life cycle, different marketing strategies are recommended. Promotion is one component of the marketing mix that changes over the life cycle of a product.

Introduction Stage. Rarely does a new hotel or restaurant open without creating some interest in the local community. The goal of all hospitality managers should be to capitalize on this natural curiosity and make it work to the advantage of the new hospitality establishment. The main focus of the promotional campaign in the introduction stage is to inform consumers in an effort to create awareness. The principal objective during this phase is to build volume within the operation by reaching individuals who are innovators and are most likely to patronize a new operation. This approach is very critical to the independently owned operation. Every effort must be made to reach potential consumers and encourage first-time patronage. All targeted segments should be identified and strategies developed to reach each of these markets.

All elements of the promotional mix are used at this point. Advertising and publicity are used to create awareness and interest in the new operation. Depending on the size of the operation, local, regional, and/or na-

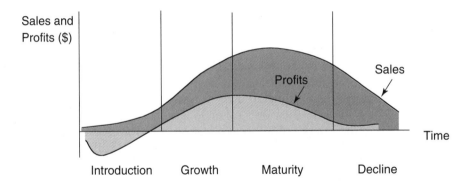

FIGURE 10.2 **The Product Life Cycle**

tional media are contacted to cover the story surrounding the opening. Personal selling is used to generate awareness and interest among intermediaries. Restaurants will contact hotels and tourist information sources that are likely to make referrals. In addition, hotels will contact tour operators and travel agents. Finally, sales promotions are used to induce trial. For example, hotels will offer familiarization trips to intermediaries, and many hospitality and travel firms will offer discounted rates to reduce the perceived risk of consuming the service.

It is very desirable to bring all management personnel with marketing responsibilities together to generate ideas for possible promotion. These idea-generating sessions should produce a wealth of potential promotions, leading to a schedule of what is to be done and when it is to be accomplished. The list of possible promotional ideas is endless; a few examples follow:

- Signs can announce "coming soon" for a new hospitality operation and perhaps indicate the number of weeks until the grand opening.
- Press releases can indicate the where, what, when, and why of the new operation.
- Mailing lists can be developed from a guest book signed by first-time patrons. This list can then be used later for direct-mail campaigns.
- Numerous media can, of course, be used. One rather novel approach involved advertising in the classified section of the newspaper and on radio for high-quality personnel for a new restaurant. The results were not only surprising, but also very successful. Hundreds of individuals applied for jobs, making the restaurant "the place" to work. In addition, the advertisements described in some detail the atmosphere, menu, and image of the restaurant, thereby informing the general public of the existence of the restaurant. The result was high-quality personnel, high guest counts, and very satisfied management.
- Community opinion leaders, such as doctors, lawyers, and restaurant reviewers, can be invited to opening-week parties and the like, all de-

signed to enhance the image of the hospitality operation. The goal, of course, is to present a positive image and influence those who can in turn influence others.

- Numerous door prizes, contests, and raffles can be used to encourage patronage. The American consumer seems infinitely willing to take a chance on getting something for little or nothing. Consider the success of Las Vegas, Atlantic City, and other locations that offer legal gambling. This approach is simply an application of psychologist B. F. Skinner's variable-interval reinforcement schedule. Individuals will continue to take chances, even though the probability of winning is very small.

- Handbills or flyers represent an inexpensive yet affective method for introductory promotion. These can, of course, be used as direct-mail pieces, or they may be distributed by other means. One new restaurant located near a large shopping mall and several office complexes distributed handbills offering a variety of discounts and freebies at these locations. In addition, the restaurant invited the secretaries of the high-ranking management personnel to a complimentary lunch and formed a secretaries' club that provided incentives and rewards to those secretaries who provided the restaurant with the largest number of reservations. The results were predictable: very high volume and the satisfaction of all parties involved.

The list of potential introductory advertising and promotional ideas is endless. Each management group must determine a sound strategy for the introductory stage of advertising and promotion.

Growth Stage.   During the growth stage, promotion and advertising is focused on building name recognition and persuading consumers to purchase your brand. If the introductory stage has been successful, a solid core of consumers has been established. With this core, the promotional objective must be twofold: (1) to reinforce and remind those consumers who have patronized the hospitality establishment, to induce repeat patronage; and (2) to reach those consumers who have not patronized the operation, thereby expanding volume with a significant number of first-time buyers.

During the growth stage, the mention of the name of the hospitality establishment brings a distinct image to the consumer's mind. Therefore, promotion and advertising should seek to reinforce the most positive aspects of this image. The strategies used during this stage include comparative advertising and stressing the special advantages offered by the product–service mix of the operation. In addition, personal selling is still used to build awareness, interest, and desire among intermediaries. However, less emphasis is placed on publicity and sales promotions as a means to build image and persuade consumers to purchase.

Maturity Stage. Only the largest and most successful hospitality organizations progress to this stage of the life cycle. The firms that achieve this level are very well established and have the tremendous advantage of nearly universal name recognition and reinforcement. The best example is McDonald's: A McDonald's advertisement need not even mention the product or service to be successful. Simply by using the word *McDonald's* or showing the restaurant and the people who patronize it, the advertisement reinforces the image and quality of the organization in the minds of consumers. The primary goal of a firm at this stage is to use the organization's size and brand recognition to remind consumers of the product's benefits and continue to differentiate it from the competition. This can be seen within the fast-food segment, as each of the largest competitors (McDonald's, Burger King, and Wendy's) attempts to differentiate itself from the others.

In addition to reminder advertising, sales promotions in the form of coupons and discounts are popular. Coupons are normally distributed through a variety of print media, by direct mail, or by service personnel at the time the bill is paid. Coupon promotions are generally most effective in increasing consumer counts. A word of caution should be offered, however: Coupons are merely short-term inducements to purchase a brand, and not a means to build long-term loyalty among customers. Rather, the consumer uses coupons as the method to shop for the best deal at any given point. If a large number of hospitality operations in a given geographic area offer coupon discounts, consumers can become conditioned to coupons as a way of life, with the result that they will patronize only the hospitality operations that offer such discounts. Finally, limited attention is given to personal selling and publicity during this stage.

Decline Stage. The goal of any firm that reaches this stage of its life cycle is to use its competitive advantage to launch new products and services that will further strengthen the organization. By adding to its product–service mix, the firm can attract new consumers and extend its product life cycle. For example, McDonald's has repeatedly used its number-one position in the fast-food segment to launch new products and services, most notably a variety of breakfast items and specialty sandwiches. These products contribute to the sales mix of the organization and serve to broaden the market appeal. All have, of course, been test-marketed prior to being introduced into the system. They are examples of ways an organization can market new products and services from a position of strength and, as a result, become stronger still.

If a firm cannot find ways to extend its product life cycle, then the appropriate strategy is to maximize short-term profit and eventually divest. This is accomplished by reducing marketing expenditures to the minimum effective level, including a reduction in the promotional budget. At this stage, there is virtually no effort in the areas of personal selling and publicity. In addition, advertising is kept to a minimum and sales promotions are used sparingly. It is assumed that these expenditures will have little effect on consumer purchasing, thereby serving only to decrease the firm's profitability.

Establishing the Promotional Budget

Promotion is an expense that must be carefully planned, monitored, and controlled. Compared with major expense items, promotion and advertising may not seem like a large percentage. However, promotional budgets must be set so as to maximize the use of the sales force, and other promotional elements such as advertising, publicity, and sales promotions. Management must carefully establish the promotion budget to maximize the productivity of the dollars spent. Some managers promote more when business volume is slow, thereby hoping to increase volume. Others attempt to reduce expenses by cutting back on promotion when a decline in volume occurs. Both approaches are subject to error because they are based on intuition rather than on a rational decision-making and budgeting process. Promotional budgets serve several useful and important functions: (1) to provide a detailed projection of future expenditures; (2) to provide both short- and long-range planning guides for management, and (3) to provide a method for monitoring and controlling promotional expenses by comparing actual expenses against projections.

Advantages and Disadvantages of Advertising Budgets. Numerous executives debate the pros and cons of budgeting promotional expenses. These are the major advantages associated with budgeting:

- Developing budgets forces management to look into the future. Although both the past and the current conditions certainly need to be considered, the future is the key. All management personnel must develop the ability to project future trends, revenues, and expenses. Failure to do so can easily lead to "management by crisis."
- Budgets serve as reference points. Budget projections need not be solid figures cast in stone. Budgeted figures and media plans are, of course, subject to modification if the marketing situation changes dramatically. The budget, however, is important as a point of reference, a goal, and a standard against which actual performance can be compared.
- When promotional budgets are established, all management personnel with marketing responsibilities should be involved in their preparation. This involvement fosters improved communication among individuals. In addition, as all managers have input into the development of the plan, support for the plan increases as each manager "owns a piece" of the plan. Once individuals identify with the budget as it is developed, this will increase their personal motivation to see that it is implemented successfully.

In addition to the aforementioned advantages, there are also some disadvantages associated with preparing promotional budgets:

- Time is money. To prepare a budget properly, a considerable amount of management time is necessary. Because the highest-paid management personnel plan the budget, the cost to the organization can be considerable. This represents time that some say could be spent more profitably performing other functions. The question to is "How much is it worth to the organization to have well-developed budgets and plans?"
- What events will shape the future? Certainly, the future is always going to be somewhat uncertain, but astute managers should be able to foresee trends and adapt to take full competitive advantage of these trends. Businesses often fail because management does not foresee changes and, as a result, the firm is unable to adapt in a timely manner. Successful management must develop a proactive rather than a reactive posture; it must foresee change before it occurs and compensate (adapt) to allow the organization to benefit from the change.

Budgeting Methods. Promotional budgets are normally either fixed or contingency. Fixed budgets, by definition, are based on predictions of sales volume and expected levels of advertising. Projected expenditures are normally held firm, even if the assumptions on which the budget was based prove to be incorrect. Contingency budgets, on the other hand, are developed based on several sets of assumptions. This development means that if situation A happens, then implement plan A; if situation B occurs, then implement plan B; and so on. This type of budget draws its name from being based on a number of contingencies, or plans developed to be appropriate for several possible outcomes.

Various methods can be used to develop a promotional budget. All of these methods fall into one of the four following categories: (1) the percentage of sales method; (2) the desired objective method; (3) the competitive parity method; and (4) the all-you-can-afford method.

The **percentage of sales** method has found very wide use in the hospitality industry. The method offers relative simplicity; a sales forecast is obtained, and a given percentage of this forecast is allocated to advertising. Within the hospitality industry, the amount of money spent for advertising is typically between 2 and 8 percent of gross sales. This method offers the following advantages:

percentage of sales after a sales forecast is obtained, a given percentage is allocated for advertising

- It is very simple and straightforward.
- Some managers prefer to view all expenses as a percentage of sales, including advertising.
- It works well if sales can be forecasted accurately and market conditions are stable.

However, the percentage of sales method also has the following disadvantages:

- This method holds that if sales decline, so too will advertising expenditures. This is not a valid argument; instead, in this situation it would be wise to increase advertising expenditures.
- Increased advertising should result in increased sales, yet this method holds that an increase in sales results in an increase in the advertising budget.

desired objective
budget developed on well-defined objectives

The **desired objective** method involves developing a budget based on well-defined objectives. Management must plan precisely what it wishes to accomplish through promotion and advertising. Based on these objectives, management must then decide what type and what amount of promotion and advertising will be necessary to achieve the objectives. Many factors must be considered, including projected sales, previous promotion and advertising, financial position of the firm, and competition within the marketplace. The advantages of this method include:

- Rather than simply allocating a fixed percentage of sales for each budget period, management must critically evaluate promotion and advertising expenditures in accordance with objectives.
- Advertising efforts are tied to specific measurable objectives, thereby making evaluation easier.
- Several variable factors, such as competition within the marketplace, are considered.

However, two major disadvantages must also be considered:

- It is difficult to determine the precise mix of promotion and advertising that will accomplish the objectives satisfactorily.
- Engaging in this type of budget preparation is very time-consuming, especially when one considers that advertising and promotion represent only one area on an income statement and only one aspect of the marketing mix.

competitive parity
establishing a budget by direct comparison with the promotion and advertising efforts of major competitors

The **competitive parity** method for establishing a budget involves direct comparison with the promotion and advertising efforts of major competitors. Based on the type and amount of promotion done by the competition, management then establishes a budget that will roughly match the activities of the major competition. The following advantages are associated with the competitive parity method:

- A relative level of equilibrium is established with regard to the competition.
- The method is simple and straightforward, especially if an industry average is used.

The disadvantages of the competitive parity method include the following:

- Relative promotion and advertising budgets, and media decisions, made by one firm usually are not applicable to other firms. For example, how can management be assured that the competition's advertising is appropriate for its hotel or restaurant?

- Basing future plans on the past performance of others is reactive rather than proactive.

The **all-you-can-afford** method is usually a last resort practiced by small firms that don't have the luxury of setting resources aside for promotion and advertising. For example, independent restaurants and lodging facilities must meet their expenses such as payroll and inventory before they can consider the allocation of resources to promotion and advertising. If a small restaurant has $1,000 that it can spare at the end of a month, then the manager or owner must determine the most efficient and effective use of that money.

all-you-can-afford
method of last resort; usually practiced by small firms with limited resources

The all-you-can-afford method is often a reality for small firms, but it isn't a sound method to use in determining the promotional budget. Once again, as sales decrease and profits are down, the firm will allocate less money to promote and advertise at a time when it would be most beneficial. Conversely, when business is good, the firm will have more money to spend on promotion. This is counter to what would make sense from a logical perspective. The main advantage associated with this method is its simplicity; it doesn't require managers to perform any formal budgeting for promotion, and spending is not related to goals and objectives.

A Budgeting Process. Those exposed to the budget preparation process for the first time can be overwhelmed. The process is often associated with corporate politics and bureaucracy. Figure 10.3 illustrates the budget process in a manner that encapsulates the process in an easily understood format. Initially, upper management must determine future objectives. At the same time, the desired future performance for advertising is projected by taking into consideration trends, future influential factors, past performance, and input from subordinates. A preliminary budget is prepared and is then compared with the short- and long-range objectives of upper management. If the budget appears to satisfy the objectives, it is adopted, and controls are established. If the budget fails to meet the objectives, then the objectives and/or the budget must be revised to bring the two into harmony.

Once the budget is implemented, a simple control process is used. If the promotional mix performs as planned, the monitoring process continues. If, however, evaluation shows that the promotional mix is not successful, several avenues can be taken:

- The promotional mix can be changed to increase the probability of satisfying evaluation standards.
- The budget can be modified based on changing market conditions.
- The short- and long-range objectives can be changed based on new available information.

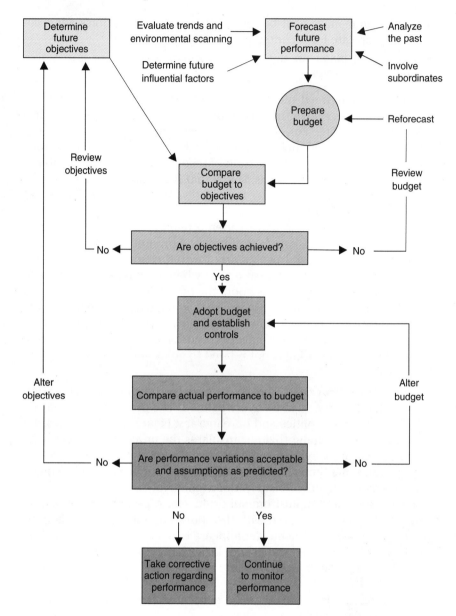

FIGURE 10.3 The Budgeting Process

▲ ADVERTISING MANAGEMENT

The American Marketing Association defines advertising as "any paid form of nonpersonal presentation and promotion of ideas, goods, or services by an identified sponsor." This definition is accepted throughout the business community. It can be broken down into four components:

1. ***Paid form.*** Any advertising is paid for and controlled by the individual or group that is the sponsor. Because someone is paying for the space (newspaper, outdoor) or time (radio, television), this individual or group has complete control over what is said, printed, or shown. Any promotion that is not paid for is called *publicity.* Because the individual or group is not paying for the time or space, those involved do not have complete control and are at the mercy of the writer or producer. A common form of publicity is a review of a restaurant in a dining or food section of a local newspaper. Publicity can obviously be either favorable or unfavorable.

2. ***Nonpersonal.*** Advertising is done through the mass media without personal contact or interaction between the seller and the potential buyer. Advertising relies strictly on nonpersonal promotion of goods, services, or ideas.

3. ***Promotion related to ideas, goods, or services.*** Advertising need not be restricted to the promotion of a tangible physical product or good. It may try to influence individuals to change their ways of thinking or their behavior.

4. ***Identified sponsor.*** All advertising has an identified sponsor.

Promotion is a broader-based term denoting efforts undertaken to induce patronage. It includes personal selling that is face-to-face communication between the seller and the prospective buyer as well as other efforts designed to increase sales. Simply stated, advertising is a form of promotion, but all forms of promotion are not necessarily advertising.

Forms of Advertising

Advertising can be divided into two broad categories, national and local. *National advertising* is aimed at a national audience by using network television and radio, or national print media such as magazines. This form of advertising normally promotes the general name of the chain, not individual locations or stores.

Local advertising is used not only by the major hospitality chains but also by second-tier chains, regional chains, and independent operations. Local advertising, including television, radio, print, and other media, is used extensively in the hospitality industry. This is where the action is, and to coin a phrase, the battle of market share is won or lost in the trenches of local advertising.

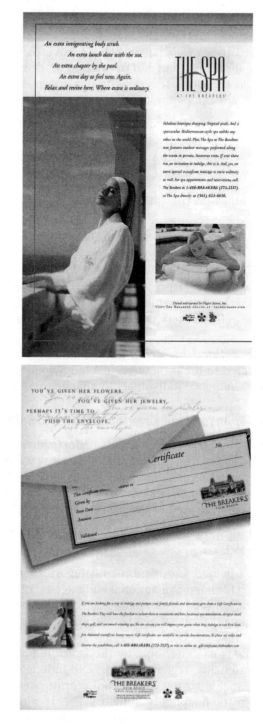

Advertising should be aimed at a particular target market. *Courtesy of The Breakers, Palm Beach, Florida*

A simple fact of business life for many managers is that specific advertising media are too expensive for the organization to use. For many managers, cooperative advertising is an excellent alternative. *Cooperative advertising*, as the name implies, involves two or more firms working together to sponsor an advertisement that provides benefit to all parties involved. For example, a group of restaurants located in a given geographic area may join together and promote dining in the area without promoting any one operation specifically. By joining together and sharing the expenses, managers are able to advertise in more expensive media and reach new audiences. Cooperative advertising is an area of tremendous promise because it allows a manager to expand the advertising media selection.

Advertising Positioning and Strategy

Advertising terms and jargon often sound like the language of war. Campaigns are launched and advertisements are aimed at target markets. Advertising need not be anything like war, but successful advertising is the result of carefully planned strategy.

A manager must first decide how to position the product–service mix. Positioning is the manner in which the consumer views the product–service mix, and each hospitality operation is positioned differently. Before any advertising decisions are made or strategy is plotted, the proper market position must be determined.

A successful advertising campaign does not result from haphazard planning and execution. A single advertisement may be very good, but prosperous companies produce consistently superior advertising. Advertising succeeds when good strategy is developed. Strategy is not a magic, secret formula. According to advertising experts Kenneth Roman and Jane Maas, strategy development revolves around five key points[2]:

1. *Objectives.* What should the advertising do? What goals does management want to achieve? For example, a new hospitality operation may set recognition among local residents as an objective, while another hospitality operation might seek to increase sales on slow nights. For the latter operation, most of the money would concentrate on promotions designed to increase volume on these nights.

2. *Targeted audience.* Who is the customer or potential customer? Advertising is not a success when used in a hit-or-miss manner. Successful advertising addresses a specifically targeted market and talks directly to that market. Many advertising programs fail because they attempt to appeal to too broad a targeted market. Figure 10.4 illustrates an advertisement that was targeted toward corporate meeting planners, to introduce a new resort property.

3. *Key consumer benefit.* Consumers can be skeptical and often need a benefit or a reason to buy before they are persuaded. This is a pitch to the consumer to come to this operation instead of another. True differences between hospitality operations are rare, but a list of products and services the operation offers should stress those different from or superior to those offered by other hospitality facilities.

4. *Support.* To have a successful advertising campaign, the key benefit must be supported in some manner. Consumers are skeptical of advertising claims—who can blame them? Included in any advertisement should be a reason for the consumer to believe in the benefit. Consumer testimonials or test results showing superiority are often used for this purpose.

5. *Tone and manner.* The advertising strategy must have a personality. This personality should blend with the image and positioning of the hospitality operation. McDonald's has been extremely successful with Ronald McDonald when advertising to children. This figure makes McDonald's seem like a fun place to be. Wendy's advertising campaign includes the owner, Dave Thomas, in ads that convey his offbeat personality. Also, Southwest Airlines and Motel 6 take advantage of the personalities of their CEOs. The tone and manner selected should blend with the overall theme that management is trying to create and should show the potential customer the nature of the operation.

Developing a Central Appeal. Developing a central advertising appeal is not an easy process. Considerable time and thought must be devoted to the creative process before a viable appeal is found. Several rules of thumb exist for the development of this appeal:

- ***A central appeal must offer some value to the consumer.*** If the central appeal does not speak directly to the needs of the primary target market, the chances for success are greatly reduced. A well-developed marketing information system should provide specific data about the marketplace, enabling management to be in tune with the values of consumers.

- ***The appeal must be distinctive.*** All advertising must compete not only with all other hospitality organizations but with advertising for everything from automobiles to washing machines. For the advertising to be effective, the appeal must offer something that separates it from everything else. Distinctive and unusual appeals are needed.

- ***The appeal must be believable.*** Claims made for the product–service mix must be backed up if the appeal is to have credibility. Because some consumers are more skeptical than others, the appeal should be believable to those who might at first have doubts.

- ***The appeal should be simple.*** Consumers are confronted each day with hundreds of advertising stimuli, and if one is to be recalled, it must be simple and straightforward. Effective and simple appeals that have been used successfully include "We do it all for you," "You, you're the one," "It's a good time for the great taste" (McDonald's), "Have it your way," "Broiling beats frying" (Burger King), and "America's business address" (Hilton Hotels).

Keys to Successful Advertising.   To be successful, advertising needs to be approached in a systematic manner. The following are several suggestions on how to improve advertising efficiency.[3]

- ***Time.*** Advertising should not be considered a necessary evil. Sales and operations are equally important and require time for an advertising program to generate satisfactory results.

- ***Budgets.*** Budgets should be developed for the needs of each operation. It makes little sense to base an advertising budget on figures and percentages that represent the national average. Generally, a manager must have the courage to spend enough to produce successful results.

- ***Study.*** A manager needs to analyze the operation and determine the operation's advantages as compared with those of the competition. Disadvantages also need to be identified so that they can be minimized or eliminated completely. The evaluation must be done constantly so that any changes in the competitive situation are noted and adjustments are made quickly.

- ***Analysis of market segments.*** Each year, many people change jobs and move, and as they do their life styles change too. No market segment is constant; they are always changing. For this reason, management must know the patrons of the hospitality operation. By doing this, management can modify the operation to meet changing consumer demands.

- ***Media.*** Media must be selected very carefully to be effective. Media used must match the intended targeted markets. Each type of medium offers advantages and drawbacks, which are discussed in the next chapter.

- ***Formation of a plan.*** Advertising cannot be successful if it is approached in a haphazard manner. It is important that continuity be established among all forms of advertising so that it gains momentum. Continuity can be established through the consistent use of logos, distinctive type styles, music, or any creative touches to make the advertising stand out from other advertisements. Managers should not be afraid of advertising and should draw up plans designed to produce results. Nothing is worse than spending too little money on advertising, so advertising expenditures should not be cut. To be successful, advertising must be used regularly, not intermittently. Successful advertising is based on repetition.

▲ PLANNING AND EVALUATING ADVERTISING CAMPAIGNS

Single advertisements may be creative or humorous and may convey a message, but by themselves, they are not able to achieve the necessary degree of advertising effectiveness. Many independent hospitality advertisers purchase print advertising or a few radio spots during certain times of the year, particularly when business is slow. This type of advertising is not likely to be as effective as it could be, because continuity between the advertisements is lost. Such advertisements are not packaged as a campaign but are instead a hit-or-miss approach. An advertising campaign includes all forms of advertising held together by a single message or overall theme. A campaign is the overall plan or strategy that guides the development of all forms of advertising.

Campaign planning is initiated by considering the competitive situation, currently targeted markets, potentially targeted markets, and market positioning. An astute manager should always be aware of the advertising activities of major competitors. This, of course, is not to say that the competition should dictate advertising activities, but awareness of competitors' activities may indicate trends. For example, what product–service attributes is the competition stressing? Is it food quality, service quality, physical facilities, extra amenities, room atmosphere, or something else? Awareness of the efforts of direct competition may allow a manager to counter the competition's benefits and gain a competitive advantage.

Both the current target markets and the potential new markets must be evaluated. How can management best reinforce the current markets to promote repeat patronage? What type of message will reach these markets most effectively? In addition, what new markets should be explored? What is the best type of message to use to overcome uncertainty and resistance and promote first-time patronage? Can these two messages be combined, or are they best kept separate? The market positioning must also be considered. How is the operation perceived by repeat consumers and by potential consumers? Is this the same perception that management wishes to project?

Types of Advertising Campaigns

Advertising campaigns come in all patterns and sizes, depending on the resources and needs of the individual hospitality organization. Generally, campaigns are organized geographically on a national, regional, or local level. Each is self-explanatory and will differ in sophistication and media selection. Local campaign planners often feel that they are at a distinct disadvantage because they have smaller advertising budgets and less marketing expertise. This need not be a disadvantage; instead, it is often just the opposite. The use of local radio spots and local print and or television advertising allows the advertiser to speak directly with the local clientele.

Often, the local advertiser has a much clearer understanding of the target market and is able to achieve a competitive advantage over regional and national advertisers.

Campaign Checkpoints. When developing the theme for a campaign, Roman and Maas suggest that the advertiser consider four checkpoints:[4]

1. Maintain visual similarity. This similarity applies to the visual media. Most common approach is to use a well-defined logo or the same layout and type style in all advertisements. Are advertisements easily recognized without looking at the organization's name? If not, perhaps the visual similarity needs further attention.

2. Maintain verbal similarity. Phrases and statements are repeated in all advertisements, reinforcing the advertiser's image and message.

3. Maintain similarity of sound. With the increased use of television and radio advertising, maintaining similarity of sound is also important. The use of the same announcer and/or the same musical logo can aid in maintaining this similarity.

4. Similarity of attitude. Projecting consistent attitude and positioning is critical to the success of an advertising campaign. All media advertisements should project a consistency of attitude in order to establish continuity.

An Advertising Planning Model

For many managers, one of the most difficult aspects involved in managing the advertising and promotional function is the detail of planning, implementing, and evaluating an advertising campaign. Figure 10.4 illustrates an advertising planning model. This visual format makes it easier to conceptualize all aspects of the process and should provide a novice planner with a structured framework from which to work. The model contains five components: (1) input from the marketing information system; (2) organizational objectives; (3) planning and strategy formulation; (4) implementation; and (5) evaluation of advertising effectiveness.

The first component, input from the marketing information system, includes information from three separate areas. First, relevant information concerning consumer behavior should be reviewed and analyzed. What are the trends in consumer behavior? How are dining habits changing? How are the travel patterns of the key market segments changing? What hospitality concepts are hot, and which ones are not so hot? Input concerning the product–service mix is also important. What are the sales trends for the various products and services offered? Information concerning the activities of direct and indirect competition is also of value in

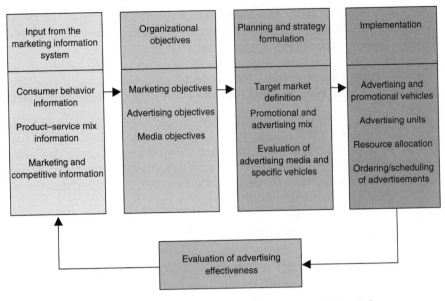

FIGURE 10.4 An Advertising Planning Model

planning the advertising campaign. The process of gathering information for marketing decisions was covered in detail in Chapter 6.

The second component, organizational objectives, should be established in three separate areas: marketing, advertising, and media. Marketing objectives focus on such things as market share and producing a specified percentage of increase in sales volume or a specified percentage of increase in repeat patronage. Advertising objectives focus on such topics as increasing consumer awareness and drawing consumers away from the competition with advertisements demonstrating the superiority of the organization's product–service mix. Media objectives focus on the selection of the individual media to achieve the marketing and advertising objectives. For example, an objective might read, "to plan media selections so that 90 percent of the target market segments are exposed to at least two of the advertisements."

The third component, planning and strategy formulation, involves the formal definition of the specific target markets. Given the limited resources available, it is virtually impossible to reach the saturation point with all target market segments. Therefore, what specific target market segments are most important? Weights should be established for all of the desired advertising and promotional activities. For example, what proportion of the total resources available should be allocated for radio, print, direct mail, and all other activities? Finally, each advertising medium and its individual vehicles are evaluated based on effectiveness and cost efficiency in reaching the target market segments.

Fourth, the advertising plan is implemented. This component includes working with each of the selected advertising vehicles, determining the advertising units (e.g., half-page print advertisements or 30-second radio spots), allocating resources to pay for the advertising time and space, and ordering and scheduling the time and space with each individual vehicle.

The fifth and final component is evaluation of advertising effectiveness. Without engaging in some form of evaluation process, how will management know to what degree the advertising efforts have met with success? There are three important explanations of why some form of evaluation procedure should be undertaken:

1. ***To gain an understanding of the consumer.*** This involves learning what consumers want, why they want it, and how best to serve these needs.

2. ***To avoid costly mistakes.*** When advertising effectiveness is tested, errors that might have gone undetected are noted, and adjustments can be made. In this way, both the effectiveness and cost efficiency of advertising is increased.

3. ***To add structure.*** Rather than viewing advertising as a business expense whose impact is impossible to measure, management can measure the impact of advertising. If sales increase by 10 percent, what is the reason for this increase? What types of advertising and promotion have had the greatest impact on sales?[5]

Evaluating an Advertising Campaign

Several years ago, the president of a large retail chain was discussing the firm's advertising efforts with a group of business people. When one person posed a question about evaluating advertising, the president responded, "I suspect that half our advertising is wasted. The only problem is that I don't know which half." This story may bring a smile to one's face, but it is often an accurate assessment of the situation. Large hospitality organizations engaged in national and regional campaigns normally have the resources to evaluate advertising effectively. Smaller advertisers and local advertisers often are not able to evaluate advertising effectiveness.

Advertising effectiveness can be measured for both its short- and long-term impact. Short-term measurements are usually given most attention because they reflect directly the income statement and the financial position of the organization. In addition, managers' tenure and bonuses are normally based on short-term performance. The long-term effects of advertising, however, should not be overlooked. Repeat patronage, brand loyalty, and an asset called goodwill reflect long-term effects. It is difficult, however, to measure the long-term residual effects of advertising within a reasonable margin for error. In the last several years, econometric techniques have advanced to the point where measuring advertising effectiveness is more precise.

The management of a hospitality operation can evaluate advertising subjectively, either alone or in conjunction with an advertising agency. Experienced management plays a key role in this type of evaluation. If management has successfully directed advertising campaigns, subjective evaluation may indeed be adequate. This is especially true of agency executives, as they often have a wealth of experience that allows them to gauge quite accurately the overall effectiveness of advertising efforts.

It is also wise to maintain a file of all advertisements. These can then be available for easy reference and reviewed periodically for winners and losers. Subjectivity does have a place in the overall evaluation of advertising effectiveness. The experience and expertise of agency personnel and hospitality managers should not be discounted. These resources are best used in combination with objective methods.

It is almost impossible to measure advertising effectiveness objectively unless well-defined objectives have been formulated prior to initiating a campaign. How would management know whether they were successful if they were not able to compare actual performance with specific objectives? As stressed in Chapter 5, clearly defined, quantifiable objectives are very important. Variances between actual performance and objectives are noted and corrective action taken. In the event that the advertising proves more successful than expected, this too should be evaluated so that the success might be repeated.

Objective testing of advertising is time-consuming and expensive. Not all operations can afford or will want this type of testing. Testing is invaluable if undertaken with care and is cost-effective if used occasionally. Following is a brief review of commonly used techniques, although they are not all suitable for all types of operations:

1. **Copy testing.** This involves pretesting the copy of an advertisement prior to running it in the media. Several advertisements are normally shown to a group of consumers, and questions are asked of the group, typically, "Which advertisement would interest you most?" "Which advertisement is most convincing?" "Which advertisement is most likely to cause you to patronize the hospitality establishment?" These questions can be asked of an entire group assembled for review a series of advertisements, or personal interviews can be conducted.

2. **Inquiry and sales.** Direct-mail advertising lends itself to the inquiry and sales method. This involves keeping a tally of each inquiry and sale. For example, if a series of advertisements were run to promote banquet business, how many people phoned or contacted the operation? How many of these inquiries were converted into sales? From these tallies, it is easy to compute a cost per inquiry and a cost per sale for this type of advertising.

3. **Coupons and split runs.** Coupons can be tallied to evaluate the effectiveness of one promotion against others. Fox example, did the sun-

dae special sell more than the special french fries promotion? Coupons are used extensively by the hospitality industry because they allow for easy evaluation. Coupons can be carried one step further and used to compare one medium against another. For example, suppose that management had a choice among three print media in which to place advertisements. Which one will reach the target market most effectively? The same advertisements and coupons could be run in the three media, with each coupon coded so that a tally could be made of the number of coupons from medium A, B, and C. In this way, a relative ranking of effectiveness is possible.

4. *Sales tests.* The level of gross sales or sales of specific items can be monitored following a specific period of advertising aimed at increasing one or the other. It is often difficult to take into account all the variables that affect sales both positively and negatively and thereby establish a cause-and-effect relationship.

5. *Consumer testing of awareness, recall, and attitude.* Through assembled groups, telephone surveys, direct mail surveys, and personal interviews, consumers can be tested to determine their relative awareness concerning a specific hospitality operation. Have they heard of the operation? Do they patronize it? If so, how frequently do they visit? Do they recall seeing any advertisements? Which ones do they recall? When shown certain advertisements, do they recall seeing these? This is known as *aided recall.*

Relations with an Advertising Agency

Should a hospitality organization hire an advertising agency? With the exception of small motels or restaurants that don't have large budgets, all larger operations should consider the use of an agency. The final decision is certainly for each organization to make, but agencies offer several advantages. First, an agency can increase the effectiveness of advertising; its work is more professional, and its use of media is better. Second, agencies can be especially helpful, if not necessary, in overcoming the special production requirements of radio and television advertising. Third, using an advertising agency is like maintaining a staff of part-time specialists—copywriters, artists, and layout professionals. Fourth, agencies are able to maintain closer contacts with media representatives than can a single advertiser. Finally, some advertising agencies are able to offer consultative services related to such advertising and marketing projects as test marketing.

Management must, however, consider the disadvantages of using an agency. First and foremost is, of course, the question of money. There is no such thing as a free lunch, and top-quality professional assistance will cost money. Furthermore, if the hospitality organization has access to adequate freelance talent and assistance, the services of an agency may not be required.

Managers have to make decisions about how advertising will be handled. These decisions should be based on the following factors:

- The amount of available time to devote to advertising
- The sizes of the target market segments
- The specific media that are being considered or have been selected
- Management's knowledge of and experience in advertising
- The amount of money to be spent on advertising

The Role of an Agency. What is an advertising agency, and what services can it provide? An agency is an independent business that works for the client that is purchasing the advertising. Agencies come in all shapes and sizes, from one-person operations to large agencies employing hundreds of individuals. Generally, a small advertiser should avoid the very large agencies because these often are not able to give the personal attention that the small advertiser needs and wants. Agencies that push out advertising in huge quantities may lack creativity and may resort to a production-line approach.

Both creative and business professionals who are specialists in various areas staff the agency. First, they apply both art and science to advertising. An agency develops and implements an advertising plan tailored to the needs of the individual client. Second, they coordinate the various functions that must take place if an advertising campaign is to be successful. They do this by coordinating the creative staff, which develops the advertisements, and the business staff, which secures the advertising time and space in the various media. An agency can actually save the client money because the fees earned by the agency are paid as commissions by the medium in which the advertisements are placed.

Types of Advertising Agencies. There are several types of advertising agencies. They can be classified based on two criteria: the type of business they handle and the range of services they offer. Agencies may serve a broad range of consumer products, or they may specialize in one field such as consumer goods, industrial products, financial services, retail sales, or real estate. Needless to say, it is wise to select an agency with a proven track record in working with service or hospitality industry clients. An advertising agency may offer specific functions such as media buying services or creative services, or it may be a full-service agency. Full-service agencies will handle not only the advertising that the client elects to purchase, but also nonadvertising activities such as sales promotional materials, trade show exhibits, publicity, and public relations.

Advertising agencies are able to provide a wide variety of professional services, including campaign planning, market research, media selection and production, public relations, and campaign evaluations. The following represents a list of most of the services that an agency should be able to provide.

- Studying the client's product–service mix to determine strengths and weaknesses and the client's relation to the competition
- Conducting an analysis of the current and potential market segments to determine future potential
- Providing direction and leadership with regard to selecting available media and the best method to advertise and promote the product service mix
- Formulating a detailed plan to reach the stated advertising and promotional objectives
- Executing the plan by coordinating the creative process (writing and designing the advertisements) and the business process (securing the desired advertising time and space)
- Verifying that the desired advertisements have been run in the media selected
- Evaluating the effectiveness of the advertising campaign and submitting a report to the client

Selecting an Advertising Agency. The agency–client relationship is very important, so the agency should be selected with great care. How should a hospitality manager go about selecting an agency? Entering into an agency–client relationship is not a move to be taken lightly, but it can be based on a rational process. A few recommendations follow.

First, make a list of the needs that an agency must satisfy. It is also wise to make a list of the major problems or symptoms unique to the character of the specific hospitality client. Begin a list of questions to ask in selecting an agency, such as "What is the reputation of the agency?" "What experience does the agency have with hospitality accounts?" "How much depth of talent does the agency have?" Other needs and criteria should be listed, but these will depend on the needs of an individual hospitality organization.

Second, make a list of prospective agencies. This will involve checking the track records of several agencies as well as informing them of the organization's interest. Some managers prefer to use an agency questionnaire to gather preliminary data from prospective agencies. Using this type of questionnaire offers both pros and cons. It allows management to gather information from a variety of agencies and then use that information in initial screening. It does, however, occasionally turn off an agency, making the agency feel that the prospective client is asking for too much information before the agency–client relationship has been established.

Third, after a list of prospective agencies has been developed, it must be narrowed to a few viable agencies. At this point management should be prepared to meet with agency representatives, review samples of their work, listen to ideas, and evaluate the agency against the organization's needs and criteria.

Agency Compensation. How are advertising agencies compensated? Typically, agencies receive payment in several ways: (1) commissions from media; (2) fees or retainers paid by client; (3) service charges for creative and production work; (4) markups on outside purchases; and (5) trade-outs. Commissions of 15 percent are normally paid to the agency by the media. For example, if an advertisement costs $1,000, the agency would collect $1,000 from the client but would pay the media $1,000 minus $150 (15 percent), or a total of $850. Agencies often do not generate sufficient revenue from small advertisers to cover production and creative costs, and therefore they charge other fees. Such fees are often monthly retainers and hourly charges for creative work.

Charges are also levied for such production work as photography and graphics. These are usually billed at a rate of cost plus 17.65 percent. If services are performed for the agency by a third party, the agency may add a mark-up to the amount billed by the third party. This mark-up would cover the costs or securing the services and coordinating the services of several third-party providers. Charges are made for advertising on which commissions are not paid, such as direct mail and local newspaper advertising.

Agencies may also accept trade-outs as a form of compensation. Trade-outs consist of trading services for services. The agency performs services for the hotel or restaurant in exchange for services in the form of food and beverages or guest rooms that are provided on a complimentary basis up to the retail value of the services provided by the advertising agency. This method is widely used by hotels and restaurants for it increases the purchasing power of each dollar spent.

Establishing a positive agency–client relationship is of critical importance. Management should be willing to work closely with the agency and be honest and open in communication. A manager should be critical of the agency's work without being overly critical of every advertisement. Attention should instead be focused on the broader overall strategy. Taking an active interest in the relationship is a very positive step in making the relationship a good one.

▲ EFFECTS OF ADVERTISING

Advertising has become a common practice by firms selling products and services in our society. Consumers marvel at the advertisements during prime-time television and special events like the Super Bowl or the Olympics. Every year, the nation is astonished at the cost of advertising for 30 seconds during these types of major events. In addition, advertisers are given awards for their creativity and special effects, and celebrities receive large sums of money to participate in advertisements. Therefore, it is no wonder that economists and consumer advocates debate the overall impact of advertising on our society.

Social and Ethical Criticisms of Advertising

Many critics of advertising raise questions about the social and ethical issues surrounding the use of advertising and other forms of promotion. The following is a list of the most common criticisms regarding advertising.[6]

Advertising as Misleading or Deceptive. Originally, advertising was a practice used to inform consumers about products and product uses. It was a way for firms to convey their messages to consumers so that they could make informed purchase decisions. Over the years, as the country prospered and more firms sold more products to more consumers with more discretionary income, advertising became a major strategic tool used to differentiate products and services. Unfortunately, in the heat of competition, some firms choose to stretch the truth in an attempt to gain a competitive advantage.

Advertising is indeed a powerful force in the marketplace, and occasionally, it may be used to deceive consumers. The government has gone to great lengths to protect the consumer. Many other groups, including the Better Business Bureau and the National Advertising Review Council, strive to limit the amount of false and misleading advertising. Also, it simply is not in the long-term interests of any hospitality operation to deceive its consumers. Advertising seeks to induce first-time and repeat patronage by making promises to consumers about specific products and services. Failure to deliver as promised hurts the advertiser's credibility and sales.

Advertising as Offensive or in Poor Taste. As mentioned before, the increase in competition has resulted in some firms engaging in questionable advertising practices in an attempt to gain market share. In addition to being misleading or deceptive, some critics have also argued that some advertising is offensive or in poor taste. For example, insurance firms use "fear appeal" to sell their products, automobile manufacturers use "sex" to sell cars, and marketers of children's products target them directly. Firms may argue their first amendment rights to free speech, but many critics feel that advertisers have crossed the line. Advertising has also been accused of creating and perpetuating stereotypes based on its depiction of certain groups of people. Proponents might argue that art imitates life.

Advertising Encourages Materialism. Rather than merely inform and educate consumers about product benefits, much advertising focuses on creating needs and promoting materialism. Products and services are being promoted as symbols of status and accomplishment, to the detriment of basic values. Celebrities are used in ads in an attempt to influence consumers and act as a point of reference. Another common practice in advertisements is to seek product placement in popular movies, many of which target impressionable youths. For example, the boy in *Home Alone 2* spent some time alone at The Plaza hotel in New York, indulging himself with the many amenities that the hotel offers. Also, cruises are advertised to people as a reward for working hard and a symbol of accomplishment, as are many tourist destinations and resorts.

Advertising Encourages People to Buy Things They Do Not Need.
Advertising seeks to persuade consumers to purchase specific products and services from the advertiser. It is the term *persuade* that bothers critics. As previously mentioned, advertising could be limited to informing and educating consumers so they can make informed decisions. Some would argue that an expensive dining experience or a night in a luxury hotel is unnecessary when a less expensive substitute would adequately satisfy their needs. Most dining out and travel is an acquired taste, and once acquired, it needs to be satisfied just as other needs are. However, proponents argue that consumers still choose the products and services that they want to purchase. Consumers are the ones who make the final decision concerning how their limited resources will be allocated. Advertising simply makes them aware of choices and attempts to encourage patronage.

Economic Effects of Advertising

Advertising has become a very important strategic tool used by companies, not only to provide information to consumers but to position themselves and gain some form of competitive advantage. There is no doubt that there are advantages to advertising at the brand level. However, some critics question the effects of advertising at the industry level or on the economy as a whole. The following is a brief discussion of the economic effects of advertising.

Effects on Consumer Choice. Most firms use advertising to differentiate their products and services from those of their competitors. Although consumers still have the option of purchasing from several different brands, in most product categories, there are advantages realized by larger firms that can afford to spend more on advertising. Therefore, some critics would argue that large firms have the ability to dominate the market and charge higher prices than their smaller counterparts. Most consumers can easily recall two or three popular brands in any product or service category, and they tend to be the brands offered by the largest competitors. As a result, larger firms may have the potential to reduce the competition based on price or product and services attributes and make it difficult for smaller firms to create brand loyalty among consumers.

The proponents of advertising would argue that firms of all sizes benefit from the ability to promote new products. Advertising is a means by which firms create awareness and interest in their products. In addition, advertising can be used to inform and educate consumers about new products and services, as well as changes in existing products. As mentioned earlier, consumers normally have several brands to choose from, so advertising has not led to monopolies or restrictions in the number of choices available to consumers.

Effects on Competition.   One of the major criticisms of advertising is its ability to create barriers of entry to firms wishing to enter a market. When large firms spend large amounts of money on advertising, it makes it increasingly difficult for new brands to enter the market with any reasonable level of success. Instead, new brands are relegated to pursuing niche strategies in an attempt to profit and survive. Large firms also enjoy economies of scale in advertising, much like they do in other areas such as ordering supplies, recruiting and training, and financing. This is especially true in the area of media buying, where firms that purchase more volume get more favorable rates. This results in large firms controlling the major media that has the most impact on consumers. Based on these assertions, some critics would argue that advertising could have an anti-competitive effect on the market.

Once again, proponents of advertising would argue that firms should be able to use advertising to provide consumers with information about their products and services, thereby differentiating their brands from the competition. Firms get large by offering good products and services at reasonable prices through convenient locations. It is naïve to believe that advertising alone creates the barriers to entry and the economies of scale that large firms enjoy in the marketplace. These benefits are merely the result of fair competition in a free market society. Also, all successful firms do not spend large amounts of money on advertising. Years ago, people believed that McDonald's was beginning to establish a virtual monopoly in the fast-food segment of the industry. Those people held that McDonald's would drive the independent operations out of business and would then consume many of the smaller regional chains. This has not been the case. McDonald's does hold a very commanding lead in annual sales, but McDonald's has experienced their own set of challenges in responding to competitive threats and changes in consumer behavior. Large chains do enjoy certain advertising advantages, but these advantages hardly create a monopolistic marketplace.

Effects on Product Costs and Prices.   Probably the most common criticism of advertising is that it results in higher costs that lead to higher prices charged to consumers for products and services. There is no question that advertising is a cost of doing business, similar to a firm's payroll, supply, building leases, insurance, and financing. It appears as a line item on the statement of income and expense, as an expense, and must be covered if a firm expects to be profitable. The concept of fixed expenses being covered by the contribution margin for products and services is presented in the pricing chapter that follows. Basically, any increase in expenses must be offset by an increase in price, or a decrease in other expenses if a firm is to maintain its current level of profitability. Therefore, it is easy to see how critics could argue that advertising leads to higher prices. A quick review of financial statements would most likely show that firms that spend more on advertising tend to charge higher prices than their competitors.

The proponents of advertising would argue that the increased prices are the result of offering higher quality products, and advertising is necessary to inform consumers of these quality differences. The fact consumers are better-informed causes firms to provide higher-quality products at lower prices. Consumers can readily compare competitive products and services, thereby putting downward pressure on industry prices.

▲ MARKETING ACTION NOW!

A large national restaurant chain has decided to open one of its restaurants in your town. Choose a particular chain and do some research to determine its menu, including prices, and its target market. Then, provide the class with a positioning statement and an analysis of the competition for this new restaurant. Try to obtain as much detailed information as possible so that you truly understand the restaurant's philosophy and mission.

Once you have gained a good understanding of the restaurant, its customers, and its competition, the next step is to determine how you would use the promotional mix leading up to the grand opening. Discuss possible strategies for advertising, public relations, personal selling, and sales promotions. How would you differentiate your restaurant from the competition? How would you go about building market share for the new restaurant?

▲ SUMMARY OF CHAPTER OBJECTIVES

This chapter reviews promotion as applied to hospitality marketing, providing a broad-based overview of the four elements of the promotional mix: advertising, personal selling, public relations, and sales promotion. The management of the promotional mix over the product life cycle is discussed, and methods for setting the promotional budget are examined. They include the percentage of sales, objective and task, competitive parity, and all-you-can-afford. A budgeting system provides an easily understood presentation of budget development.

Advertising can be national, local, or cooperative, depending on the size and scope of the firm. To reach the highest level of success, management must engage in various advertising efforts. Generally, advertising seeks to satisfy three goals: (1) to establish awareness in the minds of consumers; (2) to establish a positive perceived value in the minds of consumers; and (3) to promote repeat patronage and brand loyalty among consumers. Advertising positioning and strategy include formation of an objective, a target audience, key consumer benefits, support for the benefits, and an appropriate tone or manner. The development of an advertising appeal includes six keys to successful advertising.

In some cases, firms choose to enter a relationship with an advertising agency. The chapter provides an overview of the advantages and disadvantages of working with an agency, the role of the agency, the types of agencies, methods that can be used to select an agency, and methods for compensation.

Planning and evaluating advertising involve noting campaign checkpoints. A five-component advertising planning model includes input from the marketing information system, organizational objectives, planning and strategy formulation, implementation, and evaluation of advertising effectiveness.

Finally, the chapter discusses the effects of advertising on society. There are critics that feel advertising has many negative social consequences and economic effects on competition. In general, it is argued that advertising limits consumer choices and leads to unfair competition as larger firms create barriers to entry and enjoy economies of scale that are not available to smaller firms.

▲ KEY TERMS AND CONCEPTS

Advertising

Advertising agencies

Advertising campaign

Advertising central appeal

Advertising planning process

Cooperative advertising

Copy testing

Criticisms of advertising

Local advertising

National advertising

Personal selling

Promotional budgets

Promotional mix

Product life cycle

Public relations

Publicity

Recall

Sales promotions

Visual, verbal, sound, and
  attitude similarity

▲ QUESTIONS FOR REVIEW AND DISCUSSION

1. What are the four elements of the promotional mix?
2. How is the promotional mix used throughout the stages of the product life cycle?
3. List and discuss the various methods used to establish promotional budgets. Which is the most common? Which one is the best from a theoretical standpoint?
4. What are the three forms of advertising? Give examples of each form.
5. How would you describe the process of positioning?
6. What are the three major goals of advertising?
7. What are the pros and cons of using an advertising agency? Would you use the services of an agency?
8. How are agencies compensated for their work?
9. How would you go about selecting an agency?
10. Critique the six keys to successful advertising.
11. What is an advertising campaign? What factors should be considered when planning a campaign?
12. Cite and discuss the major campaign checkpoints.
13. What techniques are used to evaluate advertising effectiveness?
14. What are some of the social and ethical consequences associated with advertising?
15. What economic effects are associated with advertising?

▲ NOTES

[1]*Advertising Age* (May 10, 1999), pp. s4.

[2]Kenneth Roman and Jane Maas, *How to Advertise* (New York, NY: St. Martin's Press, 1976), pp. 1–3.

[3]H. Victor Grohmann, "Ten Keys to Successful Advertising," *Cornell Hotel and Restaurant Administration Quarterly*, Vol. 17, No., pp. 3–7.

[4]Kenneth Roman and Jane Maas, *How to Advertise* (New York, NY: St. Martin's Press, 1976), pp.1–3.

[5]C. H. Sandge, V. Fryburger, and K. Rotzoll, *Advertising Theory and Practice* (Homewood, IL: Richard D. Irwin, 1979) pp. 533–536.

[6]George E. Belch and Michael A. Belch, *Introduction to Advertising and Promotion: An Integrated Marketing Communications Perspective*, 2nd edition (Boston, MA: Richard D. Irwin, Inc., 1993) pp. 811–834.

11

Advertising and Media Planning

❖ Chapter Objectives

By the end of this chapter, you should understand:

1. The process of planning the media mix, including media selection and scheduling
2. The terms and concepts used in the media planning process
3. The characteristics of the various types of broadcast media
4. The characteristics of the various types of print media
5. The other forms of media that are used to support the popular media vehicles

❖ Chapter Outline

❖ Chapter Opening Profile

CHOOSING THE MEDIA MIX IS A critical part of any advertising campaign. For example, Bermuda's Department of Tourism is attempting to inform travelers of the island's unique culture.[1] In the past, travelers viewed the island as a tropical oasis, ignoring the other assets the island has to offer. However, Bermuda cannot compete with Caribbean destinations such as the Bahamas and Mexico when it comes to price. Air travel to Bermuda has declined about 7 percent over the past decade, and hotel occupancy has declined 14 percent, to a current figure of 60 percent, since 1980. As a result, Bermuda's Department of Tourism has launched a $15 million campaign focusing on the nation's other attributes such as churches, museums, and jazz.

The campaign includes six TV spots, seven radio spots, seven newspaper ads, and as many as 20 magazine ads. The ads will target individuals with certain hobbies like golfing and scuba diving, rather than focus on demographics. Also, the campaign will concentrate on five geographic markets: Atlanta, Baltimore, Boston, New York, and Philadelphia. Islanders were involved in the process by being asked to vote for the ads that they felt reflected the real Bermuda. In the end, the objective is to reposition Bermuda as a tropical island with a unique history and architecture.

▲ INTRODUCTION

No one questions that advertising is an extremely powerful force in the hospitality industry. Advertising programs must be managed with care and used to the maximum advantage of the organization. External advertising and promotion constitute a major area of marketing effort for most hospitality organizations, as numerous media are employed in an effort to communicate with selected target markets. The success of these advertising efforts rests to a large degree on the media and the manner in which they are used. Many times, advertisers spend large amounts of money without achieving the desired results. In other cases, advertisers spend only a relatively small amount, yet the results are dramatic. It is useful to remember that it is not how much is invested but how it is invested. Dollars allocated to advertising are expected to increase sales, and a positive return on an investment is expected.

Advertising is important because it can make the difference between success and failure. Management must ask three questions in initial advertising planning:

1. *To Whom Should the Advertising Be Directed?* Specifically, what target markets have been identified as primary and secondary markets? Which individuals represent opinion leaders and reference group leaders? Market segmentation data should be collected and analyzed to determine the heavy users of the product or service.

2. *Where Do These People Live?* Once the large markets are identified, it is imperative to determine where these individuals live and work. What are the best methods to reach them through advertising? In many cases, this will be as easy as determining the leaders of the business community in a small town. In other instances, determining where these individuals live and work will prove quite difficult. Suppose, for example, that a tablecloth restaurant operated in the suburbs of a major city. Where should the restaurant advertise? How should the target markets be reached? Where do these people live and work? These questions may not have self-evident answers and a considerable amount of research and discussion may be necessary.

3. *What Media Should Be Used?* Would it be best to use print advertising? Perhaps radio or television should play a major role? What about outdoor advertising, direct mail, or supplemental advertising? Should directories, such as the yellow pages, be considered?

Developing Media Plans

The stages in the media planning process are similar to the marketing planning process. First, a firm must perform some type of market analysis to determine the current situation. Second, the firm needs to establish its media objectives. That is, what the firm wishes to accomplish with its media program, such as creating awareness or increasing sales. Third, the firm must develop media strategies that can be used to attain the objectives. Media strategies would entail the development of a media mix, determining the desired coverage in regard to target markets and geographic area, and the scheduling of the specific media. Fourth, the media program will need to be evaluated on a continual basis and adapted to fit changing conditions.

Market Analysis. This stage of the process involves a thorough analysis of the market to identify the target markets that will be the focus of the media program. This decision is based on the past history of the firm, its competitors, and trends in the general population. Advertising is a key element in the positioning of firms and their products or services. Therefore, it is important to select target markets that offer potential for long-term growth and survival. These market segments then become the focus of the media program in an attempt to communicate the firm's products in a favorable light, which is consistent with the overall image of the firm. For example, all advertising might be aimed at men and women between the ages of 25 and 35 with annual incomes above $35,000. Or, advertising might be slanted toward women such that a 60-to-40 ratio of female-to-male exposures is achieved.

Establishing Media Objectives. Media objectives should be tied to the overall marketing objectives of the firm, as well as the promotion or communications objectives. The media objectives should be focused on the goals associated with the media program, and attainable using media strategies. After determining the target market(s) in the market analysis stage, a firm should establish media objectives for these markets considering the distribution of exposures (i.e., reach and frequency), the media environment, and budget limitations.[2] Some of the more common objectives for media programs are:

- To increase awareness among consumers in the target markets.
- To increase coverage in target markets.
- To have a positive impact on consumer attitudes and perceptions in regard to the firm's image.

These statements need to be developed to meet the following criteria for good objectives. Good objectives will: (1) be stated in clear and concise language; (2) include a specific time frame in which to accomplish the objective; and (3) include quantifiable terms that can be used as a standard with which to evaluate performance. For example, a local restaurant may want to reach at least 70 percent of its target audience with a direct-mail piece within the next five days.

Developing Media Strategies. Once media objectives are established, it is necessary to develop media strategies that will lead to the attainment of the firm's goals. Selecting the proper media mix, determining the target market and geographic coverage, and scheduling the media achieve this.

1. *Selecting the Media Mix.* When selecting the media mix, it is important to examine the general nature of the target market segments. Table 11.1 contains a list of the possible media vehicles and their unique characteristics. A medium should be selected based on its ability to reach the maximum number of potential consumers at the lowest **cost per thousand (C.P.M.).** However, it is also necessary to minimize wasted coverage

cost per thousand (C.P.M.) cost to reach 1,000 consumers through an advertising medium

Table 11.1	Media Characteristics	
Media Type	*Advantages*	*Disadvantages*
Newspapers	Short lead time for placing ads Low cost Good coverage Can be used for coupons	Short life span Wasted coverage Clutter Poor reproduction quality
Magazines	Quality reproduction Long life span Audience selectivity High information content "Pass along" value	Long lead time for ad placement High production costs Lack of flexibility
Radio	Personal Low cost Flexibility Low production costs Audience selectivity	Lack of visual appeal Fleeting message Clutter
Television	Large audience High impact of message Low cost per exposure High credibility	High absolute cost High production cost Fleeting message Clutter Low selectivity
Direct Mail	High selectivity/low wasted coverage Easily evaluated High information content Short lead time	Poor image Clutter High cost per contact
Outdoor and Transit	Low cost per exposure High repetition Target location	Wasted coverage Legislation/local restrictions Long lead time Lack of flexibility

while trying to maximize reach. Wasted coverage refers to advertising exposures that do not involve members of the target market. For example, if low-income households are exposed to ads for an expensive restaurant, the restaurant is wasting money because it is paying to reach consumers who are not in its target market and would be unlikely to dine at the restaurant. If one million people subscribe to a newspaper, advertisers are charged based on a readership of one million, whether the readers are in the target market or not.

Also, the objectives of the overall campaign must be considered. Is the advertiser seeking maximum impact, or is continuity with previous and future advertising more important? For example, if a well-established restaurant had used a refined and sophisticated approach in newspaper and magazine advertising, it would not make sense for it to advertise using a high-volume, high-energy advertisement, for this would break up the continuity among advertisements in different media.

In addition to these general factors, Howard Heinsius, president of Needham and Grohmann, Inc., suggests several essentials in media selection:[3]

- *Market focus.* Carefully examine your market by product–service mix category or brand and by target market segment. How does your hotel or restaurant fit in? What specific attributes do you want to advance?
- *Media focus.* Keep an open mind and listen to all media sales representatives in your area. Make note of changes, events, new programs, and the opportunities they might offer. Media time and space is perishable; keep an alert eye for special purchase opportunities.
- *Periodic media update.* Keep current information about rates and other important information such as cost per thousand and circulation. The situation can change rapidly. Be sure to stay on top of it.
- *Establish media effectiveness guidelines.* Keep tangible guidelines in mind as you examine each of the media options. This will help you to make better media selections.
- *Advertising by objective.* If specific advertising objectives have been established such as sales targets or consumer awareness levels this will aid in determining the best media combination.
- *Coordinate advertising with marketing campaigns, advertising is but one part* of the total marketing mix. Be sure that it is coordinated with the other efforts in the areas of personal selling, promotion, and public relations.
- *Develop a sound advertising budget.* Start with an amount that is within your means and then allocate it by target markets. It is important to not try to do too much with very limited funds.
- *Plan around media pollution.* All forms of media are over saturated at times. Try to select the best times to get your message across and how to rise above the pollution of other advertisements.

- *Coordinate the local efforts to match the national advertising efforts.* When a national campaign is being run, try to take advantage of this by running a local campaign that will follow.
- *Use a variety of media.* Within the limits of budgets, try to use different combinations and levels of different media to determine which is most effective.
- *Keep accurate files.* It is important to be able to review the results of each advertising campaign. Maintaining accurate records of budget, media schedules, and sales results is critical.

The media selection process involves matching available media with the firm's objectives. There may be multiple objectives and many media alternatives from which to choose. Therefore, the process is one of making choices at various levels. For example, once a decision is made to use some form of print media, the decision between newspaper and magazine follows. Then, a decision must be made regarding the particular magazines or newspapers that will be used.

2.   *Determining Target Market and Geographic Coverage.* Consideration must be given to the amount of coverage desired. The relative costs of the various media must be weighed when decisions are made. The sizes and frequency of advertisements should be analyzed carefully. Hospitality and travel firms have the option to advertise on an international, national, regional, or local level. Then, at each level, a firm must decide how long, or how often, to run an ad in a given market.

3.   *Scheduling the Media.* Each hospitality organization must tailor the scheduling of media to fit its individual needs. Figure 11.1 illustrates the three most common approaches to media scheduling. *Continuous advertising* refers to the practice of keeping the amount of advertising rela-

continuous advertising   keeping the amount of advertising relatively constant over time

FIGURE 11.1   Approaches to Media Scheduling

flighting media scheduling schedule advertising with spurts and stops

pulsing advertising constant low level of advertising with periods of blitz advertising

tively constant over time. This type is appropriate for those hospitality operations with very stable volumes. *Flighting media scheduling* involves a schedule set up in spurts and stops. Periods of blitz advertising are used, with no advertising between blitzes. *Pulsing advertising* balances the previous two approaches in that it provides a constant low-level flow of advertising with intermittent periods of blitz advertising. Ideally, high levels of continuous advertising are normally thought to be superior, but economic considerations may necessitate the adoption of either flighting or pulsing media scheduling.

▲ PRINT MEDIA

The two most common forms of print media are newspapers and magazines. Another form of print media is the Yellow Pages offered by local telephone companies. Advertising in the Yellow Pages can result in immediate action, but it is difficult to differentiate a firm's product and there is little flexibility. However, all of the print media vehicles are popular among hospitality firms because of their ability to provide detailed information and target specific markets. For example, **newspapers** offer the following advantages:

- *Short lead time for placing ads.* If a manager decides to run an advertisement on one day's notice, it can normally be scheduled in the next day's newspapers. Also, copy can easily be changed, allowing advertisements to be tailored to fit ever-changing market conditions.
- *Low cost.* An advertisement in a local newspaper is usually lower in both absolute cost and cost per thousand, in comparison to other types of media.
- *Good coverage.* Newspapers reach all demographic segments in a geographic area.
- *Can be used for coupons.* Newspapers allow for the use of coupons that can increase volume and provide information necessary for evaluating advertising effectiveness.

In general, newspapers are a valuable form of media for local hospitality and travel firms. Advertisements will reach a broad audience at a relatively low cost. However, newspapers also have the following disadvantages:

- *Short life span of the advertisement.* Newspapers generally have a one-day life span because they are published on a daily basis.
- *Wasted coverage.* Advertisers pay to reach the total number of newspaper subscribers, many of which are not in the target market based on demographics or lifestyles.
- *Clutter.* There is a lot of competition for the reader's attention within the newspaper. It is easy to have an advertisement buried amid other advertisements, decreasing readership and effectiveness.

Making the decision to open our second hotel in New York was a walk in the park.

Inter-Continental Hotels and Resorts now has a second distinctive New York location. Central Park South. With the most spectacular views along the park, classic European decor and fine dining, Central Park Inter-Continental New York is sure to be the preferred destination. And as always, Inter-Continental brings personalized, attentive service that dazzles even the most discerning traveler. We believe it will serve as a perfect complement to our East Side address. For our special grand opening rates, please give us a call at 800-327-0200.

CENTRAL PARK
INTER·CONTINENTAL
NEW YORK
112 Central Park South · New York
www.interconti.com

Magazine advertising is used frequently by hotel sales departments.
Picture courtesy of Inter-Continental Hotels, New York.

- *Poor reproduction quality.* Newspaper production and printing does not reproduce photographs with clarity. Drawings are usually a better choice.

Magazines offer these advertising advantages:

- *Quality reproduction.* Color photographs reproduce particularly well.
- *Long life span.* Through pass-along readership, magazine advertisements are seen by more people and have a longer life span than that of newspapers and other media.
- *Audience selectivity.* Some magazines are aimed at the general population, but through the use of regional and metropolitan editions as well as selective market magazines, advertisers can pinpoint specific target markets. This is especially true of city magazines.
- *High information content.* Magazines provide ample space to cover detailed topics and supply a good deal of information.

In general, magazines offer better reproduction than newspapers and allow marketers to segment on a regional basis. However, magazines have the following disadvantages as an advertising medium:

- *Long lead time for ad placement.* Magazine publishers require advertisers to adhere to closing dates far in advance of the distribution date. This does not allow for immediate changes of layout and copy if market conditions change rapidly.
- *High production costs.* Costs associated with magazine advertising are generally substantially higher than those for newspapers, including both absolute costs and the cost per thousand.
- *Lack of flexibility.* Magazines are not as well suited for local markets as newspapers, direct mail, or radio. Magazines are generally either regional or national in scope and are often of limited value to local hospitality and travel firms. Therefore, regional and national chains will normally find more benefit from advertising in magazines. However, city magazines, such as those placed in hotel rooms, do overcome this drawback.

Techniques for Successful Print Advertising

As with all types of advertising, no hard and fast rules exist, but guidelines can aid in management decisions. The following guidelines, developed over time, are generally accepted within the advertising community.

First, every effort should be made to attract the consumer's attention with the headline. Many print advertisements are ineffective because a large percentage of consumers skim through the pages and never read the entire advertisement. The headline must therefore get the attention of the reader and deliver the message.

Second, print advertising is more effective if visual components, such as artwork and photographs, are used. Although photographs do not generally reproduce well in newspapers, simple drawings can be used very effectively to increase readership. Photographs and artwork are both effective in magazines.

Third, every effort should be made to keep the layout and copy simple and straightforward. Print readers are less likely to read an advertisement that looks crowded and contains many ideas. Instead, the advertisement should have one or perhaps two points and no more. Print advertising is an example of where less is more, and this means more effectiveness.

Fourth, print advertising lends itself to the use of coupons. Coupons serve to increase volume and can be very valuable in assessing the effectiveness of print advertising media. Coupons should be designed so that they are really miniadvertisements that can be clipped out and will convey the message so the consumer does not need to save the rest of the advertisement. Placement of coupons is important both within the advertisement and on the page on which the advertisement appears. They should be placed at the edge of the advertisement, and the advertisement itself at the edge of the page to make it easier to clip them out. Simple things like coupon placement can increase advertising effectiveness dramatically.

Finally, when a given print advertisement has been effective, management should not hesitate to repeat it. The advertisement may seem old hat to the management of the hospitality or travel firm, but many potential consumers have not seen the advertisement or do not recall it. Therefore, what has proven successful in the past should be repeated.

Developing Copy for Print Advertising

For some individuals, developing advertising copy is simple and easy; for others it is painful and frustrating. This section offers a few ideas to make the task easier. Copy writing does not require the brains of a genius or the writing skills of a Pulitzer Prize winner. It simply requires looking closely at the consumer and the product–service mix.

The first step is to take a close look at the product–service mix. What does the hospitality or travel organization's product–service mix offer that is appealing to the potential consumer? It is important to avoid generalizations, such as "good food," "luxurious guest rooms," and "fine atmosphere." These phrases may be true, but what will they do for the consumer? Items that could distinguish the operation from others and give it a real competitive advantage should be listed. Emphasis should be placed on the tangible aspects of the product–service mix, such as the decor or service personnel. It is very important to try to make the intangibles seem more tangible. This will help the consumer remember the advertisement.

Second, it is important to talk directly with the potential consumer and discuss the benefits of purchasing from the hospitality or travel operation. What is the operation going to do for the consumer? What specific benefits are offered? What specific needs are being satisfied? For example, a tablecloth restaurant appealing to the business community might advertise a "lightning lunch" or "express lunch" featuring a selection of menu items that could be served immediately. It is important to back this claim with a guarantee such as "if the menu items are not served within 15 minutes, the lunch is free."

Third, the consumer benefits should be listed in priority order. Perhaps it is best to develop two or three advertisements around the top three benefits and translate them into headlines. Headlines can take many forms, as shown in Table 11.2.

Once the headline is developed, the copy for the remainder of the advertisement is written. It should reflect and support the headline and should be brief. This is not to say that long copy can never be successful. Instead, each word, each sentence, and each paragraph must say exactly what the copywriter wants it to say. All the words must count and must drive home and support the benefits to the consumer. Writing, rewriting, and further editing are the key elements in developing copy that sells. Copy should be clear; nothing is worse than vague advertising copy. When a vague phrase such as "fine food" is used, it is meaningless to the consumer. Copy should instead explain what this food will do for the consumers and how it will make them feel. It is important to make the intangibles more tangible and to talk to the consumer in terms of how the product–service mix will provide benefits that are important to the potential buyer.

Print Advertising Terms

The following terms are commonly used in print media, although some apply to other media as well:

- **Agate line.** A measurement by which newspaper and some magazine advertising space is sold, regardless of the actual type size used. There

Table 11.2	Examples of Print Headlines
Type of Headline	*Example*
Direct-promise headline	You'll love our 42-item salad bar. Your room will be perfect or you won't pay for it.
News headline	Grand Opening July 1st
Curiosity headline	Who says you can't get something for nothing?
Selective headline	To all single women...
Emotional headline	Mother's Day—What have you done for your Mom lately?

are 14 agate lines to the inch. Therefore, if a manager wanted advertising space two columns wide and three inches deep, the firm would be charged for 84 agate lines.

- *Base rate.* The lowest rate for advertising in print media. This rate is for run of paper (ROP) and means that the medium, at its discretion, puts advertisements wherever there is space.
- *Bleed.* This refers to an advertisement that extends into all or part of the margin of a page. Rates for bleeds vary with the medium used. Most media usually charge extra for bleeds.
- *Circulation.* The number of copies distributed. Primary circulation includes those who subscribe, while secondary circulation includes those who read pass-along copies. It is very difficult to measure secondary circulation.
- *Controlled circulation.* For business publications, this is now usually called *qualified circulation.* Some business publications are provided, often at little or no cost, to those individuals who qualify by engaging in a specific line of business. For example, meeting planners typically receive two or three publications targeted toward individuals who plan meetings. These publications are not available to the general public.
- *CPM (cost per thousand).* The CPM formula is the oldest means for comparing media rates. For print, the cost per 1,000 units of circulation is calculated on the basis of the one-time rate for one black-and-white page.
- *Frequency.* The number of times the same audience—listeners, readers, or viewers—is reached. It is expressed as an average, since some people may see or hear an advertisement only once, while others see it a dozen times. Placing more advertising in the media currently being used, adding more vehicles in a medium currently being used, and/or expanding into other media, such as radio as well as newspapers, can increase frequency.
- *Milline formula.* This is used to compare the costs of advertising in different newspapers. It is customary to use the cost per line per million circulation, called the *milline rate* [(Line rate $\times$ 1,000,000)/circulation = Milline rate]. The reason for multiplying by 1,000,000 is that the larger figures are easier to compare. If the rates compared are quoted in column inches, this rate can be used in the formula instead of the line rate. The same rate—baseline or column inch—must be used for all newspapers compared.
- *Reach.* The number or percentage of people exposed to a specific publication. The reach is usually measured throughout publication of a number of issues. It is the net unduplicated audience.
- *Volume rate.* Also called a *bulk rate,* a volume rate may be for total space, time used, or total dollars expended during a contract period,

usually twelve months. As more advertising is done, unit costs decrease. Newspapers generally quote their rates in agate lines or column inches. Rates get progressively lower as the number of lines increases.

▲ BROADCAST MEDIA

Broadcast media (e.g., radio and television) are distributed over the airwaves, allowing consumers to be passive listeners. The level of involvement is lower than with print media and other advertising mediums because of the sound element—the message is communicated to people who need only listen. In addition, television provides a visual element that is not present in radio. Many firms also advertise through their Web sites on the Internet, as well as the Web sites of other firms and service providers. This type of broadcast media is discussed as a form of distribution because of the relationship between advertising and sales in the growing area of electronic commerce.

Radio Advertising

Radio advertising finds extensive use in the food service segment of the industry, and in most cases, it is extremely effective. Radio is able to develop a distinct personality for a hospitality operation and it can reach consumers twenty-four hours a day. Radio advertising offers these advantages:

- *Personal.* Radio spots can be written so that they speak directly to the consumer.
- *Low relative cost.* The cost of radio is usually quite low for local advertising, especially when a package involving several spots is purchased.
- *Flexibility.* Radio copy can be changed quickly in response to rapid changes in market conditions.
- *Low production costs.* It is relatively inexpensive to create and produce radio advertising, since there is no visual element.
- *Audience selectivity.* Radio stations have specific formats that appeal to certain target markets. The demographics and psychographics of these markets can be matched with the profile of consumers that purchase the firm's product or service.

Radio advertising also offers some disadvantages:

- *Lack of visual appeal.* It is said that people "eat with their eyes," yet this is not possible on radio. Extra effort must be made when developing the copy and sound effects for a radio commercial to stretch the listener's imagination. The commercial must "sell the sizzle."
- *Fleeting message.* Once the commercial has aired, it is gone. The listener cannot refer to the advertisement to check the price, phone number, or hours of operation.

- *Clutter.* The airwaves are filled with advertisements for other hospitality operations and for every consumer product and service imaginable. Given this situation, called advertising *noise*, it is often necessary to maintain higher levels of advertising to achieve the desired effectiveness.

Techniques for Successful Radio Advertising. It is important to recognize that those listening to the radio are also engaged in other activities. They may be cleaning house, driving cars, or playing at the beach, but they are doing something besides listening to the radio. Because listeners are not devoting 100 percent of their attention to the radio, commercials should be kept fairly simple, focusing on one or two major ideas. It is not effective to bombard listeners with several ideas in each commercial; they simply will not remember these points. It is also important to mention the name of the hospitality operation and the benefit early in the commercial. Many consumers have a tendency to "tune out" commercials, but advertisers must work hard to make sure they hear at least part of the commercial.

Second, music should be kept simple, and complex lyrics should be avoided. Ideally, a jingle or short composition should trigger name recognition in the consumer's mind. Short and simple music aids in developing this recognition, especially if it is repeated as a musical logo in all radio commercials.

Third, the advertisement should suggest immediate action. Every effort should be made to get the consumer to act. Consumers will quickly forget the radio commercial, and unless the advertiser can encourage almost immediate action, the effectiveness of the advertising will be decreased.

Fourth, the advertisement should talk directly to consumers in a language and a tone that they will understand. The approach should be personal, much as if it were a conversation, albeit a one-way conversation. Many hospitality establishments, especially on the local level, have had success using live radio commercials. These can be particularly effective if a dominant radio personality does the commercials. These individuals often have loyal listeners and can have a significant influence on them.

Finally, the copy for radio commercials should be written so that it makes the listener visualize the products and services. The use of jingles and sound effects help give consumers a mental picture of the intended message.

Types of Radio Stations. The variety of choices in radio stations is very broad, both on the AM and FM bands. Stations are typically classified as progressive, contemporary, middle of the road (MOR), news–information–sports, talk, good music, classical, country and western, and ethnic.

Progressive stations, sometimes called album-oriented rock (AOR), appeal to a young audience with contemporary musical tastes. Those who listen to this type of station tend to "think young" and listen to the less conservative music that this type of station offers its listeners.

Contemporary stations offer a milder selection of rock music featuring current hits and sometimes specializing in specific types of rock such as light, classic rock.

Middle of the road (MOR), offers as close to a mass appeal format as is offered by radio. This segment was at one time dominant, but its popularity has declined. It appeals to the middle demographic segments.

News, information, and sports radio stations have proven to be very popular in the morning hours, when they attract those commuting to work. Talk-oriented stations appeal to an older audience and find their listeners in their homes during the day.

Good music stations offer a light type of music, sometimes called "background music." The sound is very relaxing and unobtrusive. This format has grown in popularity with the increase in the average age, which is the result of the aging of the baby boomers.

Classical-oriented stations are not numerous, but they do attract a very upscale audience, one that many hospitality industry advertisers would find attractive. Even within major markets, there is usually only one classical station, as the format does not enjoy wide popularity.

Country and western formats are widely popular in certain geographic sections of the country, but they tend to be less popular in major cities.

It is not possible to provide a detailed demographic profile of the type of listener that each radio formats attracts. Rather, it is best for the individual hospitality manager to compare the listener demographics of the available stations with those the hotel or restaurant is seeking to attract. In this way, the best fit between the radio stations' listeners and the potential advertiser's target market segments can be achieved.[4]

Selecting Radio Spots. Radio spots can be purchased in a wide variety of lengths, ranging from 10 seconds to 1 minute. Special attention should be paid to: (1) the number of spots; (2) the days the spots are broadcast; and (3) the times of day the spots are broadcast.

The number of spots purchased is important in achieving effectiveness in radio advertising. Consumers often require several exposures to the message before they begin to retain it. Repetition is critical to success in radio, as it is in all advertising. The days of the week selected are also important, for they suggest when the hospitality advertiser is seeking to promote business. For example, for a tablecloth restaurant, is early-week advertising more important or should the focus be on traditional weekend dining?

The time of day must also be considered. Radio should reach the consumer at a time when a decision is being made or when the advertiser is seeking to stimulate demand. Table 11.3 shows the time classifications used by radio stations. The most expensive times are morning and afternoon commuting times. A hospitality advertiser should seriously consider

Table 11.3	Radio Time Classifications	
Classifications	*Time*	*Relative Cost*
Class AA—morning drive time	6 AM to 10 AM	high
Class BB—daytime	10 AM to 3 PM	moderate
Class A—afternoon drive time	3 PM to 7 PM	moderate to high
Class C—evening	7 PM to 12 AM	low to moderate
Class D—night time	12 AM to 6 AM	low

these times, despite the increased cost, because they are likely to prove the most effective, especially for restaurants.

Producing Radio Commercials.   Figure 11.2 illustrates a time guide for producing a radio commercial. This guide can, of course, be modified, but generally a commercial should consist of introduction, commercial copy, recap of pertinent points, and musical logo. The introduction usually consists of music and copy written to get the listener's attention. It serves the same function as the headline in a print advertisement.

The copy of the commercial is the real heart of the selling proposition. The copy should explain the benefits of purchasing the product to the consumer. The recap of pertinent points should repeat points that the consumer should remember, such as a special price or new hours of operation. Finally, a musical logo is often used to fade out the commercial. Many advertisements allow five to ten seconds at the end for the announcer to read a live segment of the commercial. Both of those approaches can be very effective.

Radio Advertising Terms.   As with other forms of media, radio has its own unique terms that are used within the industry. The following are terms commonly used in radio advertising:

• ***Advertising spot.*** A short advertising message on a participating program or between other radio programs that an advertiser does not sponsor. This is what most people call a *commercial.* Advertising spots

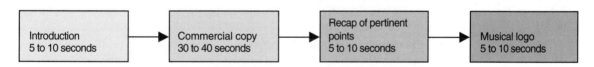

FIGURE 11.2.   **Production Guide for a 60-Second Radio Commercial**

may be (1) fixed, broadcast at a time guaranteed by contract; (2) preemptible, broadcast at a certain time unless bumped by an advertiser willing to pay a higher rate; or (3) floating, broadcast when the station decides (run of station, or ROS).

- *Drive time.* The early morning and late afternoon/early evening hours when radio has its largest audiences and highest rates.
- *Gross rating points.* Another way of comparing media vehicles and programs is by referring to gross rating points. This rating can be calculated by multiplying the rating points (percentage of households, according to surveys, listening to a program or station at a particular time) by the number of times that program or station is heard or viewed during a given period (usually four weeks). Twenty percent of a potential audience equals 20 rating points.
- *Preemptible rates.* Charged for broadcast advertising spots that may be bumped to different time periods by advertisers paying higher rates. They vary in cost by the amount of notice the station must give the advertiser before moving an advertisement; the longer the notice, the higher the rate.

Television Advertising

Each year, more and more hospitality organizations use television as an advertising medium. For some, the move into television brings increased sales and advertising success. For others, it is not such a bright picture. Television is a very demanding medium, one that delivers large audiences but requires great skill in advertising. Before a hospitality organization decides to commit resources for television, very careful thought must be given to its impact on the remainder of the organization's advertising efforts.

Advantages to television advertising include the following:

- *Large audiences.* Television, even at the local level, is able to deliver large numbers of viewers. It does not allow selectivity of target markets, but market saturation is high.
- *High impact of message.* The combination of sight, sound, and motion holds the potential for tremendous impact on viewers. This combination helps viewers to perceive the hospitality operation accurately and allows the advertiser to demonstrate the product–service mix.
- *Low cost per exposure.* Even though the absolute cost of television advertising is high, when divided by the total audience, the cost per exposure is actually very low. In this respect, television is an efficient advertising medium.
- *Credibility.* Consumers perceive claims made in television commercials as credible. Television has had a major impact on society and consumers assume only successful companies can afford to advertise on

television. Also, many of these campaigns include celebrities that enhance the credibility of the commercial.

The disadvantages associated with television advertising include:

- ***High absolute cost.*** For the vast majority of hospitality organizations, particularly small independent restaurants, the absolute cost of purchasing television time for commercials is simply too high. Venturing into television advertising necessitates such a drastic reduction in other advertising efforts that the final result is often a reduction in overall advertising effectiveness. This single disadvantage should be weighed with great care before television advertising is initiated.

- ***High production costs.*** To maintain credibility and attract the attention of viewers, it is necessary to spend a good deal of money on the production of television advertisements. Some of the costs involved include celebrities, location and sets, and special effects.

- ***Fleeting message.*** Much like radio, once a television advertisement is broadcast, it is gone, and a potential consumer cannot refer back to it.

- ***Clutter.*** Television commercials tend to be grouped together at certain times each hour. This creates a certain amount of competition for the viewer's attention and interest. During prime time less time per hour is devoted to commercials than other times, but commercial time is more expensive.

- ***Low selectivity.*** It may be difficult to segment the target audience as narrowly as preferred, leading to some amount of wasted coverage.

Techniques for Successful Television Advertising. First, the visual aspect of the commercial must convey the message to the consumer. The sound should enhance the message, but the message should be able to stand on its visual impact alone. Television is a visual medium; the visual aspect is the key to successful television advertising. Messages that hospitality advertisers try to convey include the luxury and high living of upscale hotels, or the fun people have at a restaurant. Showing people in the actual setting, not just showing the facilities or the food and beverages, does this.

Second, television advertising must capture the viewer's attention immediately, or it is doomed to failure. Facing facts, a manager must remember that consumers use commercial time to do other things, such as get snacks in the kitchen. If a commercial does not spark interest, they will not even watch.

Third, the advertisement should stay with one idea and repeat it within the time allocated. Television viewers see many advertisements throughout the day, and they cannot possibly remember all that they see and hear. Therefore, advertisements should focus on one key point. For example, both Wendy's and Burger King achieved success with campaigns centered on themes that were simple, direct, and memorable. Every effort should be made to trim commercials that talk too much. The adage a picture is worth a thousand words should be used as a guide when evaluating television storyboards.

Fourth, television advertisements should accurately project the image of the hotel or restaurant to consumers. Much time, effort, and money has been invested in the physical facilities and in staffing the operation, to create an image; advertising should not muddy that image with poor television commercials. For example, one tablecloth restaurant operating in a major metropolitan area enjoyed a fine reputation and steady clientele. In an effort to increase sales during slow periods, management ventured into television advertising. After work with the creative staff, a storyboard and script were created, and production began. The result was a commercial that featured several still photographs of the restaurant depicting dining situations. These were well done, but the announcer was talking in a hard-sell tone and at a very fast pace. This commercial cheapened the image of the restaurant and, in fact, hurt sales figures.

Types of Television Commercials. Advertisements can be creative and use several different approaches. Television commercials can be categorized into one of six types:

- ***Demonstration.*** Showing an actual part of the operation can be very effective. For example, preparing a certain menu item or banquet service in action within a hotel can help create an image.
- ***Straight announcer.*** This involves the use of only one announcer offering the benefit and support.
- ***Testimonial.*** This is a form of word-of-mouth promotion in which a series of satisfied consumers talk about elements of the product–service mix.
- ***Problem solving.*** This type of commercial offers a problem or series of problems and shows how a given hospitality operation can be the proper solution. For example, "What should you give your girlfriend for her birthday?" "How can you best celebrate your fortieth birthday?" "Why of course, come to the famous XYZ restaurant!"
- ***Story line.*** Some commercials tell a story in 30 to 60 seconds. For example, imagine the young boy sitting in a classroom at school daydreaming about a hamburger and french fries. The visual pieces and the sound discuss the benefits of the products, and when the commercial concludes, school is out, and the young boy is eating his favorite fast-food meal.
- ***Musical.*** Several successful television commercials have used the appealing visual effect of food products backed with appropriate music. If done well, this can be a very effective soft sell.

Just as radio stations divide the day into different time classifications, so does television. The television time classifications are shown in Table 11.4.

Table 11.4	Television Time Classifications	
Classification	*Time*	*Relative Cost*
Class AA	Daily, 8 PM to 11 PM	High
Class A	Daily, 7 AM to 8 AM Sunday, 6 PM to 8 PM	High to moderate
Class B	Daily, 4 PM to 6 PM Sunday, 2 PM to 5:30 PM	High
Class C	Daily, 12 PM to 4 PM Saturday, 6 PM to 4 PM	Low to moderate
Class D	Daily, 12 AM to 6 AM	Low

Television Advertising Terms. Many technical terms are used by television stations and advertisers in business negotiations. The following are terms commonly used in television advertising:

- *Dissolve.* One scene fading into the next with the two showing simultaneously for a moment.
- *Dubbing.* Recording the sound portion of the commercial separately and then synchronizing it with the visual components.
- *Fade in/fade out.* The screen goes from black to the visual material, or the final visual shot is faded into black.
- *Fringe time.* The periods immediately before and after TV prime time, 4 PM to 8 PM, and after 11 PM in all time zones except the Central time zone, where periods run an hour earlier.
- *Network.* A link of many stations by cable or microwave for simultaneous broadcast from a single originating point. The stations may be owned by or affiliated with the network. Major networks are ABC, CBS, NBC, and Fox. However, with the growth of cable television, the importance of the three major networks has declined. Other networks such as CNN, ESPN, and more targeted networks have increased their impact on the television market.
- *Prime time.* The time period when television has the largest audiences and highest advertising rates. In the Eastern, Mountain, and Pacific Time zones it is from 8 PM to 11 PM. In the Central time zone, it is from 7 PM to 10 PM.

▲ DIRECT MAIL

There are those who refer to direct-mail advertising as "junk mail." These individuals believe that direct-mail advertising is of little value and is not appropriate for the hospitality industry. These beliefs simply are not true. Direct mail can and does work for many hospitality advertisers. It is often used to solicit group and banquet business. Most hotels routinely send direct-mail pieces describing guest room and meeting facilities to potential meeting planners and then follow up with inquiries and personal calls to generate leads from the mailing. Direct mail is also used to promote special events, such as holidays or special packages, and often offer discounts.

The advantages of direct mail can be summarized as follows:

- *Highly selective/low wasted coverage.* With direct mail, an advertiser can be very selective with the target market segment and can include only the very best potential consumers on the mailing list. Direct mail need not be junk mail addressed to "occupant" or "home owner." The widespread use of personal computers has allowed even small hotels and restaurants to manage large databases and address lists that can then be merged with personalized letters.

- *Easily evaluated.* It is easy to monitor the effectiveness of direct-mail pieces by looking at inquiries and sales. Many firms include a postage-paid postcard for the prospect to use to inquire about additional information, which can be used to measure exposures and interest.

- *Short lead time.* It is relatively easy to produce and copy direct-mail pieces. Therefore, firms can keep pace with rapid changes in market conditions.

- *High information content.* There are no time or space limits, as is the case with other media. There are the limits of size or shape. Therefore, one can be very creative. The manager who develops the direct-mail piece has a great deal of control over the design, production, and distribution of the direct-mail efforts. Direct-mail pieces can contain detailed explanations and presentations.

The following disadvantages are associated with direct mail advertising:

- *Poor image.* Direct mail suffers from a poor image in the minds of many consumers. Unless the piece is able to attract immediate attention, most consumers will not read it.

- *Clutter.* In recent years, there has been tremendous growth in the use of direct mail, especially in the area of direct mail marketing of retail items. As a result, the number of direct mail pieces that the typical consumer receives each day is increasing, and it is becoming more difficult to get the desired message to the consumer.

- ***High cost per contact.*** When all the costs associated with direct mail are added up, the total is often surprising to the advertiser. Included in these costs are mailing lists, printing, word processing and letter generation, envelope stuffing, and postage.

Techniques for Successful Direct Mail Advertising

First, any direct mail piece that achieves success must capture the potential consumer's attention. Many consumers throw out direct-mail advertising without opening it; others open it but do not read it. This is obviously a waste of a firm's money. A tried-and-true approach to direct-mail advertising is based on the AIDA principle (attention, interest, desire, action). If the advertising fails to motivate the consumer to act immediately, chances are that the advertising will be set aside and eventually forgotten. Consumer action is the goal of direct-mail advertising; action leads to inquiries, inquires lead to prospects, and prospects lead to sales. Examples of copy written to spur action include, "Act within 10 days and receive a free gift" or "Call today for reservations; only a limited number will be accepted for this special evening."

Special attention needs to be given to the layout and copy writing of direct mail pieces. Generally, long paragraphs of copy should be avoided because most people simply will not read them. Research has shown that the more personal the appearance of the direct-mail piece, the greater likelihood that the recipient will read it. Many firms doing small, selective mailings will personalize them with a regular stamp and/or envelopes that are addressed by hand. Both techniques usually prove to be more effective than using bulk-rate postage and peel-off address labels.

If specific direct-mail pieces prove successful, an advertiser should run them again. The piece may seem old to the management of the hospitality operation, but to consumers, it will be new and different. If something works, there is no reason to change merely for the sake of change.

Finally, direct mail efforts are often successful because of the creativity on the part of the advertiser. Taking a familiar object and putting it to new use can create dramatic results. For example, one restaurant used brown lunch bags instead of standard envelopes. The phrase "Are you still brown bagging it?" was printed on the outside of the bag. Another restaurant used a piece that resembled a parking ticket and put them on the cars parked in certain areas. Printed on the top of the pseudo ticket was "Here's your ticket to a great lunch." Although, strictly speaking, this last promotion is not direct mail, it was very successful and used a direct-mail approach.

Mailing Lists

Maintaining mail lists is critical to the cost-effectiveness and success of any direct-mail advertising program. Only names that are truly potential consumers should be included, and names that are duplicated because several lists are used should be avoided as well. Both of these problems sound simple, but solving them is often easier said than done. A big advantage of using computer lists is the ability to check for duplication.

Mailing lists fall into two categories: in-house lists and external lists. The management generates in-house lists internally. These lists should include those who have patronized the hotel or restaurant or who have the potential to generate a significant amount of business. Many restaurants use the guest book concept very successfully. They place a guest book at the entrance and ask each individual to sign it. Another approach is to keep a large bowl, often a fish bowl, at the host's stand into which guests may place business cards. The names and addresses provided by the guests become an excellent foundation on which to build a mailing list.

Within hotels, it is relatively easy to build a mailing list based on registration cards, as well as the contacts that are made by the sales and marketing staff. External lists are obtained from companies that sell mailing lists based on demographics, socioeconomic levels, geographic areas, and numerous other variables. Costs of these lists vary depending on selectivity and size. Lists purchased externally should be guaranteed to be current. Reputable companies will guarantee lists to be 90 to 95 percent accurate and current. Mailing lists can also be purchased from clubs, associations, and other businesses.

One final word on direct-mail advertising: results may seem discouraging based on the total number of pieces mailed. Typically, the response rate on mail promotions is 1 to 2 percent. Anything more than 2 percent is very good, and more than 5 percent is outstanding. Consider a restaurant that sent a mailing to 20,000 potential consumers advertising a promotional item. A response rate of 1 percent would be 200, 2 percent would be 400, and 5 percent would be 1,000. As few as 200 extra covers can have a substantial impact on sales.

▲ SUPPORT MEDIA

In addition to the major types of media discussed earlier, other forms of media are used by firms to support, or supplement, the media effort. This section will discuss three forms of support media: outdoor advertising, brochures, and collateral materials.

Outdoor Advertising

Outdoor advertising has widespread use among those hospitality operations located near interstate highways, but it can be effective in other locations as well. One hospitality organization in a large northern city allocated a substantial portion of its advertising to outdoor advertising.

The outdoor displays were both creative and somewhat risky; the results were very successful. The advantages of outdoor advertising include these characteristics:

- *Low cost per exposure.* When the costs of producing and placing an outdoor advertisement is divided by the total number of exposures, the cost per thousand is extremely low.
- *High repetition.* Consumers who frequent a given route will see the outdoor advertising again and again. This repetition aids in recall and retention.
- *Ability to target location.* Outdoor advertising is particularly useful for hospitality and travel firms in targeting customers looking for lodging, a restaurant, or some other type of travel service (e.g., rental car, tourist information, etc.) in the immediate area.

The following disadvantages are also associated with outdoor advertising:

- *Poor audience selectivity/high wasted coverage.* While the cost per thousand is low, outdoor advertising does not lend itself to reaching small target market segments. It is a mass-market method.
- *Legislation/local restrictions.* Beginning with the Highway Beautification Act, all levels of government have discussed and often have enacted legislation to limit and tightly control the construction of outdoor billboards and signs. Legislation at all levels of government has made it more difficult for a hospitality organization to obtain the desired number of signs in the locations that are the most desirable.
- *Long lead time.* It requires considerable planning to use outdoor advertising. It takes time to create and display an outdoor advertisement.
- *Lack of flexibility.* Once outdoor advertising is in place, it is not subject to change without considerable effort and cost.

Techniques for Successful Outdoor Advertising. Three simple thoughts should influence all outdoor advertising. First, the copy should be kept brief and the print large. Those viewing outdoor advertising will be riding in buses, cabs, and cars or walking down the street. Their attention will be focused on the advertisement for only a few seconds, so, the message must be brief. A maximum of five to seven words should be used, and the fewer, the better. Information such as the telephone number or hours of operation is not likely to be remembered and should not be included.

Second, a picture or illustration is often very helpful in gaining attention. The picture or illustration should convey the message and not be used to provide clear name recognition. The best example is the McDonald's golden arches. It can be clearly seen on all outdoor advertising for McDonald's. The name recognition is instant and lasting.

Types of Outdoor Advertising. Standard outdoor advertising consists of posters and painted bulletins. Posters are blank boards on which the printed advertising is mounted. Painted bulletins are more permanent signs on which the message is painted. Both posters and painted bulletins are available in a wide variety of sizes, ranging from 6 feet by 12 feet to 10 feet by 22 feet and larger. Painted bulletins are sold individually, and posters are sold by showings. Showings refer to market coverage within a 30-day period.

A *plant* is a company that buys or leases real estate (where it erects standard-size boards) or rents walls of buildings. It then sells to advertisers use of space at these locations. A *showing* refers to the coverage of a market, not the number of posters. A 100 showing is complete coverage of a market; a 50 showing is half of it, and so on. In some communities, 10 posters might be a 100 showing, but in much smaller places, 2 posters could be a 100 showing.

When renting posters, circulation, or the number of people who will see the board, should be considered. The length of time a passer-by can see the poster clearly should be considered. Not all locations are good ones. The physical condition or the posters and painted bulletins should also be considered. Nothing will reflect more negatively on an advertiser than a poorly maintained board or one with its lights burned out.

Another type of outdoor advertising is referred to as *transit advertising*. This refers to advertising placed on vehicles used in transporting people or in public places that people encounter in their daily travel routines. For example, most cities sell advertising space on buses, taxis, and subways, as well as on walls in the stations where people wait for these forms of transportation.

Brochures and Collateral Materials

Brochures are developed and used to supplement other forms of advertising, as well as personal selling efforts. Normally, brochures are used in direct-mail campaigns in addition to being placed in hotels, restaurants, tourist attractions, and tourist information centers. Other forms of collateral materials include meeting planner guides and video brochures. Hotels, cruises, and resorts use video brochures that provide a quick four-to-six minute tour of the property. However, written brochures are still the most common item for creating awareness and interest among potential consumers.

Creating Effective Brochures. Brochures play a vital role in the advertising and promotional efforts of hotels, and they can be of benefit to restaurants and travel firms as well. They can be used in a wide variety of situations. It will not be possible to tell the entire story within a brochure, as there are space restrictions. The most important point to remember is to communicate your facility's positioning. It is imperative that you create and maintain an image in the consumer's mind. Once you have determined the type of positioning statement you want to communicate, you can move on to the key benefits and support that the brochure will communicate. The following guidelines will lead to more successful brochures:

1. *Brochure cover.* First, the cover design is very critical. It should communicate where your property is located and your positioning statement. The cover is valuable space and it should be used to convey your primary selling message and the key consumer benefit. The photograph used on the front cover should grab the attention of potential guests, capturing their interest.

2. *Photographs.* All photographs should help to stretch the potential guests' imagination. They should be able to see themselves in the setting. Photographs of activities are more useful than photographs of just the facilities. If you plan to use food in the photographs, use close-up photos of finished products, not just the ingredients. Avoid the use of standard types of photographs that are all too common in hotel brochures. These include the smiling chef standing beside the buffet table and service personnel serving food in a restaurant. Strive for a fresh approach.

3. *Information.* Potential guests need information that will help them to better understand things about your product–service mix. The use of maps and or graphics on the brochure helps the reader to gain a better understanding of where you are located, as well as some specifics about the types of products and services offered. Basic information such as address, telephone, and chain affiliation should also be included.

4. *Copy.* Just as with any type of advertising, the copy used in a brochure must talk to the consumer in his or her own words and must speak directly in terms of benefits that are important. The use of a professional copywriter may be useful. It is important to avoid cliches, as these will actually turn off potential guests.

Specialty Advertising

In addition to the basic media used by hospitality and travel firms, specialty advertising materials bearing the firm's name and logo can be given or sold to a targeted consumer. There are literally thousands of specialty items, including pens, pencils, calendars, rulers, paperweights, jewelry, matches, programs, candy jars, travel bags, and T-shirts.

Some of the advantages of specialty advertising are:

- *Retention.* If the item is of value or usefulness to the recipient, it is likely to be retained, and the advertising message is seen repeatedly.
- *Selectivity.* Most specialty items are distributed directly to consumers in the firm's target market. For example, hotel pens and children's cups in restaurants are kept by customers, and hotels, restaurants, and airlines all sell shirts and hats bearing the firm's name and logo.

Collateral materials can be used in direct mail advertising or as inserts in print advertising. Courtesy of NE Restaurant Company, Inc., Maynard, Massachusettes.

- **Low cost.** When purchased in large quantities, many specialty advertising items can be fairly inexpensive per unit.

Some of the disadvantages associated with specialty advertising include:

- **Image.** It is important to use items that are consistent in quality to the overall quality perceptions that consumers have of the firm. If the items are cheap, it will have a negative impact on the image of the firm.
- **Clutter.** Many firms distribute specialty items such as pens and key chains. Firms must develop unique items that will be of some value to consumers.

▲ MARKETING ACTION NOW!

Every city or town has its share of media that can be used for advertising. First, discuss some of the media vehicles used by hospitality and travel firms in your area. What similarities and differences exist among the different types of firms? How do the characteristics of these vehicles affect the firms' decisions? Second, contact some of the local media and ask them how they charge for advertising. Also, ask them how much it costs to produce a typical advertisement (i.e., the cost range) and the lead time to place the ad. Finally, compare the information obtained by the various individuals, or groups, in the class.

▲ SUMMARY OF CHAPTER OBJECTIVES

This chapter covers the vast area of external advertising and promotional media. These media constitute an invaluable resource, which if managed properly, can generate increased sales and handsome profits. Managed poorly, these media will drain away advertising resources and leave little or nothing to show in return. As with all investments, management must evaluate advertising for its return on investment.

The relationships between a hospitality client and an advertising agency involve both positive and negative aspects. Management should consider several factors when selecting an agency and should consider compensation practices within the industry.

Media selection involves several factors. These include the nature of the target market, the campaign objectives, the desired amount of coverage, and the activities of direct competition. Media plans must be developed to achieve maximum effectiveness. These plans must consider the target markets closely to blend the media to achieve the desired results. Media scheduling includes the following approaches: continuous, flighting, and pulsing advertising.

External advertising media include newspapers, magazines, radio, television, direct mail, outdoor, and supplemental advertising. Each of these media has its appropriate use, advantages, drawbacks, and techniques that generally are successful. An understanding of advertising terms allows a manager to communicate more intelligently with media and advertising agency personnel.

▲ KEY TERMS AND CONCEPTS

Agate line

Base rate

Bleed advertisement

Brochures

Circulation

Collateral materials

Continuous, flighting, and pulsing media scheduling

Controlled circulation

Cost per thousand (CPM)

Demonstration

Drive time

Dubbing

Fade in/fade out

Frequency

Fringe time

Gross rating points

Media planning process

Milline formula

Outdoor advertising plant

Preemptible rates

Reach

Showing

Specialty advertising

Testimonial

▲ QUESTIONS FOR REVIEW AND DISCUSSION

1. What factors affect the selection of advertising media?
2. Discuss the media planning process.
3. What are the methods of media scheduling? Which one do you consider the best? Why?
4. Compare and contrast the various types of media based on their respective characteristics.

▲ NOTES

[1]Beth Snyder, "Bermuda ads from JWT recasts isle in new light," *Advertising Age* (May 10, 1999) p. 12.

[2]David W. Nylen, *Marketing Decision-Making Handbook* (Englewood Cliffs, NJ: Prentice-Hall, 1990) p. G-150.

[3]Howard A. Heinsius, "How to Select Advertising Media More Effectively," in *Strategic Marketing Planning in the Hospitality Industry*, edited by Robert L. Blomstrom (East Lansing, MI: Educational Institute of the American Hotel and Motel Association, 1983) pp. 256–258.

[4]Harry A. Egbert, "Advertising for Hotels," edited by Robert L. Blomstrom (East Lansing, MI: Educational Institute of the American Hotel and Motel Association, 1983) pp. 280–284.

12

Sales Promotions, Merchandising, and Public Relations

❖ Chapter Objectives

By the end of this chapter, you should understand:

1. The concept of sales promotion and its role in marketing strategy
2. The various types of sales promotions and the advantages and disadvantages associated with their use
3. How to manage sales promotions
4. The concept of merchandising
5. The concept of public relations and its role in marketing strategy
6. The various public relations techniques

❖ Chapter Outline

   I. Chapter Opening Profile
  II. Introduction
 III. Sales Promotions
     A. Role of sales promotions
     B. Type of sales promotions

❖ Chapter Opening Profile

RETAIL STORES FIRST STARTED OFFERING TRADING stamps to consumers with purchases in the late 1800s. Thomas Sperry and Shelley Hutchinson (S&H) offered their "green stamps" to various retailers with the idea that they could be redeemed for merchandise at a central distribution point. This concept continued until the use of trading stamps peaked in the 1960s, with many grocery stores, gas stations, and other retail establishments participating. Then, in response to high inflation and the energy crisis in the 1970s, the popularity of trading stamps began to wane. Consumers were more interested in actual cost savings than sales promotions (i.e., premiums) like trading stamps. Trading stamps all but disappeared by the 1980s, until a similar concept was adopted by the airline industry: frequent flyer programs.

Much like trading stamps, the objective of frequent flyer programs is to reward consumers in relation to the amount of products, or services, that they purchase. Trading stamps were distributed based on the amount of money a customer spent, and frequent flyer miles are currently distributed based on the number of miles a customer travels. This type of non-price promotion, or premium, has been adopted by other sectors of the hospitality and travel industry. Hotels offer frequent guest programs and restaurants offer frequent diner programs. In addition, many hospitality and travel firms have formed relationships around the trading-stamp concept. For example, if you stay at a Marriott hotel or rent a car at Avis, you can earn frequent flyer miles for United Airlines. Credit card companies, such as American Express have developed broad-based mileage and merchandise credits in cooperation with airlines, hotels, and retailers. Nearly all credit card providers have adopted some type of mileage program, with American Express Mileage Plus™ being the most popular program.

Frequent-customer programs have become very popular as a means for firms to build repeat business and brand loyalty. However, these programs do have some drawbacks. For instance, frequent-diner programs can be inexpensive to maintain, but the start-up costs can be high (e.g., $20,000 for computer equipment and printing).[1] Also a great deal of time and effort is required to plan the program's structure and benefits. Customers find ways to "cheat" the program, and restaurants risk alienating customers when changes are made to the programs. Finally, customers may get bored with the program, and it could become difficult to track diner visits and points over time. And, in the case of airlines or hotels, customers redeeming points could displace paying customers during periods of high demand. In fact, airlines have started offering merchandise such as magazines and event tickets as a means to divert some of the points from airline travel. As airline load factors increased, blackout dates became more common. As a result, some passengers were not able to secure free tickets on the flights they desired. Allowing passengers to redeem mileage points for merchandise and special events increases customer satisfaction and reduces the demand for free tickets on flights with high load factors.

▲ INTRODUCTION

The hospitality industry is a people-oriented business. Hospitality operations promote hospitality, yet hospitality cannot be purchased, cannot be traded, and does not appear on the menu. Hospitality is intangible, yet it is absolutely necessary for success. When service personnel project the "spirit of hospitality," the results can be dramatic: increased sales, increased profits, increased consumer satisfaction, and, yes, increased employee satisfaction and motivation. Food service operations also sell atmosphere, convenience, entertainment, escape, and social contact. All of these are related to the spirit of hospitality and are equally intangible. All deserve consideration as promotable items.

Role of Sales Promotions

In recent years, most companies have devoted an ever-increasing percentage of their budgets to sales promotions and have reduced the percentage devoted solely to advertising. **Sales promotions** seek to accomplish several broad objectives and can be used for several reasons:

sales promotions
short-term inducements to get consumers to purchase products

- ***To increase consumer awareness.*** This is the first step in attracting new guests or customers. To attract a guest, one must first stimulate interest and a desire to act. Advertising seeks to increase awareness as well, but sometimes it takes a targeted promotion to turn that awareness into consumer purchasing action.

- ***To introduce new products and services.*** Every hotel and restaurant launches new products and services. The best way to ensure that the target markets are aware of these products and services is to initiate a special promotion to draw attention to them. When McDonald's or Burger King launches a new product, you can be sure that they support the introduction with extra advertising and special promotions designed to promote trial of the new product. Merely introducing the new product or service to the target markets is not enough; you need to beat the drums, create interest, and stimulate trial purchases and future demand for the new products and services.

- ***To increase guest occupancy and customer counts.*** With increasing competition and tight supply and demand in many markets, one of the few avenues for market share growth is to take business away from the direct competition. To accomplish this, it is necessary to feature promotions that offer consumers a better deal, or greater value than they can receive elsewhere. Promotions are used to spread the word to potential guests.

- ***To combat competition.*** If the direct competition is gaining market share at the expense of your hotel or restaurant, you may be forced to match their promotion or to add one of your own with a new twist. For example, Marriott Hotels was among the first hotel companies to offer a frequent guest program. Their program proved to be so successful that other competing hotel chains were forced to offer frequent traveler programs to compete with Marriott.

- ***To encourage present guests to purchase more.*** Total sales can be increased by packaging (bundling) different products and services at a total price that is less than the cost of purchasing the components separately. Promotions can also be used to encourage guests to trade up to more expensive products and services by of offering a discounted price on the more expensive product or service. The primary purpose is to increase sales by encouraging present guests to purchase more.

- ***To stimulate demand in non-peak periods.*** All hotels and restaurants have periods when demand is weak. Promotions can be used to increase weekend business for a business-oriented hotel, or stimulate off-season and shoulder-season business at a resort. Within the food service segment, promotions can be used to increase sales during periods of the day or days of the week when demand is slow. For example, many restaurants stimulate early evening business by offering a discount to senior citizens who dine between 5:00 and 7:00 PM, when business is often slow. They take advantage of the fact that seniors usually try to dine earlier and are often more conscious of the price–value relationship. Early dining promotions directed at this target market are often quite successful.

As is the objective with all forms of promotion or advertising, the ultimate goal is to stimulate attention, interest, desire, and action **(AIDA)**. Sales promotions are most effective as short-term inducements to purchase a particular brand. As such, they can lead to desire and action, but sales promotions are normally not effective as long-term strategies.

AIDA process that consumers experience involving attention, interest, desire, and action

Types of Sales Promotions

Within the broad sphere of sales promotion two strategies are commonly used: push promotion and pull promotion. Push promotion is used when the marketing manager wants to push the product–service mix through the service delivery system or channels of distribution. This approach encourages increased purchases and increased consumption by consumers. Pull promotion, on the other hand, is aimed at stimulating the interest of consumers and having them pull the product through the channels of distribution. This in turn puts additional pressure on the retail outlets or hospitality facilities to supply the products and services most in demand by consumers. Some of the more commonly used push and pull techniques include:

Push Techniques

- *Point-of-sale (POS) displays.* These displays, usually seen at the counter of fast-food restaurants or as table tents in other types of restaurants, are designed to stimulate increased sales. Similarly, signs, banners, and table tents are displayed by hotels in their lobbies, restaurants, and guest rooms.

push techniques promotions aimed at channel members to get them to move products through the channel of distribution

- *Cooperative advertising.* A national chain normally provides advertising at the national and local levels for its outlets. Also, franchisees will often get help with local advertising, in addition to the chain's national advertising, as part of the franchise agreement.

- *Advertising materials.* To encourage the local property to run advertising, the national chain will supply camera-ready advertising materials as well as prepared radio commercials.

- *Traditional and electronic collateral material.* Many firms supplement their other promotional efforts with materials such as brochures, flyers, or directories of other outlets within the chain. Beyond the traditional print collateral, firms use Web-based promotions via the Internet to communicate with current and prospective customers.

- *Convention and managers' meetings.* National chains use these meetings as a method to introduce new products and services to those who will be working in the individual units. These meetings are used for sales and service training.

pull techniques promotions aimed at consumers to create demand for products

Pull Techniques

- *Sampling.* This technique can be used very effectively by food service managers. For example, samples of menu items can be distributed in the lobby area of a fast-food store, thereby encouraging customers to try the new product. The goal is to convert this trial into regular use and repeat purchase. Within the lodging field, this technique is common as well. Meeting planners often visit the potential hotel meeting site to "sample" the product service before they make a final decision about the host hotel for the upcoming meeting.

- *Price reduction promotions.* Price reductions for a limited time can encourage trial and increase sales. A successful use of this type of promotion was Marriott Hotel's "Two for Breakfast Weekend," in which two guests could experience a get-away weekend at a heavily discounted price and receive a complimentary breakfast for two. As with all promotions of this type, restrictions should apply and a definite time period should be stated.

- *Price reduction coupons.* These are certificates that entitle the consumer to receive a discount when presented at the retail outlet. They can be distributed in newspapers, magazines, face to face, or via direct mail.

- *Combination offers or bundling.* This involves combining two or more products or services and offering them for a price less than the price if they were purchased separately.

- *Premiums.* These are extra merchandise or gifts that the hotel or restaurant gives away or sells at a very favorable price to guests. Examples include such items as hats, tote bags, glassware, and T-shirts with the logo printed on them. If the hotel or restaurant is able to cover the direct costs of the item, the premium is called *self-liquidating.*

- *Contests and sweepstakes.* The attraction of contests and sweepstakes is the highly desirable prizes that consumers can win. There is one minor difference between a contest and a sweepstakes. A contest requires some skill on the part of the participant, while a sweepstakes is based solely on chance. In all states, lotteries are illegal. Lotteries consist of three elements: (1) the element of chance; (2) consideration, giving something in return, for example, having to make a purchase in order to enter the sweepstakes); and (3) a valuable prize. To avoid illegal activities in most localities, it is necessary to eliminate one of these elements. By simply not requiring a purchase to enter the sweepstakes, it is not classified as a lottery and is therefore legal in most localities. Contests, because they require some skill on the part of the participant, are not considered to be lotteries because there is no element of chance involved.

Commonly Used Techniques

The most common sales promotion techniques in the hospitality industry are: coupons, sampling, premiums, and contests or sweepstakes.[2] The following sections provide a more complete discussion of these techniques.

Coupons.   The primary objectives for coupons are to stimulate trial of your products and services by reducing the price, encourage multiple purchases, and generate temporary sales increases. Coupons offer several advantages:

- The coupon represents a tangible inducement, offering a savings or benefit.
- The price reduction is for a limited time and will not affect profit margins in the long term.
- Coupons can be used to accomplish specific objectives, such as boosting business in nonpeak periods.
- The maximum cost of the promotion can be calculated in advance. For example, based on past experience, the percentage of the coupons likely to be redeemed.

Coupons have disadvantages as well:

- Some employees will be tempted to defraud the business. It is possible for them to take cash and substitute coupons. The higher the value of the coupon, the more supervision is necessary.
- Redemption rates are not easily predicted. Among the environmental factors that can affect the redemption rate include value of the coupon, timing, and competitive activities. This is most common with new promotions because there is no prior history to judge future redemption rates against.

Sampling.   Encouraging trial of new products is the primary objective of sampling. If consumers will at least try the product, it is believed that they are more likely to purchase in the future. Sampling also is an excellent way to persuade consumers to trade up to more expensive products and services. Sampling can also be tied in with other types of promotions. For example, airlines routinely offer upgrades to first class for frequent travelers as a reward for their frequent use of the airline. Not only is this a reward, but after flying in first class, travelers may decide to book themselves into first class for subsequent flights, thereby increasing sales and profits. Airlines help the traveler to rationalize this additional cost by awarding additional mileage points when the traveler flies in first class. Sampling offers these advantages:

- Getting consumers to try the product is superior to getting them to look at an advertisement. It provides the consumer with instant feedback.

- It represents value to the consumer. Many consumers like to think that they can get something for free. For example, including small portions of entree and appetizer items within the offerings for "happy hours" is an excellent way to stimulate dining room business.

Some disadvantages of sampling follow:

- Giving away products can become a major expense if it is done for an extended period of time.
- Samples of food products must be served when they are freshly prepared. If the products are to be held for any period of time, care must be taken to ensure that the quality can be maintained.

Premiums. Premiums, giving away something, are used to bring in new guests, to encourage more frequent visits by current guests, and to build positive word-of-mouth about the operation. Advantages include the following:

- Most consumers like to get something for nothing or for a good price. It helps to build good will for your business, especially if the premium is highly valued by the consumer.
- If the premium is clever or unique, it will build positive word of mouth as consumers tell others where they found the premium. When your logo is included on the premium, the message is always in front of the consumer.

Disadvantages of premiums include these:

- Storing and handling the premium items can be a challenge if they are large or bulky.
- Employees and others may take the premiums for their own use or for their families and friends.
- The quality of the premium must be equal or superior to the image of the hospitality facility. If the premium does not work properly or breaks, it will diminish the image the consumer has of the facility or organization.
- Anticipating demand for premiums is difficult. If they are to be advertised as being available, it is imperative that a sufficient inventory be maintained so consumers are not disappointed. Raising expectations and then not delivering will result in negative consumer perceptions.

Contests and Sweepstakes. These are being used with increasing frequency, especially within the more competitive segments of the industry such as fast food. They are designed to increase the number of customers and build market share, often at the expense of the competition. Advantages of **contests** include the following:

- Consumers are more involved in the process because there is some element of skill and thinking required, thereby presenting an opportunity to create and support a more lasting positive image in the consumer's mind.

- Those who enter have already shown an interest in your products and services and are more likely to purchase them. This eliminates the potential for chance winners that don't normally purchase the product.

Disadvantages of contests include these:

- There can be some difficulty in judging entries because the criteria are often subjective. Those selected to judge must take the responsibility seriously, because the contestants will be serious about the outcome.

- Often the rules and guidelines for the contest are lengthy and may turn off potential participants.

The advantages of **sweepstakes** include the following:

- Entry is very easy; no purchase is necessary. The names and addresses of those who enter can be stored in a database and used in future direct mail advertising efforts.

- Because the rules are usually quite simple, attention can be focused on the prizes in advertising.

- Sweepstakes will attract more participants than contests because it is easier to enter. No skill is involved, and it takes little time or effort to complete the entry.

- Selection of the winner is easy and judging is not required.

Disadvantages of sweepstakes include these:

- The entry box may be stuffed. It is possible for a consumer to reproduce the entry blank and enter thousands of times. For this reason, the rules should prohibit the mechanical reproduction of the entry forms.

- An individual's chances of winning the large prizes are very small, so people may get discouraged and not enter.

Managing Successful Promotions

When developing a sales promotion campaign, the marketer must consider several major aspects. First, it is necessary to determine the size of the incentive that needs to be offered to get consumers to participate. The larger the incentive, the more likely it is to attract attention. Second, the firm must establish the conditions for participation. Hospitality and travel firms often limit offers to certain times of day or days of the week. In addition, offers may require reservations in advance and depend on availability. Third, the marketer must determine the timing of the promotion, including its duration. Will it be combined with other promotion such as advertising, will it be offered during peak or nonpeak periods, and how long will the sales promotion be available? Finally, it is necessary to determine how consumers will be informed of the promotion and estimate the total budget for the promotion. Coupons are normally distributed by mail, and other promotions are advertised at the point of purchase or via some other media vehicle. Coupons can also be distributed via the Internet, allowing additional promotions to the consumer as well.

The hospitality industry trade journals are filled with terrific ideas for promotions. There is never a need to reinvent the wheel. Rather, simply modify the ideas that others have used successfully before. With this in mind, an excellent source that managers might want to review is *Fifty Promotions That Work,* published by the American Express Company. This publication was an outgrowth of *Briefing,* a newsletter that American Express provided to restaurateurs across the country. Like anything else managers do, planning a promotion calls for careful planning, execution of the plan, and evaluation. The steps to a successful promotion are:

1. ***Select the Target Market for the Promotion.*** When the sales records are analyzed, the most likely targets for a special promotion can be identified, as those segments that offer the greatest potential for increased sales.

2. ***Establish Specific Objectives for the Promotion.*** Objectives should be very specific, detailing exactly what the promotion should accomplish. Expected results should be quantified.

3. ***Select the Promotional Technique.*** Based on the situation and the advantages and disadvantages of each of the techniques, select the one best suited to the situation.

4. ***Brainstorm about the Potential Offer.*** There are hundreds of excellent ideas. Make a list of those being considered and seek input from others. All potential offers should be examined carefully from two perspectives: the potential appeal to the target market, and the potential sales increase in light of the projected costs and expenses.

5. ***Create the Promotional Theme.*** This is the area where one can be very creative. What will the promotional copy line or tag line be? Does it capture the interest of potential guests? Can it be used both internally and externally in the promotion? For a promotion to achieve the maximum potential, it needs to be carried forward both outside and inside the operation. Externally, it should build business. Internally, it should create excitement among the staff and build morale.

6. ***Develop the Promotional Budget.*** A projection of the total anticipated costs should be prepared to include all internal and external costs. To be able to evaluate the promotion, all costs, both direct and indirect, must be measured. It is wise to project the impact on costs and revenues at several different levels of consumer participation.

7. ***Select the Advertising Media and Vehicles to Support the Promotion.*** Based on your knowledge of the media, those that will best sup-

port the total promotional campaign should be contacted. Advertising space and time should be secured.

8. ***Develop an Implementation Timetable.*** Promotions require attention to detail so that all phases are integrated and implemented properly. To accomplish this, a timetable is required. Specific dates should be established for each task. Assigning responsibility to a specific individual or team for the completion of these tasks will increase accountability.

9. ***Conduct Internal Training of the Entire Staff.*** Just prior to the implementation of the program, the entire staff should be briefed so that they are familiar with the details of the promotion. Items of interest are how long the promotion will last and how the details will be handled by the different members of the staff.

10. ***Work the Plan.*** Put the promotional plan into action and follow the timetable.

11. ***Monitor Results.*** Feedback should be followed very carefully and should be compared with the timetable. Are things progressing as planned? Is the level of consumer participation within the projected ranges? Are the staff members working as planned? Attention to detail is very important. All information collected should be retained for future use in other promotions.

Evaluating the Impact of Sales Promotions. There are several elements of a sales promotion that must be evaluated in order to determine the actual impact of the final promotion. The following is a brief description of the major elements:

- *The administrative costs associated with conducting a sales promotion.* Some costs are directly related to conducting a sales promotion, such as printing, mailing, and advertising. The firm should estimate these costs prior to launching a sales promotion to determine this fixed cost. For example, the opening profile for this chapter refers to the computer costs and other administrative costs associated with offering a frequent-customer program in restaurants.

- *The cost of displaced sales.* A certain number of customers would have consumed the service at the actual, or regular, price. When these customers participate in a promotion, such as a coupon or some other form of price discount, the firm loses revenue equal to the difference in price multiplied by the number of consumers. For example, some consumers order pizza delivery from the same provider time after time. If the firm offers a $1.00 off coupon that is redeemed by 200 regular customers, the firm loses $200 dollars in revenue.

- *Additional revenue from new customers.* One of the main objectives of sales promotions is to induce trial among new customers, with the eventual goal of having them become repeat customers. Any revenue received from new customers is positive and will offset the administrative costs and losses from displaced sales. For example, the pizza delivery restaurant may have had 200 new customers pay an average of $10 per order, resulting in additional revenue in the amount of $2,000. In our example, after accounting for displaced sales, this would leave $1,800 to cover the administrative costs of offering the promotion.

It is important for firms to consider all of these costs to determine the necessary budget, as well as the viability of a particular sales promotion. The elements listed earlier are short-term in nature and should be evaluated in conjunction with the potential long-term effects of having additional customers. The increase in revenues may be accompanied by a decrease in unit costs as the overall volume increases. In some cases, a hospitality or travel firm may be content to break even or actually lose some money on a sales promotion in the short run, in order to achieve its long-term objectives.

merchandising creating an atmosphere to enhance consumer interest and service delivery

▲ MERCHANDISING

When the consumer comes through the front door of a hospitality operation, all the attention of management and the service employees should be focused on satisfying the consumer. Hospitality is a form of retail business and, as such, adequate effort should be placed on merchandising hospitality services to consumers once they enter the establishment. All too often, the service employees show about as much enthusiasm for selling as for changing a flat tire. Instead of performing as professional salespeople, they often serve as little more than order-takers. They saunter up to the table with a guest check in hand and ask unsmilingly, "Ya ready to order?" When asked a simple question such as how an item is prepared, the answer is often, "I don't know; I'll ask the chef." When they bring items to the table, they often ask, "Who had the roast beef?" while the plate is passed from one guest to the next. Sound familiar?

Missed Selling Opportunities

Lack of professional selling on the part of a service organization's employees results in lower sales and less satisfied consumers. All of this is simply a matter of missed opportunities. For example, consider the following situation in which four friends were planning to have dinner at a restaurant. They were seated by the host following this greeting: "Do you have reservations?" After they had waited about five minutes for a server to approach the table, Sally appeared, presented each guest with a closed menu, and asked, "Would anyone like anything from the bar?" Each responded "no," and Sally said that she would be back in a few minutes to take their dinner orders. She returned in a few minutes, asking "You ready to order?" When a guest inquired about any special items or recommendations, Sally responded, "There isn't a special today; I guess the chef just wasn't in the mood. Everything on the menu is good. Can I take your order?" The guests then placed their orders, which Sally took without speaking except to ask about the type of vegetable and salad dressing that each guest would like. What was wrong with this situation, and who is at fault?

Clearly, Sally failed to sell; she merely took the orders. She failed to suggestive-sell a round of drinks, a bottle of wine, an appetizer, or a specialty of the house. Simply stated, Sally failed to do her job. Less clear is who is at fault. Management is at fault, not Sally. Management has the responsibility to recruit, train, supervise, coach, counsel, and motivate the service personnel. If they fail to do their jobs, management must accept the responsibility. Figure 12.1 summarizes the loss of potential revenue from the table that Sally serviced. The total lost revenue is $45 for the party of four. Although it is doubtful that the party of four would have spent an additional $45, they might easily have spent an additional $10, $20, or $30.

The point is that the service people are salespeople. They must be taught to suggestive-sell, to increase the check averages, to deliver additional profits, and to ensure satisfied guests. If employees suggestive-sell, they have a 50 percent chance of being successful. However, if they do not suggestive-sell and do not say anything, the chances of being successful are nearly zero percent. Suggestions for ways to effectively suggestive-sell are shown in Figure 12.2.

This example was focused on a food service operation, but similar examples can be seen in other segments of the hospitality business. For instance, cruise lines could upsell passengers to book higher-priced cabins, purchase trip insurance, or buy excursion packages for ports of call. Similarly, rental car agencies could offer promotions that will encourage customers to upgrade their vehicles or extend their rental periods.

Drink sales	4 @ $3.00	=	$12.00
Wine sales	1 bottle	=	15.00
Trading up/suggestive selling a more expensive entrée or accompanying item	4 @ $1.50	=	6.00
Dessert or after-dinner drink sale	4 @ $3.00	=	12.00
	Potential lost revenue	=	$45.00
	Potential lost gratuity (@15%)	=	$6.75

FIGURE 12.1 Potential Impact of Missed Selling Opportunities

1. Develop a positive mental attitude. Not everyone will accept the suggestions, but all guests will appreciate the desire to serve and attend to their needs.

2. Do not try to manipulate the guest; simply make positive and upbeat suggestions

3. Suggest favorite items or aspects of the product–service mix with which the employee is most familiar. This makes the suggestion more personal and sincere, increasing the chances of success.

4. Use props to support suggestive selling. For example, it is relatively easy to turn down an offer for dessert, but if a dessert tray is brought to the table and the server offers the right suggestion, sales of desserts will increase. Offering samples of wine will increase the sale of wine by the glass. Some restaurants offer "flights of wine" in which several small samples are provided at about the same cost as a glass of wine. Some guests will merely try the samples, but others will purchase additional wine after trying the samples.

5. Always make positive suggestions; always focus on the positive aspects of the product–service mix. If a guest makes a negative comment, acknowledge the comment, but try to turn the negative into a positive.

6. Always be attentive to guests' needs. Some will be very receptive to suggestive selling, but others will want speedy treatment with a minimum of extra conversation and suggestive selling. Do not use a "canned presentation" to suggestive-sell. Stay tuned to the guests' needs and vary the suggestive selling presentations.

7. Never make excuses for why suggestive selling will not work or has not worked in the past.

FIGURE 12.2 **Suggestions for Effective Suggestive Selling**

Training Guest-Contact Personnel

Management has the responsibility to recruit, orient, train, supervise, coach, counsel, and motivate the service personnel. This is no small task, and it does not happen by accident.

When recruiting, it is imperative that management view potential guest-contact employees as the lifeblood of the organization, for they can make or break the hotel or restaurant. Managers should seek to hire individuals who "come alive in front of the guest." Recruiters and interviewers should look for enthusiasm, a high level of empathy, good organizational skills, obvious ambition, high persuasiveness, experience, verbal and communication skills, and a "can do" and "will do" attitude.

A wide variety of training methods can be used, but the overall focus should be on the following. Four basic aspects of training guest-contact and service personnel are product–service knowledge (cognitive aspect), physical skills (psychomotor aspect), attitude (affective aspect), and reassurance (affective aspect). Each of these is discussed in the following paragraphs.

Product-Service Knowledge (Cognitive Aspect).   This refers to the learned or memorized job knowledge, such as how specific menu items are prepared or presented, specific attributes related to guestrooms, or other ingredients of the product–service mix.

Physical Skills (Psychomotor Aspect).   These are learned physical skills, such as how to prepare a tableside salad or how to present, open, and pour a bottle of wine.

Attitude (Affective Aspect).   These are more difficult to teach because they are related to an individual's perceptions and beliefs, which are not easily changed. Attitudes affect the individual's behavior and motivation to provide service to the guest. Even if training in the first two areas results in exceptional employee performance, poor attitudes can and do result in unsatisfied guests. All employees must be trained, coached, counseled, and led by example in displaying the spirit of hospitality in serving guests. Bear in mind that in today's service economy, poor employee attitude is the number-one complaint of consumers. Consumers will tolerate minor problems, but they will not and should not be expected to deal with poor employee attitudes. The focus of training employees should be that the firm is able to tolerate any employee mistake except rudeness to a guest.

Reassurance (Affective Aspect).   The service person should be trained in how to reassure guests. This can take many forms. For example, if a guest in a dining room orders an item, the server might respond, "That's our most popular item, you'll enjoy it" or "All of our desserts are fresh baked, but that one is my favorite." Service personnel also need to be trained in how to effectively handle guest complaints. Some guests will complain no matter what you do to please them, but this group represents a very small minority. The vast majority of guests who complain have good reason, and every effort should be made to correct the error and make sure they are satisfied. It is wise to think of a guest's complaint as the tip of the iceberg, because for every complaint you hear, there are likely to be others that you do not hear. It is imperative that employees receive specific training in how to handle guest complaints. Part of the training should also provide guidance in how an employee can get the manager involved in resolving the complaint so that the guest is satisfied.

Training service personnel is of critical importance if internal promotion is to be successful. An employee must be aided in developing product–service knowledge, physical skills, a positive attitude, and the ability to reassure and effectively handle all guest situations.

Entertainment

Entertainment can generate increased sales and more satisfied guests. Entertainment during the last several years has taken on many new forms, including in-room movies and video games, large-screen television, various forms of disk jockey and music video entertainment, comedy clubs, and other forms of media entertainment. Many forms of entertainment are suitable, but live entertainment has long been regarded as the most powerful form.

Live entertainment is not the best approach for all hospitality operations, but it can be considered for some, based on the following questions:

- What impact will the entertainment have on volume, both in sales and the number of guests?
- Is the physical layout of the facility suitable for live entertainment?
- How will the cost associated with live entertainment, such as payment to performers and increased advertising, be covered?

First, the impact that entertainment will have on sales volume should be analyzed closely. The break-even point should be calculated. Different methods to cover the costs of entertainment are feasible; these include charging higher prices for food and beverage to offset the increased cost, instituting a cover charge or a cover charge and a minimum purchase, and covering costs through increased sales.

Second, the physical layout of the facility must be examined closely. Is the configuration of the facility suitable for live entertainment and perhaps for dancing? Many operators have discovered that their facilities were simply too small for live entertainment but did not discover this until after they had made the commitment.

When entertainment of any type is selected, the marketing concept should be a paramount concern. Management should focus on the needs and wants of the guests and attempt to satisfy the guests rather than themselves. If the guests want rock music, yet the management prefers jazz, there should be no question as to which type of entertainment is selected.

Other Merchandising Techniques

Many other techniques should be considered for promoting your hotel or restaurant. These include brochures and meeting planner guides, directories, flyers and in-house signs, and tent cards. All of these techniques offer a great deal of potential when they are used properly and directed toward the appropriate target audience.

Brochures are not as easy to design as one might think. When hotel brochures are placed in a rack with others, it becomes clear how difficult it is to design a brochure that will stand out from the others, capture the potential consumer's interest, and spark further inquiry or action. If a brochure is able to accomplish this, it truly is successful. Nykiel offers several suggestions for designing an effective brochure:[3]

- ***Identification of the facility, including logo.*** It is important to emphasize the chain affiliation if one exists. The consistent use of logos is very important in developing an image.

- ***Descriptive facts on the facility.*** Too many brochures use pretty faces and flowery copy and do not provide enough description of the facts related to the facility.

- ***Map and directions for how to get to the facility.*** This is particularly necessary if the facility is not as easily reached as the competition. It needs to be strongly emphasized that you can reach the facility. A map showing travel mileage and times from major cities or other attractions is also useful.

- ***Basic information.*** Be sure to include address, telephone number, and other pertinent information, such as hours of operation.

- ***Person to contact for further information.*** This might be the director of marketing, catering, or another department, depending on the purpose and intended target audience for the brochure. In addition, with the increasing importance of the Internet, providing the URL for a prospective guest to seek further information is important. An ever-increasing number of consumers use the Internet as an important source of information concerning all types of products and services.

- ***Products, services, and amenities offered by the facility.*** It is important to emphasize those aspects of the facility that will help to differentiate it from the competition.

- ***Attractions and interesting things for guests to do while they are in the area.*** Attract guests to your establishment by listing some of the main tourist attractions and activities in the region.

- ***Transportation information.*** This would include limousine service, rental car companies, airlines, and other forms of transportation that could be used.

▲ PUBLIC RELATIONS

The term *public relations* is widely misunderstood and is often misused within business, and the hospitality business is no exception. Every business interacts with a variety of "publics" representing consumers, the general public, the financial community, the organization's employees, government, the media, suppliers, and many others. Public relations is the process by which the relationships with each of these publics is managed. All businesses must realize that the general public is affected by everything that companies say and do. Public relations are most obvious in the event of a disaster, such as a hotel fire, but public relations encompass many other facets and can and should take a positive tone as well. The following section will discuss aspects of public relations, offering guidelines for effective public relations, techniques that can be used effectively to manage public relations and finally, a specific application of public relations: the opening of a hotel.

It requires great skill to effectively manage public relations, which is why many firms use external consultants and agencies to assist them with this effort. Public relations should be an integrated part of the overall marketing plan. Just as objectives, strategies, tactics, action plans, target audiences, implementation schedules, and methods for evaluation are a part of the development of a marketing plan, the same approach should be applied to public relations. Positive and beneficial public relations do not just happen by chance; they must be the result of individuals making it happen according to a plan.

One of the basic needs of public relations is for the organization to be able to provide accurate information. The development of a press kit can help to accomplish this goal. The essential components of a press kit follow:[4]

- **Fact sheet.** This should contain basic information about the facility and the companies that own and operate it. The type of information necessary would include such things as property name, address, telephone number, names of contact personnel, a list of hotel facilities and amenities, and detailed specifications for meeting facilities.

- **Description of the local trading area.** Where is the facility located, and what are the surrounding areas like?

- **Special features of the product–service mix.** Are there special aspects of the facility that should be mentioned, such as architecture, type of suites offered, type of food and beverages, or special services?

- **Specific details about the product–service mix of the facility.** This should provide information about each of the retail outlets.

- **Photographs.** Stock photographs should be maintained of both the exterior and interior of the facility, showing the facilities being used by guests.

- **Biographical sketch of the general manager.** A brief description of the general manager and his or her background.

The press kit is useful when interacting with members of the media, as well as the other publics. Table 12.1 provides a list of those members of the media with whom the public relations personnel should be familiar.

Public Relations Techniques

Public relations can be applied in several ways. Some of the more common techniques include the following:

Table 12.1	**Public Relations Media Contacts**
Print Media	*Broadcast Media*
City editor	Station manager
Food editor	News director
Travel editor	News announcer
Finance editor	Station personalities
Style section editor	
Travel editor	
Business editor	
Feature columnists	

- *News releases.* These should be routinely sent to the media, providing information about people and events of potential interest. Certainly, not all of the releases will result in positive coverage, but some will.
- *Photographs.* These will be particularly effective if they feature a famous personality or create a human-interest angle.
- *Letters, inserts, and enclosures.* Letters might be sent to governmental officials urging them to take some type of action. Inserts can be used as envelope stuffers in employee paychecks, or they can be sent with follow-up correspondence with guests or clients.
- *House organs and newsletters.* These can be both internal and external but should be focused on a specific target audience. The purpose is to communicate positive images, increase sales, and influence public opinion.
- *Speeches and public appearances.* Members of the management staff should be encouraged to speak before groups with either professional or civic applications. Special care should be taken to ensure that the speech is well prepared and delivered.
- *Posters, bulletin boards, and exhibits.* These help draw attention to your organization.
- *Audiovisual materials.* Videotapes can be distributed to the media and travel professionals.
- *Open houses and tours.* Inviting the media and travel professionals to your property can increase awareness and create interest.

Guidelines for Public Relations

It is difficult to provide a complete list of possible public relations techniques. However, the following guidelines offer several good ideas for increasing the effectiveness of public relations activities. The editors of *Hardware Retailing* magazine developed the following guidelines:

1. Always identify individual photographs when submitted so that recipient does not play "editor's bingo" in guessing who's who. Only send photos of people involved, not the person making the announcement. In group shots, identify individuals from left to right, standing, etc.

2. Do not fold, staple, crease or otherwise mutilate photos, or write on the front or back with a heavy hand, thereby damaging the photo.

3. Know the publications that you send material to so that you do not waste your company's money or the editor's time. Don't develop a reputation for sending out worthless material or your important releases may one day be overlooked or discarded.

4. Always provide pertinent information such as company's name and address (not just the public relations or ad agency's name and address), retail price or cost of the product so that the reader can evaluate its appeal and marketability, etc. Just the facts, no puffery.

5. Do not send too many releases at one time and then complain that the publication did not select "the most important one." If one is more important from a product, marketing, design or production standpoint, send it separately or identify it properly. It is really best to space out releases. Few publications maintain files of releases since they receive hundreds each week.

6. Be brief and provide a summary of the release so that it can be judged quickly (and properly) and written efficiently by someone who is not an expert in your field. Complete information can be briefly stated without reams of company history!

7. Do not confuse trade magazines with *Playboy* or *Playgirl* and use scantily dressed models. Editors frequently choose not to use a picture if models are too obviously selected to trap the viewer with blatant sex appeal.

8. Be careful when placing logo-type, model number, etc., on photos, so that it can be cropped off without destroying the product image. Providing this information in a corner of the photo may solve your product or brand identification problem. Otherwise, your photo may not be used at all.

9. Remember the timing of magazine publishing, and do not send out releases a week or so before promotion takes place, expecting them to be used in time. You should not ask a publication to run a new product or display item before you are in production and/or your sales organization has told the trade about it in regular personal calls.

10. Do not threaten editors with loss of advertising if they do not run your items or bait them with promises of advertising if they do.

Public relations requires careful planning and attention to detail. Unlike advertising, in which the sponsor controls the content and the timing of the message, public relations requires coordination with many other parties. These parties do not have the interests of the hotel or restaurant as their primary objective. Table 12.2 provides an example of a timetable developed to plan the public relations for the opening of a new hotel. It should be noted that the plans provide a framework around which more specific action plans and specific responsibilities can be developed. This schedule begins six months before the hotel opens, at which time the announcement of construction plans and the groundbreaking ceremony will have been completed.

Table 12.2	**Public Relations Timetable for Hotel Opening**
150–180 Days Before Opening	*60–90 Days Before Opening*
1. Hold meeting to define objectives and to coordinate public relations effort with advertising; establish timetable in accordance with scheduled completion data. 2. Prepare media kit. 3. Order photographs and renderings. 4. Begin preparation of mailings and develop media lists. 5. Contact all prospective beneficiaries of opening events. 6. Reserve dates for press conferences at off-site facilities.	1. Launch campaign to local media and other media with a short lead time, emphasizing hotel's contribution to the community, announcement of donations and beneficiaries, etc. 2. Send third and final progress bulletin with finished brochure. 3. Commence behind-the-scenes public tours. 4. Hold hard-hat luncheons for travel writers. 5. Set up model units for tours.
120–150 Days Before Opening	*30–60 Days Before Opening*
1. Send announcement with photograph or rendering to all media. 2. Send first progress bulletin to agents and media (as well as corporate clients, if desired). 3. Begin production of permanent brochure. 4. Make final plans for opening events, including commitment to beneficiaries.	1. Send preopening newsletter (to be continued on a quarterly basis). 2. Hold soft opening and ribbon cutting ceremony. 3. Hold press opening. 4. Establish final plans for opening gala.
90–120 Days Before Opening	*The Month of Opening*
1. Launch publicity campaign to national media. 2. Send mailings to media. 3. Send second progress bulletin. 4. Arrange exclusive trade interviews and features in conjunction with ongoing trade campaign. 5. Begin trade announcement.	1. Begin broadside mailing to agents. 2. Hold opening festivities. 3. Conduct orientation press trips.

Source: Jessica Dee Zive, "Public Relations for the Hotel Opening," *The Cornell Hotel and Restaurant Administration Quarterly.* Vo. 22, No. 1, p. 21.

Evaluating Public Relations

As with the other promotional program elements discussed previously, it is important to evaluate the effectiveness of the public relations effort. In general, public relations programs are effective because they require little cost (in both relative and absolute terms), they are not subject to the same clutter as advertising and sales promotions, and they have the ability to generate interest in a firm's product or service. Also, the source is credible and well-managed public relations programs can improve the image of the firm. However, the firm does not determine the message that is sent to consumers because there is no exchange of money, and the publicity can be negative.

The public relations efforts of firms need to be evaluated to ensure an effective long-term program. The following is a list of possible methods that can be used to evaluate these programs.

- *Personal observation.* All members of a firm should take an active interest in the image that is being portrayed by the media. Both positive and negative publicity should be conveyed to proper authorities within the organization. Some companies hire public relations firms or designate employees that are responsible for this task.
- *Public opinion surveys.* Firms can conduct their own studies of public opinion, or purchase the results of syndicated research performed by independent agencies. These studies enable firms to track their progress over time.
- *Use objective measures.* Firms or their representatives can simply count the number of impressions over a certain time period. More specifically, these impressions can be separated into positive and negative categories. Percentages can be calculated for each category as a percent of the total, and the ratio of positive to negative impressions can be examined as well.

Firms should use a combination of all these types of evaluation techniques. As more companies hire public relations firms and organize public relations departments, more emphasis will be placed on this activity. Public relations is no longer considered a passive practice that cannot be controlled by firms.

▲ MARKETING ACTION NOW!

One concept that has become popular in the restaurant industry is the early bird special for consumers who are willing to dine before the peak dinner hours. Consumers are offered a selection of meals at lower prices if they order before 6:00 PM or 7:00 PM, depending on the restaurant and the market. This is a type of price promotion that targets consumers who tend to be more sensitive about price. It is particularly popular in resort areas or destinations that are frequented by tourists. Normally, restaurants will offer only a few menu items at the reduced price and may serve smaller portions or eliminate an accompaniment such as a salad or side order.

1. What market segments or consumers tend to take advantage of early bird specials?
2. Why do restaurants limit the number of menu choices at the reduced price?
3. How would you evaluate the impact of this type of promotion? Discuss the relevant effects.
4. Why do restaurants serve smaller portions or eliminate an accompaniment?

▲ SUMMARY OF CHAPTER OBJECTIVES

This chapter focuses on the important aspect of promotions and public relations. The elements of the promotional mix are presented and a communications model is illustrated. The role of sales promotion is discussed and includes increasing consumer awareness, introducing new products and services, increasing guest occupancy and customer counts, combating competition, encouraging present guests to purchase more, and stimulating demand in nonpeak periods.

The two basic types of sales promotion strategies are push and pull. Push strategies attempt to push the product–service mix through the service delivery system, while the pull strategy encourages increased purchases and consumption by consumers. Several common techniques are discussed, including coupons, sampling, premiums, and contests, and sweepstakes. Recommendations for managing and budgeting for successful promotions are also discussed.

Merchandising techniques are also reviewed. A discussion of the lost revenue potential from missed selling opportunities is presented, as well as suggestions and recommendations for how these missed opportunities could be avoided. Specific material presented includes suggestions for training guest-contact employees include product–service knowledge (cognitive aspect), physical skills (psychomotor aspect), attitude (affective aspect), and reassurance (affective aspect). Methods by which guest-contact employees could be trained are presented.

The broad field of public relations is introduced. Public relations involve the management of relationships with the "publics" with whom the firm comes in contact. Specific material presented includes the development of a public relations press kit, as well as the most commonly used public relations techniques.

▲ KEY TERMS AND CONCEPTS

Broadcast media

Collateral material

Contests and sweepstakes

Coupons

Cooperative advertising

Merchandising

Point-of-sale displays

Premiums

Print media

Public relations

Pull techniques

Push techniques

Sales promotion

Sampling

Suggestive selling

▲ QUESTIONS FOR REVIEW AND DISCUSSION

1. What are the elements of the promotional mix?

2. Illustrate the components of the communications model. How can this model be used to improve communications?

3. What is the role of sales promotion?

4. What are several of the objectives of sales promotion? Which one(s) do you believe is (are) the most important? Why?

5. What is the difference between push and pull strategies? Use an example to illustrate the difference.

6. Cite and discuss the pros and cons of each of the major sales promotional techniques discussed in the chapter.

7. If you were given the job of designing and managing a sales promotion, how might you use the guidelines presented in the chapter? What would you do differently?

8. What are the skill areas in which guest-contact employees must be trained? Which of these, in your opinion, is the most important? Why?

9. What is public relations? What do public relations personnel do?

▲ NOTES

[1]Melanie A. Crosby, "Rewarding Regulars: Frequent-Diner Programs Keep Customers Coming Back for More," *Restaurants USA* (September 1998), pp. 12–17.

[2]American Express, *Handbook of Restaurant Promotions*, pp. 3.1–3.4.

[3]Ronald A. Nykiel, *Marketing in the Hospitality Industry* (New York: Van Nostrand Reinhold, 1983) p.130.

[4]Jacques C. Cosse, "Ink and Air Time: A Public Relations Primer," *The Cornell Hotel and Restaurant Administration Quarterly*, Vol. 21, No. 1, pp. 37–40.

13

Personal Selling

❖ Chapter Objectives

By the end of this chapter, you should understand:

1. The fundamentals of selling and the profile of successful salespeople
2. The basic markets for hotel group sales and their decision factors
3. The personal selling process and its role in promotion
4. The art of negotiating and key account management
5. The ethical issues in personal selling

❖ Chapter Outline

I. Chapter Opening Profile
II. Introduction
   A. Sales roles
   B. Profile of a successful salesperson

❖ Chapter Opening Profile

A current trend in sales is to shorten the sales cycle by providing salespeople with the names of qualified prospects rather than have them do cold calling to look for leads, who need to be qualified before a sale can be made.[1] This is especially appealing in light of the 80/20 rule: 80 percent of business comes from 20 percent of a firm's customers. Telemarketing can be used to get information about the prospects in a company's database so that salespeople can be informed when they make sales calls. This allows salespeople to spend more time selling activities and can help improve their success rates.

Many salespeople spend less than 50 percent of their time in actual sales work. When they do get the time to make sales calls, they spend a good portion of it making cold calls and looking for prospects. This is alarming when you think that the main reason salespeople are hired is because of their ability to communicate with customers and close sales. If they could be provided with qualified prospects and spend more of their time making sales presentations, there is no doubt that the company's sales would be improved. This chapter will discuss some of the methods that can be used to qualify leads. Hotels are becoming more adept at obtaining lists of qualified customers so sales managers can devote more time to selling and be more effective at meeting their sales quotas.

▲ INTRODUCTION

In the competitive world of hospitality sales and marketing, the ability to effectively identify potential business, qualify the prospects, engage in personal selling activities, and eventually book the business are critical to the success of the property. The term *selling* is often used synonymously with the term *marketing*. Marketing encompasses all of the activities that are necessary in creating an exchange between a buyer and a seller. These activities include promotion, pricing, product design, and distribution. **Personal selling** is merely one component of the promotion mix, which refers to the personal communication of information to persuade a prospective customer to buy something (e.g., a product or service) that satisfies that individual's needs.[2] The range of activities that are under the umbrella of personal selling is quite broad. Sales managers communicate with clients and prospects by means of the telephone, personal sales calls resulting from appointments, cold sales calls without appointments, and contacts with clients at trade shows, professional meetings, and conventions.

Sales Roles

Sales jobs can vary widely in their nature and requirements, even within the same company or industry. This chapter focuses mainly on hotel sales, but the fundamentals and techniques can be applied to any type of hospitality or travel sales. One of the main factors that can be used to classify sales positions is the extent to which the salesperson is responsible for creating sales and developing new accounts. **Order takers** are salespeople who ask customers what they want or respond to purchasing requests. This type of salesperson is most common in organizations that have high demand for their products and services, or organizations that engage in a great deal of mass advertising and use the pull strategy for promotion. In other words, customers seek them out. **Order getters** are salespeople who are responsible for creating sales and developing new accounts. They still service their existing accounts, but they are also expected to use sales strategies to obtain new accounts.

> **order takers** salespeople who attend to customer inquiries and repeat purchases

> **order getters** salespeople who are responsible for creating sales and developing new accounts

Many resort hotels and luxury properties enjoy good demand and have many repeat customers. The salespeople in these establishments are able to spend more time in the office responding to inquiries and following up with repeat customers. The goal is to create a good mix of customers who will maximize the firm's potential revenue over the long run. Conversely, hotels that don't have high demand because of various components of their product–service mixes find it more challenging to obtain group business. When there is excess room capacity, lodging facilities require salespeople to be good order getters and create sales. It is important to note that some hotels do not target group markets, and even with excess capacity, they might choose to have only one salesperson, who acts as an order taker.

telemarketing use of telecommunication technology to conduct marketing campaigns aimed at certain target markets

Some firms employ both order takers and order getters to obtain a customer mix. For example, **telemarketing** systems use the hotel's telecommunication technology, and trained personnel conduct marketing campaigns aimed at certain target markets. Hotels advertise a toll-free number that can be used by customers to contact the hotel. When calls are received, they are sent through the proper channels. Transient customers can be handled by reservations, and group business can be directed to the sales department. Once in the sales department, it can be determined whether to use an order taker or an order getter. Hotels that focus on group business tend to have separate toll-free numbers for the sales department. A **sales blitz** is another type of personal selling activity that targets specific groups within a condensed time frame. A sales blitz can be done in person or over the telephone, and hotels will often use staff members from different departments within the hotel. The goal of most sales blitzes is to make a large number of sales calls in a short period of time, with the objective of generating as large a number of qualified potential buyers as possible. Blitzes are often used to requalify prior clients who have not booked any business for a year or more.

sales blitz selling activity that targets specific groups within a condensed time frame

The importance of sales has increased as the competitiveness of the group meetings business has intensified. Today, through the efforts of the major hotel corporations and professional associations such as the Hospitality Sales and Marketing Association International (HSMAI), sales and marketing professionals employed within the hospitality and tourism industry are better trained than ever before. They have to be to be successful.

Profile of a Successful Salesperson

What makes a salesperson successful? A profile of a successful salesperson would reveal several factors that all contribute to the individual's success. Courtesy pays a big part in making an individual successful. It is imperative that the sales manager always strives to make certain the client is satisfied. This means having to expend some extra effort or occasionally doing something that is not routine. It might even mean bending the rules or standard operating procedures to ensure client satisfaction. Courtesy also means being able to smile and handle a difficult situation even when those around you are angry or in a panic.

A second aspect in the profile of a successful salesperson is complete knowledge of the product–service mix that is being sold. The salesperson should know every square inch of the hotel property and should be able to answer questions that the prospect might raise. The salespeople should be knowledgeable about all facets of the hotel, including items such as meeting room set up, booking policies and procedures, weight capacity of freight elevators, audiovisual capabilities of the hotel, and food and beverage skills and talents of the hotel's staff.

A third part of the profile is professional appearance and behavior. This does not mean that the individual needs to be a "pretty face." Rather, the sales manager should present a professional appearance. This requires professional clothing, such as business suits, and good personal grooming. First impressions are critical in selling, and professional appearance can be a real asset in establishing rapport with a prospective client.

The desire and willingness to work is a fourth characteristic in the profile of a successful salesperson. Only a small percentage of sales calls and contacts will result in sales or signed contracts. A successful salesperson must have the perseverance to keep going and to keep asking for the business, even when many others have said no. Keep in mind that if 1 call out of 10 results in a signed contract, a sales manager has been told no 9 times before making a sale. For this reason, when a prospect says no, the sales manager should say "thank you," knowing that the next prospect might say yes. A conversation with one of the leading salespeople for a major manufacturing company revealed an interesting philosophy when he stated, "I'm not in sales, I'm in rejections. I get rejected a lot more than I make sales."

Another quality that is a real asset in sales is organizational ability. Keeping in constant communication with dozens of clients and keeping all of the many separate details straight calls for superior organization. The use of contact management software such as Act, Maximizer, or Microsoft Outlook is a tremendous asset in helping sales managers maintain profiles of each client. In addition, contact management capability is often part of a hotel sales office software solution such as Delphi. The ability to recall names and faces is also important. When a salesperson meets clients it is imperative to remember their names, who they work for, and other pertinent details. Following up with trace dates and the details of each client's contract calls for superior organizational skills.

A final quality that is an asset to the successful salesperson is a strong personality. This does not mean that to be successful in sales, one must be extroverted and the life of the party. Rather, it means that the individual needs to have some warmth, some empathy, and the ability to make others believe in and trust you. If prospects do not feel comfortable with the salesperson, it is very unlikely that they will make a purchase.

Several studies have been conducted with the purpose of identifying the characteristics or traits of successful salespeople. The results of one such study are shown in Figure 13.1.[3] Hotel sales and marketing is a dynamic environment in which to work. It is demanding and full of challenges, but the rewards are commensurate with the efforts required. In the hotel industry, salespeople are normally referred to as *sales managers*, and the person responsible for the sales function is referred to as the *director of sales*. In larger hotels, the director of sales reports to the *director of marketing*, and in some smaller hotels the two positions are combined into a *director of sales and marketing*. The remainder of the chapter will explore aspects of hotel sales and personal selling.

Impression Criteria

    Appearance—neat and clean cut

    Dress—conservative and in good taste

    Demeanor—confident and with a sense of humor

    Attitude—friendly and sincere, possessing a "consumer is number one" orientation

    Voice and speech—talks to express and not to impress; has well developed listening skills

"Can do" Criteria

    Grades—upper 25 percent of graduating class

    Curriculum—tendency to take advanced and more difficult courses

    Extracurricular activities—has contributed to organizations, held offices, and volunteered

    Related work experience—part-time and summer jobs; internships

    Career goals—interest in marketing and well developed reasons for this interest

"Will do" Criteria

    Character—integrity, self-reliance, loyalty, idealism, principles

    Motivation—drive, perseverance, sense of responsibility

    Ability to get along with others—likes people, cooperative, has constructive attitude and maturity

FIGURE 13.1 Characteristics of Successful Sales Personnel

▲ SELLING TO GROUP MARKETS

Before a single telephone call or personal sales call is made, the sales manager must begin to develop a clear understanding of the nature of the buyer: the meeting planner. A **meeting planner** is someone who plans meetings that will be attended by all sorts of individuals. Meeting planners represent a vast array of different groups, from large national associations to small local civic groups. With this diversity comes a huge gap in talents and skills. Many meeting planners, especially those representing large associations and companies, are very knowledgeable professionals. They usually know as much or more about the operation of a hotel as an entry-level sales manager. At the other extreme are those individuals who only occasionally plan meetings and whom the sales manager must educate as well as sell. Such is the challenge faced by the sales and marketing team—selling to many different individuals, each holding the title of meeting planner.

If sales managers are to effectively sell to the meeting planner, several things are necessary. First, sales managers must thoroughly understand the product–service mix that they are representing. They must know everything or be able to find the answers quickly to questions raised by the meeting planner. Second, they must know how to sell. Selling is a skill that is first learned and is then refined. Few individuals are born to be in sales; for nearly everyone, selling is a learned skill. Selling in the hospitality industry is just like selling in other industries, especially service industries: One must learn to sell effectively.

FAB Selling Technique

One of the most common approaches to selling is to focus on the benefits that a product or service offers consumers. In selling benefits, the salesperson relates a product's benefits to the consumer's needs by stressing its features and advantages. This technique can be referred to as the **FAB Selling Technique.** The *F* refers to product features, or the physical characteristics of the product. The *A* refers to the advantages, or performance characteristics, that will be of benefit to the buyer. And finally, the *B* refers to the benefit, or favorable outcome, that the buyer experiences. In other words, salespeople take the product's features and demonstrate how they can be advantageous to the buyer, resulting in the end-benefit that is being sought.

FAB selling technique emphasizes features, advantages, and benefits

Features. All products have physical characteristics like price, shape, color, and size. Hotel services are no exception. In the past, many firms attempted to sell products and services based on features, until they realized that it was more effective to focus on the benefits provided by the product or service. Many hotels have front desks, guest rooms, restaurants, pools, meeting facilities, and parking lots. Consumers can fill their basic needs at any of these establishments, but those that are superior in terms of performance have a competitive advantage when it comes to benefiting consumers. Figure 13.2 provides a **property analysis checklist** that can be used to evaluate a hotel's basic features.

Advantages. Once the basic features are determined, it is necessary to compare these features with competitors to assess a firm's strengths and weaknesses. This analysis provides salespeople with the information that they need to persuade buyers. The salespeople should focus on the firm's strengths or the advantages associated with the product and stress its benefits to the consumer. However, it is important to determine consumer needs and the benefits that they are seeking.

Hotel chains train salespeople to know the property's physical characteristics, but it is also necessary to train them to know the property's performance characteristics. For example, the following product advantages could exist:

- The hotel has the best location in town
- The hotel's restaurant has been rated the best in town

- The hotel has free or less expensive parking
- The hotel's banquet facilities are the largest
- The hotel's guestrooms have been recently renovated
- The hotel has been given an award for service quality

As you can see, there are many ways to gain a competitive advantage over the competition. However, it is critical to match a hotel's advantages and benefits with markets that value those particular attributes highly.

Location
- ➢ Rural or urban; location within city or town
- ➢ Type of area: industrial, agricultural, political
- ➢ Accessibility by highway and major carrier; by membership
- ➢ Facilities for sharing and overflow; attractions for free time

Guestroom Accommodations
- ➢ Total number and amount that can be committed; when they can be committed
- ➢ Types of rooms: singles, doubles, suites, etc.; special rooms: nonsmoking, handicapped accessible
- ➢ Rate schemes: rack rates, discounted rates (volume, time of purchase, etc.), upgrades

General Facilities and Services
- ➢ Public dining and lounge facilities
- ➢ Entertainment, recreation, and fitness facilities
- ➢ Business or corporate services: faxing, copying, shipping, etc.
- ➢ Other services: room service, valet parking, laundry, etc.

Meeting Facilities
- ➢ Total number and dimensions of meeting rooms; possible setups
- ➢ Location and dimensions of exhibit areas
- ➢ Equipment: tables, podiums, audiovisual, etc.
- ➢ Banquet rooms and reception areas

Outside Facilities and Services
- ➢ Restaurants and tourist attractions
- ➢ Sports and recreation facilities (e.g., golf, tennis, etc.)
- ➢ Additional business services

Transportation
- ➢ Mass transit and taxis
- ➢ Rental cars, charters, and sightseeing vehicles

FIGURE 13.2 Property Analysis Checklist

Benefits. To sell products and services to consumers, salespeople must be able to tell consumers how their needs will be fulfilled. Benefit selling can address a consumer's personal motives by answering the question "what's in it for me?" In discussing benefits, salespeople should stress the favorable outcomes that will result if the consumer purchases the product or service. To sell effectively, the sales manager must possess a thorough understanding of the needs of the prospective client. The sales manager should be a professional in identifying client needs and then showing how the hotel's product–service mix will help to meet those needs. It is much easier to sell when you are demonstrating how your product–service mix will solve the client's problems than when you are merely trying to push your product–service mix.

Knowledge of the meeting planners' needs begins with background information about the group that the meeting planner represents, as well as the more specific needs directly related to the meeting. For example, the needs of most meeting planners will fall into the following categories: costs, location, image and status, professional service, adaptability and flexibility, and professional operations and management.

Costs. A meeting planner's desire to keep costs reasonable and within the allocated budget is a major need or objective. All meeting planners must operate within a restricted budget, yet they want to obtain the best "deal" for their dollars spent. In short, they want to book meetings with the hotel that will be able to provide the best price-value relationship. This does not necessarily mean the cheapest price, simply the highest perceived value for the dollars that are spent.

Location. Most meeting planners have a general idea of the type of location that they prefer. This will depend on the type of meeting being planned. Not every hotel needs to be located next to an airport, a lake, or a golf course, or boast of a great location. It is simply a matter of showing meeting planners how the location of a specific hotel will meet their immediate needs. Location includes both geographic location and the general environment surrounding the property. For example, a resort property may not be as easy to reach as a downtown hotel, yet it may have the type of environment that offers the opportunity for both meetings and recreation.

Image and Status. Meeting planners typically want to hold meetings at hotels that reflect the image and status of the client organization. This does not mean that the image must be upscale and exclusive, although this is certainly desirable for many meeting planners. An image of budget and no frills is important to some groups. If the groups can be booked on a consistent and continuing basis, the profits will follow. The role of the sales manager is to link the image and status needs of the meeting planner to the perceived image, status, and positioning of the hotel, thereby creating a reason to buy.

Professional Service.

Likely to be at the top of a list of complaints of nearly all meeting planners is the absence of professional service. The quality of service has been widely criticized within the United States. It is imperative that the sales manager be able to show the skeptical meeting planner that the hotel will be able to provide the level of service desired and expected by the client.

Adaptability and Flexibility.

Every hotel has **standard operating procedures**, yet at the same time to effectively sell to meeting planners, the sales manager must be able to demonstrate that the hotel will be flexible enough to meet the special requirements of the group. No meeting planner likes to be told, "We can't do that because it is not within the policies of the hotel." Meeting planners are not asking the hotel to do anything illegal or immoral; they simply want to work with sales managers that adapt and work hard to meet their needs and special requests. The truly professional hotels that are indeed guest- and service-oriented will go out of their way to adapt to meet the needs of the meeting planner.

Professional Operations and Management.

A hotel is only as good as the staff and management that run the operating departments of the hotel. If the operations side of the business is poor, no amount of effort by the sales and marketing team will result in repeat bookings. Simply stated, the operations managers and the entire staff must function as a team, working with the sales and marketing staff to deliver to the meeting planner's groups the explicit level of products and service that were promised. Satisfying meeting planners means not only meeting their expectations but exceeding the expectations as well.

If a sales manager is to be successful, he or she must help the meeting planner solve the problems faced in planning the meeting. This includes finding answers to all of the critical decisions that confront the meeting planner. The role of the salesperson begins with preplanning, which can be very important if the meeting planner is not experienced. The sales manager can assist the meeting planner with the following:

- Defining the purpose of the meeting and identifying who will attend and the total number of attendees
- Identifying and managing the expectations of those who will attend the meeting
- Developing a central theme for the meeting or themes for specific events within the entire meeting
- Developing a schedule for the events that are planned
- Developing a budget for all meeting expenses such as rooms, food and beverage, and other expenses
- Developing criteria by which to select a geographic location and hotel site

- Deciding on first, second, and third most preferred meeting dates

In most cases, the meeting planner will have already done much of this preplanning before visiting with the hotel sales manager, but even so, the discussion related to some of these issues will serve to qualify the prospective client and establish the meeting planner's expectations.

Once the preplanning is completed, the role of the sales manager becomes more critical. The meeting planner needs to make decisions about the type of guest room accommodations needed. This will include several particulars:

- Determining the total number of rooms that should be blocked, as well as the arrival and departure patterns of the attendees,
- Assessing the need for hospitality suites and suites for VIPs and speakers,
- Making decisions about the billing procedures, such as each guest being responsible for individual charges, all of the charges being billed to a master account, or some combination of the two methods,
- Finalizing a meeting schedule to include the necessary meeting room configurations, meeting lengths, food and beverage functions, coffee breaks, and the proper audiovisual requirements.

Once these issues have been discussed and determined, further discussion with the meeting planner is necessary to work out the details of the meeting room set-ups and meeting logistics. Some examples of the details that should be discussed follow:

Meeting Room Rental Fees and Set-up Charges. If the group is meeting during a high demand period and is not generating sufficient room revenue and/or food and beverage revenue, a meeting room rental may be charged. This rental fee is often negotiable. Additional setup fees may be charged if special setup is required, for example, the 8×10 foot booths set up for exhibits. Those often require additional utility connections for the exhibitor's displays.

Meeting Room Set-Ups and Configuration. Theater-style meeting rooms, in which chairs are placed in rows, are appropriate for large groups. The schoolroom set-up is used for groups in which a good deal of note taking is expected; this set-up provides rows of tables and chairs all facing in one direction. For smaller groups, the tables and chairs can be arranged in a variety of configurations such as T-shape, U-shape, hollow-square, and oval.

Once the meeting has been booked into the hotel, the catering sales staff begins to work more closely with the client in planning the food and beverage functions, such as breakfasts, lunches, dinners, receptions, coffee breaks, and entertainment for any of these functions. Creativity is of the utmost importance in this area. Every hotel needs to try and outdo the competition. In the weeks and final days before the meeting is held, the ho- tel staff needs to work closely with the client to work out the final details concerning the meeting. The final details will include several areas:

- Registering attendees and providing them with the necessary informa- tion packets
- Distributing welcome gifts and or baskets for dignitaries and VIPs
- Determining guarantees for food and beverage functions. Most hotels require final guarantee counts for food and beverage functions 48 to 72 hours before the actual event. A guarantee count is the number of guests for which the hotel will prepare and which the client will be billed. Most hotels will prepare for 5 percent over the guarantee count, and the client will be billed for the actual number of attendees or the guarantee figure, whichever is greater.

If the sales manager is to build a long-term relationship with the client, it is necessary to build a solid working relationship. This relationship is built on trust and the ability of the hotel's staff to deliver consistent prod- ucts and services that meet or exceed the expectations of the meeting planners. While this may seem to be a very simple concept that every ho- tel should be able to deliver, it is much more difficult in the real world. However, the truly great hotels are able to do it every day.

Meetings Market Segments

Selling to any group begins with understanding the needs of the prospec- tive client and then showing the client how your hotel's product–service mix can satisfy those needs. To do this well, the sales manager must have a great deal of background information about the client's group, the group's needs, past meeting behavior and patterns, and objectives and plans for future meetings. The second step is to link the features offered by the hotel's product–service mix with benefits that the client will find at- tractive and that will satisfy the stated client needs and objectives.

Each group is different, and it may be incorrect to stereotype specific types of groups. However, some broad generalizations about each group market segment can be made. According to the 1998 Meetings Market Re- port, the meetings market accounted for $41.8 billion in total expenditures in 1997.[4] Table 13.1 provides a breakdown of the meetings market by the three main categories: association meetings, association conventions, and corporate meetings. It is interesting to note that although corporations ac- count for the largest number of meetings and attendees, associations and conventions account for more in total expenditures. The reason for this will be clear after reading the following sections.

Association Market Segment. The association market is very broad, ranging from large national and international conventions attended

Table 13.1	**1997 Meetings Market**			
	Corporate	*Convention*	*Association*	*Total*
Number of Meetings (in thousands)	783.9	11.3	189.5	984.7
Expenditures (in billions)	$10.8	$16.7	$14.3	$41.8
Number of attendees (in millions)	49.9	11.7	17.9	79.5

by thousands of individuals to very small but expensive board of directors' meetings. When we think of the association market, we tend to think of the large conventions, but this is only a small segment of the total associations meeting market. Associations hold several different types of meetings each year, including the following:

- *Annual convention for the entire membership.* This meeting is usually the largest that the association will hold. It will often include exhibits, especially within the trade association market.
- *Board of directors' meetings.* These are typically held three or four times a year and are often quite elaborate. The expenditures per attendee are higher than other association meetings.
- *Seminars and workshops.* Associations provide continuing education for the members, and these meetings are held throughout the year.
- *Committee meetings.* Associations operate by means of a volunteer committee approach and each of the committees may need to meet several times a year.

The decision-making process and long lead time for the association market can be quite frustrating for the hotel sales manager. This market segment is often assigned to the most experienced sales manager or the director of sales because that individual's additional experience will prove beneficial in working with this market segment. The meeting planners working with the larger associations are normally quite experienced and professional, so the hotel's representative must be equally knowledgeable and experienced. The decision-making is scattered among several people within association. For example, the meeting planner may decide where to hold small meetings and workshops, but decisions about larger meetings like annual conventions normally involve the executive committee and/or the board of directors. For this reason, the sales manager must be prepared for a lengthy decision-making process. The initial contact may be with the association meeting planner, but it may take several weeks or

Hotel sales departments are responsible for filling public spaces as well as guest rooms with corporate and association groups. *Courtesy of The Breakers, Palm Beach, Florida.*

months before the board of directors makes a final decision concerning the location for a large meeting.

The lead time for planning meetings can also be quite long. For the largest of the national associations, it is common for the site of the annual convention to be selected five to ten years in advance. Even smaller associations typically plan their annual conventions one to three years in advance. This lead time creates some real challenges for the sales and marketing staff. Even if a large annual meeting is booked now, the revenue will not be realized for quite some time in the future.

Associations often use the annual convention as a revenue-producing event, the revenue then being used to fund some of the association's annual operating expenses. For this reason, associations will be sensitive about such negotiable items as meeting room rental, complimentary room policies, food and beverage prices and, in some cases, room rates. Keep in mind that association attendees will be paying their own expenses to attend meetings and may be very sensitive about prices for guest rooms, suites, and food and beverages.

SMERF group social, military, educational, religious, and fraternal groups that often have meetings but are working with limited budgets

Another popular member of the association market is the **SMERF group.** SMERF stands for a combination of several market segments: social, military, educational, religious, and fraternal. SMERF meetings are frequently held in conjunction with nonprofit groups that are often working with a very limited budget. They usually do not have a professional meeting planner. Some of the SMERF meetings are small, but the number of meetings that the SMERF market segment generates makes the overall contribution significant.

Corporate Market Segment. This market segment is very broad and is widely solicited by hotels. The corporate market is quite different from the association market segment. The differences include needs and objectives, the type and number of individuals in attendance, and the lead time required. Corporations hold many more meetings than associations. The meetings tend to be smaller, have a much shorter lead time, are less price sensitive, are subject to quicker site decisions, and involve fewer individuals in the decision making process.

Corporate meetings are attractive to hotels for several reasons: They are held throughout the year rather than being concentrated in certain periods or months, and they do not require as extensive a use of meeting rooms as the association market segment. The typical corporation meeting involves fewer than 50 attendees, and the types of corporate meetings vary widely, including the following:

- *Training meetings.* With the advent of new technology, corporations are always holding meetings to train new staff and provide update training for current staff. This type of meeting is perhaps the most common. Many hotels located near the offices of major corporations will solicit this type of meeting on a continual basis.

- *Sales meetings.* Most corporations maintain a sales staff that meets on a frequent basis. These meetings serve both to provide information to the sales staff and to motivate them. This is an excellent type of meeting to solicit because the group is normally less concerned about price than other types of meetings. The organization is concerned about providing attendees with convenience and comfort.

- *New product introduction meetings.* When a corporation introduces a new product, it is often done with great fanfare. The meeting is likely to be attended by dealers, corporate sales staff, and the media. This type of meeting can be very extensive and very price insensitive.

- *Management meetings.* Management staff often needs to get away from the place of business to meet and discuss issues in a quiet environment, where they will not be interrupted by telephones and distractions of the office.

- *Technical meetings.* Technical specialists need to meet to discuss items of mutual concern. This type of meeting is less elaborate than the other types of corporate meetings.

- *Annual stockholders' meeting.* All publicly held corporations are required to have annual stockholders' meetings that may be attended by a large number of individuals. Some food and beverage events associated with this type of meeting can be very extensive.

- *Board of directors' meetings.* These are perhaps the most elaborate and expensive, and often feature extensive food and beverage presentations. They also require more expensive and specialized meeting rooms within the hotel.

Meeting planning within corporations is typically spread among several departments. Larger corporations tend to have many meetings and may have established meeting planning departments. However, in most corporations, meetings are planned by people with other areas of respon-

incentive trips meetings held at resort properties in exotic locations or abroard cruise ships as a reward for outstanding performance

sibility such as marketing or human resources, or independent planners are used. The decision making is usually rapid and does not involve as many individuals as the association market. If the meeting planner is not the final decision-maker, he or she is usually highly influential.

In addition to business meetings, corporations also plan **incentive trips** for their employees as a reward for outstanding performance. Incentive meetings tend to be held at resort properties in exotic locations and aboard cruise lines. In many ways, incentive meetings are similar to association meetings. For instance, location and climate are very important, and there is an emphasis on recreation and relaxation. Also, attendance is voluntary, spouses often attend, and the trips must be heavily promoted to encourage employees to perform well in hopes of "winning" a place on the trip. The lead time for planning incentive trips is a year or more, they last 4 to 5 days on average, and they can be attended by anywhere from 10 to 1,000 people (the average is around 100). Business meetings are normally scheduled for tax purposes (so participants don't have to report trips as taxable income), but they are often cancelled or ignored by the meeting attendees. However, incentive trips do resemble corporate meetings in that the decision making is centralized, a master account is used for billing, service is important, planners are not price sensitive, and there are established guarantees for rooms and meals.

Decision Factors. The association and corporate markets are natural segments for the group business market in hotels because of their clear distinctions in meeting characteristics. In addition, sales managers need to understand the factors that are important to each meeting planner in selecting a facility. Table 13.2 contains a comparison of the factors considered important by meeting planners for the two types of meetings. Although it is important to deal with each meeting planner on an individual basis, these responses for the average planner will provide a place to start.

As you can see, there are differences in the factors that are most important for the various types of meetings. Corporate planners are most concerned about the quality of food, followed by the ability to negotiate rates and the number, size and quality of meeting rooms. Convention planners are most concerned about the number, size and quality of the meeting rooms and sleeping rooms, and the ability to negotiate rates. Finally, association planners tend to be in less agreement as to the most important factors, but the ability to negotiate rates received the most "very important" responses. These planners are also worried about the meeting rooms, quality of food, and the cost of the facilities. The top four in rank are the same for the three types of meetings, but the factors differ somewhat in importance. It should also be noted that convention planners placed some importance on exhibit space, but it was not included due to the lack of importance among association and corporate planners.

This information can be useful in applying the FAB technique. Hotel sales managers can determine what features are important to a particular

Table 13.2	Factors Considered Very Important in Selection of a Facility/Hotel		
	Corporate	*Convention*	*Association*
Quality of food service	80%	78%	71%
Negotiable food, beverage, and room rates	77%	83%	76%
Number, size and quality of meeting rooms	74%	93%	72%
Cost of hotel or meeting facility	72%	76%	73%
Efficiency of billing procedures	64%	62%	56%
Meeting support services and equipment	63%	61%	47%
Efficiency of check-in and check-out procedures	61%	60%	50%
Number, size, and quality of sleeping rooms	60%	83%	55%
Assignment of one staff person to handle all aspects of meeting	53%	55%	45%

Source: Sarah J. F. Barley, editor, "The Big Picture," *Meetings & Conventions,* October 1998.

meeting planner then discuss the advantages provided by these features. By focusing on these performance characteristics, the sales manager can demonstrate to the meeting planner how having a meeting at the hotel will be of benefit. The next section provides a detailed explanation of the entire personal selling process.

▲ THE PERSONAL SELLING PROCESS

As mentioned earlier, personal selling is an interpersonal process whereby the seller ascertains, activates, and satisfies the needs and wants of the buyer so that both the seller and the buyer benefit. Selling need not be one-sided; it can satisfy both parties. Prospective clients can derive benefits in that the burden of planning, organizing, and directing the various aspects of a group meeting function is shared by the hotel. For most clients, this is a tremendous relief, as they no longer are directly responsible for the event. Of course, the hotel also benefits through increased sales and profits.

Why should a hotel operation engage in personal selling? First, it allows the operation to be presented in an interpersonal manner to a prospective client. The sales presentation need not be supported by expensive visual aids. Sales calls and presentations can be as simple as having a sales manager engage in telephone and personal solicitation. These sales calls give the hotel operation exposure and provide the prospective clients with another choice when arranging group meetings and banquet functions. Second, sales calls allow for two-way communication between the hotel sales manager and prospective clients. Prospects are able to ask questions, and the representative has the opportunity to present the hotel operation more thoroughly than is possible through advertising. The representative can personally demonstrate how the operation will be able to satisfy the specific needs of the prospect.

Sales calls should be made on prospective clients as well as previous clients. Previous clients should receive follow-up calls to cultivate an ongoing business relationship. If the previous experiences did not satisfy the client, there is all the more reason to follow up with a sales call. Perhaps the situation can be corrected and negative word-of-mouth publicity prevented. Often the mere attention to the client's needs and a sincere effort to improve will be enough to convince the client that the hotel should be given some additional business. The goal is to continually meet or exceed customer expectations, thereby ensuring their satisfaction.

Three basic types of sales calls are follow-up calls, initiating calls, and blitz calls. Follow-up calls are arranged with representatives of groups and organizations that have previously been clients of the hotel. Their main purpose is to remind the client of the hotel's willingness to be of service in the future. Initiating calls are made on people who have not been clients in the past but represent solid prospects for future business. The purpose of these calls is to create awareness of the products and services and to encourage a site visit so that the prospective client may see first-hand what the facility has to offer. Few bookings are made at the time of initiating calls, but it is the first step in cultivating a better relationship. And, as mentioned earlier, a sales blitz saturates an area by making many times the normal number of sales calls and distributing literature describing the product–service mix. A successful blitz reaches as many potential clients as possible. Sales blitzes often use a varied approach involving not only personal sales calls but also telephone selling us well as other forms of advertising using the mass media.

Successful salespeople generally focus on four components of successful selling: (1) prospecting and qualifying; (2) planning and delivering sales presentations; (3) overcoming objections; and (4) closing the sale (see Figure 13.3).

Prospecting and Qualifying

Identifying prospective clients is a critical activity if the sales manager's efforts are to be successful. Generally, 20 to 30 percent of all telephone sales calls are scheduled with prospective clients—those who have not previ-

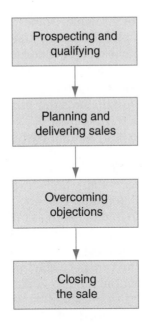

FIGURE 13.3   The Personal Selling Process

ously booked a banquet or a meeting function with the hotel. No hotel can rely entirely on repeat business, so the organization must commit itself to seeking and cultivating new business and expanding its market.

In the process of identifying and qualifying prospects, hotel sales managers should determine whether prospective clients represent good prospects before they invest a large amount of time. The following questions are helpful in determining whether a prospect is a good one:

- ***Does the prospect have needs and wants that can be satisfied by the products and services of the hotel?*** If the needs and wants of the prospect differ substantially from the product–service mix of the hotel and personal selling is undertaken anyway, sales managers are likely to be wasting both their own time and that of the meeting planner. In addition, it can create a poor image for the hotel, because the sales manager has not done enough background checking and homework to determine if the hotel "fits" the prospect's needs.

- ***Does the prospect have the ability to pay?*** It is important to determine whether the prospect has income or credit reserves to pay for a meeting or banquet function. This is a particularly important question to consider when dealing with small associations, corporations, and SMERF groups.

- ***Does the prospect have the willingness to pay?*** In some cases, the meeting planner may have the ability to pay for the nicest hotels but not the willingness. For example, some corporations have policies against using luxury hotels because they feel it is too extravagant, even though they have deep pockets. Or, a corporation may have contracts set up with various hotel chains, limiting the list of potential sites.

- ***Does the prospect have the authority to sign a contract and commit the organization for the meeting function?*** Although it is not a total waste of time, it is terribly frustrating for a sales manager to cultivate prospective sales only to find that the individuals with whom they have been dealing do not have the authority to sign a contract and commit the organization for a function. It is important to know what the decision-making process is, who is involved, and when a decision will be made. If this information is not available from the hotel's records, the best way to find out is to ask the meeting planner.

- ***Is the prospect readily accessible?*** It is important that the sales manager be able to contact the meeting planner by telephone and schedule an appointment with the prospect. Part of the prospecting is determining the best time and method to contact the prospect. It may be difficult to schedule a sales presentation with company presidents so they may prove to be poor prospects.

Locating suitable prospects is a task confronting all sales representatives. What methods can be used to obtain leads that will result in good prospects? The following list represents a few potential sources:

- ***Inquiries.*** Often individuals visit or call the hotel operation and request information concerning banquets and or meeting facilities. These individuals and the groups they represent are ready-made prospects.

- ***Names given by existing clients.*** This approach is sometimes called the *endless chain* or networking. Simply ask each of the existing clients to supply the names of additional individuals, groups, or companies that might be prospective clients. The resulting list is then qualified to determine the most attractive prospects, and personal selling begins. It is important to follow up with a thank-you letter to the individual who supplied the name of the prospect, especially when the lead results in booked business. The mutual contact also serves as a means of introduction with the new prospect.

- ***Centers of influence.*** Every community has its own leaders and influential people. These individuals make excellent prospects because they tend to be active in the community; they are "joiners." Additionally, it is an excellent idea for the sales manager and other members of the management staff to belong to community and civic organizations. In this way, they can establish personal relationships with these community leaders.

- ***Developed lists.*** Often, lists of prospects are simply developed from sources such as the telephone directory, chamber of commerce, and local clubs and organizations. These lists should then be qualified to identify the most likely prospects.

- **Direct mail prospecting.** Lists can also be used to initiate direct-mail prospecting. Promotional material is mailed to a list of prospects, and the sales manager can either follow-up with a telephone call seeking an appointment or wait for an inquiry.

- **Corporate sales offices.** All of the major hotel chains maintain national and regional sales offices. One of the responsibilities of these offices is to direct prospective leads to the chain's hotels that are in the best position to service the prospective clients. In addition, hotels within a chain may refer potential business to other hotels within the chain. For example, if a sales manager has made a contact with a meeting planner and learns that the group is planning to meet in another city, the sales manager should refer the client to the sales department of the chain's hotel in that city.

- **Cold calls.** Finally, personal sales calls can be made without prior arrangements or appointments. These are called *cold calls*. The sales manager simply contacts the prospect by telephone or may make a personal call to the prospect's office and ask to see the prospect. Rarely does this type of call result in a signed contract, but it does open some doors for future contact with the prospect. When made as personal sales calls, however, cold calls are quite time-consuming and, as a result, are very expensive.

Planning and Delivering Sales Presentations

Soon after qualifying a prospect as a good candidate for the product–service mix of the hotel, a sales manager should make contact. This is usually done by telephone. Subsequent contact may also be by telephone, the sales manager may make a personal visit to the prospect's place of business, or the prospect may visit the hotel to inspect the facilities. Sales managers should be assertive and honest. They should introduce themselves to the prospect, identify the hotel they represent, and the reason for the call. Mentioning a mutual acquaintance or a common interest may help to break the ice, but sales managers should be honest and up-front. They should not attempt to schedule the appointment under false pretenses, as this will only hurt in the long run.

The overall goal of any personal selling activity is, of course, to promote purchase on the part of the prospect. Rarely, however, does this occur without a well-planned sales presentation. The AIDA (awareness, interest, desire, and action) approach is one that has long been used in training sales personnel. To sell the prospect successfully, the sales manager must help move the prospect through each of the four steps of the AIDA model. Supplemental materials such as magazine advertising and direct mail can help create awareness and to some extent, interest, but it is the responsibility of sales managers to create desire and action.

Before making the sales call, a sales manager should develop an outline of the presentation. What are the prospect's needs and objectives for the meeting or function? How can the hotel's products and services help the organization meet its needs and objectives? It is important to make the products and services offered by the hotel as tangible as possible and to link them directly with the stated needs and objectives of the prospect. What points should be stressed? How should they be presented so that the hotel operation is perceived positively? What should the sales call accomplish?

It is not advisable to prepare a canned sales pitch that is merely replayed for each new prospect. Instead, a sales manager should be natural and straightforward, not waste words, and get right to the point. The sales presentation should begin with a formal introduction followed with questions probing the prospect about his or her needs and objectives. These needs and objectives can then be used as the basis for the remainder of the sales presentation, focusing on how the property's features and performance characteristics match the buyer's needs. It is important to let the prospect know that the hotel values, wants, and deserves the prospect's business. It may be best to use a checklist of points to be covered, for it is better to refer to a list than to appear disorganized during the presentation.

It is also important to be aware of the nature of the prospect. Some individuals have come to sit and talk; others are too busy. A sales manager should be able to vary the presentation to suit the needs of the prospect. Every effort should be made to make the prospect comfortable by establishing rapport. Every effort should also be made to emphasize the strong selling points of the hotel operation's product–service mix, while linking these strengths to the stated needs and objectives of the prospect.

Finally, one of the most important skills that can be acquired by sales managers is the art of listening. Often, sales managers feel that they must do all the talking if a sale is to be made. Nothing could be farther from the truth. Selling also requires concentrating on what the prospect is saying and on nonverbal behavior. A good sales manager allows the prospect to ask uninterrupted questions and does not try to anticipate questions and jump in with a canned response before the prospect has finished asking the question. *Active* listening is a learned skill, and one that is critical to successful selling. Selling means focusing attention on prospects and learning to hear what they are really saying.

Active listening requires a salesperson to hear and understand what the buyer is trying to say, from the buyer's point of view. The key is that the salesperson actually needs to understand the buyer, not merely hear what the buyer is saying. It is important to let the buyer know that you are listening and that you know what he means. There are four techniques that can be used in active listening:[5]

- *Encourage talking.* Let prospects know that you are listening and that you want them to continue talking. This can be done with verbal and nonverbal signals. You can say things like "I see" and "go on," or you can nod your head and use facial expressions.

- *Take notes.* Note taking gives the prospect the message that you are interested in what he is saying and that you are concerned about getting the details correct. It is important to maintain eye contact while you are taking notes and not overdo it.

- *Paraphrase the customer's meaning with a confirmation question.* State in your own words what you think the prospect meant. This will help to clarify any misunderstandings and give the prospect a feeling of assurance that you are concerned about accuracy.

- *Express an understanding of the customer's feelings and perceptions.* In addition to rephrasing the content of the prospect's message, it is helpful to express similar opinions or feelings. This is especially helpful when the prospect has feelings of doubt or frustration. Let the prospect know that his feelings are understandable and allow him to elaborate.

All of these techniques will go a long way toward building the prospect's level of confidence with you and your organization. In addition, listening and obtaining feedback will provide valuable information to use in the sales presentation.

Overcoming Objections

No matter how good a sales manager may be, sooner or later (and probably sooner) a prospect will object during the sales call. Before you proceed, you need to determine if the prospect's response is a request for more information, a condition of the sale, or an actual objection. In most cases, objections can be anticipated based on past experiences with other prospects, and a thorough knowledge of the property and the competition. Most objections fall into one of the following categories:

- *Price.* The perceived value of the products and services being offered may not be high enough. This calls for the sales manager to reassure the prospect and to continue to negotiate.

- *Products and services offered.* The prospect may not feel comfortable with the assurances that the sales manager has made about the quality or consistency of the products and services provided by the hotel staff. It may be easy to show the prospect first hand how the hotel performs.

- *Hotel.* The prospect may hold a negative image or impression about the individual hotel property or the entire chain. If this is the case, efforts must be taken to change the perceptions, and ask the prospect for a second chance, especially if the prospect represents a sizable piece of business.

- ***Pressure to decide***. Sometimes the prospect simply doesn't like being put under pressure to make a decision immediately. This can occur when another group is thinking of booking the same space on the same days, or when sales managers are pressuring the prospect to decide in order to make a quota.
- ***Individual sales manager.*** Once in a while there can be a personality conflict between the sales manager and the prospect. Sales managers need to be flexible and able to work effectively with a wide variety of individuals.

For the sales call to be successful, of course, these objections must be overcome. A simple yet effective approach directs the sales manager to use these steps:

1. Listen; allow the prospect to explain the objections fully.
2. Reflect or rephrase the prospect's feelings to assure the prospect that you fully understand the objection.
3. Handle the objection. Several methods are used to effectively handle the objections that prospects will raise.

   a. ***Agree and counter.*** Acknowledge the prospect's objection but then offer support for why the objection really is not important or is not an objection. It is important to offer support or a reasoned argument for your response. If the prospect has incorrect facts, that is easily remedied. If the prospect has an incorrect perception, this is much more difficult to change. Perception represents an individual's view of reality, and this is not easily changed.

   b. ***Turn the objection into a reason for buying.*** For example, if the prospect objects to the price it might be useful to talk about the hotel's employee-to-guest ratio and how this allows the hotel to provide a higher level of service than the competition and therefore is justification for the higher price.

   c. ***Seek more information.*** Often the stated objection is not the full reason why the prospect is not ready to make a commitment. The sales manager must probe further to determine if the meeting planner's facts are incorrect or incomplete, or if the objection is based on a bad experience in the past. Sometimes, prospects appear to be objecting when they are actually trying to obtain more information.

   d. ***Postpone the objection.*** If the prospect raises an objection early in the sales presentation and it would be best dealt with later, ask to defer it for a few minutes, indicating that it will be discussed at length. For example, if the prospect objects to the price, it is unwise to discuss price until the hotel's product–service quality is well established in the prospect's mind. It is imperative that objections be dealt with. Do not just ignore them, hoping that prospects will forget about them—they will not.

4. Get a commitment from the prospect that the objective has been met. If this is the case, it is advisable to ask for the business and attempt a trial close. The following types of questions can be used to determine if the objections have been properly handled:

- That's the answer you're looking for, isn't it?
- Do you agree that we've covered your question and given you a way to handle it?
- That solves your problem, doesn't it?

After attempting the trial close, if you cannot overcome an objection or close the sale because of an objection, you will either need to return to your presentation or consider walking away if it seems insurmountable. If your trial close suggests that you have overcome the prospect's objection(s), then it is time to close the sale. The next section covers some common closing techniques.

Closing the Sale

Despite otherwise successful sales efforts, many sales managers fail to get a firm commitment from the prospect. They simply fail to close the sale. Closure can be as simple as saying, "Can we confirm your meeting for October 15th?" Closure involves summarizing the major selling points and striving for agreement on the part of the prospect. Simply stated, closure involves asking for business. A number of methods can be used to close a sale. Among the most common are:

- ***Continued affirmation.*** If the sales manager can ask questions to which the prospect will answer yes, this can set up prospects for closing the sale. They have already responded positively to a series of questions, and the sales manager has led them to a point where he or she can then ask for the business.
- ***Prestige or status close.*** This is often used by upscale or exclusive properties. The sales manager discusses the other groups that have met in the hotel, and by affiliating the prospect's group with the other more prestigious groups encourages the prospect to decide to hold the meeting or function at the hotel.
- ***Assumptive close.*** This is a bold approach in which the sales manager simply assumes that the sale is closed and asks the prospect questions that relate to details of the contract or hands the prospect the pen and ask him or her to sign the contract.
- ***Closing on a minor point.*** This is useful when the prospect has raised an objection that the sales manager has successfully dealt with. If there

is agreement on a minor point, the sales manager can then ask for the business. This approach involves offering the prospect choices and asking "which" questions rather than "if" questions. In this way, the prospect will not respond with "no," but rather will agree and offer an explanation.

• ***Standing room only.*** If another group is looking at the same dates and space in the hotel, it may be useful to tell the prospect that he or she will need to make a decision quickly in order to reserve the meeting space and a block of guest rooms.

▲ PERSONAL SELLING TOOLS

A number of tools can be developed and used by salespeople to improve their performance. These tools increase the efficiency and effectiveness of sales presentations. We have chosen to discuss two such tools: key account management and negotiating skills.

Key Account Management

There is a rule that has been applied to sales for some time called the 80/20 rule. This proposition holds that 80 percent of the profitable business will be generated by 20 percent of the customers. Not all prospects, guests, or meeting planners should be treated equally. Rather, special attention should be given to those who are producing the largest share of the revenue and profits or who have the potential to do so. The groups that make up this 20 percent are termed *key accounts.* They deserve special attention and extra-personalized selling efforts.

Each sales and marketing department should keep a very close watch on the level of business provided by each account. Trends should be studied to determine which accounts are growing and which are declining. An analysis of each account should be conducted periodically to determine the total revenue and contribution margin for each account. Based on this analysis, accounts can be classified as shown in Figure 13.4.

Based on this analysis, key accounts can be identified and strategies and action plans developed to foster the development of exceptional accounts. Accounts with the most current business and greatest potential must be given extra attention, while those that are marginal should not consume too much of a sales manager's time and effort. Keep in mind that resources are limited, and they should be directed toward the accounts with the most profit potential.

Negotiating Skills

In today's environment, salespeople should be ready to negotiate with buyers from both consumer and industrial markets. There is a prolifera-

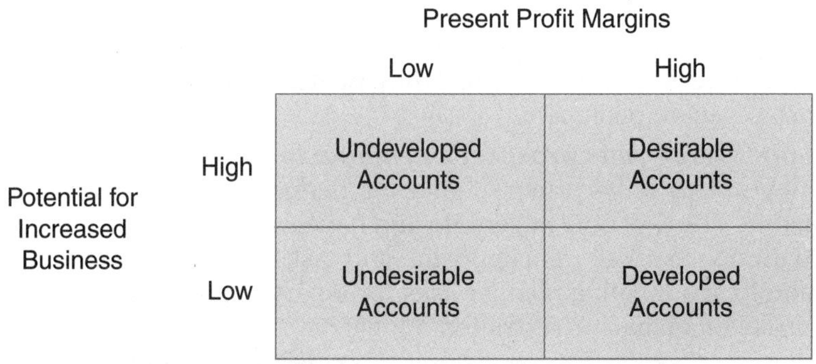

Present Profit Margins

		Low	High
High		Undeveloped Accounts	Desirable Accounts
Low		Undesirable Accounts	Developed Accounts

Potential for Increased Business

FIGURE 13.4   Account Profile

tion of information available to consumers, including tips and suggestions for getting the "best deals" from manufacturers and retailers. Advances in technology make this information easy to access, thereby allowing consumers to compare alternatives easily. The negotiation process is particularly critical in industrial markets because of the high volume. For example, if a hotel sales manager is negotiating the room rate for 500 rooms over 4 nights (2,000 room nights), a reduction of $5 in price results in a decrease in revenues of $10,000. This transaction could take place over a matter of seconds.

The goal of any negotiation is to achieve a win–win situation. It is important not to view the negotiation process as a competition because someone will end up losing. Dissatisfied customers do not return, and they provide negative word-of-mouth to their colleagues. Rather, it is important to create an exchange that results in the mutual satisfaction of the involved parties. A good sales manager will plan for the sales presentation and the inevitable negotiation process. A complete knowledge of the competitive environment will provide useful parameters for steering the negotiations. In addition, the sales manager should develop acceptable ranges and options for negotiating to ensure profitability. Finally, the following tips will improve the sales manager's potential for success in negotiating.[6]

- ***When you give something up, try to gain something in return.*** Once you show a tendency to negotiate, prospects will try to negotiate on every item. Therefore, make it clear that you expect something in return for making concessions. For example, a hotel sales manager could say "I'll lower the room rate by $5 per night if you guarantee 100 rooms for 4 nights."
- ***Look for items other than price to negotiate.*** As mentioned earlier, a small reduction in price could result in a large decrease in revenue when dealing with volume business. Hotel sales managers can focus on items other than room rates. For example, planners could be given free

meeting space, room upgrades, reduced meal prices, or free audiovisual equipment. All of these items would have a much smaller impact on the hotel's bottom line, and they provide meeting planners with a sense of accomplishment.

- *Do not attack your prospect's demand; look for the motive behind it.* Try not to tell a prospect that his demand is ridiculous or unreasonable. This will only anger him and have a negative impact on the negotiations. Instead, remain calm and ask for an explaination. For example, if a meeting planner asks for a very low room rate, it may be because of a small or restricted budget.
- *Do not defend your position; ask for feedback and advice from the prospect.* If you meet resistance to your offer, don't get defensive. Simply ask the prospect why he thinks that it is unreasonable. Asking, "what would you do if you were in my position" is often beneficial in this situation.

▲ ETHICAL ISSUES IN PERSONAL SELLING

As with most other areas of business, there is also the potential for unethical behavior by salespeople. A firm's policies and practices should provide salespeople with a good understanding of acceptable behavior, or conduct. When these policies are written and used in training, salespeople are more likely to uphold the firm's ethical standards. The following is a brief description of the most common types of unethical behavior among salespeople.

- *Sharing confidential information.* Salespeople and customers build close relationships over time that lead to the disclosure of confidential information based on trust. There is a potential for salespeople to share this information with a customer's competitors, either voluntarily or involuntarily. Salespeople need to be cognizant of this possible breach and realize that it may backfire in the eyes of the competitor. This behavior speaks to the character of the salesperson.
- *Reciprocity.* This refers to the mutual exchange of benefits between buyers and sellers. If a firm has a policy of reciprocity, it can be viewed as an exclusive tying arrangement, which is illegal. For example, a hotel may purchase supplies only from firms that agree to use its services for corporate travel.
- *Bribery.* Bribes in the form of monetary payoffs or kickbacks are unethical, if not illegal. Many U.S. firms find themselves at a disadvantage in international markets because their corporate policies and U.S. laws forbid them from offering bribes in countries where it is accepted as a normal business practice. Some meeting planners have coaxed hotels into giving them kickbacks from the room revenues for their meetings.

- *Gift giving and entertainment.* There is a fine line between gift giving, entertainment, and bribery. If the gift is being used to obtain the customer's business, then it amounts to a bribe. Gifts should only be given after contracts are signed as a symbol of the firm's gratitude. Meeting planners are inundated with gifts in the form of hotel coupons and frequent guest points, or even frequent flier miles. Wining and dining clients is another popular sales technique. "Fam," or familiarization, trips provide meeting planners with free hotel rooms, airline travel, and entrance to tourist attractions or special events. In response, some firms have policies regarding the acceptance of gifts and entertainment by meeting planners and travel agents.

- *Making misleading sales claims.* In their pursuit of sales and quotas, salespeople may decide to provide customers or prospects with misleading information. It is not uncommon in hotel sales for a sales manager to promise meeting planners things that the food and beverage department cannot deliver. This results in some difficult negotiations at the time of the meeting. Another practice that is found in hotel sales departments is *blind cutting*. This refers to the practice of promising a certain quantity of rooms in a contract, but then setting the actual room block at a lower amount to account for slippage or artificially high estimates from meeting planners.

- *Business defamation.* Salespeople sometimes make disparaging comments about their competitors when dealing with customers. Not only does this reflect poorly on the salesperson and the hotel, but in some instances, it is actually illegal (e.g., slander or libel). It is very tempting to take a cheap shot at a competitor when making comparisons between properties or firms. However, salespeople should constrain themselves to answering specific questions with factual information.

The extent to which a firm is successful in deterring unethical behavior on the part of its employees will depend on how it treats employees who violate its policies and the level of support for the policies throughout the organization.

▲ MARKETING ACTION NOW!

If you really think about it, everybody engages in selling in some form or another. Children sell and negotiate with their parents, adults raise money for charities, employees sell and negotiate with their superiors for desirable assignments, promotions, and raises, and people sell themselves to others in relationships. Therefore, a general knowledge of personal selling is advantageous for everyone.

Most of the students in this class have, or will, go through the interview process for employment. In essence, you are selling yourself to an organization that is also selling itself to you. Go through the four stages of the personal selling process and explain how each one pertains to stages in the job interviewing process. Be specific and provide detailed examples of what would occur at each stage. For instance, what objections would you anticipate, and how would you handle them? Which closing techniques would work, and which would not? Begin with the first stage, prospecting and qualifying, and proceed through the entire process.

▲ SUMMARY OF CHAPTER OBJECTIVES

This chapter focuses on the vital link in hotel sales and marketing, the sales and solicitation of group business. The initial section of the chapter examines the selling function and the attributes that make a sales person successful. These attributes include courtesy, knowledge of the products and services, professional appearance, a strong desire for and willingness to work, and finally a strong personality.

The role of the meeting planner is reviewed. Each meeting planner is different, and the needs and objectives of each group will be different, presenting a real challenge for the sales manager. However, common needs of meeting planners include costs, location, image and status, professional service, adaptability and flexibility, and professional operations and management. In working with a meeting planner, the sales manager should strive to build a solid working relationship based on trust and the hotel's ability to meet the meeting planner's needs and objectives. The sales manager should become a problem solver.

Selling effectively to group markets is discussed at length, especially as it relates to the needs and objectives of the association and corporate market segments. Characteristics of each of these markets are discussed and generalizations made. The FAB selling technique is introduced as a means of tying product features to advantages and benefits that can be marketed to prospective customers.

The personal selling process is presented as including four important steps: prospecting and qualifying, planning and delivering the sales presentation, handling objections, and closing the sale. Each step is explained and techniques are provided for achieving the efficiency and effectiveness necessary to succeed. The importance of listening is discussed, and several options are presented for handling objections and closing the sale. In addition, some additional personal selling tools are presented. Key account management helps salespeople expend their effort where the potential payback is greatest, and some tips are provided for improving negotiating skills.

Finally, the chapter discusses the ethical issues surrounding the personal selling process. There are many areas for potential abuse, including the sharing of confidential information, reciprocity, bribery, gift giving and entertainment, and business defamation. It is important for hotels and travel firms to establish a written code of ethical behavior that is conveyed to its employees during orientation and job training. There must be penalties for violating the firm's ethical standards, and the entire firm should support them.

▲ KEY TERMS AND CONCEPTS

Active listening	Order getter
AIDA model	Order taker
Association market segment	Personal selling process
Convention	Property analysis checklist
Corporate market segment	Prospecting and qualifying
FAB selling technique	Sales blitz
Incentive trip	SMERF group
Key account management	Standard operating procedures
Meeting plannners	Telemarketing
Negotiating skills	

▲ QUESTIONS FOR REVIEW AND DISCUSSION

1. Cite and discuss the attributes of a successful sales manager. Which one do you consider to be the most important? Why?

2. What do you see as the pros and cons to a career in sales?

3. What is the role of the meeting planner? How does this individual interact with the hotel sales and marketing staff?

4. Cite and discuss the nature of the association and corporate market segments, including decision making, lead-time, types of meetings, and site selection criteria.

5. What are the steps in the personal selling process? Provide a brief description of the activities at each step.

6. Discuss some of the procedures that can be used to qualify a prospect.

7. When a sales manager encounters objections, how might these be handled?

8. What does it mean to close a sale? What methods can be used to accomplish this?

9. What is account management? How can it be done?

10. What are some common negotiating skills?

11. List and discuss the ethical issues in personal selling.

▲ NOTES

[1]Howard Feiertag, "Qualified customers yield better results on sales calls," *Hotel & Motel Management* (May 3, 1999) p. 42.

[2]Charles M. Futrell, *Fundamentals of Selling: Customers for Life* (Chicago, IL: The Mc-Graw-Hill Companies, Inc., 1996).

[3]Nancy L. Scanlon, *Marketing By Menu* (New York: Van Nostrand Reinhold, 1985) pp. 72–75.

[4]Sarah J. F. Bailey, editor, "The Big Picture," *Meetings and Conventions* (October 1998) pp. 2–35.

[5]Gerald L. Manning and Barry L. Reece, *Selling Today*, 6th edition (Upper Saddle River, NJ: Prentice Hall, Inc., 1995) pp. 256–258.

[6]Charles M. Futrell, *Fundamentals of Selling: Customers for Life* (Chicago, IL: The Mc-Graw-Hill Companies, Inc., 1996) p. 243.

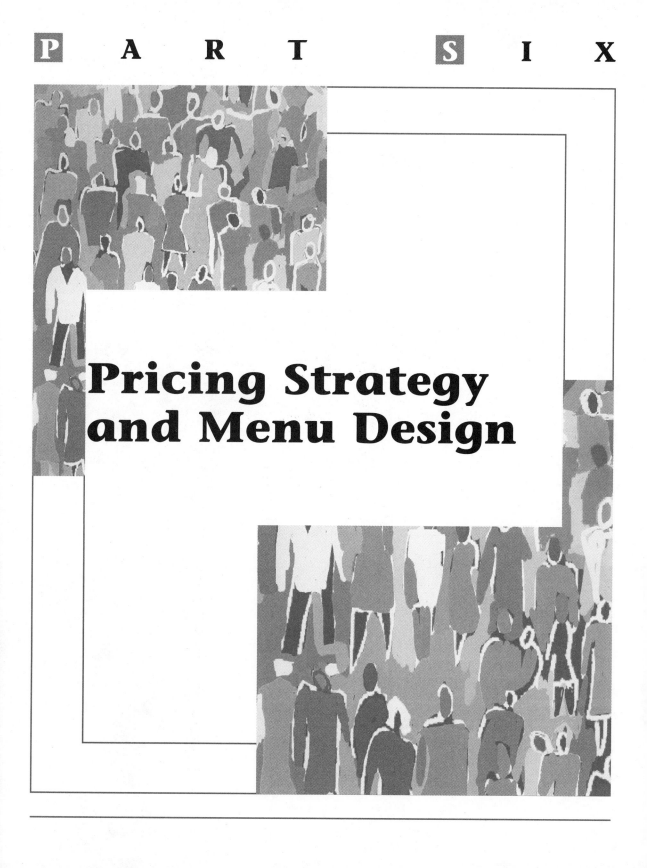

Pricing Strategy and Menu Design

14

Pricing Strategy

❖ Chapter Objectives

By the end of this chapter, you should understand:

1. The meaning of price and its use in strategic marketing
2. The impact of pricing objectives, consumer price sensitivity, and the external environment on pricing decisions
3. The broad pricing strategies that can be used by a firm based on the relationship between price and economic value
4. The use of price in segmenting consumer markets
5. The relationship between costs, price, and demand and the basic pricing techniques
6. The legal and ethical issues surrounding pricing decisions

❖ Chapter Outline

  I. Chapter Opening Profile
  II. Introduction

❖ Chapter Opening Profile

THE CONSOLIDATION OF HOTEL FIRMS HAS resulted in an increase in price competition with a focus on revenue management and cost controls. "You can still make money owning and operating a hotel, even though you may not be making it by growing," said Robert Mandelbaum, director of research for PKF Consulting.[1] Rate management is an important component in maintaining profits during the slowdown and into the year 2000 and beyond, according to Mendelbaum. In the past, hoteliers tended to start discounting rates at the first sign of a drop in occupancies, but since 1996, rate growth in most cities has kept up at two or three times the pace of inflation even when occupancies dropped. "You can even lose a couple of points in occupancy as long as you're able to maintain good pricing, which in the hotel industry means room rates," Mandelbaum said. "If you can maintain good rate growth, you'll still see profit growth."

Most of the demand for hotel rooms is still during peak periods (e.g., Tuesday through Thursday for business travelers, and summer for leisure travelers). One of the main objectives of rate management is to charge premium rates for those periods. If you are able to maximize revenue for the peak days of the week and peak periods, loss of occupancies on weekends will not have as much of an impact on overall average daily rates. In addition to yield management, PKF recommends increased cost controls. Costs are the other factor in the profit equation, and decreases in costs at the same or higher prices will result in increased profits. Hotels must choose appropriate strategy based on the price sensitivity of their consumers.

▲ INTRODUCTION

Price is a component of the marketing mix and the vehicle used in free enterprise to allocate limited resources. The other three components of the marketing mix—promotion, product, and distribution—create value and appear on the firm's income statement as expenses. Conversely, price is the firm's tool for capturing value and it affects the revenue section of the income statement. As such, price can be defined as the value given to a product or service by consumers.

Various names are associated with price such as *fee*, *tuition*, and *premium*. The important thing to remember is the concept of exchange. In other words, the buyer and the seller have to be mutually satisfied for an exchange to take place, and this exchange does not have to include a monetary unit. The early system of exchange was referred to as **bartering**, where individuals or organizations exchanged goods and services with one another. Even nonprofit organizations are in the business of selling a sense of goodwill, or charity, in exchange for donors' contributions.

Pricing strategy integrates marketing and finance in an attempt to create an atmosphere of mutual satisfaction. The product or service attributes are combined with price so as to provide enough value to satisfy customers, while enabling the firm to cover costs and make an adequate profit. The rest of this chapter is devoted to the process of strategic pricing, including the factors that will influence pricing decisions.

▲ FACTORS THAT AFFECT PRICING DECISIONS

The pricing decision is a critical component of the marketing mix and the positioning of a product or service. Pricing is a continual process that requires a firm grasp of the market and its environments. The dynamic nature of the market and its environments creates a formidable challenge for even the most experienced managers. Therefore, it is best to take a systematic approach to pricing, including establishing of pricing objectives that are consistent with the overall objectives of the firm, assessing consumer price sensitivity, and monitoring the external environment.

Pricing Objectives

Many possible pricing objectives can be grouped into four major categories based on goals related to financial performance, volume, competition, and image. These objectives are consistent with the organizational objectives discussed in Chapter 5 and must be considered when setting prices. The following is a brief summary of the categories.

Financial performance objectives focus on areas such as the firm's level of profitability, rates of return on sales and equity, and cash flow. Most large companies continually monitor these performance measures and find it easy to use these measures as benchmarks, or objectives. It is relatively easy to see the role of price in these measures of firm performance.

Volume objectives focus on sales and market share. These measures can be based either on the number of units sold or the dollar amount of units sold. The sales measure looks at the firm individually, while the market share measure views the firm relative to the competition. Volume objectives are particularly common in the early stages of the product life cycle when firms are willing to forego profits in exchange for building long-term sales and market share. In addition, price competition is strong in the maturity stage in an attempt to hold market share.

Competition objectives focus on the nature of the competitive environment. A firm may want to maintain competitive parity with the market leader, widen the gap between itself and market followers, or simply survive. There is a good deal of head-to-head competition in the hospitality and travel industry. For example, airline companies match each other's price changes so closely that the industry is often under investigation for price collusion.

Image objectives focus on the firm's overall positioning strategy. A firm's position in the market is a direct result of its price–quality relationship as perceived by consumers. The hotel market can be segmented by price into economy, midmarket, and premium categories. Also, airline companies offer bereavement fares for emergency travel, and hotels offer discounts for guests with family members in the hospital. These discounts enhance the image of the firm.

Consumer Price Sensitivity

An important factor in setting price is the price sensitivity of consumers, or how they react to changes in price. There are many situational factors that will affect a consumer's price sensitivity, and these factors can actually vary from one purchase decision to another. For example, a married couple may be less price sensitive when choosing a restaurant for a special occasion than they would be if they were having a normal meal after work. The following is a summary of the most common effects on consumer price sensitivity.[2]

Price–Quality Effect.   In many situations, consumers use price as an indicator of a product's quality, especially when they don't have much experience with the product category. In this case, consumers will be less sensitive to a product's price to the extent that they believe the higher prices signify higher quality. For example, overseas travelers often use price as a gauge of quality because they lack familiarity with the travel products in foreign countries. This would pertain to all components of the travel product such as hotels, restaurants, rental cars, and tourist attractions. This lack of information, along with the perceived risk of making a bad choice and the belief that there are quality differences between brands are the main reasons that consumers would use price as a signal of quality.

Unique Value Effect.   Consumers will be less price sensitive when a product is unique and doesn't have close substitutes. If a firm is successful in differentiating its product from those of its competitors, it will be able to charge a higher price. Consumers must be aware of the differentiation and convinced of its value in order to pay the higher price. In essence, the firm's strategy is to reduce the effect of substitutes, thereby eliminating the consumer's reference value for the product. This strategy is used by resorts and health spas in marketing themselves as one-of-a-kind properties. Similarly, many fine dining restaurants use this approach and differentiate themselves on attributes such as the chef, the atmosphere, and/or the menu. Airline and rental car companies would have a more difficult time using this strategy because of the homogeneity of the products.

Perceived Substitutes Effect.   Consumers will be more price sensitive the higher a product's price relative to the prices of perceived substitutes for the product. Consumers must be aware of the other products and actually perceive them as substitutes. The prices for the substitutes help consumers form a reference price, or the reasonable price range, for the product. There are many perceived substitutes for products such as fast food, airline travel, rental cars, and hotel rooms. When there are a number of substitutes that consumers are aware of, there tends to be a downward pressure on price, resulting in a relatively narrow acceptable range for prices. For example, there are no significant price differences between products in fast-food restaurants or airline tickets for a popular route.

Difficult Comparison Effect. This effect is closely related to the perceived substitutes effect. Consumers may be aware of substitutes for a product, but they will tend to be less price sensitive the more difficult it is to compare brands. Therefore, many firms try to differentiate themselves from the competition on certain attributes that are difficult to compare. Bars may serve drinks in different quantities, or resorts may package products in an attempt to make direct comparisons more difficult. However, rather than spend the time and effort to make comparisons, many consumers are content to simply choose a brand that will be satisfactory. Franchises benefit from this phenomenon because they focus on providing consistent products and services under a recognizable brand name. Even though they haven't made direct comparisons or familiarized themselves with all of the alternatives, consumers will feel safe in choosing one of these well-known brands.

Shared-cost Effect. Consumers will be less sensitive to price if another organization or individual is sharing in the cost of a product. The smaller the portion of the price paid by the consumer, the less sensitive to price the individual will be. This sharing could be in the form of a tax deduction, a business reimbursement, or some type of sales promotion (e.g., coupon or rebate). When business travelers stay in hotels, eat at restaurants, or rent cars, they tend to be less sensitive to price because their firms normally pay for most of their travel expenses. Hospitality and travel firms that target business travelers often charge higher relative prices for their products. However, it is interesting that business travelers usually pay lower prices within a hotel than individual, or transient, travelers due to the overall volume of the business segment.

Expenditure Effect. Consumers will tend to be more price sensitive the larger the amount of the total expenditure. This amount can either be measured in absolute terms or as a percentage of income. For example, a consumer booking a cruise at a price of $5,000 will be more sensitive to price than if she were eating a meal in a restaurant. The cost of the cruise is a relatively a large travel expenditure, whereas the cost of a meal pales in comparison. However, a consumer with an income of $500,000 a year would normally not be as price sensitive regarding the cruise as one with an income of $50,000 a year. Also, consumers with higher incomes place a greater value on their time and may decide to accept higher prices without evaluating alternative products.

End-benefit Effect. A product may only represent one component of the purchases necessary to attain a desired benefit. The end-benefit effect is composed of two parts: derived demand and the share of total cost. Derived demand refers to the relationship between the desired end-benefit and the consumer's price sensitivity for something that contributes to that end-benefit. This is most popular in industrial markets where firms purchase products to resell to other consumers. The more price sensitive the firm's consumers are, the more price sensitive the firm will be in purchasing components of the end-benefit. For example, tour operators determine the type of hotel or rental car included in a package based on the price sensitivity of the target segment.

In the retail market, consumers tend to be more price sensitive the larger the portion of the total cost represented by the price of the component. Consumers would be less sensitive to beverage or dessert prices at an upscale restaurant where dinner for two can cost $100 or more. Similarly, a consumer may not be as price sensitive to hotel parking rates when they are spending $200 a night in a downtown hotel. The use of packages, or bundles, by resorts and tourist attractions attempt to extract as much consumer surplus as possible by "backing in" to the consumer's value for the end-benefit.

Environmental Factors

As discussed in depth in Chapter 1, management must keep abreast of the developments in the external environment. These developments can affect pricing decisions because they affect a firm's costs, the demand for its products, and the competition. However, even though firms can't control the external environment, they should monitor it on a regular basis. The components of the external environment include the economic environment, the social environment, the political environment, the technological environment, and the competitive environment.

Economic Environment. There are constant changes in the state of the economy as measured by indicators such as business growth, inflation, consumer spending, unemployment rates, and interest rates. Firms' pricing strategies should reflect changes in the economy if they are to compete and earn an acceptable profit. Firms that compete in international markets must consider the state of the economy in the foreign markets as well as the domestic market. Foreign exchange rates can affect a firm's income statement drastically and influence the future of the firm. Prices will have to be changed in accordance with changes in income and consumer spending, as well as with variations in a firm's costs resulting from changes in the economy.

Social Environment. Consumers' tastes often change over time, and firms that do not adapt go out of business. Changes in cultures and subcultures throughout the world are affecting many societies. Different cultures have different spending patterns and saving practices. For example, many Asians tend to save more of their incomes than other nationalities, but they also tend to purchase name brands that are associated with high quality. Therefore, the Asian market is less price sensitive than some of its counterparts. As cultures mesh, they influence each other's eating habits. For example, consumers in the United States are eating more sushi and drinking more tea than in the past.

Political Environment. All levels of government have a tremendous impact on the operation of hospitality firms throughout the country. Changes in minimum wage laws affect the costs of restaurants, while changes in tax laws related to business expenses affect the demand in restaurants. Both of these areas need to be considered in setting menu prices. Similarly, hotels must consider the impact of hotel taxes on consumers when setting their prices. For example, hotels in New York City were very concerned about the impact on group and convention business when local hotel taxes were raised. At one point, the total taxes on guest rooms added up to more than 21 percent. This however, has been lowered to make New York City a more attractive destination for group business. In addition, governments impose many fees on businesses, and firms operating in international markets must contend with additional fees and tariffs.

Technological Environment. Another area of concern for managers is keeping up with advances in technology. Many of the new technologies in the hospitality and travel industry are intended to improve the efficiency of firms, thereby reducing costs. For example, when food servers use hand-held terminals to place orders, they no longer have to enter the kitchen or move to a stationary terminal in another location. These new point-of-sale systems also enable firms to track costs and demand for particular food items. This information is invaluable in setting prices. Similarly, hotels and airlines use sophisticated systems to capture costs and demand that help them maximize revenues through price setting.

Competitive Environment. Finally, it is critical to know what is happening in the competitive environment. New firms entering the market will change overall supply, thereby changing the market structure and putting downward pressure on prices. Competitors also engage in promotional campaigns offering price discounts or free merchandise that will affect consumers' perceptions of value. For example, the airline industry is notorious for its short-term price wars in a battle for market share.

▲ BROAD PRICING STRATEGIES

Once a firm's pricing objectives are set, it is necessary to identify the role that price will serve in the product's overall marketing strategy. Price can be set high to restrict the firm's market to a limited segment of buyers (e.g., luxury hotels and fine dining restaurants), set low to attract buyers (e.g., economy hotels and fast-food restaurants), or kept neutral to emphasize other aspects of marketing (e.g., mid-scale hotels and theme restaurants). These approaches represent three broad strategies that a firm can adopt: skim pricing, penetration pricing, and neutral pricing.[3] Table 14.1 illustrates these strategies based on the relationship between price and economic value for the "middle market" of consumers. **Economic value** can be defined as the sum of a product's **reference value**, or the cost of the competing product that the consumer perceives as the closest substitute, and a product's **differentiation value**, or the value to the consumer (both positive and negative) of any differences between a firm's offering and the reference product.

Skim Pricing

This strategy involves setting high prices in relation to the product or service's economic value to most potential consumers. This strategy is designed to capture high profit margins from an exclusive segment of consumers that places a high value on a product's differentiating attributes. Skim pricing is a preferred strategy when selling to the exclusive, price-insensitive market, and it results in higher profits than selling to the mass market at a lower price. For example, luxury hotels and resorts market hotel rooms with many amenities such as valet parking, laundry service, and golf. Most consumers are not willing to pay the higher prices associated with this level of service, but there is a smaller segment of consumers that places a high value on the additional amenities and will pay the higher prices.

Many service firms have limited capacity, and it may be necessary to maximize profits by managing supply and demand by charging higher prices. Skim pricing also tends to be used by firms whose variable costs represent a large portion of total costs and the product's price. There is little incentive to decrease cost per unit by increasing volume under this cost structure. From a competitive standpoint, skim pricing works best

economic value sum of a product's reference value and its differentiation value

reference value cost of the competing product that is perceived as the closest substitute

differentiation value value to the consumer of any differences between a firm's offering and the reference product

Table 14.1	**Strategies Based on Price and Economic Value**

	Relative Price	
Economic Value	Low	High
Low	Neutral	Skim Pricing
High	Penetration Pricing	Neutral

when a firm's product is unique, or superior to competitive products in perceived quality.

Penetration Pricing

This strategy involves setting low prices in relation to the firm's economic value to most potential consumers. This strategy works best on price-sensitive consumers who are willing to change product or service providers to obtain a better price. Firms using this strategy choose to have lower profit margins in an attempt to gain high sales volumes and market shares. Penetration pricing is common among economy hotels that market to consumers who view the product as merely a place to sleep, and have no need for additional amenities.

Most of the costs of providing the rooms in economy hotels are fixed. Normally, an economy hotel won't have a restaurant with room service, or a concierge to help guests with travel plans. Similarly, fast-food restaurants don't have chefs and food costs are relatively low. In both cases, the furniture and décor is fairly basic. The higher volume generated by the lower prices is expected to result in economies of scale and a lower cost per unit of providing the service. From a competitive standpoint, penetration pricing works best when a firm has a significant cost advantage over its competitors or when the firm is small and not considered a threat by its competitors. Charter airlines and small commuter airlines are examples of firms that can adopt a penetration pricing strategy and not are considered a threat by larger airline companies.

Neutral Pricing

This strategy involves setting price at a moderate level in relation to the economic value to most potential consumers. In other words, the firm makes a strategic decision to use attributes other than price to gain a competitive advantage. A neutral strategy can be by default, when a firm cannot use skim pricing or penetration pricing because its cost structure or the market conditions. However, this strategy has become more popular with the growth in the value segment of consumers. In the hotel industry, many consumers do not want to pay high prices, but they do want some amenities like restaurants and pools. Finally, a high price can actually be a neutral price when product value justifies the price to most potential consumers.

▲ PRICING TECHNIQUES AND PROCEDURES

When management establishes prices, three approaches can be used either individually or in combination with one another: cost-oriented pricing, demand-oriented pricing, and competitive pricing.

Cost-Oriented Pricing

As the name implies, cost-oriented pricing uses a firm's cost to provide a product or service as a basis for pricing. In general, firms want to set a price high enough to cover costs and make a profit. Two types of costs can be considered: fixed costs and variable costs. Fixed costs are incurred by a company to be in business, and they do not vary with changes in sales volume. For example, restaurants must invest in a building, kitchen equipment, and tables before they even begin to serve customers. Variable costs are the costs associated with doing business, and they vary with changes in sales volume. For example, restaurants incur costs for food, labor, and cleaning that are directly related to the level of sales.

Break-even analysis can be used to examine the relationships between costs, sales, and profits. The break-even point (BEP) is the point where total revenue and total cost are equal. In other words, the BEP in units would be the number of units that must be sold at a given contribution margin (price-variable cost) to cover the firm's total fixed costs:

$$\mathrm{BEP}_{\text{units}} = \frac{\text{Total fixed costs}}{(\text{Selling price} - \text{Variable cost})}$$

The break-even point in dollars can be calculated by multiplying the break-even point in units by the selling price per unit. Break-even analysis is a seemingly easy method for analyzing potential pricing strategies, but one must be careful to use only costs that are relevant to the decision so that the results are accurate.

Figure 14.1 illustrates the relationships between costs, sales, and profits. As mentioned before, fixed costs are incurred regardless of sales. Therefore, they remain constant with changes in sales volume and are represented by a horizontal line. The total cost line intersects the fixed cost line where it begins on the vertical axis and increases with volume to account for variable costs. The total revenue line begins at the origin and increases with volume. The break-even point in units is the point where the total revenue line intersects the total cost line. When firms operate at volumes less than the break-even point, losses are incurred because total revenue is not enough to cover the total cost of producing and marketing the product. When volume exceeds the break-even point, firms will make a profit because total revenue exceeds total cost.

For example, suppose a family purchases a large home and renovates it to be used as a bed and breakfast. The total fixed costs would be the $300,000 purchase price plus the $100,000 spent on renovations, or a total of $400,000. The owners estimate the variable cost to clean the room, restock supplies, and feed the guests to be approximately $25 per day. If the owners were to charge guests $75 per night to stay at the bed and breakfast, the break-even point in units would be 8,000 room nights

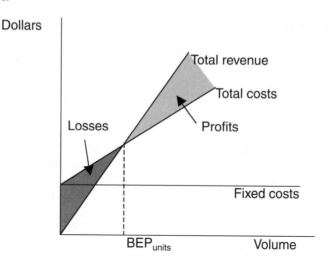

FIGURE 14.1   Break-even Analysis

(400,000/(75 – 25)). If there were a total of 20 rooms, and they obtained an average occupancy of 50 percent throughout the year, it would take 800 nights (a little over two years) to recoup their original investment. However, it is more likely that the purchase was financed over time, and the owners receive tax credits on the interest, expenses, and depreciation. Therefore, assuming the owners did not take salaries or hire additional workers, it is more likely that the yearly fixed costs are in the neighborhood of $30,000. The new break-even point would be 600 room nights (30,000/(75 – 25)), which would represent 60 days at an average occupancy rate of 50 percent.

This example illustrates the benefit of using break-even analysis for setting the prices for new products. However, break-even analysis does not account for the price sensitivity of consumers or the competition. In addition, it is very important that the costs used in the analysis are accurate. Any changes in the contribution margin or fixed costs can have a significant impact on the break-even point. For instance, if the owners overestimated the price, and consumers are only willing to pay $50 a night, then the break-even point would change to 1,200 nights, or double the original estimate. Finally, the break-even formula can be easily adjusted to account for a desired amount of profit. The desired amount of profit would be added to the numerator (total fixed costs) and would represent the additional number of units that would need to be sold at the current contribution margin to cover the desired amount.

Cost-plus pricing is the most widely used approach to pricing in the industry. The price for a product or service is determined by adding a desired mark-up to the cost of producing and marketing the item. The mark-up is in the form of a percentage and price is set using the following equation:

cost-plus pricing
price is determined by adding a desired mark-up to the cost of producing and marketing an item

$$\text{Price} = \text{ATC} + m(\text{ATC})$$

where: ATC = the average total cost per unit
$\quad\quad\quad m$ = the mark-up percentage / 100%

The average total cost per unit is calculated by adding the variable cost per unit to the fixed cost per unit. The fixed cost per unit is simply the total fixed costs divided by the number of units sold.

This approach is popular because it is simple and it focuses on covering costs and making a profit. However, management must have a good understanding of the firm's costs in order to price effectively. Some costs are truly fixed, but other costs may be semi-fixed. Semi-fixed costs are fixed over a certain range of sales, but vary when sales go outside that range. In addition to the problem of determining the relevant costs, the cost-plus approach ignores consumer demand and the competition. This may cause a firm to charge too much, or too little.

Target-return pricing is another form of cost-oriented pricing that sets price to yield a target rate of return on a firm's investment. This approach is more sophisticated than the cost-plus approach in that it focuses on an overall rate of return for the business rather than a desired profit per unit. The target-return price can be calculated using the following equation:

target-return pricing set price to yield a target rate of return on a firm's investment

$$\text{Price} = \text{ATC} + (\text{desired dollar return} / \text{unit sales})$$

The average total cost per unit is determined the same way as in the cost-plus approach, and it is increased by the dollar return per unit necessary to provide the target rate of return. This approach is also relatively simple, but it still ignores competitors' prices and consumer demand.

Demand-Oriented Pricing

The demand-oriented approaches to pricing use consumer perceptions of value as a basis for setting prices. The goal of this pricing approach is to set prices to capture more value, not to maximize volume. A price is charged that will allow the firm to extract the most consumer surplus from the market based on the **reservation price**, or the maximum price that a consumer is willing to pay for a product or service. This price can be difficult to determine unless management has a firm grasp of the price sensitivity of consumers. Economists measure price sensitivity using the **price elasticity of demand**, or the percentage change in quantity demanded divided by the percentage change in price. Assuming an initial price of P_1 and an initial quantity of Q_1, the price elasticity of demand (ε) for a change in price from P_1 to P_2 can be calculated by:

reservation price maximum price a consumer is willing to pay

price elasticity of demand percentage change in quantity demanded divided by the percentage change in price

$$\varepsilon_p = \frac{(Q_2 - Q_1)/Q_1}{(P_2 - P_1)/P_1}$$

law of demand
inverse relationship between price and quantity demanded

prestige pricing setting high prices for products that have high quality images

odd/even pricing setting prices just below even dollar amounts to give the impression that it is less expensive

price lining having a limited number of products available at different price levels based on quality

The price elasticity of demand is usually negative because price increases tend to result in decreases in quantity demanded. This inverse relationship between price and quantity demanded, referred to as the **law of demand**, is representative of most products and services. However, the demand for products and services can demonstrate varying degrees of elasticity (see Figure 14.2). The demand for products is said to be *elastic* if a percentage change in price results in a greater percentage change in quantity demanded. Conversely, the demand for products is said to be *inelastic* if a percentage change in price results in a smaller percentage change in quantity demanded. *Unitary elasticity* occurs when a percentage change in price results in an equal percentage change in quantity demanded.

In a market with elastic demand, consumers are price sensitive, and any changes in price will cause total revenue to change in the opposite direction. Therefore, firms will tend to focus on ways to decrease price in an attempt to increase the quantity demanded and total revenue. In a market with inelastic demand, consumers are not sensitive to price changes, and total revenue will change in the same direction. In this situation, firms will tend to focus on raising prices and total revenues, even with a decrease in quantity demanded. In markets with unitary demand, price changes have no effect on total revenue and firms should base pricing decisions on other factors such as cost.

Some popular demand-oriented pricing approaches are based on consumer perceptions of value. **Prestige pricing** is used by firms that have products with strong price–quality relationships in markets with inelastic demand. These firms set high prices and try to build value through other quality-related attributes such as service and atmosphere. This approach is common among five-star hotels and fine-dining restaurants. **Odd/even pricing** involves setting prices just below even dollar amounts to give the perception that the product is less expensive. For example, car rental agencies set prices like $49.95 rather than $50, and hotels use prices like $99 instead of $100. Also, many menu items are priced with odd endings such as $3.99 or $10.95. Theory has it that people read and process prices from left to right, rounding to the lower number. **Price lining** refers to the practice of having a limited number of products available at different price

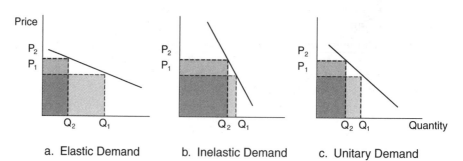

FIGURE 14.2 Price Elasticity of Demand

levels based on quality. Demand at each price point is assumed to be elastic, whereas demand between price points is assumed to be inelastic. The products at each price level are targeting a different market segment. For example, rental car companies have economy, mid-size, full-size, and luxury categories.

Competitive Pricing

As the name implies, competitive pricing places the emphasis on price in relation to direct competition. Some firms allow others to establish prices and then position themselves accordingly, either at, below, or above the competition. This method assures that the price charged for products and services will be within the same range as prices for competitive products in the immediate geographic area. This method, however, has several drawbacks. First, consider the case of two similar firms. One is new and the other has been operating for several years. The new establishment is likely to have high fixed costs such as a mortgage with a high interest rate that must be paid each month. On the other hand, the established firm might have a much lower mortgage payment each month and fewer costs. Because of these differences, the established firm would have lower fixed operating expenses and could charge lower prices, even if all other expenses were equal. Second, other expenses might also vary among different firms. Labor costs might be higher or lower depending on the skill level of the personnel, their length of service in the operation, and numerous other factors that may come into play. For this reason, it is extremely risky for managers to rely on the prices of a direct competitor when setting their own prices. Each operation is unique and has its own unique cost and profit structure. Although management does need to monitor the competition, prices should never be based solely on prices charged by a competitor.

▲ SEGMENTED PRICING

The importance of price varies among consumers, and firms often use this variation as a means for segmenting markets. Then, a firm can choose to target one or more of these markets with specific marketing strategies tailored to each market. The appropriate strategy will depend on the firm's costs, consumers' price sensitivities, and the competition. Several tactics can be used to segment markets on the basis of price.[4]

Segmenting by Buyer Identification

One method that can be used to segment by price is to base it on some form of buyer identification. That is, in order to obtain a discounted price, a buyer must belong to a certain group that shares similar characteristics.

Consumers must identify themselves as belonging to a certain group in order to get a discounted price. For example, hotels and motels have many discounted rates available for consumers belonging to groups like the American Automobile Association (AAA) or the American Association of Retired Persons (AARP). Another variation is for consumers to save coupons that can be presented at a later date for a discount. Many restaurants put coupons in newspapers or direct-mail pieces that must be saved and brought to the establishment to get a discount within a certain time period. However, only a particular type of price-sensitive consumer will take the time and effort to save, file, and redeem coupons for price discounts.

Segmenting by Purchase Location

It is possible to segment consumers based on where they purchase a product or service. Some restaurant chains will vary their prices in different geographic locations to account for differences in purchasing power and standard of living. For example, fast-food restaurants often charge more for menu items in large cities, food courts, and major highway locations, than in suburban and rural locations. Also, hotel, restaurant, and car rental chains charge different prices in international markets based on a country's standard of living. Finally, a general practice by theme parks is to charge more for tickets purchased at the gate, and less for tickets purchased at nearby locations (e.g., hotels and supermarkets) or through various organizations (e.g., government agencies and AAA).

Segmenting by Time of Purchase

Service firms tend to notice certain purchasing patterns based on the time of day, week, month, or year. Unfortunately, it is not always possible to meet the demand during these peak periods. One way to smooth the demand is to offer discounted prices at off-peak times. Restaurants offer "early-bird" specials for patrons who are willing to eat earlier in the evening, airlines offer "supersaver" rates for consumers who are willing to travel at nonpeak times, and hotels offer lower rates for weekends and slower seasons throughout the year. This results in a shift in demand from peak times to off-peak times by the most price-sensitive consumers. **Yield management** programs are used by airlines and hotels to set prices that will maximize revenue, based on the costs of providing services and the price sensitivities of the consumers.

yield management programs used to maximize revenue based on the costs of providing services and the price sensitivities of consumers

Segmenting by Purchase Volume

One of the most common forms of price segmentation is to vary price based on the quantity purchased, offering discounts for larger orders. The majority of firms, both small and large, will negotiate price discounts for larger volume orders. Hospitality and travel firms will normally start discounting prices for groups of ten or more people. In particular, hotel sales-people are responsible for filling the hotel with groups by offering discounts that tend to increase with the size of the group. Hotels and restaurants use the same tactics to sell catering functions such as weddings and banquets.

Segmenting by Product Design

Another form of price segmentation is based on the actual product or service. It may be possible to segment consumers by offering simple variations of a firm's product or service that appeal to the different segments. For example, airlines found that they could charge substantially more for first-class seating by widening the seats slightly and providing a little more service. Similarly, hotels offer suites and concierge floors that are slightly larger and/or provide some additional services. None of these variations by airlines or hotels have a significant impact on the cost of providing the service, but the firms are able to charge significantly higher prices to a small segment of the market that values the additional amenities and services.

Segmenting by Product Bundling

The last form of price segmentation involves packaging products and services into price bundles. Offering several products at a packaged price enables consumers to get a better deal than if they were to purchase the bundle components separately. Fast-food restaurants offer bundled meals that include a sandwich, an order of french fries, and a soft drink. They also allow consumers to increase the size of the components for a small amount more. An alternative form of product bundling is to offer premiums, or free merchandise, with the purchase. Fast-food restaurants put free game pieces and pull-tabs on their packaging, and they give children free toys with a child's meal.

These are some of the basic tactics that can be used to segment markets on the basis of price. The various tactics can be used alone or in combination with one another to achieve a firm's desired goals. Today's consumers can obtain information about competitive products and services very easily, resulting in a large, value-conscious market. Firms will need to find ways to segment the price-sensitive consumers from the quality-oriented consumers so they can extract the most consumer surplus and revenue from the marketplace.

▲ YIELD MANAGEMENT

Yield management refers to a technique used to maximize the revenue, or yield, obtained from a service operation, given limited capacity and uneven demand. This technique was first used by airline companies, and then adopted by lodging and cruise firms. Within the hospitality and tourism industry, yield management has come into more widespread use with the expansion of computerized property management systems. In its most basic form, yield management uses a firm's historical data to predict the demand for future reservations, with the goal of setting prices that will maximize the firm's revenue and profit.

Yield management is widely used within the hospitality and travel industry for several reasons:

- *Perishable inventory.* As discussed in Chapter 2, hospitality and travel services are highly perishable. If a hotel room is not occupied one evening or an airline flies with empty seats, the potential revenue for those services cannot be captured at a later date. In other words, there are no inventories for services.

- *Fluctuating demand.* Most hospitality and travel firms experience demand that rises and falls within a day, week, month, or year. During high demand periods, services are sold at or near full price. During the low demand, or nonpeak periods, capacity is left unused.

- *Ability to segment customers.* Firms must be able to segment customers based on price, as discussed earlier in this chapter, and offer a discounted price to a selective group of customers.

- *Low variable costs.* Hospitality and travel firms often have a large ratio of fixed to variable costs, which would favor a high-volume strategy. The marginal cost of serving an additional customer is minimal as long as there is excess capacity.

Selective Discounting

One of the cornerstones of yield management is the ability to offer discounts to only a selective group of customers. Rather than offer one price for a given time period, either peak or nonpeak, firms are able to discriminate between consumers. This minimizes the effect of lost revenue resulting from consumers who are willing to pay full price being able to pay the discounted price. To accomplish this, service firms normally place restrictions on the discounted price so that consumers must sacrifice something in return for the discount. For example, airline companies require passengers to book in advance (up to 21 days), stay over Saturday night, and accept a no-cancellation policy to obtain the discounted fare. Similarly, hotels require guests to stay over weekends, during nonpeak seasons, or for a minimum number of nights.

Historical Booking Analysis

One of the major problems facing service firms using yield management systems is the determination of the amount of capacity to make available at the discounted rate. As mentioned earlier, yield management makes use of historical data in predicting future trends. A curve can be constructed using data from the same period the previous year, and adjusting for recent trends seen in the most recent periods. The following curve illustrates a typical pattern for a large conference hotel:

% of Rooms Sold

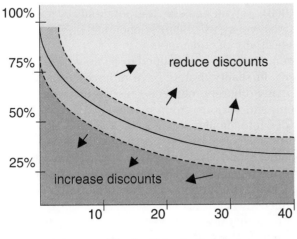

Weeks Prior to Date

The solid line represents the historical pattern for room sales prior to the date in question. In general, the hotel would determine a comfort zone or construct a confidence interval around the actual occupancy rate. If prior sales are within this interval, then the hotel continues to use its current discounting policy. If the occupancy rate exceeds the upper level, then the hotel will temporarily reduce the number of discounted rooms and rates. If the occupancy rate falls below the lower level, then the hotel will offer more discounted rooms and rates until the occupancy rate is brought back within the predicted interval.

Yield Management Equation

As stated earlier, the goal of yield management is to maximize the revenue, or yield, from a service operation. The following equation is a simplified version of the calculation used in actual programs.

$$\text{Maximize} \left[\frac{\text{Actual revenue}}{\text{Potential revenue}} \right]$$

The potential revenue for a hotel would be the number of total rooms available for sale multiplied by the rack rate for those rooms. For instance, if a hotel had 200 rooms that all had a rack rate of $100, the potential room revenue for that hotel would be $20,000 per night. However, if the hotel had an occupancy rate of 70 percent and an average room rate of $80, then the actual revenue would be $11,200 [(.7×200)×80]. The yield in this case would be .56 (11,200/20,000). The goal is to maximize this figure or to get it as close to 1.0 as possible. What if this hotel offered more discounts and had an occupancy rate of 80 percent and an average room rate of $75? The actual revenue would have been $12,000 [(.8×200)×75], or a yield of .60 (12,000/20,000). As you can see, the potential revenue remains the same, but the actual revenue will change depending on the level of discounts and the price sensitivity of consumers.

This example is overly simplified to demonstrate the basic use of yield management. In reality, hotels have different rooms with different rack rates, and many different market segments, including business and pleasure transient, and various group markets. Each of these major segments can be divided into smaller subsets. For instance, the group market can be segmented into association, corporate, and incentive travel. Hotels have created positions and, in some cases, departments that are responsible for revenue management. These individuals perform historical booking analysis and confer with the hotel's executive committee to determine discounting policies.

Another area that needs to be considered in determining a hotel's discounting policy is the additional revenue that is generated from guests, other than the room revenue. For example, hotels can earn additional revenue from guests in the restaurant, the bar, fitness centers, parking, laundry services, room service, corporate services like faxing and shipping, and by catering for groups. Rather than analyze each individual, hotels look at the major market segments and calculate a "multiplier" that can be used to adjust room revenue for additional revenue potential. This is important because hotels must maximize the revenue they receive from all sources. For instance, it would be a mistake to take a transient guest who paid $10 more a night than a business traveler, if the business traveler is likely to spend more than $10 a day for additional services. Similarly, turning down a group because of high demand among transient customers may result in a loss of revenue from catering services that would have been purchased by the group. However, in high peak demand seasons, such as fall in New England, hotels can charge considerably more to transient customers than groups, and it would be a mistake to book a group well in advance and forego this additional revenue.

Yield management has had a major impact on the hospitality and travel industry. Advances in computer technology have improved the ability to estimate demand and revenue. In addition, it has become easier to segment markets and employ selective discounting through vehicles like the Internet. In the future, yield management programs will become more affordable for smaller operations. In fact, yield management systems can be developed using ordinary spreadsheet software. Finally, companies are working on resource management models that will analyze the revenue contribution from all sources in the hotel, rather than focus only on guest rooms.

▲ PRICING LAW AND ETHICS

Pricing practices are normally illegal if they are found to be anticompetitive or if they take unfair advantage of consumers. However, ethical standards are not as clear as legal standards developed through case law. Many people feel that although it is legal to maximize profits through pricing, it may not always be ethical. First, we will discuss the legal issues surrounding pricing decisions, and then, we will present a typology that can be used for considering the ethical constraints on pricing.

Legal Issues in Pricing

The federal government has sought to ensure fair price competition since it passed the Sherman Act in 1890, followed by the Clayton Act in 1914. These two pieces of antitrust legislation were enacted in response to growing concerns for small businesses with the advent of large corporations competing on a national level. Most of the laws are open to interpretation and often difficult to enforce, especially in regard to services. The Robinson-Patman Act, passed in 1936, to strengthen the Clayton Act, targeted unfair pricing practices. Most laws focus on goods or commodities, for which grade and quality can be easily determined, whereas services vary greatly. Therefore, the government has devoted most of its resources on monitoring the pricing of tangible products. Pricing practices that are potentially illegal can be placed into four groups: explicit agreements, nonexplicit agreements, price discrimination, and tie-in sales.[5]

Explicit agreements are formal agreements among firms to set the same prices or to use the same formula in setting prices. This practice of price-fixing is generally regarded as illegal and will be enforced. It is illegal for competitive hotels to discuss prices, even if they are accommodating guests for the same conference. For example, a Marriott hotel and a Sheraton hotel have formed a "connection" in Springfield, Massachusetts, to compete for meetings requiring more rooms than either hotel contains. The two hotels are physically connected, and they operate as two wings of one hotel for larger conferences. Guests can charge meals and other services from either hotel to their rooms. However, each hotel must negotiate price separately with the meeting planner without any contact, or it would be illegal.

Nonexplicit agreements take the form of concerted actions by competitors that are not formal but represent some level of collusion. The courts look for a pattern of uniform business conduct, or *conscious parallelism*. It is not enough for competitive firms to exhibit parallel behavior, they must also be found guilty of making a conscious effort to engage in that behavior. Airline companies have been investigated, and prosecuted, for this behavior in the past. Even today, it is not uncommon to be quoted identical fares on competitive airlines for the same routes. As with explicit agreements, it is unlawful for firms to exchange price information if it is intended to affect prices, or if it identifies specific customers. Convention and visitors bureaus are able to provide aggregate price information on hotel rates in their regions, as long as they don't identify the rates for specific customers, including groups for meetings and conventions.

Price discrimination laws forbid firms from charging purchasers different prices for commodities of like grade and quality in an attempt to substantially lessen competition. There are two legal defenses for discriminatory prices. The *cost justification defense* allows firms to charge different prices when the costs of providing the product differ between purchasers, and the *meeting competition defense* allows firms to charge different prices to meet the lower price of a competitor. As mentioned earlier, it is difficult to use these criteria to evaluate the pricing practices of service firms. Every service experience is different and, with the consumer being part of the production process, firms could argue that the cost of providing the service differs between purchasers. There is a fine line when it comes to the price segmentation techniques applied in the yield management programs used by hotels and airline companies, but services have remained largely untouched by the price discrimination laws as stated in the Robinson-Patman Act.

Tie-in sales refer to the practice of sellers requiring that, as a condition of purchasing one product, customers must buy other products exclusively from the seller. Tying arrangements were deemed unlawful by the Clayton Act if the arrangements were meant to substantially lessen competition. The courts have been lenient in allowing tying arrangements that are voluntary or result in procompetitive benefits. For instance, courts have allowed franchisors, like McDonald's, to require franchisees to purchase products from them that were necessary to maintain standards of performance and a consistent image.

Ethical Issues in Pricing

Ethical standards are much more difficult to evaluate and uphold than legal standards in the area of pricing. Peoples' views regarding ethics can be as diverse as their cultural or socioeconomic backgrounds. At one end of the continuum, there is a view that as long as a practice is legal, it is ethical to charge a price that will result in the maximum amount of profit. At the other end, there is a view that individuals and firms should not exploit one another for personal gain and that societal benefits should be stressed over those of any one entity. Table 14.2 illustrates the levels comprising the continuum from the legal perspective to the societal perspective.

Table 14.2	**Pricing Ethics**					

	Level of Ethical Restraint				
	Low			→	High
	1	*2*	*3*	*4*	*5*
Price is paid voluntarily	X	X	X	X	X
Price is based on equal information		X	X	X	X
Price is not exploiting buyers essential needs			X	X	X
Price is justified by costs				X	X
Price provides equal access to goods regardless of one's ability to cover costs					X

Level one assumes that all exchanges are voluntary and it is the responsibility of the buyer to obtain as much information as necessary to make a good decision. The legal principle of caveat emptor, or let the buyer beware, is the cornerstone of a capitalist economy. This principle enables firms to compete and results in a larger variety of products offered at lower prices. However, services cannot be physically held or evaluated until after they are purchased and consumed. This, along with the high level of variability associated with services, provides a high degree of risk and uncertainty for consumers in purchasing hospitality and travel products.

Level two suggests that consumers should not be exposed to making purchases under conditions of asymmetric information. That is, the seller should be required to disclose pertinent information to buyers, so they are not at a disadvantage. For example, airline companies are required to disclose any restrictions placed on tickets for air travel, such as the fact that "supersaver" rates are nonrefundable. Similarly, hotels must disclose room cancellation policies to would-be guests.

Level three imposes an additional restriction that sellers cannot earn excessive profits by charging artificially high prices for essential products. The best example of this practice would be when pharmaceutical companies charge high prices for life-saving drugs that are unaffordable for those without insurance or people with lower incomes. Airline companies and hotels offer discounted prices for certain consumers who must travel and find lodging away from home (e.g., funerals, family illnesses, accidents). Also, restaurants often donate food to soup kitchens and food banks.

Level four condemns the practice of segmented pricing even when the product is nonessential. It states that prices shouldn't be segmented based on value, and firms should not take advantage of consumers during periods where there are shortages, even for nonessential products. Hotels engage in questionable practices when they charge higher than normal rates during periods of high demand such as college graduations and special events. They often require minimum stays and charge a price above the published rate (rack rate). Additionally, some restaurants use different menus with higher prices for holidays and other special events.

Level five would seem extreme to most people because it is not consistent with free markets in a capitalist economy. Instead, this ethical restraint resembles a standard that one would find in a socialist society. It suggests that every member of the community, or society, should share with one another to ensure a minimum standard of living. This standard would be more applicable to underdeveloped countries or religious communities, where the members are committed to a societal goal. This ethical restraint would normally result in less variety of products and services of lower quality.

In closing, one's approach to the world would certainly affect his belief as to the appropriate level of ethical restraint. Obviously, there is a trade-off between what is best for an individual with what is best for society. The more levels of restraint imposed, the smaller the gap between the higher and lower incomes in a society. There is not as much incentive for people to invest, resulting in a lower overall standard of living. Therefore, the correct level of restraint is probably somewhere between levels one and five as determined by the respective society.

▲ MARKETING ACTION NOW!

You are the general manager of an independent restaurant that has been very successful in the past. Sales have been good, and the restaurant has been profitable. However, in the last two years, profits have begun to decrease. There has been increased competition from national chain restaurants and your pricing strategy has been to "hold the line" on prices. In fact, prices have not been changed in over two years. You've spoken with the owners about increasing prices, but they are reluctant to do so for fear that it will result in a decline in sales. You've reviewed the most recent income statements for the restaurant and feel that some action must be taken to increase prices and restore healthy profits. What should you do in preparation for your meeting with the owners?

▲ SUMMARY OF CHAPTER OBJECTIVES

Price is an important component of the marketing mix because it directly affects the revenue of a firm. Price is also a critical element in segmenting markets and positioning a firm's products and services. As such, firms must consider all of the factors that affect price, like the objectives of the firm, consumers' price sensitivity, and the external environment. Government regulations, trends in demographics and purchasing patterns, economic conditions, technological advances, and changes in the competitive environment all impact prices.

Consumers' perceptions of value are the basis for making pricing decisions. After all, price must be an accurate representation of the value that a consumer places on a product or service, or an exchange would not occur. The three broad pricing strategies—price skimming, price penetration, and neutral pricing—are based on the relationship between price and economic value. Firms attempt to differentiate their products from one another, and then focus on those segments of the population that value their product–service mixes. Price segmentation should concentrate on those attributes that are valued differently by various segments of the population.

The most common pricing techniques are the cost-oriented, demand-oriented, and competitive pricing approaches. Cost-oriented approaches base pricing decisions on the cost of providing the product, starting with the break-even point and then adding a mark-up or target return. Demand-oriented approaches focus on consumer price sensitivity and market demand, including certain psychological tactics. Competitive pricing involves setting prices in relation to a firm's competition. The firm must choose to price at, below, or above the competition.

Finally, legal and ethical issues surround product pricing. Laws exist to protect consumers and ensure fair competition. Firms cannot collude to fix prices and take advantage of consumers and other competitors. In addition to the legal standards, firms often must deal with ethical standards imposed by society. These standards will vary somewhere between "let the buyer beware" in a pure capitalist economy and a socialist economy, which restricts profits for personal gain.

▲ KEY TERMS AND CONCEPTS

Bartering	Penetration pricing
Break-even analysis	Prestige pricing
Competitive pricing	Price discrimination
Consumer price sensitivity	Price elasticity of demand
Cost-oriented pricing	Price lining
Demand-oriented pricing	Pricing objectives
Differentiation value	Reference value
Economic value	Reservation price
Law of demand	Segmented pricing
Neutral pricing	Skim pricing
Odd/even pricing	Yield management

▲ QUESTIONS FOR REVIEW AND DISCUSSION

1. What is price? What are some of the major factors that affect pricing decisions?

2. What are the major pricing objectives discussed in the chapter?

3. What are the most common effects on consumer price sensitivity?

4. What are the three broad pricing strategies? When is it appropriate to use each strategy?

5. What are the advantages and disadvantages of using break-even analysis?

6. What is economic value? Give an example of how you would determine the economic value for a particular hospitality service.

7. Discuss some of the price segmentation strategies that can be used by hospitality and travel firms.

8. What are the three major pricing techniques? Can you use more than one? Explain.

9. What is yield management?

10. What are some of the legal and ethical issues surrounding pricing decisions?

▲ NOTES

[1] Kathy Seal, "Economic conditions lead to concentration on basics," *Hotel & Motel Management*, January 11, 1999, pp. 65.

[2] Thomas T. Nagle and Reed K. Holden, *The Strategy and Tactics of Pricing: A Guide to Profitable Decision Making*, 2nd edition (Englewood Cliffs, NJ: Prentice-Hall, Inc., 1995) pp. 77–94.

[3] Thomas T. Nagle and Reed K. Holden, *The Strategy and Tactics of Pricing: A Guide to Profitable Decision Making*, 2nd edition (Englewood Cliffs, NJ: Prentice-Hall, Inc., 1995) pp. 152–161.

[4] Thomas T. Nagle, "Economic Foundations for Pricing," *Journal of Business*, Vol. 57, N. 1, Part 2, pp. S3–S26.

[5] Thomas T. Nagle and Reed K. Holden, *The Strategy and Tactics of Pricing: A Guide to Profitable Decision Making*, 2nd edition (Englewood Cliffs, NJ: Prentice-Hall, Inc., 1995) 366–381.

Using Menu Design as a Marketing Tool

❖ Chapter Objectives

By the end of this chapter, you should understand:

1. The importance of menus in food service marketing.
2. The guidelines used in selecting and categorizing menu items.
3. The process for designing and producing actual menus.
4. The potential pitfalls associated with menu planning.
5. The methods and guidelines used in evaluating menus.

❖ Chapter Outline

❖ Chapter Opening Profile

RESTAURANTS ALL OVER THE COUNTRY HAVE been serving children oily, salty, and fried foods with games and puzzles for years. The restaurant industry is attempting to change this pattern by encouraging its members to develop more nutritious kids' meals that taste better.[1] This is particularly important given the fact that the food kids learn to love in their early years will have a great impact on what they choose to eat as adults. Most restaurants offer the standard chicken fingers/nuggets, pizza, hot dogs, hamburgers, grilled cheese sandwiches, and macaroni and cheese. Restaurant chains conduct a good deal of research regarding menus and consumer tastes, but they still seem to ignore the nutrition issues surrounding this $9 billion market.

There are a couple of reasons for this lack of enthusiasm about kids' menus. First, many parents let their children choose the restaurant or have something to say about the choice, and Americans currently spend more than half of their food dollars on food prepared away from home. Younger children prefer the standard kids' fare and restaurants couple this with marketing gimmicks like toys, puzzles, games, and crayons. It is no secret that these devices are meant to distract children from the main task at hand—eating. The simple fact is, kids only eat with adults, and most adults choose to take their children to restaurants that have let them know children are welcome.

The second reason for the lack of nutrition and taste in kids' meals is the low contribution margin on these meals. Most family and quick-service restaurants charge $3 to 4 for a kid's meal, which often includes a drink and a dessert. The low price forces restaurants to reduce portions and the cost of ingredients to make even a small profit margin. In fact, in many cases, the kid's meal is priced as a loss leader to attract the more profitable adults. However, this strategy can also backfire because restaurants that target children may actually drive away adults without children.

In the future, successful restaurants will be those that find a way to attract children without having them take over the restaurant. Children tend to get bored with kids' menus as they reach 8 or 9 years of age. This boredom and the current trend toward healthy eating will provide an incentive for restaurants to become more creative and find ways to continue to attract the child market. It is in the restaurant industry's best interest to develop more nutritional meals for children while maintaining a focus on marketing.

▲ INTRODUCTION

The printed menu used by a food service operation affords management one of the best methods to communicate with the customer. The menu should provide more than a mere listing of the food and beverage offerings. The menu should influence the customer's selection of food and beverage items. Planning is crucial when creating menus; a successful menu does not result from chance. Careful planning and attention to design principles are needed at each step of the design process. No quick and easy formulas apply to all food service operations, but basic principles may be modified to fit the needs of each individual food service operation. The menu should complement the organization's other marketing activities. That is, it should be designed to satisfy specific marketing objectives.

One of the main goals of the menu is to increase customer repeat patronage. This can be accomplished by providing not only items that have proven to be highly popular but also a wide enough selection to prevent menu monotony. The menu can also provide a competitive advantage in appealing to new target market segments. By closely studying menu census data, marketing information systems, and market research data, management can identify trends and alter the menu to take advantage of changing consumer tastes. The menu might also be used to expand the market, as a restaurant does when banquet services are promoted within the regular menu. The promotional piece draws customers' attention to additional product service offerings that they may not otherwise have considered.

The Role of Menus in Marketing

A successful menu should, in fact, satisfy four major marketing objectives. First, the menu should further the goals of the marketing concept. Recall that the marketing concept holds that the needs and wants of the consumer should be given the highest priority. If the hospitality organization is successful in satisfying these needs and wants, then the marketing concept holds that financial success will naturally result. In short, if consumers are happy, the organization will experience increasing volume and should succeed. It follows that if consumers are not satisfied, volume will decrease and the operation will not succeed. Therefore, every effort should be made to design the menu to include food and beverage items that the target market segment(s) will find appealing. Establishing consumer needs and wants can be accomplished in some part through market research and analysis of internal marketing information systems and national menu census data.

Second, the menu should contribute to establishing the perceived image of the operation. For example, a menu used by an operation that appeals to young singles desiring a fun-filled atmosphere might include humorous names for menu items and cartoon drawings on the menu to establish the perceived image. A Mexican restaurant might use the drawings of a building with Mexican-style architecture on the front of its menu. The menu is one of the initial communication vehicles that the customer en-

Menus can help restaurants establish a perceived image among customers. *Courtesy of Red Lobster Restaurants, Orlando, Florida.*

counters after entering the hospitality operation. The menu's impact in the formation of a positive perceived image should not be discounted.

Third, the menu should act as a means to influence customer demand for menu items. Through menu clip-ons, menu item descriptions (copy), positioning of menu items on the menu, and artwork, the menu planner can influence customer demand. Extremely popular or profitable items are given extra attention or more prominent positioning, thereby making the customer more likely to select them. Attempting to influence customer behavior in this manner can result in a menu mix that not only increases the number of some menu items sold but can also substantially increase sales and gross profits. Experimenting with different menu mixes can result in substantially different levels of gross profitability, even without an increase in the total number of menu items sold.

Fourth, the menu is a vehicle to gain a competitive advantage. A successful operation often has selected menu items for which it is noted; these are called **signature items** and are promoted heavily on the menu, further adding to the competitive advantage. Hospitality operators should attempt to create certain signature items to enhance the perceived image of the operation and to create a distinct competitive advantage.

signature items selected items for which a food service operation is noted

Desktop Publishing

The improvement in computer technology has had a great impact on the restaurant industry regarding menu design and printing. Powerful software packages enable restaurants to make menu changes in a fraction of the time and expense than in the past. Most restaurants have a computer system with menu designing software and a laser-quality printer that allows them to produce menus with various fonts and type styles. In addition, clip art files with stored graphics can be easily inserted into any menu. The software packages also have more sophisticated proofing tools such as spell checkers and grammar checkers that reduce the amount of time spent proofreading final documents. Restaurants can now produce menus that rival the more expensive alternative of using a professional designer and print shop.

A wide range of products is available for restaurants to use in publishing their menus. For example, they could use basic word processing software or purchase more sophisticated menu design software. Printers can also range from low-end laser quality to higher-end color laser printers. Regardless of the level of product, it is very easy to make changes and view them before making a final decision. Restaurants can test different paper stocks, type styles, and menu layouts without incurring any major costs or taking a great deal of time.

In addition to using computers for menu design and production, restaurants use accounting and other software packages to improve the operation of the business. Once again, restaurants can use basic software packages, such as Microsoft Office or purchase specific software made for the restaurant industry at a greater cost. Computers make it easy for restaurants to chart expenses, conduct sales analysis, and analyze operational data. This ability to link menu design to performance will enable restaurants to become more competitive and customer-oriented.

▲ MENU-PLANNING CONSIDERATIONS

Several factors should be taken into consideration during initial stages of the menu-design process. Perhaps the most obvious factor is the consumer. What are the likes and dislikes of those who patronize the operation? What food items currently on the menu do they like most or least? A detailed sales history and other data provided by the marketing information system are invaluable in menu planning. Any menu must satisfy the consumer in order to be successful; therefore, a hospitality manager must fully understand consumer behavior and must always keep the consumer in the proper perspective. The entire business should be organized so that the consumer will derive satisfaction. Managers must always strive to provide consumers with exactly what they want to buy, not just what management wishes to sell. If the consuming public is demanding fast-food items, then a prudent hospitality manager should provide them, even though a manager may, in fact, prefer to produce something else. Management selects specific target market segments, and the needs and wants of these market segments must always be the first consideration when planning a menu.

Once the consumer's desires are determined, another consideration arises. What is the availability and cost of the needed food and beverage products? Many food items are seasonal, and some fresh ingredients may be difficult to obtain at a reasonable price on a year-round basis. Once a hospitality manager has determined that consumers desire a certain product, a consistent source of supply must be located.

The skills of production and service employees must also be considered. If new menu items are introduced, do the current employees possess all the talents and skills necessary to prepare, present, and serve each new item correctly? If they do not, what training measures must be undertaken to teach them the necessary skills? Should additional employees be hired? These are important questions that a hospitality manager must ask during the initial stages of the menu-planning process.

The physical layout and design of the operation must also be considered. The layout and design of the kitchen is particularly important. Is the food service equipment capable of producing the new menu items? Decisions regarding space limitations, equipment capacities, and layout must be made. Modifications in the layout of the kitchen and service areas may be necessary to facilitate production and serving of new menu items. In other instances, additional equipment may have to be purchased to produce and serve the new items. For example, if a manager decided to switch from American table service to a combination of French and Russian table service, a considerable investment would have to be made in equipment.

Menus should provide consumers with the opportunity to select a nutritional meal. Certainly, institutional operations have a much stronger obligation to satisfy the nutritional needs of the clientele than do commercial operations. This is not to say, however, that commercial operations can ignore nutritional considerations. Every effort should be made to provide the consumer with the option of a meal that will satisfy one-third of the **recommended dietary allowance (RDA)**. It is also important to remember, as numerous studies have shown, that consumers are more concerned and more knowledgeable about nutrition than ever before.

Finally, menus must be balanced. Menus will achieve increased success if they balance several aesthetic factors. Food and beverage items must be selected so that overall the menu is a balanced variety of the following:

- *Flavor.* Sweet, sour, spicy, hot, bland
- *Color.* Dark brown, golden brown, light green, dark green, white, red, orange
- *Texture.* Firm, soft, chewy, crisp
- *Shape.* Cubed, solid, ground, strips, balls, sliced
- *Method of preparation.* Broiled, fried, baked, braised, boiled
- *Sauces.* A variety of both sauce and non-sauce items should be included.

Selecting Menu Items

Before the managers of a food service operation begin the layout and planning of a menu, they should give careful thought to the selection of menu items. A restaurant's menu policy should define the number of items and the type of food that the restaurant intends to offer consumers. Figure 15.1 provides an example of a **menu policy flow chart** that can be used in selecting menu items.[2] The first step is to formulate a list of menu groups that will be included on the menu. Second, management must choose the group classifications within each menu group. Third, group specifications must be included under each group classification. Finally, the exact specifications are determined for each item that will be included on the menu. This process must be followed for every menu item and all four of the factors in the flow chart are equally important.

menu policy flow chart process used to select the items included on a menu

The final selection of menu items should be based on a thorough analysis of the restaurant's sales. Once this listing is comprehensive enough to meet the operation's needs, management should rank-order each item in each category for its customer popularity and profitability. Based on these combined priorities, knowledge of the food service operation, and experience, management should begin to finalize the selection of menu items to be included on the new menu.

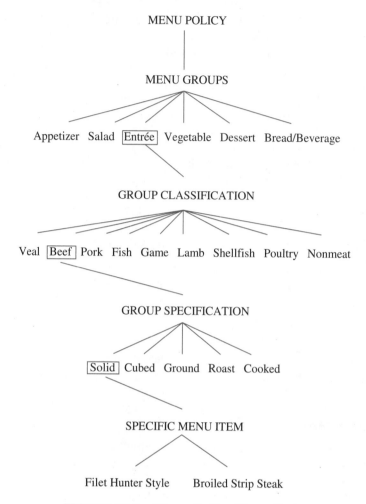

MENU POLICY

MENU GROUPS

Appetizer Salad Entrée Vegetable Dessert Bread/Beverage

GROUP CLASSIFICATION

Veal Beef Pork Fish Game Lamb Shellfish Poultry Nonmeat

GROUP SPECIFICATION

Solid Cubed Ground Roast Cooked

SPECIFIC MENU ITEM

Filet Hunter Style   Broiled Strip Steak

FIGURE 15.1 Menu Policy Flow Chart

menu census data
based on national re-
search studies food and
beverage trends

Management should also consider **menu census data** in selecting food and beverage items for the menu. Several of the industry trade journals publish menu census reports. These reports represent the findings of national research studies undertaken by respected market research firms. Both *Restaurant & Institutions* and *Restaurant Business* magazines, for example, publish this type of data and reports. Menu census reports usually contain useful information relating to (1) key menu trends, such as a concern for freshness; (2) trends that allow for regional differences and uniqueness; (3) best-selling items in American hospitality; and (4) menu census data broken down by type of operation.

Although menu census data published by industry trade journals will not provide data specific to one operation or one narrowly defined geographic location, these reports represent excellent sources for monitoring

WYNSOR'S

Grill & Bar

Wine by the Glass

Artesa ., Chardonnay	*$7.00*	*Btl $33.00*
Frog's Leap, Chardonnay	*$8.50*	*Btl $40.00*
Clos Du Bois, Chardonnay	*$6.00*	*Btl $28.00*
Kendall Jackson, Chardonnay	*$6.50*	*Btl $30.00*
Liberty School, Cabernet Sauvignon	*$6.50*	*Btl $32.00*
Columbia Crest, Merlot	*$7.50*	*Btl $28.00*
Kendall Jackson, Cabernet Sauvignon	*$7.50*	*Btl $32.00*

Appetizer

CRAB CAKE SAUTÉ
With Assorted Mixed Greens and Cuban Black Bean Relish.
$9.25

MUSHROOM RAVIOLIS
Served with Portobello Mushroom Essence.
$8.50

SHRIMP COCKTAIL
Jumbo Shrimp served with Cocktail Sauce and a Fresh Lemon Wedge
$9.50

PASTRAMI-SMOKED SALMON
With Red Onions, Capers and Sour Cream
$8.95

BLACKENED AHI TUNA
With Vegetable Julienne and Ponzu Dressing.
$9.75

CHICKEN CROQUETTES
With Seasonal Mixed Greens. Served with a Light Curry Sauce
$7.25

ENDIVE AND RADDICIO SALAD
With Goat Cheese and Caramelized Pecans in a Sherry Vinaigrette.
$9.50

ANGEL HAIR PASTA
With Maine Lobster Morcels and Chipotle Sauce.
$10.75

ONION SOUP
With Cheese Croutons and Crispy Onions
$4.75

SOUP OF THE EVENING
$4.50

WYNSOR'S CLASSIC SALAD & DESSERT BUFFET
$15.75

Enjoy the classic salad & dessert buffet with your main course
for only $7.50

Dessert buffet with entree $6.50

Main Course

HOME-MADE JERK CHICKEN
With Yukon Mashed Potatoes, Seasonal Vegetables and Mango Chutney
$17.75

MOUSSAKA
(100% Vegetarian) Grilled Carrots, Potato, Bell Peppers Wrapped in Grilled Yellow and
Green Zucchini.
$14.75

PAN FRIED MOSKOVY DUCK BREAST
With Minnesota Wild Rice, Baby Carrots and Braised Endives.
Served with a Port Wine Ginger Sauce.
$22.50

PAN SEARED SALMON
On a Bed of Saffron Potatoes, Green Onions and Shitake Mushrooms.
Served with a Cabernet Butter Sauce. (Crispy Potato Julienne for Garnish).
$20.50

SEA SCALLOPS AND CRAB CLAWS
Served with Asparagus, Mashed Potatoes and a Spicy Creole Sauce.
$21.25

GRILLED MONSTER SHRIMP
Stuffed with Crabmeat. Served with Baby Red Pear Tomatoes and
Broccoli Florets in a Citrus Herb Sauce.
$27.50

STRIPED SEABASS (PAN-FRIED)
With Mashed Potatoes, Yellow Summer Squash, Pear Tomatoes and
Baby Spinach. Served with Chive Beurre Blanc.
$21.50

FILET MIGNON
Served with Mashed Potatoes, Yellow Wax Beans, Chippolini Onions and
Shitake Mushrooms. With a Merlot infused Demi-Glaze Reduction.
$22.00

BLACK ANGUS PRIME RIB
Served with Au Jus, Fresh Horseradish, Oven Roasted Red Russet Potatoes and Seasonal
Vegetables.
12 oz $20.00   16 oz $22.50

GRILLED NEW YORK STEAK
On a Bed of "Rosti" Potato and Baby Spinach. Served with Madagascar Sauce.
$20.25

VEAL MEDALLIONS SAUTÉ
Nested on a Melange of Roasted Corn, Green Peas, Red Onions, Black Olives, Pine Nuts
and Spinach with an Oven Roasted Garlic Sauce. (Crispy Potato-Fan Garnish).
$22.95

GRILLED T-BONE STEAK
Succulent Beef, Served with Mashed Potatoes, and Fresh Vegetables Du Jour.
$25.95

COLORADO LAMB CHOPS
Served with French Andouille Sausage-Risotto.
$26.75

MAINE LOBSTER (3Lbs)
Served on a Bed of Wild Rice Melange with Lentils, Asparagus and Baby Carrots. Served
with a Lobster Beurre Blanc Perfumed with Courvoisier.
$36.00

Hotel restaurants must choose menu items that will appeal to their customers.
Courtesy of the Wyndham Hotel at Los Angeles Airport

both geographic trends (national and regional) and trends by type of operation. When those data are combined with internally generated sales histories, marketing information systems, and managerial judgment, the result is a solid basis for decisions concerning menu item selection.

Managing Price Increases

One of the most critical decisions facing restaurant managers is raising menu prices. There are many factors to consider. First, how often should prices be increased? There is a point where customers will become disenchanted with a restaurant if it raises prices too often. Second, how much should prices be increased? Customers have a certain range of price increase that is acceptable without a decrease in sales volume. Third, how many menu items will be affected by the price increase? Some restaurants increase the prices of a few menu items at a time, whereas others raise the prices of the entire menu at one time. In other words, some choose to increase prices for the most popular items, or those for which the cost of ingredients has risen, and others attempt to cover the cost increases by spreading it among all of the menu items.

It is important to examine all of these factors when making a decision to increase prices. However, one thing is certain: the less attention drawn to a price increase, the better. The following is a list of common marketing practices used to disguise menu price increases.

- *Avoid making price increases across the board.* This is very noticeable to customers and can have a major backlash.
- *Try to avoid listing prices in a straight line.* When prices are aligned in a straight line on one side of the menu, they stand out from the menu copy and become the focus of attention.
- *Don't list items according to price.* Once again, this will cause price to become the focus of attention and make the price range readily apparent.
- *Never cross out prices or write over them.* This will signal any price increases and it looks very unprofessional.
- *Use odd-even pricing.* The most common prices end in a 5 or a 9. Research has shown that consumers perceive a price like $7.95 as being closer to $7.00 rather than $8.00. This is because many people process numbers from left to right. Also, it is more difficult to notice an increase involving an odd amount.
- *Trade-off portions with price changes.* Profit is a function of both price and cost. A price increase can sometimes be avoided by reducing the portion or the cost of ingredients. Items that have ingredients that fluctuate greatly in cost should not be priced on the menu, they should be listed as "market price." Also, packaging entrees with other items can disguise price increases. This is an approach called product bundling,

in which menu items are bundled with other items, often at price that is less than if the individual items were ordered separately. This is common practice in the food service business, and it is especially common in the quick-service segment.

- *Avoid raising prices when introducing a new menu.* Customers will look for price increases when a new menu is introduced. It is better to phase in price increases before a major change in menu design. Similarly, menu items with increased prices should be placed in less obvious locations on the menu.

▲ PRODUCING THE PRINTED MENU

All food service managers like to consider themselves professionals. Food service, like any other field, requires certain unique skills and expertise. However, not all managers possess all the necessary skills that the field demands. When a menu is planned and designed, layout, copy writing, and artistic skills are needed, yet many hospitality managers do not have a great deal of talent or skill in these areas. A wise manager recognizes these shortcomings and seeks professional assistance.

A wide variety of sources are available. Some sources can complete the entire menu from initial planning to final production and printing. Others may be able to offer expertise dealing with only certain aspects of the menu. The first source of assistance is a firm engaged solely in menu layout and design. Many design firms offer stock menus as well as custom-designed menus tailored to each individual operation. In developing a custom-designed menu, they will completely design and produce the concept, design, typesetting, paste-up, photography, and printing. These services are not inexpensive, but the investment in professionally designed and produced menus is normally rewarded by increased sales and by the achievement of the manager's menu objectives.

Advertising agencies may also be able to assist in menu design. Agencies have individuals on staff who can produce photographs and artwork suitable for a hospitality menu. They also employ copywriters who may be able to add the extra flair that a menu needs to make it unique and to produce increased sales.

If a hospitality manager chooses to design a menu personally, the only outside help necessary is a top-quality printer. Most printers will be able to do the job adequately, but it is wise to work closely with a printer who has experience with menus. When selecting a printer, consider the following questions: Is the printer's equipment capable of producing the size, color, and style of the menu exactly as desired? Is the printer able to provide quick service on short runs when prices or menu items change?

The Menu Cover

First impressions arc vitally important, so the design of the cover is critical. It sets the tone, creates the mood, and establishes the image of the food service establishment in the mind of the consumer. The cover is the first part of the menu that is seen by the customer, and it should contain the restaurant name and logo. Additional items depend on the size of the menu and the atmosphere that is being conveyed. In essence, the menu cover introduces the customer to the restaurant.

The choice of cover designs is nearly limitless, but a number of factors may limit the selection process. Cost limitations may force a manager to select a more conservative and less expensive menu cover. If cost is of great concern, then only one color should be printed on a solid-color background. This can still have a dramatic effect, yet it remains relatively inexpensive. The length of service desired for the menu is another factor that should be considered when selecting a menu cover. If a long service life is desired, heavyweight and grease-resistant paper stock should be used.

No concrete rules dictate exactly what should be included on a menu cover, so the following are only guidelines. The name of the food service operations and any artwork should appear on the front. The address, phone number, hours of operation, and credit cards accepted should be included on either the back cover or within the menu. The cover should reflect the theme and atmosphere of the hospitality operation and should be as creative as possible.

Writing Menu Copy

The words appearing on the menu are referred to as *copy*. These words must be carefully chosen and must be designed to sell, rather than merely list the available food items and prices. A well-written menu has a definite flair that can be translated into higher check averages and increased profits. As all managers are interested in increased sales, menu copy is an excellent starting point for reaching this goal. Menu copy can be divided into three main categories: (1) listings of menu items and prices; (2) descriptive selling of menu items; and (3) copy relating to extra services, special cuisine, or special features of the product-service mix offered.

Listing menu items and prices is the first and most basic step in developing menu copy, but it is important to consider the organization and sequencing of the items as well. In what order should the items appear on the menu? Should all the items receive equal attention? To answer the first question, one school of thought holds that the items should appear on the menu in the same order in which the customer would eat them. For example, appetizers should be first, followed by soups and salads, entrees, and desserts. If a hospitality operation does not follow a rigid pattern of service, similar menu items should be grouped together. This might mean grouping sandwiches, side orders, pizzas, beverages, and complete din-

Menu layout and item descriptions help to increase revenues.
Courtesy of NE Restaurant Company, Inc., Maynard, Massachusetts.

ners. All menu items should not receive equal attention on the menu. Not all items are equally popular with consumers, nor are they equally profitable to the operator. For example, why should a cup of coffee selling for $.95 be given the same amount of space and copy as a highly profitable entree selling for $17.95? Items that should be given special and bolder attention are those popular with consumers, profitable for the operation, or preferably, both.

Another school of thought is that menu items should be positioned so that the items that are the most popular and most profitable are seen first by the consumer. This will initiate the dining experience in a positive manner. Figure 15.2 illustrates the eye-movement pattern typical with threefold menus. Generally speaking, a consumer looking at a single-page menu will first focus slightly above the middle of the page. With a four-page menu, a consumer will focus slightly above the middle of the right-hand page when looking at the inner two pages.

Many hospitality managers merely list the menu items and the corresponding prices. The consumer's first reading of the menu copy is the "moment of truth" for any restaurant. The consumer is going to make a selection based on the presentation of the items on the menu. The menu should be designed with flair and should predominantly feature popular and profitable items. A menu lacking any descriptive selling of its items is dull, for if menu items and prices are merely listed the menu looks like a telephone book, with names in one column and numbers in the other. Today's hospitality consumers are becoming more sophisticated and are demanding more. Consumers have been exposed to many innovative operations and are increasingly less likely to patronize operations with

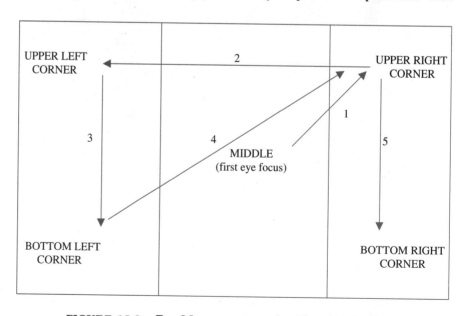

FIGURE 15.2 **Eye Movement on the Threefold Menu**

dull and mundane menus and presentations. The menu should not merely list—it should sell!

All menu items cannot be given an extensive description, but most items can be given some extra copy. Copy can easily be developed to show an item's preparation, ingredients used, portion size, quality of ingredients, or any other special features. It is not difficult to add flair to a menu. The copy need not be amusing, only accurate.

The third category of menu copy is related to extra services, special cuisine, or other interesting features. A hospitality menu should never contain any blank pages. Pages that do not contain menu items should be used to promote such extra services as banquets, takeouts, or other features. Menus should be treated as advertising space. Blank pages are a waste of money because they could be used in some way to promote the operation. This copy may actively promote such profit-makers as banquets, or it may reinforce the operation's image by discussing the quality of products used or by describing any special furniture or paintings the hospitality operation might own. Use the space to the greatest promotional advantage. It is better to have a patron reading about the aging process for beef, rather than glaring across the dining room at a service person or reading where the silverware is manufactured.

Type Style and Paper Stock

Through careful selection of type style and paper stock, a manager can greatly improve a menu. Type style and paper stock can be used in combination to create the desired impression. The menu is one of the few communication links with the consumer, so it must be both readable and attractive.

When selecting type style or paper stock, it is advisable to view the samples under the same conditions as those experienced by a consumer. For example, do not select type style or paper stock under bright fluorescent lighting if the lighting in the dining room is low-level incandescent or candles.

Many different type styles are available in a wide range of sizes. Most printers have a wide enough selection to satisfy the needs of most food service operations. A few guidelines should be followed to make the final menu both readable and attractive. Type size is measured in points; type size ranges from 6 to 72 points. Most menus should not be printed in less than 8 to 10 point type because smaller sizes are difficult to read. To help you get a better understanding of point size, consider the following:

This is 8 point type

This is 10 point type

This is 12 point type

This is 18 point type

It is also advisable to use a larger type size for headings, so that they will be bolder and will stand out better. A combination of lowercase and capital letters should be used because a menu made entirely of capital letters is more difficult to read.

The primary consideration when selecting paper stock is the length of service desired. If a menu is going to be changed weekly, it would not have to be printed on stock as heavy as one that will be changed monthly. For menus a manager is planning to use for an extended period of time, lamination may be applied to make the menu impervious to liquids and grease. Also, a vinyl cover or leather cover can be used to protect high-quality paper stock and increase the life of a menu.

Menus can be expensive to design and print, and the cost of the paper will represent roughly one-third the cost of printing a menu. It is, however, a false economy to use a menu after its useful life is over. The image of the restaurant will suffer if consumers receive dog-eared or stained menus. Prices that have been crossed out and written in by hand only draw unnecessary attention to price increases. A menu is an important communication tool. Its appearance should be the very best that a hospitality operation can offer.

Wine Lists and Promotions

Wine has two major attributes. First, it offers a chance for romance and enjoyment. Second, it can be highly profitable, especially when a substantial volume is sold. These two attributes mark wine for special attention. Many aspects of menu design apply to the design of a wine list as well. The successful selling of wine depends not only on a well-planned wine list but also on personal selling by the service personnel. Several factors should be considered when designing a wine list.

First, an idea successfully used by many hospitality organizations is to link specific wines with individual entrees on the menu. Usually, two wines are suggested as being complementary to each entree. This copy is included directly on the menu, indicating either the names of the wines or the bin numbers of the recommended wines. Of the two wines suggested, one should be in the low-to-moderate price range and the other in the moderate-to-high price range. By offering different price ranges, the guest is given a choice without having to feel as though the higher-priced wines are being promoted exclusively. Suggestive selling of wines to accompany each entree is highly recommended.

Second, a description of the wine on the actual wine list assists the guest, especially the novice wine drinker, in selection. Despite the increasing per-capita consumption of wine in the United States, many restaurant guests are unsure of themselves when they order wine. In many cases, where the name and vintage of the wine are the only listings, the guest does not have enough information to make an informed decision. If a description of each wine is included, the guest will feel more certain of the selected wine and will not feel nearly as anxious.

Finally, the most neglected aspect of selling wines is the service personnel. Often, they do not have the tools necessary to sell the wine properly. They need to be adequately trained not only in presenting, opening, and pouring the wine but in selling it. Extra attention must be given to training the service personnel. In particular, they must be shown how to approach the guests and evaluate their potential for ordering wine. The next step is to get the wine list in the hands of the guest who is the decision maker, captivate the guest's interest by talking abut the wines and how they will complement the selected entrees, and offer positive suggestions about which wines to recommend. To accomplish these tasks, the service personnel will need to receive training that focuses on product knowledge, the handling and serving of wine, and most important, techniques for selling wine successfully. It is very important that such personnel learn how to ask for the wine sale: If they don't ask for the sale, they will rarely receive it.

The marketing and promotion of wine is an aspect of menu planning and design that often does not receive adequate time and attention to detail. Wine is a profitable aspect of the operation, and professionally planned wine lists are a real asset.

Banquet Menus

Within hotels and restaurants that have targeted group business as a substantial part of their volume, the selling of group meal functions is critical. One of the aids to selling this type of group is the banquet menu. First and foremost, planning banquet menus is in many respects very similar to planning other types of menus. However, banquet menus do not have to be boring. The entree selections do not have to be limited to several varieties of roast beef, chicken, and ham. A great deal can be done with food and beverage presentation and the flair with which items are presented and served. This type of banquet presentation can make the occasion memorable.

The variety of menus and presentations offered by the leading hotels is nothing short of amazing. Theme parties of endless variety help turn simple group meal functions into memorable events. Smaller hotels and restaurants that are active in the banquet business can use this same approach on a smaller scale. Presentation of banquet menus often consists of a packet of information along with all menus offered.

▲ OTHER ISSUES SURROUNDING MENU PLANNING

The preceding discussion revolved around the techniques used in planning menus and how the menu can be useful as a marketing tool. This section will focus on some of the major issues surrounding menu design and planning. First, the potential pitfalls that can occur with menu planning will be presented. Second, there is a discussion about the ethical issues regarding accuracy in menus. Finally, the reader is introduced to the concept of using cycle menus to minimize customer boredom.

Menu-Planning Pitfalls to Avoid

Despite the best efforts of hospitality managers, mistakes are made in menu design and production. The following are common menu pitfalls:

- *Being the wrong physical size.* Often a menu is too small to accommodate all the items. The result is overcrowding, which makes the menu difficult to lead. On the other hand, some menus are so large that they become difficult for the guest to handle, particularly at a crowded table. Management should strive to achieve a happy medium.
- *Using too small a type size.* Often the type size is too small for many people to read easily. Not everyone has 20/20 vision, and many consumers are somewhat vain and do not want to put on glasses just to read a menu.
- *Failing to sell.* Many menus lack any sort of descriptive selling copy. These menus fail to communicate fully with the guest.
- *Treating all menu items equally.* Do not treat all menu items equally on a menu. A hospitality operation does not make an equal profit on all food and beverage items. To increase sales, special attention should be given to items that are popular and or profitable.
- *Using tacky clip-ons.* Make certain that any menu clip-ons do not cover any part of the regular menu. If this is not possible, it is advisable to use table tents to showcase specials and feature items. It's also advisable to have the service personnel personally describe and sell special or signature items. It is also advisable to have the clip-on printed on the same paper stock and in the same type style as the regular menu. In this way, the clip-on will appear to be an integral part of the menu, not as an afterthought.
- *Forgetting the basics.* Be sure to include on the menu such basic information as hours of operation and whether credit cards are accepted.

Accuracy in Menus

With the growing sophistication of hospitality consumers has come an increased emphasis on accuracy in menus. Simply stated, this means serving exactly what the menu says will be served. For many years, restaurants have been subject to licensing, minimum wage, tax, and sanitation laws and codes, but the words placed on the menu were not legislated or controlled to any great extent. Consumer groups have, however, become more active in this area, and consumers are now more aware of potential violations in menu accuracy.

Accuracy in menus is centered on several areas where potential problems might arise, including the following:

- *Representation of quality.* If food products are merchandised on the menu by weight or volume, then that is the exact amount that must be served. Steaks are often merchandised this way. Also, sometimes an implication of size is made on the menu. For example, a cup of soup is less than a bowl.

- *Representation of quality.* Federal and state standards are sometimes used on a menu for products such as beer, poultry, eggs, fruits, and dairy products. If claims are made on the menu about a specific grade or standard, this is exactly what must be served. For example, if a steak is merchandised as being prime, it must be USDA prime, not USDA choice or any lower grade. By USDA definition, ground beef is just that, ground beef. It cannot contain any type of extra fat, water, or extenders.

- *Representation of price.* The menu should be very specific about what is included at the stated price. For example, if there is an extra charge for an "all white meat" chicken entrée, the menu should clearly state this. If a 15 percent service charge is automatically added for parties of six or more, this should be stated on the menu.

- *Representation of brand names.* Brand names must be accurate as well. Blue cheese may not be substituted for Roquefort cheese. If Jello™ is listed on the menu, then Jello™ brand must be used, not another gelatin product. Containers of products, such as ketchup, that are placed on the tables must contain the brand name stated on the label.

- *Representation of product identification.* The exact product stated on the menu must be served. A cheaper product should not be substituted. Examples of products that might cause an accuracy-in-menu problem include maple syrup and maple-flavored syrup; whipped topping and whipped cream; butter and margarine; turkey and chicken; light meat tuna and white meat tuna; flounder and sole; ground beef and ground sirloin of beef.

- *Representation of point of origin.* The point of origin must be exactly as stated on the menu. If challenged, the restaurant manager should be prepared to substantiate the menu claim by showing packing labels or other documentation. Examples include Idaho potatoes, Maine lobster, Long Island duckling, Wisconsin cheese, Smithfield ham, Gulf shrimp, and Chesapeake Bay oysters.

- *Representation of merchandising terms.* Merchandising terms such as "our own special salad dressing," "chef's special sauce," or "finest quality" must not be used when the operation is unable to substantiate such statements. Commercially prepared salad dressing or sauces may not be called "house specialties." Other merchandising terms that may cause a problem include fresh daily, ground daily, and baked each day on our premises.

- *Representation of means of preservation.* Food products may be preserved in a wide variety of forms, such as fresh, frozen, canned, or chilled. If these terms are used on the menu, they must be accurate.

- *Representation of food preparation method.* The method of preparation represented on the menu must be accurate. If a menu item is represented as charbroiled, it must be exactly that and nothing else. Other preparation methods include sauteed, baked, broiled, deep-fried, smoked, poached, and microwaved.

- *Representation of verbal and visual presentation.* Any representations by means of a picture or a server's comments must be accurate. For example, if a picture on the menu of a dessert shows whole strawberries, then it would be improper to use sliced strawberries in the item that is served. If a server states that the fish is fresh, then it must indeed be fresh, not frozen.

- *Representation of nutritional claims.* Menu merchandising terms such as *low calorie* must be able to be substantiated.

Figure 15.3 is the position paper of the National Restaurant Association concerning accuracy in menus that is still used today. This is a standard that all food service operations would do well to uphold. Compromising standards is unethical and an example of poor marketing.

Accuracy in menus should be a major concern when a manager is writing or reviewing a menu. The following are guidelines:

- *Read your menu!* Check the details on the menu with what your kitchen staff actually serves. If you have made changes in purchasing or preparation but have not listed them on the menu, take immediate action to bring the menu up to date.

- *Talk to your service personnel.* Are they aware of what you serve and where it comes from? Do they describe your menu items correctly? Remember that accuracy in menus include the oral statements of employees as well as the printed menu. Perhaps a manager should conduct a menu review session with the entire staff.

- *Evaluate consumer comments and complaints related to accuracy in menus.* As with any area of marketing, consumer perceptions are important. Managers should be concerned whenever consumers feel that certain claims are inaccurate.

- *Institute a training program in handling consumer complaints.* Standard operating practices should be developed for all possible situations.

Consumers expect and demand honest representation of food and beverages, and they have a right to get it. Programs to support accuracy in menus represent legitimate efforts by ethical business people and national and state restaurant associations.

POSITION STATEMENT

Accuracy In Menu Offerings

The food service industry has long recognized the importance of accuracy in describing its products, either on menus, and through visual or oral representation, both on ethical grounds and from the standpoint of customer satisfaction. The National Restaurant Association incorporated standards of accuracy in all representations to the public in its Standards of Business Practice, originally adopted by the Association in 1923. We reaffirm and strongly support the principles therein expressed.

"Truth in dining" or "truth in menu" laws and ordinances have been proposed in some government jurisdictions, and in a few cases adopted, in the belief that representations on restaurant menus present a unique problem in consumer protection. The National Restaurant Association believes that such legislation is unnecessary as Federal, state and many local governments have laws and regulations prohibiting false advertising and misrepresentations of products, and providing protection from fraud. In an industry such as ours, where economic survival depends upon customer satisfaction, misrepresentation is most effectively regulated by the severe sanction of customer dissatisfaction and loss of patronage.

To be equitable, the complexity of such legislation would be staggering. It is conceivable that standardized recipes for each menu listing would be required if regulatory refinement followed its logical course. The problems of enforcement, and proof if due process is observed, would be monumental, if not impossible.

The "truth in dining" movement is not confined to the proposition that restaurant menus be absolutely accurate in their representations. Legislation and ordinances have been proposed that would require the identification of a specific means of preservation, method of preparation or statement of food origin. Such requirements could unjustly imply that certain foods, processes or places of origin are unwholesome or inferior.

Government action must be confined to problems where its intervention can be effective and at a cost commensurate with the benefits to be gained.

Adopted February, 1977

One IBM Plaza/Suite 2600
Chicago, Illinois 60611
(312) 787-2525

FIGURE 15.3 National Restaurant Association Position Statement concerning accuracy in menu offerings. *Courtesy: The National Restaurant Association.*

Cycle Menus

Many managers of institutional operations such as hospitals feel that marketing does not play a part in the menu planning and design process. Rather, their major focus is on the nutritional needs of the clients. Marketing should, however, be a major concern, in addition to nutritional concerns, because one of the biggest problems in institutional operations is menu monotony and lack of interest on the client's part. Management of institutional operations must give careful consideration to merchandising and marketing to increase client satisfaction.

Cycle Menu Patterns. Central to the menu-design process in institutions is the cycle menu. Institutional operations have developed and used many different forms of cycle menus. For example, a very short cycle of perhaps five to seven days might be used in a hospital setting. A much longer cycle, perhaps four to six weeks, might be used for a university food service operation. This longer cycle is necessary to maintain customer interest. Cycle menus can be designed using several patterns:

- *Typical.* This cycle begins on the same day. For example, the cycle might start on Monday and end on a Sunday, beginning a new cycle on Monday.
- *Typical break cycle menu.* This type of cycle menu begins each new cycle on a different day so that the same foods are not repeated on the same day of the week. This helps to avoid the problem of serving meatloaf on Mondays. An example of this type of menu is shown in Figure 15.4.[3]
- *Random cycle menu.* This type of cycle is used for extended "captive" customers, such as those found in schools or long-term hospital patients, In this type of cycle, each menu is assigned a letter and then the letters are picked at random and assigned to the individual day. An example is shown in Figure 15.4.

For marketing, cycle menus are most important because they can be used to reduce consumer boredom. Cycle menus should be constantly updated with new menu items to maintain consumer interest. In institutional settings, this is of critical importance. Once consumers become bored with the menu selection, it is not long before negative feelings begin to develop in other areas, such as food quality, sanitation, and price.

Marketing Cycle Menus. In addition to producing a printed cycle menu, management should give careful consideration to the merchandising and marketing of the menu. Many managers use innovative names for menu items, ones that spark consumer interest and accurately reflect the nature of the food items. In addition, management should plan special events to maintain consumer interest. These special events should be periodically scheduled throughout the cycle (perhaps once a month). Special events might be used in a university hospitality operation to include the following:

- Ethnic dinners (Mexican, Asian, or English)
- Special decorations and decor changes in the dining room to reflect seasonal changes
- Special entertainment in the dining room

TYPICAL BREAK CYCLE

WEEK 1	MONDAY DAY 1	TUESDAY DAY 2	WEDNESDAY DAY 3	THURSDAY DAY 4
WEEK 2	MONDAY DAY 5	TUESDAY DAY 6	WEDNESDAY DAY 1	THURSDAY DAY 2
WEEK 3	MONDAY DAY 3	TUESDAY DAY 4	WEDNESDAY DAY 5	THURSDAY DAY 6
WEEK 4	MONDAY DAY 1	TUESDAY DAY 2	WEDNESDAY DAY 3	THURSDAY DAY 4
WEEK 5	MONDAY DAY 5	TUESDAY DAY 6		

RANDOM CYCLE MENU

DAY 1 A	DAY 2 J	DAY 3 L	DAY 4 Z	DAY5 C	DAY6 D	DAY7 M
DAY 8 P	DAY 9 I	DAY 10 B	DAY 11 Q	DAY12 N	DAY 13 E	DAY 14 W
DAY 15 F	DAY 16 O	DAY 17 H	DAY 18 R	DAY 19 V	DAY 20 K	DAY 21 S
DAY 22 U	DAY 23 G	DAY 24 X	DAY 25 T	DAY 26 Y	DAY 27 A	DAY 28 J

FIGURE 15.4   Samples of Cycle Menu Patterns. *Courtesy: Nancy Loman Scanlon*, Marketing by Menu (John Wiley & Sons, Inc., 1985).

- Special presentation of food items, such as a meat entrée (steamship round of beef) carved in the dining room
- Extended hours of service offering coffee, soft drinks, and light snacks during exam week, perhaps until midnight
- Birthday cakes presented to residents on request
- Dinners offered in separate dining rooms for identified groups, such as residents of a dormitory floor, thereby promoting unity
- "Sick baskets" delivered to students who have been hospitalized because of illness or accident
- "Build your own sundae," featuring several varieties of ice cream and toppings
- Hors d'oeuvres featured in the lounge before dinner begins

Cycle menus need not be dull. They should be designed with four objectives in mind: (1) to provide the consumer with the menu items desired; (2) to achieve the financial goals and objectives of the organization; (3) to adequately provide for the nutritional needs of the consumers; and (4) to maintain consumer interest and relieve monotony.

▲ MENU EVALUATION

When managers design a menu, they seek to accomplish specific objectives. As with any effort, however, it is often difficult to ascertain the degree of success. Some measure of evaluation must therefore be used. Performance criteria must be established prior to implementing a new menu, and actual performance must be measured against these criteria. For example, management may give special treatment to a single menu item, such as prime rib, with the objective that this entree should constitute 30 percent of all entree sales. A simple method to evaluate this objective would be to calculate the percentage of total entree sales of prime rib. In the same manner, it would be possible to determine the degree to which each objective was achieved. After the menu has been in use for some time, perhaps a month or two, the degree of success for all objectives should be analyzed.

Menu Sales Mix Analysis

Numerous methods can be used to evaluate menu effectiveness. The selection of one method over another is usually a function of time and money. The simplest method used to evaluate menu effectiveness is simply to count the number of times that each item is sold. In most food service operations today, this information is readily available from the detailed tape printout and readings taken from *point-of-sale registers*. Based on this information, management can add or delete menu items or change the merchandising focus of the menu. Another common approach is a comparison with menu census data. Menu census data allow management to compare sales figures and sales trends with regional and national data.

A more sophisticated approach would be to perform a more in-depth analysis of the menu items, including their sales and costs. Some of these methods used in **menu engineering** resemble the growth-share matrix introduced in Chapter 8. In the case of a menu, each item is treated as its own strategic business unit. The two axes are item contribution margin in dollars and the number sold of each item. Items with larger contribution margins would be considered good growth prospects that warrant more marketing effort and resources. Items with larger sales figures would be considered high share items and a good source of revenue. The axes would be divided to form four quadrants using the average contribution margin and the average number sold (see Figure 15.5).

menu engineering
analysis of menu items based on cost, volume, and profitability

Each menu item would be plotted on the matrix based on its contribution margin and the number sold during the time period in question. Based on these two criteria, menu items are classified as dogs, question marks, stars, or cash cows. Each quadrant has some baseline strategies that can be used for the menu items that are positioned in it. Once again, this is similar to the Boston Consulting Group's growth-share matrix. There are other variations of this methodology, but this one was chosen because it is consistent with the approach used in product management. The important thing to remember is that any approach should take into account food costs, food prices, and sales volume. In this case, the contribution margin is the difference between menu price and food cost.

Dogs. These menu items have low sales volumes and low contribution margins. They don't warrant much attention and should be placed in less desirable locations on the menu. In an attempt to increase the contribution margin, management can consider raising the prices on these items and/or lowering the food costs of preparing the items. In the long run, management should consider finding a substitute for this item. The substitute could be an item that is already on the menu that can be promoted more or a new item that can be added to the menu to take its place. If the contribution margin cannot be improved, then the item may need to be removed from the menu.

Question Marks. These menu items have low sales volumes and high contribution margins. They have the potential for growth and should receive management's attention. Given the high contribution margin, an increase in sales volume would greatly benefit the restaurant. These items should be placed in prime locations on the menu and be strongly promoted. For example, waiters could be instructed to focus on them in their suggestive selling, and the items could be highlighted on table tents and other in-store promotions. Other strategies that could be employed in-

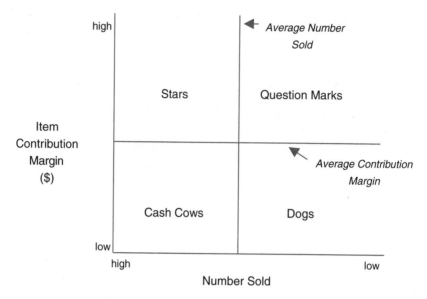

FIGURE 15.5   Sales Mix Analysis Matrix

clude making it a signature item, or offering special deals to create awareness and trial.

Stars.   These menu items have high sales volumes and high contribution margins. They should occupy prime locations on the menu and be a major focus of promotional efforts. These menu items should be promoted through in-store displays and suggestive selling efforts. It is important to maintain current levels of quality and price. Any significant changes could hurt the sales of these items, which would impact greatly on the profitability of the restaurant. These menu items are often signature items for restaurants and should be carefully managed until newer items (i.e., question marks) can be phased in.

Cash Cows.   These menu items have high sales volumes and low contribution margins. They tend to be menu items that have been around for a while and, in many cases, they are used as loss leaders. Whether they are signature items or not, these menu items attract customers and can be used to sell other items. Management should experiment with price increases or ways to decrease food costs. However, if customers are sensitive to changes in price, it is advisable to focus more on costs. For example, it may be possible to substitute less expensive ingredients or serve smaller portions, thereby increasing the contribution margin. In the long run, it is possible to find different items that are similar and offer larger contribution margins. Over time, these menu items can be moved to less prominent locations on the menu.

▲ MARKETING ACTION NOW!

Most people have dined at restaurants in various segments, including fine-dining, family-style, casual, and quick-service restaurants. Each of these types of restaurants uses a different type of menu design. First, compare and contrast the various styles of menus for each of these restaurant segments. Focus on the elements described in the section on producing the printed menu. Choose examples of these restaurants in your area and be specific.

Next, try to get a copy of a menu from one of your favorite restaurants or a restaurant where you work (or have worked). Examine the menu in relation to the basic guidelines used in menu design and evaluation. What are the strengths and weaknesses that you see in regard to the menu design? Finally, try to perform a menu sales mix analysis for this restaurant using the matrix approach. It may be necessary to make some assumptions based on the consensus of the people in your class, or based on your experience working in the restaurant.

▲ SUMMARY OF CHAPTER OBJECTIVES

This chapter is an overview of several important factors dealing with menu planning and design. The achievement of marketing objectives through the menu-design process must be considered. These objectives usually focus on the marketing concept, the enhancement of the operation's image, influencing the consumer's selection of menu items, and using the menu as a means of gaining a competitive advantage.

Several factors that must be considered when planning a menu include consumer likes and dislikes, availability and cost of food and beverages, personnel skills and talents, physical layout of the hospitality facility, and the need for a nutritionally balanced menu. A simple technique can show how to select priorities for both profitable and popular menu items. Data from a national or regional menu census can also be used. Managers who lack the time and/or talent to produce high-quality menus should refer to sources of expertise for design assistance. The design and production aspects of the actual menu include menu cover, copy writing, type, paper stock, wine lists, and accuracy in menus. Managers should avoid common pitfalls of the menu-design process.

Selected aspects of cycle menus include both patterns and suggestions for improved marketing and promotion of cycle menus. Evaluating menu effectiveness is important, and widely used methods of evaluation are available. The menu is of critical importance in the marketing efforts of a hospitality manager. It communicates, sells, creates the mood, and establishes the tone. The chapter introduces the reader to the use of the menu sales mix analysis for menu engineering.

▲ KEY TERMS AND CONCEPTS

Clip-ons

Cycle menu

Menu census data

Menu copy

Menu cover

Menu engineering

Menu policy flow chart

Menu sales mix analysis

Paper stock

Point-of-sale cash register (POS)

Recommended dietary allowance (RDA)

Signature item

Type style

Type size

▲ QUESTIONS FOR REVIEW AND DISCUSSION

1. What factors must be considered when planning a menu? How do they impact the menu design process?
2. How should a manager select items to be included on the menu?
3. If you were a food service manager, what professional assistance would you seek when developing a new menu? Why?
4. How will length of service desired affect the menu cover selection?
5. What is menu copy?
6. What are the three categories of menu copy?
7. Of what value is descriptive copy?
8. Cite and discuss the guidelines for accuracy in menus.
9. What is menu sales mix analysis?

▲ NOTES

[1]Michael DeLuca, "Are kids' menus getting any better?" *Restaurant Hospitality*, (June 1998), Vol. 82, No. 6, p. 18.

[2]Jack E. Miller and David V. Pavesic, *Menu Pricing & Strategy*, 4th edition, (New York: Van Nostrand Reinhold, 1996) pp. 157–19.

[3]Nancy L. Scanlon, *Marketing by Menu*, (New York: Van Nostrand Reinhold, 1985) pp. 72–75.

Index